The California Psychological Inventory Handbook

Edwin Inglee Megargee

Foreword by Harrison Gough

THE
CALIFORNIA
PSYCHOLOGICAL
INVENTORY
HANDBOOK

 Jossey-Bass Inc., Publishers
San Francisco • Washington • London • 1977

THE CALIFORNIA PSYCHOLOGICAL INVENTORY HANDBOOK
by Edwin Inglee Megargee

Library of Congress Catalogue Card Number LC 76-186581

International Standard Book Number ISBN 0-87589-122-5

Manufactured in the United States of America

JACKET DESIGN BY WILLI BAUM

FIRST EDITION
First printing: April 1972
Second printing: June 1977

Code 7206

The Jossey-Bass
Behavioral Science Series

Foreword

As Edwin Megargee points out in his chronology of the California Psychological Inventory (CPI), it was in 1951 that the item pool was first brought together within the confines of a single booklet, 1956 when the test was first published for general use, and 1957 when the first review (by Laurance Shaffer) appeared. The remoteness of those days, if proof is needed, may be inferred from the fact that Megargee himself was an undergraduate student at Amherst when the last of these events took place. Now that this perceptive and scholarly book on the CPI has been completed, it is clear that fate smiled on the CPI and its author when Megargee chose Berkeley as the place to initiate his graduate studies in 1958.

In my own teaching and writing on the CPI I have always found the most difficult task to be that of conveying the spirit of the enterprise. Perhaps for this reason I have written more on the empirical and statistical validation than on the underlying theory of the inventory. Megargee gently chides me for this imbalance, and I am forced to acknowledge the justice of his comments. More important is the fact that his book furnishes the kind of analytic and in-depth background that the user of the inventory should have available.

Some of these basic ideas concerning the CPI can now be stated quite simply, hard as they were to discern and formulate fifteen to twenty years ago. One of these fundamentals pertains to the aims of the test, which, briefly put, are to forecast what people will say and do in defined contexts and to foretell what others will say about them. These are the primary claims of the instrument, and its evaluation should attend to them. A second set of guidelines pertains to the concepts via which these predictions are to be made, stipulating that the dispositions selected for scaling should be easy to use and to comprehend, and relevant to interpersonal behavior in any time or place. In observance of these guidelines, the inventory is scaled for what are often called folk concepts, descriptive and classificatory notions concerning behavior and disposition that people everywhere use easily in their daily interaction with one another.

A third intention is that the set of variables be small enough to allow application of the inventory in everyday settings but at the same time large enough to permit forecasting of a wide variety of behaviors either by a single scale or (more frequently) by some simple and readily interpreted combination of scales. Multiple regression technique offers a convenient method for identifying these combinations, but analysis need not be restricted to linear models; that is, "signs," patterns, and interactions between and among variables should all be considered in attempts to attain practical levels of accuracy in forecasting criteria.

As might be expected, early test use was very often addressed to more or less obvious problems, such as scholastic achievement, graduation from high school or college, dropping out between high school and college, and performance in particular school subjects such as mathematics and psychology. In the last five to ten years usage has become increasingly diversified. For example, in the personnel field there have been studies of air traffic controllers, stock market speculators, managerial effectiveness, and creativity among architects and mathematicians; in medicine, studies of blood lipid variability, drug usage, response to vasectomy, contraceptive practices, employability of epileptics, and performance in the psychiatric residency; in cross-cultural work, validational studies from France, Israel, Italy, Japan, Poland, Switzerland, and Taiwan; and in counseling, studies of choice of college major, response to therapy, performance in honors programs, and attainment in particular schools or specialties such as dentistry, medicine, nursing, and education. Laboratory investigations are also beginning to appear, including studies of performance under monitored and unmonitored conditions, verbal learning as influenced by social reinforcement, and Megargee's own experiments on dominance, which show the significant role of context in determining the manner in which this disposition is manifested.

The pages to follow, it can be asserted, contain information and analyses invaluable to anyone who uses the CPI or wishes to become familiar with this test. The book also points the way toward future developments and (one hopes) improvements in the inventory, as difficulties and deficiencies are candidly confronted. Personally, I have gained much from reading this book; it is beyond doubt the most systematic and authoritative document on the CPI now available. It is, in fact, a volume that should be read and studied by anyone who uses or plans to use the inventory.

Berkeley, California   HARRISON GOUGH
January 1972

Preface

The female cuckoo has a singularly unpleasant habit of laying her egg in the nest of another, smaller bird and leaving it there to be hatched and raised by unwitting, involuntary foster parents. Although I must confess that I have not spent a great deal of time pondering on the cuckoo, I have, from time to time, wondered how these foster parents react to the appearance of this large, voracious offspring, who stridently demands such a disproportionate share of the nest and the food that they must spend all their time serving him to the neglect of his apparent siblings. Does the poor wren curse the day he became a parent, or does he feel a perverse pride in having sired what appears to be the largest wren in avian history?

I now have some understanding of what it is like to act as father to a cuckoo egg, for I have become the unwilling author of a book entitled *The California Psychological Inventory Handbook*. It did not start as a book on the CPI, much less a CPI *handbook*. Originally, the manuscript was to be a single chapter in a textbook surveying all the major structured personality inventories, with chapters planned on the Minnesota Multiphasic Personality Inventory (MMPI), The Sixteen Personality Factor Questionnaire (16 PF), The Guilford-Zimmerman Temperament Survey, the Edwards Personal Preference Schedule, and the Strong Vocational Interest Blank (SVIB) in addition to the CPI. I had been collecting material and reading extensively on all these instruments, and I began writing fully intending to prepare a book with chapters on each of these devices.

Unfortunately, the CPI chapter refused to stay within the fifty pages allotted to it. One or more books had been written about all the other tests such as the MMPI, 16 PF, and SVIB so I could refer the reader to these primary sources for detailed information. Not so the CPI. Despite the fact that two decades have passed since the CPI was introduced, despite the fact that some 250,-000 answer sheets are filled out each year, despite the fact that over six hundred published and many unpublished studies using the CPI have accumulated, despite the fact that the inventory has been translated, in whole or in part, into two dozen languages and dialects, and despite the fact that, in the most recent *Mental Measurements Yearbook,* Kelly (1965, p. 169) hails it as "one of the best, if not the best, available instrument of its kind," no book has ever been written describing and evaluating the CPI.

Because no basic text or handbook was available on the CPI, I found myself writing more detailed descriptions of the theoretical basis and the derivation of the CPI scales than I had originally planned. The two-page integration of factor analyses of the CPI became twenty-six pages of text and five tables. Thus, like the fledgling cuckoo, the CPI "chapter" began to grow at a disproportionate rate, consuming more and more of my energy and resources as I neglected the other chapters. If things had continued at this rate, I would have soon been author of the world's longest chapter. Novelists sometimes have the experience of a character running away with the story; here a test was running away with the book. Apparently I had either to stop, throw away 80 per cent of what I had written, and then rewrite everything at a much more superficial level, or to give up the struggle and proceed with the full-length book on the CPI that was demanding to be written. The former course seemed to be about as easy as suggesting to a woman in hard labor that perhaps she ought to think twice about having a baby. Although I was not consciously aware of it, my decision had apparently been made a long time before I started writing and I was just now learning about it.

In retrospect, if there was a moment of conscious choice, it came shortly after I read in an article certain details I had hitherto been unaware of about the derivation of one of the CPI scales. Although I had interpreted many CPIs and had even taught courses covering the CPI, I had never got around to reading this rather obscure article before. Yet these details altered my whole perception of the meaning of the scale and explained many puzzling facts about the way in which it related to other variables. I then knew that I would not be content unless I summarized the methods and samples used in the construction of each scale for the benefit of readers who, like myself, had not yet put forth the effort required to locate and read the original accounts of the construction of each scale (not all of which had been formally published). Once I devoted this much space to scale construction procedures, I could not still cover the range of topics I wanted to within the confines of a fifty-page chapter. At that point I finally realized I was raising one obnoxious cuckoo rather than a nest full of well behaved wrens.

Since, like it or not, I appeared to be in the process of writing a book on the CPI, I resolved to do the best job I could. I attempted to write a resource volume that would have in it all the basic information anyone using the CPI would require, whether he was a counseling psychologist, a clinician, or a researcher. At the same time I tried to write in such a way that the beginner would find the *Handbook* easily comprehensible even if he did not have a strong background in psychological testing. In short, rather than make the book easy by leaving out the hard parts, I tried to make the hard parts understandable. If I have succeeded, this handbook should be useful to everyone who needs to learn about the CPI, from the rankest beginner to the most sophisticated expert.

At the same time, I did not want the *Handbook* to be simply a compendium of facts, a lengthy annotated bibliography, or an almanac. My goal was to do more than describe; I also wanted to integrate and evaluate the material presented. Throughout the book I present my opinions about various aspects of the CPI and the research literature; at the same time I try to present the reader with the data he needs to decide whether he agrees with my opinions. If readers who disagree with my conclusions are able to buttress their arguments by pointing to data provided in the book, I will feel that I have succeeded in this objective. I also take note of opposing points of view and alert the reader to areas of controversy. For example, the chapter on interpretation of the individual CPI profile explains how I go about the interpretative task. My approach differs in some respects from that suggested by Harrison Gough, and these areas of disagreement are delineated. The whole idea of individual interpretation was abhorrent to at least one actuarially oriented colleague, who took me to task for including such an anachronistic chapter in what he regarded as an otherwise sound book. I duly note his opinion too. In short, then, insofar as possible, I have tried to write a book which has a definite viewpoint but which is not dogmatic.

The *Handbook* follows a definite progression, each part building on what preceded it; it should, therefore, be read in sequence. Some readers tend to skip directly to the chapter on interpretation, and I chastise and scold these people at suitable points in the text. The chapters on the interpretation and on the applications of the CPI are toward the end because I am convinced that one must have a thorough understanding of the basic structure of the inventory and its empirical relations before one attempts to interpret it or to apply it to various problems.

In the first part of the *Handbook*, I place the CPI in its proper context. I believe that one cannot fully understand an assessment device without some understanding of the approach to testing espoused by the test author and of the historical and social forces that impinged upon and influenced its development. Therefore, after a brief global description of the CPI, the remainder of Part One examines Gough's philosophy of assessment and discusses how it influenced the choice of constructs to be scaled and the general methods of scale development and validation used.

Part Two examines in detail and evaluates each of the eighteen CPI scales. Gough's purpose in deriving each scale is first stated, followed by a summary of the test construction procedures used in selecting the items. The item composition of the resulting scale is then described. Information as to the amount of item overlap and the reliability of each scale is provided. Finally the literature bearing on the validity of each scale is reviewed. The final chapter in Part Two describes some of the new CPI scales briefly, and an appendix lists the item composition of many of them.

Part Three examines the correlates of the various CPI scales and the interpretation of the individual profile. Chapter Nine discusses the correlations of the CPI scales with each other and reviews and integrates the results of twenty factor and cluster analyses of the CPI. In Chapter Ten, the pattern of correlations which were obtained between the various CPI factors and the scales on other tests and various demographic variables is discussed, and the results of adjectival analyses of the eighteen scales are presented in an effort to increase our understanding of the various scales and to derive interpretive principles. The final chapter of Part Three describes the interpretation of the individual profile sheet and provides numerous case examples.

Part Four turns to an examination of the application of the CPI in various areas. Whereas the characteristics of the individual scales were the primary objects of attention in the first three parts of the *Handbook*, Part Four discusses the use of the CPI as a whole. For example, Part Two discusses the validity of the Achievement via Conformance and of the Socialization scales: Part Four describes the overall test patterns associated with academic achievement and juvenile delinquency and presents multivariate approaches to various prediction problems through the use of techniques such as multiple regression analysis. In the course of this treatment, various factors that influence the nature of these relationships become apparent. For example, the vast literature on the prediction of academic achievement with the CPI demonstrates that one must consider the setting (grade school, high school, college, or graduate school), the level and the distribution of IQ in the sample, whether overall achievement or achievement in some delimited area such as mathematics is being predicted, and whether the CPI is being used alone or in conjunction with other tests. Other factors that one must take into account include whether the study was performed in the United States or abroad (the CPI being used widely in cross-cultural research) and the criterion of achievement used. One must consider similar parameters in applying the CPI to other areas such as leadership, social deviance, conformity, and creativity. (Applications of the CPI in three broad areas—vocational-educational, clinical-counseling, and personality-social research—can be examined.)

Finally, the Epilogue reiterates the important points made in the text and describes the important directions for future research.

Over the years many people helped with this project, first at the University of Texas and later at the Florida State University. A series of student assistants aided in the library research; chief among them were Mary Quinn Burkhart, Richard Frohwirth, Robert Levine, Judith McGuire, Guerry Peavey, and Charles A. Wheeler. Other student assistants helped in the tedious business of preparing tables and figures, transcribing numbers, checking them, and rechecking them: Dave Gilbert, Ann Trawick, Cameron MacDonald, Roylynn Hamilton and Mary Daniel.

Several secretaries struggled with the task of transforming my manuscripts, with their multicolored arrows, illegible directions, and scrawled insertions stapled to the sides, into legible copy for me to deface again. Chief among them was Lynn Wernlund, who coped with every draft from the first dictated version to the semifinal, final, definitely final, positively final, and absolutely final revisions. Before her Ann Fountain typed numerous notes and detailed outlines (before wisely seeking another position), and later Sara Lyon typed several chapters as well as most of the tables and the reference list. Julie Wiley helped with the frontmatter and index and, along with Sara Lyon, played a major role in proof-reading.

Throughout this period, I was fortunate in working in an atmosphere extraordinarily conducive to scholarly activity. This was due in large measure to Joseph Grosslight, chairman of the Florida State University Psychology Department and to Charles Spielberger and Wallace Kennedy, who served as directors of the Clinical Training Program.

Several colleagues examined the manuscript and commented on it. Three in particular, Harrison Gough, Lewis Goldberg, and Wallace Hall, all spent several days meticulously evaluating the manuscript and writing over forty single-spaced pages of notes and comments that were an invaluable aid in preparing the final revisions. In addition, Gough kindly provided me with references, reprints, unpublished papers, correspondence, and reminiscences. I also received less detailed comments from Stanley Brodsky, William Henry, Robert Hogan, and Wayne Holtzman. In addition, two classes of students in clinical psychology read the *Handbook* in manuscript form and wrote comments in the margin. Painful though it was, I had to agree with most of the critical comments and revise the manuscript accordingly. Even when I disagreed and chose not to follow the advice given, consideration of a different viewpoint helped me think through and clarify my position.

I also want to thank Harrison Gough and Consulting Psychologists Press for special permission to print sample items from the CPI and to reproduce the profile sheet and Table 5 from the CPI *Manual*. This material is copyrighted and published by Consulting Psychologists Press.

To all these people who gave so freely of their time and energy, my thanks. I hope they find the *Handbook* worthy of the effort they put forth.

I dedicate this work to my wife, Ann, who in many ways is the one who made it possible.

Tallahassee   EDWIN INGLEE MEGARGEE
January 1972

Contents

APPENDICES

List of Tables

List of Illustrations

Let us have tests and instruments which are relevant to life and true to life, and let us have users of these tools who possess the talent, the training, and the integrity to interpret them validly and with creative insight.

HARRISON GOUGH

The
California
Psychological
Inventory
Handbook

PART I

In an important paper, Harrison Gough, creator of the California Psychological Inventory (CPI), proposes that assessment instruments be subjected to a "conceptual analysis." According to Gough (1965a), this analysis involves three distinct stages. The first consists of determining "what criteria are principally relevant to the test, how well it predicts what it seeks to predict, measures what it proposes to measure, or defines what it is intended to define" (p. 295). The second stage "seeks to discover the psychological basis of measurement, to specify and clarify the meaning of that which is measured" (p. 295). The third level focuses on the importance of the instrument, which stems not only from the degree to which it is successful in measuring what it seeks to measure and in defining a psychological dimension, but also from any serendipitous relationships that are found.

In this book, the CPI is subjected to a thorough conceptual analysis. The development of each scale is described in full, and the literature relating to its reliability and validity is critically evaluated. Moreover, the correlates of each

2

THE CALIFORNIA PSYCHOLOGICAL INVENTORY

scale, the factor structure of the test, and the uses that have been found for the individual scales and the test as a whole are explored, thereby providing the reader with the data he needs for secondary and tertiary evaluation of the inventory.

However, although the writer agrees with Gough that all these data are necessary for an adequate understanding of an assessment device, he does not feel that they are sufficient. To fully appreciate a personality inventory such as the CPI, one must not stop at what the test assesses; one must understand why it assesses these particular variables in this particular manner. In his article, Gough implies that we should start our inquiry with the test instrument; the present author, however, feels that we should start our inquiry with Gough and with the intellectual atmosphere that gave rise to the CPI. Therefore, after a brief description of the CPI, this part is devoted to a discussion of its creator and to a consideration of how his philosophy of personality assessment shaped the development of the CPI.

CHAPTER 1

Description of the Inventory

In 1948 Harrison Gough published the first scales of what was to become the California Psychological Inventory (CPI). Over the next few years he and his associates derived other scales, and he published the first copyrighted edition of the CPI, including fifteen scales, in 1951. Five years later Consulting Psychologists Press published the full eighteen-scale CPI. In its first edition, the CPI *Manual* (Gough, 1957) listed fifty-four studies that had used or had investigated the CPI. As the *Manual* was reissued in 1960 and revised in 1964 and 1969, the number of investigations steadily increased so that, a quarter of a century after the initial scale construction, the literature contained more than six hundred CPI studies.

Concomitant with this growth in the research literature has been a widening use of the CPI in counseling centers, clinics, schools, and correctional agencies. Editions are available in Australia, France, Italy, and Japan, and the inventory has been translated, in whole or in part, into Afrikaans, Australian English, Chinese (four dialects), Czech, Dutch, French, German, Hebrew, Hindi, Italian, Japanese, Korean, Norwegian, Polish, Portuguese, Punjabi, Sinhalese, Spanish, Swedish, Tagalog, Tamil, and Turkish. Normative data are available on thirty-one groups totaling 15,294 individuals. In a single study of the Socialization scale, 26,824 subjects were tested in ten countries. Kleinmuntz (1967, p. 239) states, "The CPI is already well on its way to becoming one of the best, if not the best, personality-measuring instrument of its kind." Anastasi (1968, p. 448) hails it as "one of the best personality inventories currently available," noting that "its technical development is of a high order, and it has been subjected to extensive research and continuous improvement." And Goldberg (in press) concludes, "Eventually . . . the CPI may become obsolete. But . . . the knowledgeable applied practitioner should be able to provide more solid nontest

4

predictions from the CPI than from most other comparable instruments on the market today." By any criterion, the CPI has achieved the status of a major personality assessment instrument.

Yet, the CPI remains one of the most poorly understood of the principal personality inventories. One reason is its apparent simplicity. In contrast to The Sixteen Personality Factor Questionnaire with its scales for Parmia and Alexia and the Minnesota Multiphasic Personality Inventory (MMPI) with its enigmatic K and F scales, the CPI measures such everyday traits as dominance and responsibility, characteristics that "everybody" knows and understands. This familiarity often gives the student such a false sense of security that he fails to take the time to study the "folk concept" theory that is the bedrock of the CPI.

Another pitfall is the superficial resemblance of the CPI to the MMPI. In constructing the CPI, Gough built on the foundation laid by the authors of the MMPI. Indeed the two tests share 178 virtually identical items (Goldberg and Rorer, 1964; Jones and Goldberg, 1964). These similarities led Thorndike (1959) to dub the CPI "the sane man's MMPI," implying that the CPI is merely a collection of eighteen scales designed for use in normal populations. This is not the case, and those who fail to comprehend the unique characteristics that differentiate the CPI from other inventories are unable to understand or to use the instrument fully.

The basic facts about the CPI are easy to outline. It is a self-administering paper-and-pencil personality test. Designed for group administration, it also can be taken individually or even by mail. While it is important to gain rapport with the subjects, standardized testing conditions are not essential. No time limit is imposed, but most subjects finish in about an hour. The test requires fourth-grade reading ability unless the items are read aloud to the respondents. The CPI has been administered to subjects ranging in age from twelve to seventy, but some of the items do not apply to elementary school or junior high school students. The content is geared more to students and young adults than to older groups.

The reusable question booklet contains 468 statements, twelve of which appear twice for a total of 480 items (Goldberg, in press). Most of the content consists of reports of typical behavior patterns and customary feelings, opinions, and attitudes about social, ethical, and family matters. Compared with the MMPI, the CPI is notable for its lack of symptom-oriented material. By and large, the content is much less objectionable than that of the MMPI, and the vocabulary and grammatical constructions are generally easier to understand.

The respondent indicates on a separate answer sheet (designed for hand scoring) whether he thinks each statement is true or false for him or whether he agrees or disagrees with it by placing an X in a box labeled T or F. Scorers place opaque plastic templates over the answer sheet and, for each scale, count the number of Xs that appear in the clear plastic windows. Computerized scoring services are also available. They require the respondent to answer on special devices such as the National Computer Systems (NCS) or the Dela Data answer sheets.

Once computed, the raw scores are transferred to a profile sheet. (See Chapter Eleven for samples of CPI profiles.) By plotting the raw scores on the profile sheet, one converts them to T-scores: standard scores with a mean of 50 and a standard deviation of 10. These standard scores are based on norms collected for more than over six thousand men and seven thousand women. Although not a true random or stratified sample of the general population—whites are overrepresented, for example—the sample did include subjects of widely varying age, socioeconomic status, and geographical areas (Gough, personal communication, 1971). The results are then ready to be interpreted by a skilled clinician based on his understanding of the derivation, reliability, validity, and empirical correlates of each scale, and on his knowledge of how the scales interact with one another. (Interpretation of the individual CPI profile is described in Chapter Eleven.)

The CPI is typically scored for eighteen scales that Gough has divided into four groups as an aid to profile interpretation. The six Class I scales measure poise, ascendancy, self-assurance, and interpersonal adequacy. The scales included are for Dominance (Do), Capacity for Status (Cs), Sociability (Sy), Social Presence (Sp), Self-Acceptance (Sa), and Sense of Well-Being (Wb). The Class II measures assess socialization, maturity, responsibility, and intrapersonal structuring of values. They also include six scales: Responsibility (Re), Socialization (So), Self-Control (Sc), Tolerance (To), Good Impression (Gi), and Communality (Cm). Class III groups together three scales relating to achievement potential and intellectual efficiency: Achievement via Conformance (Ac), Achievement via Independence (Ai), and Intellectual Efficiency (Ie). The last category, Class IV, is a grab bag which, for want of a better term, is described as measuring intellectual and interest modes. The three scales included are Psychological Mindedness (Py), Flexibility (Fx), and Femininity (Fe). Of these eighteen scales, fifteen are designed as measures of these various personality traits, and three, Wb, Gi, and Cm, as validity scales which also have interpretive significance.

The four classes are groupings designed to facilitate clinical interpretation of the profile rather than psychometric factors or clusters. However, Class I and Class II do roughly correspond to the first and second factors that emerge from factor analyses of the CPI, described in detail in Chapter Nine. Such analyses typically yield five factors. Factor 2 consists of scales Do, Cs, Sy, Sp, and Sa. Factor 1 is usually the largest and includes Wb, Re, So, Sc, To, Gi, Ac, Ai, Ie, and Py. However, a number of these scales also have high loadings on other factors as well. The third factor is considerably smaller than the first two and is defined by scales To, Ai, Ie, Py, and Fx. The fourth consists of So and Cm, and the fifth of but a single scale, Fe.

Various investigators have devised other CPI-based scales and measures for special purposes in addition to the eighteen standard scales. Some of these are factor scales or rationally derived summary scores, such as the mean of the T-scores on the factor 1 scales. Such scales are offered by those who object to the interrelatedness or redundancy of many CPI scales or who wish to emphasize the common factor variance and minimize the specific variance. Other scales measure traits not included in the original inventory such as empathy and anxiety.

However, there has been much less scale proliferation in the CPI than in the MMPI. MMPI researchers usually devised a new scale whenever existing scales were found to be inadequate for the assessment of some trait. Although Gough originally viewed the CPI as an open-ended inventory like the MMPI and the Strong Vocational Interest Blank (SVIB) (Gough, 1965c), he has since adopted the position that "a basic tenet for multivariate instruments such as the CPI is to move on to patterns and combinations in any setting in which the relationships for individual scales are too low" (Gough and Kirk, 1970, p. 227). Following this precept, Gough has taken the lead in using multiple regression techniques to derive weighted combinations of CPI scales that can assess such diverse factors as social maturity, achievement in medical school, and success on parole. Many of these equations include in the prediction not only CPI variables but also data from other tests or case histories. The more heterogeneous the array of potential prediction variables the better the chances of assessing a complex criterion (compare Megargee and Menzies, 1971). In Chapters Twelve, Thirteen, and Fourteen, in which the application of the CPI to various assessment problems is discussed, a number of the equations offered by Gough and other investigators are presented.

These multivariate studies exemplify Gough's persistent efforts to refine, correct, and improve the CPI—efforts which have won the praise of most reviewers. According to one authority, "the most impressive feature of the CPI has been its adopters' and its publishers' relentless efforts at collecting pertinent research data and . . . its developer's responsiveness to criticism" (Kleinmuntz, 1967, p. 240).[1] The *Manual* is revised at approximateley three-year intervals, and between revisions supplementary bibliographies are sent free to CPI users.

While the technical adequacy of the CPI is generally well regarded, some reviewers have questioned the constructs Gough chose to assess and the methods of scale construction he selected (Cronbach, 1959; Thorndike, 1959; Kelly, 1965). Why, for example, did he choose to measure such traits as responsibility or to construct a scale for achievement via conformance? Why not measure "more psychological" dimensions and assign labels less loaded with value connotations? Why choose test-construction methods that result in an instrument with a large number of "redundant" scales that correlate highly with one another and with measures of response set and response bias? Why not take steps to ensure the factorial purity of each scale?

The answers to questions like these depend on a deeper understanding of the construction of the CPI than can be gained from the *Manual* or from the articles reporting the derivation of particular scales. They are firmly rooted in Gough's theories of personality, his philosophy of testing, and his beliefs regarding the proper goals of a personality-assessment inventory. While he has

[1] For example, inflated biserial correlation coefficients based on the comparison of extreme groups were erroneously cited as validity coefficients in the first edition of the *Manual* (Gough, 1957). Gough was roundly and legitimately scored for this error by Thorndike (1959) and by Cronbach (1960), and he promptly removed the offending coefficients in the next revision of the *Manual* (1960). The ghosts of those biserial *r*s still haunt him, however. Vingoe (1968) recently cited them as a reason for questioning the validity of certain CPI scales, and Cronbach (1970, p. 543) in the third edition of his *Essentials of Psychological Testing* repeated the objections to their usage that he had voiced in the second edition (1960, p. 482), without noting that they had been removed ten years earlier.

alluded to some of the theoretical assumptions of the CPI (Gough, 1965a, 1965c, 1968a), he has not as yet published a digest of the precepts for which he argues so trenchantly in private. This lack of a published theory makes it difficult for the test user to evaluate the merits of the CPI properly because, in the final analysis, whether one shares these values determines whether he regards a given test characteristic, such as redundancy, as good or bad.

In the next chapter, we shall explore the philosophical basis for the CPI and some of the influences on Gough that helped shape the personality inventory he developed. This background makes many of the characteristics of the instrument understandable.

CHAPTER 2

Philosophical Basis of the CPI

In the mind of the layman, there is generally a clear distinction between art and science. Art to him is a subjective, personal expression of the artist, while a technological or scientific discovery is viewed as something objective and mechanical in which human feelings or values play a minimal role. However, on close examination, he would soon find a tremendous amount of technology in art, and a great deal of art in science. When painters talk shop, they do not discuss each other's work in the lofty, abstract terms found in the typical museum catalog; instead they are more likely to confer about the technical details of surfaces and media, of how light, texture, contrast, and composition can be used to produce artistic effects. Similarly, sculptors discourse for hours about materials, kilns, temperatures, and the like. Scientists, conversely, are popularly supposed to think and talk as they write —that is, in a logical, unemotional fashion with all decisions reached solely by reference to scientific laws or empirical data. However, as any scientist knows, that stereotype is just so much hokum. Certainly the scientist has a commitment to reason and logic; but most of the major decisions, such as the choice of problems to investigate for the next ten years, are based on a mixture of human values. They include such consideration as whether his choice is a worthwhile way to spend his time and whether he will enjoy this particular investigation. There are also practical considerations such as whether he can get a grant for this research and whether his project requires too much space.

Despite the image of scientific-technological objectivity the values and philosophy of the test author do strongly influence the test.[1] The construction,

[1] In this discussion, the term *test* is being used in its broad sense to refer to any

9

development, and promotion of a major assessment device are so arduous and time-consuming that they usually occupy a major portion of the author's professional career. Often the test becomes his life work. An able and gifted man does not make such a commitment unless he believes that his approach is of such value to psychological science that it is worth the years of effort and thousands of dollars required. He must be convinced that his predecessors were mistaken and that he is correct. If David Wechsler had been satisfied with the Stanford-Binet, the Wechsler-Bellevue would never have been born, just as Wayne Holtzman had to be convinced of the psychometric inadequacy of the Rorschach before he proceeded to develop the Holtzman Inkblot Technique.

Because of this investment, test authors are of necessity individualists with deeply held convictions who become very involved with their creations. In many ways the test becomes an extension of the man, embodying many of his basic values and most cherished beliefs. Just as the art student must study the artist to understand his paintings, so too the psychologist must comprehend the philosophy of the test author to appreciate fully his test.

Gough is one of the few test authors who has formally articulated his values and his philosophy of testing; unfortunately, the most cogent expressions of his principles are contained in unpublished papers and personal correspondence. In this chapter we will present Gough's principles of testing and place them in their intellectual and personal contexts, as well as spell out their implications for the construction and subsequent development of the CPI.

Selection of Variables

An artist must first decide what his subject will be. To some extent he is guided by opportunity: Paul Cezanne could hardly have painted the back side of the moon. But the painter's personal values are even more relevant in such a decision. Despite the fact that he summered by the sea, Henride Toulouse-Lautrec almost invariably painted people indoors—in cafes, brothels, theaters, and dance halls. Robert Wood, however, paints seascapes almost exclusively; any human figures are simply incidental parts of his compositions.

Just as an artist must choose a subject, the would-be test constructor must decide what to assess. Usually a number of good reasons can be adduced to justify his choice, but the basic decision is usually determined by a subjective value judgment.

According to Gough (1965c) the author of a personality test can go about the task of selecting traits to assess personality in one of three ways. The first is to measure traits that have been postulated in some existing psychological theory. A Freudian might choose to assess oral dependency, penis envy, or castration anxiety; a Jungian would be inclined to build scales measuring introversion-extraversion; a follower of Henry Murray would construct scales for need achievement and press rejection. Insofar as these scales could serve as valid operational definitions of these constructs, this approach would be exceedingly valuable for those wishing to do research testing the predictions generated by a particular

---

assessment device. In a narrower sense it can be argued that the CPI is an inventory and not a test.

theoretical frame of reference. Such scales could also be used in the prediction of behavior if the theory were valid.

According to Gough (1965c, p. 4) there are advantages and disadvantages in constructing a theory-based inventory:

> To turn to a theory or to the variables promulgated by a significant man is the modal answer today and the one endorsed by most books and authorities. . . . The measures tied to a theoretical system have meaning in a context which itself may have great power. But history usually shows even the greatest thinkers to have been in error, and if a test is linked solidly to such systems the test must go down when the system goes down. An inventory scale for animal magnetism might have been popular with followers of Mesmer in the late 1700s but would be of little interest to most researchers today.

As we shall see, Gough never adopted a formal theoretical position. This may have been because of the atheoretical intellectual atmosphere, the so-called dust bowl empiricism at the University of Minnesota, where he reviewed his undergraduate and graduate training, or simply a result of his own independent streak. However, Gough is also quite skeptical of the validity of many theoretical positions in the interpretations of normal interpersonal behavior. Many theories of personality are based on clinical observations of disturbed people, and he maintains that the behavior patterns observed in the clinic represent too narrow and atypical a range of functioning to serve as the basis for any general theory of personality. One might just as well construct a theory of music on the basis of extended observations of tone-deaf individuals with 80 per cent decibel loss, he argues. Self-analysis and introspection are even narrower standards for drawing general conclusions; often what emerges from them is nothing more than an attempt to evaluate everyone from a standard based on the theorist's projected self-image.

One can always depart from established theoretical frameworks and construct a new system. Instead of assessing the variables that others have postulated as being of fundamental importance, one can seek to determine for oneself what the important variables are. That is what Gough regards as the second alternative basis for test construction. The research program of Raymond Cattell, creator of the Sixteen Personality Factor Questionnaire, is a prime example of this second approach, in which observations are made, their relationships are determined, and, through use of the tool of factor analysis, hypothetical constructs are identified and scales for assessing them are developed. However, this approach also has its limitations: "The *de novo* approach can sharply disengage itself from dead and dying systems of the past but may have a problem in winning adherents in the present; another way of stating it is that the new dimension may not be relevant to the needs of the user and may not predict whatever it is he wishes to have predicted" (Gough, 1965c, p. 4).

Gough prefers a third approach which consists of examining the setting in which the test is to be used and developing measurements based on the constructs already in operational usage there. Thus the Strong Vocational Interest Blank is meant to be applied in vocational counseling and the variables assessed are drawn from the normal workworld. The MMPI was designed to be used in neuro-psychiatric settings and the variables scales drawn from the world of psychopathology. Thus the third approach, the practitioner's approach, has general direct relevance and salience because it deals with concepts having already attained a degree of functional validity (Gough, 1965c, p. 4).

Gough places the CPI in this third category. But what is the context of usage for the inventory? What concepts already exist in the realm of interpersonal behavior? The answer is the descriptive terms now applied by people to one another to describe their everyday behavior patterns and traits: concepts such as responsibility, tolerance, sociability, and so on. These terms Gough calls folk concepts.

Gough criticized theory-based tests on the grounds that if a theory does not stand up over time, the test also dies. One might find it inconsistent for him to have then turned to the popular lexicon, with all its vagaries, as a source of traits to assess. However, a folk concept is not simply a term that is in popular usage. A folk concept must transcend a given era or a particular society. The trait of dominance for example, was as relevant to Plutarch in his description of Julius Caesar in the first century A.D. as it was to Arthur M. Schlesinger, Jr., in his portrayal of John Kennedy in the twentieth. Sociability and responsibility are important dimensions of interpersonal behavior from Alaska to Zanzibar.

> Because the instrument is intended for the diagnosis and comprehension of interpersonal behavior, the concepts selected are those that occur in everyday social living and, in fact, arise from social interaction. Most simply, such variables may be described as "folk concepts"—aspects and attributes of interpersonal behavior that are to be found in all cultures and societies, and that possess a direct and integral relationship to all forms of social interaction [Gough, 1968a, p. 57].

How does one identify and find folk concepts? One starting point is in natural language. This approach was pioneered by Gordon Allport (Allport and Odbert, 1936) and later by Cattell (1943, 1946, 1957), who explains:

> The first source—and the only immediate practical one—for a "total realm" of personality traits is to be found in language. Over the centuries, by the pressure of urgent necessity, every aspect of one human being's behavior that is likely to affect another has come to be handled by some verbal symbol—at least in any developed modern language. Although some new words for traits constantly appear, a debris of equivalent but obsolete words constantly falls from the language. Consequently, it seems likely that a plateau in the growth of the total number of necessary symbols was actually reached in English some centuries ago, at least by the time of Shakespeare [Cattell, 1957, p. 7].

Moreover, linguistic studies can provide a rough measure of the importance of a trait. The greater the number of synonyms the more important a characteristic is in a given society (Goldberg, 1970). (One may take some comfort from the fact that the thesaurus provides 30 per cent more synonyms for *love* than for *hate*.)

Although Gough prefers not to base a test entirely on a single theory of personality, he would be foolish to ignore theory entirely. The writings of psychological and sociological theorists can also contribute to valid constructs as can anthropological and ethnological reports.

In the final analysis, however, the selection of concepts by which to scale personality is subjective. In the CPI it is based in part on Gough's educated guess about the variables that would be most likely to have a high payoff in accurate predictions. Expedience also plays a role—the availability of certain subject populations, the needs of specific research projects, and the availability of certain criterion measures naturally influences the development of the inventory.

The first published version of the CPI had fifteen scales; later *Sp, Sa,* and *Sc* were added to bring the total to eighteen. However this should not be regarded as a definitive list of folk concepts. One could no doubt think of other concepts —such as generous-stingy—which appear to fit Gough's description of folk concepts just as well, if not better, than those he selected. In a personal communication (1971), Gough writes:

> The claim for the CPI is not that all folk concepts have been assessed, or even that the most important ones are scaled. The claim is simply that the eighteen variables do correspond to what people everywhere appeal to when they talk about themselves and others and that as a set the eighteen variables can predict —one scale at a time or via combinations—just about everything that happens in interpersonal life. Note that this claim does not mean perfect prediction; in many circumstances the forecasts will be very modest, and in every situation they will be enhanced by taking into account other factors, particularly environmental factors.

Gough (1968a, p. 58) maintains that scales based on his selected folk concepts have several important advantages:

> One of these advantages is an immediate relevance for cross-cultural measurement. If, for example, self-control is a universal variable in interpersonal living and if in fact all societies and all cultures recognize this variable as well as individual differences in its expression, then a scale developed in any one culture has at least presumptive relevance for the diagnosis of behavior in any other culture. . . .

> A second advantage in working with folk concepts as a basis for scaling is that the variables are meaningful and readily comprehended by the user. Any scale will carry latent and potential implications, which the skilled interpreter must learn to appreciate, but at the same time no special instruction or insight is required to recognize the main thrust of scales seeking to appraise such interpersonal qualities as dominance, sociability, responsibility, tolerance, social presence, and flexibility. . . .

> A third advantage lies in what might be called the power of these folk variables. Deriving from interpersonal living and tied to consistent and characteristic modes of reaction, they can in turn validly forecast future behavior in the same context. . . .

To summarize the above, we may say that the theoretical basis for scaling in the CPI is found in the ongoing processes of everyday social life, more specifically in what may be called folk concepts. This emphasis ensures the relevance of the inventory to problems and issues in interpersonal behavior and, for validation, points unmistakably to cross-cultural, longitudinal, and life-centered inquiry. The purpose of each scale is to reflect to a maximum degree some theme or aspect of interpersonal behavior—one that has clear visibility and is conceptually recognized by all people, everywhere. The desideratum for the set of scales is that any social behavior, of whatever variety, can be forecast and comprehended by either a single scale of the inventory or by some simple and meaningful *combination* of scales.

Not all psychologists share Gough's enthusiasm for folk dimensions. Cronbach (1959, p. 98) objects:

> The variables describe character in value-loaded terms. Teachers and principals very likely will approve this, but the inventory seems to encourage the idea that there is just one ideal type. Such scale titles as Responsibility, Tolerance, and Socialization have a pronounced ethical overtone which suggests that low scores reflect faults, rather than symptoms of needs, skills, and cultural pressures. Because of this implicit conflict with modern views of personality, it would be deplorable if CPI profiles were interpreted by principals, teachers, parents, or students without guidance from a psychologically trained person.

Gough has vigorously maintained that the CPI must be interpreted only by qualified professionals. While there is perhaps more danger of amateur analysis when lay language is used, the major question is whether words in everyday usage have acquired so much excess meaning that it is impossible to operationalize them or limit them to an exact scientific definition. Physicists, for example, trying to explain their special use of such terms as *work* or *energy* often wish they had chosen to invent new terms rather than redefine old ones. Cattell, who has chosen to scale such traits as rhyathymia and parmia, can be more confident than Gough that his students will not have erroneous preconceptions about his definitions of these terms. Gough would probably respond that while it is true that folk concepts such as self-control may have different connotations for different people, relabeling concepts to increase precision results in such loss of relevance that the original aim, an increase in communication, is lost. Moreover, he would probably argue that it is the culturally defined construct, with all of its subtle connotations as well as its formal denotation, that he wishes to assess.

Even psychologists who agree that folk concepts are at least worth using on a trial basis become uncomfortable when Gough suggests that those concepts are culturally or temporally universal. Skepticism at any suggestion that a given pattern is universal has become as automatic in psychologists as the knee jerk. The claim of universality has so often been promulgated by frauds and quacks, by people who suggest overly simple solutions to complex problems, that most psychologists have learned to shy away from axioms such as "a once-burned baby avoids a hot stove."

Gough recognizes that he must back up his claims with data. For this reason, cross-cultural research has been an essential part of the validation of the

CPI, and relationships found in the United States are often tested in many other countries. Most of these studies have found that the CPI travels well and predicts behavior abroad almost as well as it does at home.

Gough's approach to psychological assessment thus represents a unique blend of idealism and practicality, the abstract and the concrete, the idiographic and the nomothetic. Much of this eclecticism stems from his joint education in sociology and psychology at the University of Minnesota. As an undergraduate sociology major graduating in 1942, Gough was excited by the important social problems tackled by sociologists. However, he was strongly influenced by F. Stewart Chapin and Elio Monachesi, who, unlike many sociologists at that time, brought quantitative as well as qualitative research methods to bear on sociology. His exposure to psychologists such as Richard M. Elliott and Donald G. Paterson reinforced his empirical bent, so that he gradually became convinced that psychological research methods had to be applied to the socially significant problems identified by the sociologists. When Gough left the University to enter military service in 1942, he had not formulated the approach he would use in pursuing those research goals. His service experience and his postwar graduate education played a strong role in influencing such decisions.

Strategy of Test Construction

Once an artist has chosen his subject matter, he must decide on the methods he will use to render it. Wil he use watercolors, acrylics, or oils? Paper, board, or canvas? Brush, sponge, or knife? The approach is determined partly by the subject, partly by his own training and preferences, and partly by what he has at hand to work with. So, too, with test construction by a psychologist.

Once he has decided on the attributes he wishes to scale, he must select a method for building his test. According to Anastasi (1968, p. 21), "A psychological test is essentially an objective and standardized measure of a sample of behavior." The value of the test depends on how this limited-behavior sample relates to some large behavioral domain. The behavior domain Gough wished to predict was how an individual would act under specified conditions and how others would respond to him. His task was to select some limited set of objective, standard behavioral observations that would enable him to make these predictions.

Many samples of behavior have been used for personality assessment. They include the client's behavior in artificially contrived situations, his artistic productions, his responses to unstructured stimuli, his story-telling behavior, and his patterns of psychophysiological autonomic nervous system responses, to name a few. The behavior sample that Gough selected was the pattern of true and false answers to a series of questions about social behavior, attitudes, and interpersonal relations. This sample has the advantage of objectivity, ease of scoring, and the potential for large-scale administration. The disadvantages are that it lacks the richness and, perhaps, the subtlety of less structured behavior samples.

Given Gough's background, it would have been remarkable if he had chosen any other behavior samples. According to Wernick's account (1955, p. 98) of Gough's early life, "By the time Gough was ready for school, the state of Minnesota had gone test happy, and from the age of six he was used to spending many hours being subjected to the crude psychometric evaluations of that era. He loved it and still does. To this day he cannot resist signing up for any test he hears about, including those for civil service psychologist, which he always passes triumphantly."

Gough attended the University of Minnesota while Starke Hathaway and J. Charnley McKinley were deriving and publishing the first MMPI scales. In 1942, the year the Depression and Psychasthenia scales were published (just in time to measure the depression and anxiety resulting from World War II), Gough got his bachelor of arts degree in sociology and enlisted in the Army. In one of the few recorded instances of accurate Army selection, he was assigned to duty as a classifications officer and later as a clinical psychologist in a neuro-psychiatric clinic. It is likely that this military experience, during which he had to test large numbers of men, further inclined him toward the structured test approach. His graduate education in psychology at the University of Minnesota during the postwar years, when much research on the newly published MMPI was taking place, convinced him. From 1946 to 1949 he immersed himself in the course of study developed at Minnesota by Paul Meehl and Hathaway, taking every course they offered. By the time he had completed his Ph.D. and accepted an appointment at Berkeley in 1949, Gough had already published ten articles dealing with the application of the MMPI to the assessment of achievement, prejudice, social status and delinquency—starters in his campaign to bring the measurement techniques of psychology to bear on socially relevant problems. Further studies deriving scales for the assessment of responsibility, dominance, femininity, social participation, and test-measurement distortions appeared, culminating in the publication of the CPI. Thus while the CPI was born in Berkeley, it was conceived in Minneapolis, and much of the prenatal development took place while its creator was under the influence of the Minnesota intellectual atmosphere.

This atmosphere influenced not only the decision to develop a structured rather than a projective measure of folk concepts but also guided the item-writing and item-selection techniques. The Minnesota approach, sometimes characterized as "dust bowl empiricism," placed primary emphasis on the relationship between the item and the criterion. Unlike the rational or intuitive methods, in which the test author or a committee of judges decides which items should be included, the empirical approach emphasizes the administration of a large item pool to carefully selected groups at the extremes of the behavioral dimension in question. Those items that consistently differentiate such groups are selected for inclusion on the scale, regardless of whether the manifest content of the item makes sense. That procedure had been used by E. K. Strong in the selection of items for the scales of the Strong Vocational Interest Blank and was also followed by Hathaway and McKinley in the construction of many of the MMPI scales. The emphasis is on practical utility rather than psychometric elegance or factorial purity. It is the approach of the Midwestern farmer who fixes his fence with baling wire and judges it not for its beauty but on the basis of whether it keeps his neighbor's cows out of his cornfield. (Thus, "dust bowl" empiricism.)

The third and final decision a test author must make is how the test should be used. This decision is rarely, if ever, discussed in textbooks on testing, yet it guides much of the subsequent validation and application of the testing instrument. Gough (1965c, pp. 1–2) states his position on this issue clearly and succinctly: "To me, the first and cardinal principle is that tests are made to be used, and a subsidiary principle is that they are to be used in the analysis and conceptualization of the individual case."

Gough himself is a gifted test interpreter whose skill at describing a client on the basis of a CPI or MMPI profile is famous. In the service he was impressed by the clinical case formulation of Leopold Wexberg, the Viennese Adlerian psychiatrist. In the postwar years at Minnesota, the MMPI came to be used for the clinical interpretation of the individual case with virtuoso performers such as Gough being called on to demonstrate their skill in free-wheeling, multifaceted clinical interpretations based on profile analysis. For those who regard structured personality inventories as being diametrically opposed to projective techniques, it is instructive to sit in on one of these sessions. They find, often to their horror, that Gough, despite his reputation as a representative of the nomothetic approach, is using the CPI in much the same way that Bruno Klopfer uses a Rorschach protocol.

Gough's emphasis on building a test to be used by the individual test interpreter has influenced much of the subsequent research and development of the instrument. The profile sheet was designed to simplify the task of the interpreter—and not strictly on the basis of factor analysis. Similarly much research has gone into adjective checklist analyses which are relevant not only for the conceptual analysis of the CPI but also in their ability to facilitate the acquisition of interpretive skills.

However, the principle that the CPI was made for practical use reaches much further than this. Much of Gough's subsequent research with the test has focused on the application of the test in the prediction of important, everyday behavior patterns. "Issues such as school progress, graduation versus dropout, scholastic achievement, leadership, interpersonal effectiveness, social maturity, professional performance, and creativity should all be proper concerns of the test; indeed, encouraging and provocative studies have been completed on all of these topics" (Gough, 1965c, p. 7). Insofar as the test can contribute to the valid prediction of such behavior patterns, Gough regards its validity as justified. Thus, because of his conviction that tests should be useful and useable tools for the prediction of behavior, he has placed greater emphasis on what Campbell (1960) has termed practical validity than he has on trait or construct validity.

> The purpose of each scale *is to predict what an individual will do in a specified context and/or to identify individuals who will be described in a certain way.* These aims are important both theoretically and practically and should be distinguished from the more common goal in inventory measurement of trait specification. If a scale is intended to define a unidimensional trait of personality, then it must meet minimal statistical requirements of internal homogeneity, domain reliability, and factorial independence. However, if the purpose of a scale is to forecast what a person will say or do, and/or how he will be described by those who know him well, then these statistical considerations become relevant if, and only if, it can be shown that the predictive utility of the measure is improved by their fulfillment.

Reference to another well-known test, the Strong Vocational Interest Blank (Strong, 1943), may help to make clear what is being said. An occupational scale on the *Strong*, such as minister, is not intended to define a trait of ministerialism, but rather to identify individuals whose outlook resembles those in the profession and who might (therefore) feel at home in the indicated environment. Similarly with the CPI, a high score on a scale for a social status does not mean that the individual tested has a trait of high status, but rather that in viewpoint and outlook he tends to resemble people of high status or possessed of those talents and dispositions that will lead him toward such attainment.

The significance of the point that is being emphasized lies principally in the kind of evidence to which one should turn for an evaluation of the worth of the measure. For the scales of the CPI this evidence should come from the context of application: do the scales for achievement motivation forecast scholastic attainment, does the scale for dominance predict ascendent behavior, does the scale for socialization forecast behavior on parole or in other settings where observance of rules and prohibitions is essential, and does the scale for social presence identify people who are at ease, self-assured, and natural in their dealings with others [Gough, 1968a]?

Gough is annoyed by those who criticize the CPI because it fails to measure up to criteria that he feels are irrelevant. To be sure, the CPI scales lack factorial purity and many are highly correlated with one another. There are also imbalances in the true-false keying, and some correlate highly with measures of social desirability. Gough would respond by saying, "So what?" to such criticism, for he feels it demonstrates the critic has confused the ends of test construction with the means used to achieve those ends. If statistical analyses improve behavior prediction, they should be incorporated in the instrument. They are not goals in themselves. Certainly they are not the criteria by which a test should be evaluated.

The problem is that although Gough's goal is behavioral prediction, many CPI users, including the present writer, use the inventory scales to define constructs. When a scale is being used as the operational definition of a trait, then construct validation should be used to establish whether the scale is related to what it purports to measure.

However, in any validity study of constructs, the relevance of the various criteria must be judged. For example, one of the most frequent criticisms of the CPI is that it contains too much overlap between scales and not enough homogeneity within them. Cronbach and Meehl in their classic description of construct validation (1955, p. 288) state, "Only if the underlying theory of the trait being measured calls for high item intercorrelations do the correlations support construct validity." Since Gough has never maintained that folk-concept scaling calls for high item intercorrelations, such item data seem irrelevant. Similarly, when a nomological net of predictions fails to be confirmed, one must determine whether it is because the scale failed to assess the trait and thus lacks construct validity or because the theory generating the prediction was in error. The studies of Megargee and his colleagues on the Dominance (*Do*) scale (Megargee, 1969b; Megargee, Bogart, and Anderson, 1966; Fenelon and Megargee, 1971) show how various situational factors can lead to erroneous predictions from a valid scale.

Thus the CPI must be confirmed in regard to both practical validity, (that is, concurrent and predictive validity) and trait (construct) validity. The proof of the pudding is in the eating, but we must also analyze the ingredients to determine whether the concoction should be properly called pudding. No matter how tasty the alleged pudding is, if it is round and has a crust on top and bottom and filling between, it should be called pie.

Gough recognizes this problem with nomenclature, and despite the fact that the main thrust of his research has been on practical applications of the CPI, he has devoted considerable thought to naming the scales and has renamed them when the evidence suggested that the original name was inappropriate. Thus the Social Participation scale became Sociability and Social Status was re-named Capacity for Status on the basis of further research after the scale was constructed.

This subsequent research is part of what Gough (1965a) terms the con-ceptual analysis of the test scales. Conceptual analysis is an explicit program of scale validation and refinement that includes, but goes beyond practical and trait validation. It includes three steps or stages which must be followed if an adequate understanding of a scale is to be achieved.

> The first of these emphases may be designated the *primary evaluation*. The task here is to determine what criteria are principally relevant to the test, how well it predicts what it seeks to predict, measures what it purports to measure, or defines what it is intended to define. Most of what is said about test validity in textbooks and manuals may be classified under this first heading. . . . *Secondary evaluation* seeks to discover the psychological basis of measurement, to specify and clarify the meaning of that which is measured. . . . The task is to uncover and hence illuminate the underlying psychological dimensionality that is inherent in any test or measure possessing primary utility. . . . *Tertiary evaluation* is perhaps more difficult to define than the other two concepts. It is concerned with the justification for developing a particular measure or for calling attention to a measure. Part of this justification will come from the in-trinsic significance of the primary aim of measurement and part may come from the range of implications delineated in the secondary analysis. But additional and possibly even greater significance may come from the spectrum of life settings, beyond any envisaged under its primary validity, for which the tech-nique has predictive and explanatory relevance [Gough, 1965a, p. 295].

Because Gough designed the CPI to predict everyday social behavior by assessing folk concepts, the bulk of the primary evaluation has focused on the degree to which the various scales, singly or in combination, can forecast various criteria such as academic achievement or parole success in the United States and other cultures.

The secondary analysis has relied on observation of individuals scoring at different points on the various scales. Studies such as these have disclosed a nar-cissistic component in *S*s with extremely high Self-Acceptance scores and a volatile element in people with very high Flexibility scores. Secondary evaluation also involves correlating scales with other tests and inventories and making inferences on the basis of the resulting patterns, as well as the basic review of the original scale-development procedures and analysis of item content.

Tertiary evaluation relies on serendipity and thus one cannot plan for it; however, by keeping alert and following up unexpected relationships during the primary and secondary stages, one can discover new uses for a scale. For example, the Socialization scale was originally designed to identify potential delinquents, but it has also been found to forecast academic underachievement among highly gifted students (Gough, 1965a).

Much of the theory Gough has outlined in his essay on conceptual analysis is basic to the historical development of any personality-assessment device. The unique aspect of it is that Gough has specifically outlined his approach and provided us with a rationale for it, just as he has attempted to explain how he chose the variables to be scaled.

Considering all the elements to be taken into consideration, one can sense the immensity of the task that confronts anyone who attempts to construct and establish a major personality-assessment device. Myriad decisions must be made, and chaos would soon result if these decisions were not guided by a unifying philosophy of testing. In the case of the CPI the character of the instrument was shaped by Gough's decision to build a structured inventory for the prediction of social behavior by scaling the functional concepts used in interpersonal relations. This decision led to the selection of folk concepts rather than theoretical constructs, to empirical methods of test construction, to an emphasis on practical validational procedures, to rejection of test characteristics that do not contribute to improved prediction and subsequent research in conceptual analysis, and to practical applications designed not only to provide validational data but also to make the CPI maximally useful to the psychologist interpreting the individual case.

It is possible to take issue with Gough's approach on two levels. First, one can disagree with his basic values. One can take the position that inventories should be constructed on the basis of theory rather than usage or that adherence to certain psychometric guidelines should be the first yardstick for evaluating a scale. The more basic the disagreement, the less likely it can be resolved, because no agreement can be reached regarding the criteria by which a test should be judged. The second level of disagreement could arise with regard to judging how well Gough achieved the goals he set for himself. This can be decided by referring to empirical data.

The remainder of this book concerns the second level and seeks to determine how well the various CPI scales, singly and in combination, forecast behavior. In essence then, we follow Gough's plan for a conceptual analysis of the test. One of the first steps in such an analysis is to review the methods by which the test was constructed. That is the subject of the next chapter.

CHAPTER 3

CPI Development

∫∩∫∩∫∩∫∩∫∩∫∩∫∩∫∩∫∩∫∩∫∩∫∩∫∩∫∩∫∩∫∩∫∩∫∩

It is a basic article of faith for most clinicians that to understand a person thoroughly one must examine his childhood development; indeed, it is believed to be best to start by studying his parents in order to get a feel for his early environment and genetic raw material. However, psychologists rarely use that approach in familiarizing themselves with a new test. Instead of examining the early history and genealogy of each test, they often treat them all as having emerged from identical, sterile incubators. While clinicians skeptically probe a client's account of his present functioning, they may accept uncritically the claims made in a test manual concerning its application, often skipping the material about derivation, standardization, and validation in getting to the pages describing administration and interpretation. However, just as a child's conception, gestation, and early development imprint it with certain indelible characteristics, so the construction of a personality inventory permanently endows it with unique strengths and weaknesses that must be digested if the test is to be properly understood and used.

Just as parents never use the exact same methods in rearing each one of their children, no two CPI scales were derived and standardized in an identical fashion. Those construction differences between the eighteen scales are discussed in Part Two. The focus now will be on the general methods employed to derive them.

General Methods of Inventory Construction

Although different descriptive labels are used, most authorities agree that the basic methods used for selecting items for structured inventories can be classified as follows:

21

In the intuitive or rational method, the test author decides which items should be included. While all rational, intuitive, or logical methods share this basic characteristic, there are important variations. Hase and Goldberg (1967) have subdivided the rational approaches according to whether item selection is based on an intuitive understanding of the trait or is guided by some formal psychological theory. Another way of differentiating such tests is by determining whether the test author alone selected the items, as in the Rogers Personality Inventory, or whether they were chosen by a group of judges, as with the Heilbrun need scales of the Adjective Check List or the Taylor Manifest Anxiety Scale.

The present writer finds it most useful to differentiate the rational approach according to whether the selection was purely intuitive or partly empirical —that is, guided by data at some point. A primary example of the latter approach is *internal consistency analysis,* in which the test author intuitively selects a pool of items that appears to reflect the trait in question. (Internal *consistency* analysis should not be confused with internal *criterion* analysis.) He then administers the entire item pool to a group of subjects and obtains their scores on this preliminary test scale. Next he computes correlations between the item scores and the total scores for all the items in the pool. These correlation coefficients serve as the criteria for final item selection, the items with the highest item-total correlations being chosen for the final scale. This method was used in the derivation of four of the eighteen scales.

Empirical data can also be used to guide the elimination of undesirable items. On Jackson's new Personality Research Form, the basic criterion for inclusion of an item on a scale was agreement by the test authors that the item measured the trait in question. However, items were excluded on the basis of empirical data showing overly high correlations with scales measuring other traits or undesirable response styles. By this means, Jackson was able to increase the discriminant validity of his test. (See Campbell and Fiske, 1959).

Of the various methods of item selection, the rational approach is most likely to have high content validity. It usually reflects a consistent approach and can result in a scale closely related to a formal psychological theory. Of course the validity of such a scale depends on the ability of the test authors to predict how people with the traits in question will respond to the various items. Moreover, there is always the possibility that the diagnosis of response patterns that can be reached by the test author may also be reached by the respondents, making the scale subject to possible dissimulation or distortion.

In the external criterion method, item selection is guided solely by the empirically determined relationship between the test item and a particular criterion measure. (Because of this emphasis, it is sometimes referred to as the *empirical* method, although the factor analytic and internal criterion methods are equally empirical.)

Once an initial item pool is assembled (usually on a rational basis), it is administered to groups of individuals who differ on the dimension to be assessed. Ideally these two criterion groups are equivalent in every salient respect except for the characteristic or dimension in question. The frequency of true and false responses for each group is determined for each item, and the statistical significance of any differences determined. Those items that significantly differentiate the two groups are selected for a preliminary scale. This scale is first applied against the original criterion groups; if the results are satisfactory, it is then cross-validated on new samples. Poor items that may be working against the discrimination are identified and eliminated. This shortened and refined scale should also be cross-validated.

The advantage of the external criterion method is that it transcends the intuitive ability of the test constructor and can detect discriminating items that may be far from obvious. One might expect a delinquent to answer true to the item, "I have been quite independent and free from family rule" because numerous studies of the home life of delinquents have shown that to be the case (Glueck and Glueck, 1950; Rosenquist and Megargee, 1969). Empirical item analyses have shown just the opposite. Despite the fact that delinquent youngsters are in fact more independent, they answer false to this item significantly more often than do nondelinquents (Meehl, 1945). Similarly, a clinician who is aware of the characteristic lack of guilt ascribed to the sociopath would expect him to answer false to the item, "Much of the time I feel I have done something wrong or evil," when in fact a true response is more characteristic.

These examples illustrate several facts about the external criterion method: 1) it is the empirical relationships and not the manifest content that determine whether or not an item is included. Even if an item's relationship to the criterion is obscure, or even if the direction of the scoring appears absurd, it will be included if it reliably differentiates the criterion groups; 2) the psychologist is not interested in the literal truth of the response—that is, whether or not a respondent is in fact more free and independent, but rather is more interested in how the response may prove to be reliably related to other behavioral dimensions; 3) as a result of the above, empirically derived scales can be quite subtle and may be more difficult for a respondent to falsify than rational scales; 4) because of the lack of "face" or content validity, empirically derived scales are often less acceptable to test takers and more difficult to explain to laymen who naturally assume that the psychologist is interested in the factual content of responses;[1] 5) failure to match the derivation groups adequately can result in undesirable artifacts. In the case of the MMPI *Pd* scale, for example, the criterion group of

---

[1] In his criticism of the use of the empirically derived MMPI in Peace Corps selection, Congressman Cornelius Gallagher objected to the inclusion of such items as, "I have had no difficulty starting or holding my bowel movement," and pointed out that if the Peace Corps required such information it should be obtained by a physician during a medical examination. When Peace Corps Director Sargent Shriver attempted to explain that despite the item's appearance on the test, the psychologists were not interested in what it might tell them about the respondents' colonic characteristics, the Congressman was understandably confused. However, such objections can be avoided if all the items in the initial pool have adequate face validity. Of course, they then may not be subtle.

delinquents was younger than the normal contrast group, with the result that nondelinquent teenagers tend to obtain somewhat elevated scores simply because of their ages.

As might be expected, the method of external criterion selection is used most often in tests that stress the practical prediction of various criteria, such as the Strong Vocational Interest Blank (SVIB) and the MMPI. The CPI follows that tradition and the method was used in the derivation of thirteen of the eighteen scales.

INTERNAL CRITERION ANALYSIS

This method is used most by factor analytic personality researchers who, having identified a factor that appears to be a basic personality dimension, wish to construct a paper-and-pencil scale to define and assess it. A small item pool is constructed which consists of items that appear to be closely related to the particular factor. (Then items are initially selected on an *a priori* basis.) These items are then administered to a group of *S*s, often along with other measures that have been identified as relating closely to the factor. The items are intercorrelated and the resulting matrix is factor analyzed and rotated. Then the correlation of each item with the factor (the item's "factor loading") is determined. The items with the highest loadings are selected for the scale. This method, often called the *factor analytic* method, was used in the derivation of such instruments as the Guilford-Zimmerman Temperament Schedule, the 16 Personality Factor Questionnaire, and the Maudsley Personality Inventory. As might be expected, the scales that are derived with such a technique are usually factorially pure and homogeneous, in contrast to the heterogeneity and factorial complexity often found in scales constructed by other methods. Because of the high item homogeneity, one can be confident that equal scores represent equivalent test performances. On the other hand, clinicians who emphasize practical validity often maintain that such scales may not relate as closely to complex behavioral patterns.

Obviously there are considerable differences of opinion about the best method of test construction. Despite the importance of this dispute and the significance of these issues for assessment in both the laboratory and the clinic, few empirical studies have been designed to determine which method is best. An exception is the program of research by Hase and Goldberg (Hase, 1965; Hase and Goldberg, 1967; Goldberg and Hase, 1967; Goldberg, Rorer and Greene, 1970; Goldberg, 1971). Those investigators have constructed experimental inventories by each of the methods discussed and have compared their validity levels. The first reports from this project indicated that no strategy produced a set of scales that was clearly superior to the sets of scales produced by other methods. More recently, the intuitive or rational procedures have been reported to have an edge on the others. This finding needs replication using other samples, particularly because the empirical scales, unlike those produced by other strategies, were not specifically derived for the purpose of this research. Until more investigations of this type are made, the particular subjective biases in the way tests are constructed will continue to play the primary role in the choice of test construction strategy.

Scale Derivation

Thirteen of the eighteen CPI scales were derived using the external criterion method. Four were derived using rational procedures of internal consistency analysis. (The method used to construct the eighteenth scale, Communality, does not fit neatly into any of the other methodological categories.)

EXTERNAL CRITERION METHOD

Once the construct to be measured has been chosen, the first step in building any scale is selection of an initial item pool. For his early adventures in test construction, Gough naturally turned to the MMPI item pool. However, he often found the MMPI items too oriented toward psychopathology for the folk dimensions he wished to assess, so he supplemented them with additional, especially written items.[2]

In the course of developing the CPI, about 3500 items were evaluated. Later, special item pools composed of new items and MMPI items came into consistent use. Because of that procedure, 178 of the 480 items on the CPI are virtually identical to MMPI items and thirty-five others are quite similar (Goldberg and Rust, 1963; Jones and Goldberg, 1964). The proportion of MMPI items on the various CPI scales ranges from a low of 4 per cent for the Communality (Cm) scale, to a high of 91 per cent for the Well-Being (Wb) scale (Megargee, 1966b).

The next step, after the initial item pool has been selected, is to choose external criteria. The criteria used in the empirical derivation of CPI scales varied considerably from scale to scale. A common procedure was to ask a group of friends and acquaintances to nominate members of their group who were high and low on the trait in question. Usually these judges were provided with a written description of the behavior patterns the test author had in mind, as in this example from the Responsibility scale (Gough, McClosky, and Meehl, 1951, p. 74):

> The responsible person is one who shows a ready willingness to accept the consequences of his own behavior, dependability, trustworthiness, and a sense of obligation to the group. Others would describe the responsible person in such terms as "you can depend on him," "he is a straight shooter," "he always does his part," etc.

> The responsible person will not necessarily be a leader in his group, or of higher than average intelligence (although he might well be characterized in this way), but will be primarily a person who does seem to have a sense of commitment to the group and others, who is dependable, and who possesses integrity.

[2] Item writing is an art, and even those psychologists who disagree with Gough's approach to assessment generally acknowledge his skill in writing items. Few, if any, item writers can match his ability to construct items that accurately reflect the subtle nuances of expression and phraseology found in everyday language. As a result, the CPI item pool is unusually acceptable to test takers since the items are rarely objectionable and usually make sense to most respondents.

The second group, those low on responsibility, need not be irresponsible, but they should be the ones you can readily judge as lacking the qualities mentioned, or deficient in them. Be careful not to confuse responsibility with popularity. Also, be careful to make your ratings on the basis of the person's *actual behavior,* and not according to the way you think he would like to behave, or be seen.

The number of nominations received by each person in the group would be tallied and the group rank ordered; such rankings were then used as criteria.

For other scales, more objective criteria were used. For the Femininity scale (Fe), the responses of women were contrasted with those of men. The Sociability (Sy) scale was based on the number of extracurricular activities in which a student participated, while the Achievement via Conformance (Ac) and the Achievement via Independence (Ai) scales used the gradepoint average of high school and college students, respectively. The Socialization (So) scale was derived by contrasting the scores of delinquents with nondelinquents. Two of the validity scales, Well-Being (Wb) and Good Impression (Gi), compared protocols obtained under normal conditions with those produced when the subjects were asked to malinger or to "fake good."

For several scales, Gough used the scores obtained on other tests to select criterion groups for subsequent item analyses. Among the CPI scales having other tests as criteria were Intellectual Efficiency (Ie), for which IQ scores served as the criterion; Tolerance (To), for which the California Ethnocentrism (E) and Fascism (F) scales were used; and Capacity for Status (Cs), for which evaluations of socioeconomic status based on the Sims Score Cards were employed.

Upon first studying the CPI, one is struck by the fact that, for each of several scales, the criterion appears to be just the opposite of what one would expect. For example, a record of juvenile delinquency seems a strange criterion for a scale called Socialization. This came about because Gough derived several of the scales for other purposes and published them before he integrated them into the CPI. Thus the Socialization scale began as a scale for the prediction of juvenile delinquency (Gough and Peterson, 1952). With additional research, Gough became convinced that not only did high scores reflect delinquency, but that low scores indicated superior socialization. So the *Delinquency* scale came to be regarded as a bipolar Delinquency-Socialization scale. When the CPI was assembled in 1957, it seemed desirable to have the scale arranged so that high scores on all eighteen reflected either positive or negative behavior. Because the inventory emphasized factors contributing to interpersonal and social effectiveness, Gough chose to key all the scales so that high scores reflected favorable dimensions. Consequently the Delinquency scale was renamed *Socialization,* and keying reversed. (That is, all the true items were keyed false and vice versa.) At the same time, and for the same reasons, his Prejudice scale became the Tolerance (To) scale, Impulsivity became Self-Control (Sc), Dissimulation became Well-Being (Wb) and Infrequency was transformed into Communality (Cm).

Other scales were renamed when subsequent research indicated the first label was inappropriate. Participation in extracurricular activities served as the original criterion for one scale, so Gough named it *Social Participation.* Later research showed that high scorers were seen as more sociable by their friends and acquaintances and that this sociability was a more salient characteristic than their willingness to participate in other activities. Consequently it was renamed *Sociability (Sy)*.

Although the CPI has the reputation of being an empirically derived inventory, five of the eighteen scales were constructed rationally. Of these, four used the method of internal consistency analysis described above: Social Presence *(Sp)*, Self-Acceptance *(Sa)*, Self-Control *(Sc)*, and Flexibility *(Fx)*. The typical procedure was to select a number of items that appeared to relate to the characteristic in question, then administer those items to a particular sample group and compute item-total correlations. Those items with the highest correlations were then selected for inclusion in the scale. Next, the relation of the scale scores to other tests and measures of behavior was determined in order to test the new scale's validity.

In contrast to most of the empirically derived scales, little material has been published on the development of those that were rationally constructed. The only reports the writer has encountered are the brief descriptions recently published by Gough in a discussion of the interpretation of the CPI (Gough, 1968a). Such details as the samples used, the exact criteria for including items, and, in some cases, the size and nature of the initial item pool, are unspecified.

The last CPI scale, Communality *(Cm)*, was also selected by means of a mixed rational-empirical procedure. Formerly known as Infrequency, the items included on the scale were ones that only 5 per cent of the normative sample respondents had answered in the keyed direction. The purpose of the scale was to identify individuals who were giving an excessive number of atypical answers, possibly indicating a failure to understand or comply with the directions. Although the scale was renamed and the keying reversed, it is still the low or atypical scores that are meaningful. Indeed, the standard score conversion tables (Gough, 1969b) show the *Cm* scale to be heavily skewed, with the *T*-scores that can be obtained ranging from a low of 1 to a maximum of only 63.

Whatever the method of item selection, the subsequent steps in scale development are fairly standard. All scales are subjected to validation. As we have noted, Gough has two basic criteria that he uses to gauge a scale's validity. First, it must identify people who will behave in a specified way. The *Do* scale, for example, must identify people who will act in what would be considered a dominant fashion *in any culture*. Second, people with high scores must impress others as having the quality in question. High scorers on *Do* must be described as dominant, forceful, self-assured and the like.

In addition, Gough subjects the scales to a conceptual analysis to clarify what it is that each scale is assessing as well as to explore them for unexpected relationships and uses. As described in the previous chapter, the conceptual analyses include formal validational studies, but proceed beyond them to determine as fully as possible the characteristics of the scale and the people who score at different levels on it.

As with most tests, the bulk of the research on the CPI has focused on testing what Campbell and Fiske (1959) have termed "convergent validity," determining whether a scale relates to the variables to which it is supposed to relate. Relatively little effort has been expended determining the discriminant validity, that is, ascertaining whether a scale relates significantly to others with which it is not supposed to be correlated. As long as the *Do* scale predicts who will display leadership, Gough is not terribly upset if it also correlates with measures of popularity or intelligence. Gough would take note of these facts in his conceptual analysis, but would not try to remove this variance by deleting items unless he could be sure that he could do so without lowering the correlations with criteria of dominance.

In addition to validational studies and conceptual analyses, other more mundane chores must be carried out by the test author. One such chore is the devising of a form summarizing an individual's test performance. In keeping with his Minnesota background, Gough devised a profile sheet on which an individual's raw score could be plotted in order to yield standard scores. The first CPI profile sheet printed in 1951 had fifteen folk concept scales on the left side and three validity scales on the right. Standard scores had a mean of 100 and a standard deviation of 10. That profile sheet proved unsatisfactory. Some scales were keyed so that high scores reflected positive traits; on others high scores were negative. This led to a chaotic, up and down, roller coaster effect when an individual case was plotted, making the interpreter's task quite difficult and obscuring the natural configurations in the data.

A number of changes were introduced in the present profile sheet adopted in 1957. *T*-scores with a mean of 50 and a standard deviation of 10 were used in place of the old standard scores, and scales were rekeyed where necessary so that the conventionally desirable pole was at the top.[3] The validity scales were integrated with the concept scales and the relations of the major and minor axes realigned to give a more aesthetically pleasing appearance. (See profile sheets in Chapter Eleven.)

To facilitate clinical interpretation of the profile the order in which the scales appeared was changed and they were grouped into four clusters. Class I includes six scales that assess poise, ascendancy and self-assurance. Class II contains six scales that measure socialization, maturity and responsibility. Class III includes three scales of achievement-potential and intellectual efficiency, and Class IV contains three scales reflecting intellectual and interest modes. The selection of those groupings was guided in part by the results of numerous factor and cluster analyses, but the primary criterion for the groupings was facilitation of individual score interpretation; such clinical considerations took precedence over statistical factors.

Another task is the collection of normative data. The *T*-scores on the profile sheet are based on norms for over six thousand men and seven thousand

---

[3] These scores are calculated by the formula $T = 50 + \dfrac{10\ (Xi - M)}{SD}$, where Xi is the raw score, and M and SD the mean and standard deviation of the normative group. These are the same type of standard scores that are used on the MMPI and other structured tests. (Some statisticians term these scores Z standard scores with a mean of 50 and a standard deviation of 10.)

women. In addition, norms are available on twenty samples of men and twelve samples of women representing a variety of occupational, clinical, and educational groups. As is typical of inventories developed during the 1950s, whites are overrepresented in the normative samples. However, studies reporting data for blacks, orientals, chicanos and other ethnic minorities have begun to appear in the literature (Abbott, 1970; Ellsworth, 1968; Benjamin, 1970; Rusk, 1969; Mason, 1967; Gill and Spilka, 1962; Tremble, 1969).[4]

The determination of reliability is another required step. An inventory such as the CPI, which is designed to assess enduring personality characteristics (as opposed to transient mood states), should have high coefficients of stability. Of course, the larger the time interval between test sessions, the lower the coefficient of stability will probably be. In Table 1, long and short-term test-retest correlations noted by Gough in the CPI *Manual* and in a personal communication are reported along with short-term coefficients for eleven CPI scales investigated by Hase and Goldberg (1967).

The short-term coefficients reported by Hase and Goldberg (1967) are reasonably high, ranging from .71 to .90 with a median of .83. Not surprisingly, lower correlations are the rule among the prisoners, with correlations there ranging from .49 to .87 with a median of .80. The long-term coefficients are mostly in the .60s and .70s, indicating moderate stability over one year, even among adolescents. (Goldberg and Rorer [1964] have also reported the test-retest reliability for all of the individual CPI items. Also included in their monograph are item means, standard deviations and endorsement frequencies.)

No coefficients of internal consistency are reported in the *Manual*. The writer has calculated estimates of internal consistency by applying Kuder-Richardson Formula 21 to the means and standard deviations for the largest normative group presented in the *Manual*: 3572 high school boys and 4056 high school girls. These coefficients vary considerably, ranging from a low of .22 to a high of .94. Hase and Goldberg (1967) reported coefficients of internal consistency calculated by applying Kuder-Richardson Formula 20 to the responses of 179 University of Oregon freshmen women and to eleven of the eighteen CPI scales. In addition, Gough has supplied corrected and uncorrected split-half correlations for 550 men and women in another personal communication. These data are all presented in Table 2.

The data show considerable variability in internal consistency. Oddly enough, the scales derived using internal criterion analysis are not notably higher than the scales constructed using external strategy. Generally, the scales in Cluster IV (*Py, Fx,* and *Fe*) are substantially lower than those in other clusters.

Given the advent of modern computers, a factor analysis has now become almost a standard part of the development of a new inventory. Although Gough (1964b) has reported that he performed five factor or cluster analyses as a guide

---

[4] Ellsworth's (1968) data on ghetto blacks, along with other studies, indicate that the profiles of minority group members tend to be low compared to the standardization sample. The mean on most scales was in the 30s and 40s. It may be sufficient to evaluate minority group members relative to special norms; however, it is possible that new scales may have to be derived for use with such groups; that is, an item analysis contrasting high and low dominance blacks may have to be conducted, for example.

Table 1.   Coefficients of Stability

	Short Term (1–4 weeks)		Long Term (1 year)		
Scale	200 Prisoners[a]	179 Freshmen Women[b]	125 High School Girls[a]	101 High School Boys[a]	234 Men and Women[c]
Do	.80	.89	.72	.64	.63
Cs	.80	.79	.68	.62	.68
Sy	.84	.90	.71	.68	.68
Sp	.80	—	.63	.60	.65
Sa	.71	—	.71	.67	.65
Wb	.75	—	.72	.71	.71
Re	.85	.83	.73	.65	.71
So	.80	.88	.69	.65	.72
Sc	.86	—	.68	.75	.72
To	.87	.88	.61	.71	.66
Gi	.81	—	.68	.69	.66
Cm	.58	—	.44	.38	.41
Ac	.79	.81	.73	.60	.69
Ai	.71	.81	.57	.63	.60
Ie	.80	.85	.77	.74	.76
Py	.53	.74	.49	.48	.48
Fx	.49	—	.67	.60	.63
Fe	.73	.71	.65	.59	.85

[a] Data reprinted from CPI *Manual* (Gough, 1969b, p. 19).
[b] Data reported by Hase and Goldberg (1967, p. 236.
[c] Data supplied by Gough on new, shorter form of scale (personal communication).

to dividing the scales into classes, the results have not been published. However, other investigators have more than made up this deficit so that at present at least a dozen and a half factor analyses of the CPI have been published. They will be reviewed in Chapter Nine.

IMPLICATIONS OF PROCEDURES

At the beginning of this chapter, it was stated that in order to understand a test such as the CPI, it is first necessary to study its development. Now that the general methodology of its construction has been described, what are some of the implications for the finished test?

We have seen that Gough, being above all a pragmatist, used different techniques for the derivation of the various scales. Some variations were dictated by theory and some by expediency. One might liken his approach to the (Mid-

Table 2. Internal Consistency Coefficients

| | KR–21 | | KR–20[b] | Split-half | |
Scale	3572 High School Boys[a]	4056 High School Girls[a]	179 Freshman Women	500 Men and Women[c] Uncorrected	Corrected
Do	.70	.71	.80	.67	.80
Cs	.61	.68	.59	.65	.79
Sy	.74	.75	.80	.63	.77
Sp	.74	.75	—	.61	.76
Sa	.51	.58	—	.54	.70
Wb	.76	.79	—	.75	.86
Re	.72	.70	.67	.70	.82
So	.68	.67	.78	.72	.83
Sc	.82	.85	—	.77	.87
To	.74	.75	.74	.75	.86
Gi	.77	.77	—	.65	.79
Cm	.70	.52	—	.46	.63
Ac	.69	.94	.65	.65	.79
Ai	.54	.56	.63	.62	.75
Ie	.81	.74	.72	.68	.81
Py	.22	.23	.44	.45	.62
Fx	.56	.51	—	.55	.71
Fe	.62	.29	.30	.57	.73

[a] Computed by present writer from data in *Manual.*
[b] Data from Hase and Goldberg (1967, p. 236).
[c] Data supplied by Gough (personal communication).

western) farmer who adapts his basic farming techniques to the particular crop, soil, weather, and market conditions he encounters each season, and who continually modifies his approach in the light of past experience. Thus Gough used both empirical and rational techniques, and selected his external criterion groups by a variety of methods. As a result, the CPI is a heterogeneous instrument. Each of the different scales has its own particular quirks and characteristics. This is one reason why the CPI, despite its apparent simplicity, requires interpretation by a trained psychologist, just as do more esoteric tests such as the Rorschach.

Throughout our discussion of the derivation of the CPI, it was apparent that Gough placed primary emphasis on the prediction of behavior. In building the test he stressed convergent validity, leaving the question of discriminant validity to take care of itself. This resulted in two characteristics that have received considerable criticism: redundancy, and high correlations with measures of response bias and response set.

Redundancy occurs when two or more scales measure the same thing or co-vary to some extent. Symptoms of redundancy include items that fall on two or more scales, and scales that correlate highly with one another and have high loadings on the same factors. As is the case with most personality inventories, including some factor analytic instruments, the CPI exhibits all of these symptoms.

While many noted psychometricians deplore redundancy and maintain that test scales should be independent of one another, it is apparent that Gough placed much less importance on independence although he did attempt to sharpen the distinction between constructs in his instructions to raters as well as in his selection of criterion groups. For example, the description of responsibility given to the raters made a distinction between responsibility and leadership or intelligence. However, Gough did not eliminate overlapping items or those that showed excessive correlations with scores on the *Do* or *Ie* scales, nor did he have qualms about constructing separate scales for similar constructs such as socialization and self-control.

Some critics have suggested that the eighteen CPI scales should be replaced by four or five independent, factorially pure scales that would tap most of the common variance. This would naturally increase the discriminant validity, but Gough is reluctant to take this step lest it also lower the convergent validity—which he feels is far more important.

During the zenith of the response set research, tests such as the CPI were often criticized because of high correlations with measures of social desirability (SD) or acquiescence (Acqu.). In part, this stemmed from the intellectual environment because the testing atmosphere of the decade from 1947 to 1957, during which most development of the CPI was carried out, preceded the great emphasis on response sets in the next decade from 1957 (Edwards, 1957; Jackson and Messick, 1958) to 1966 (Block, 1965). Inventories devised during the response set decade, such as the Edwards Personal Preference Schedule and Jackson's Personality Research Form, were often subjected to procedures designed to eliminate or minimize unbalanced keying or high correlations with measures of social desirability. Gough maintained that selecting items on the basis of their relations with response set measures rather than external criteria the scales were designed to predict merely confused the ends of testing with the means adopted to achieve those ends. He also pointed out that the CPI included an excellent measure of social desirability, the Good Impression scale, antedating Edward's *SD* scale, and that the CPI also contained scales to identify random answering and malingering. Moreover, the evidence accumulated since 1965 suggests that unbalanced keying has little influence on CPI items, and that the role of social desirability was exaggerated (Block, 1965; Dicken, 1963b; Rorer, 1965; Rorer and Goldberg, 1965).

Turning to other characteristics of the CPI which stem from the methods of test development, we have noted that most of the scales were constructed by means of external criterion analyses to assess complex, multiply-determined behavior such as achievement, self-control, and the like. One would expect that scales able to predict such complex functioning would themselves be complex, and this indeed is the case. Of course, the greater a scale's complexity, the lower its internal homogeneity. In general, the CPI scales have less unidimensionality and lower coefficients of internal consistency (split-half and Kuder-Richardson coefficients) than is felt desirable by those who prize such characteristics. (See Table 2.)

In his external criterion analyses, Gough generally used extreme groups whose behavior defined the opposite poles of the dimension he wished to assess. Because of that, most of the resulting scales are also bipolar with high and low scores that are equally interpretable. (This differs from MMPI procedures, in which a group manifesting a disorder was contrasted with an average group of Minnesota normals. Thus, in the derivation of the MMPI Hypochondriasis scale, for example, a criterion group of psychiatric patients manifesting numerous psychosomatic complaints was contrasted not with a group exhibiting superior health, but with a sample of normals displaying an average number of physical complaints. Consequently, low scores on the MMPI have little or no meaning.)

Most of the scales were derived and cross-validated using large samples of high school and college students. While norms are available on a variety of groups (Gough, 1969b), the CPI is most applicable to students and young adults, not only because the larger size of these samples provides more stable normative data, but also because the language and content of the items is more relevant to younger groups. There are more items dealing with studying and dating than with working or raising a family, and few of the items reflect the problems of older people such as retirement, reduced physical capacity, and death. These characteristics could lower the face validity and lessen the rapport in samples of older people; further research should be done to determine the empirical validity of the instrument with older groups.

Although Gough's folk culture theory has led to considerable cross-cultural and cross-national validational research, only recently have studies been undertaken to explore the validity of the CPI among blacks, chicanos or other domestic minority groups in the United States. Recent research showing marked deviations for normal blacks on several MMPI clinical scales emphasize the need for similar studies to be performed on the CPI. This is particularly important if the CPI formulas predicting academic achievement are to be used as an aid in selecting minority group Ss for educational programs.

In review, Gough's approach to test construction emphasized the building of scales for the purpose of predicting socially relevant behavior patterns. As a result, the development and validation of the CPI has aimed at maximizing predictive and concurrent validity even at the expense of other test attributes such as factorial purity and discriminant validity. The failure of some CPI scales to have the latter attributes is of more concern to personality researchers who wish to use the CPI for trait measurement than it is to those who wish to predict practical criteria, such as the likelihood a student will be graduated from high school. The Tolerance scale can serve as a good example of those two approaches to the test. Gough's goal was to construct a scale that would differentiate people who behaved in a tolerant fashion from those who displayed minority group prejudice. If the CPI scale succeeds in doing so, both in the United States and in other cultures, then he regards it as a successful measure. Others, however, may wish to assess a personality trait dimension of tolerance-prejudice. If they use the To scale for this purpose, their study can be criticized by someone who points out that 91 per cent of the CPI To items are keyed false and notes that CPI is thus assessing not tolerance, but "naysaying." Or someone might point out the high correlation with the MMPI K scale ($r = .63$), and suggest that To really measures faking good. Obviously, the personality researcher's life is much simpler if he does not have such annoying covariations to worry about. However, the personnel officer who wants a measure that will help identify bigots couldn't care less about these extraneous relationships—as long as the scale works.

The reader might have gotten the impression that practical validity can be achieved only by sacrificing psychometric elegance. This need not be the case. Some of the most successful CPI scales have high homogeneity, low overlap with other trait scales, and minimal correlations with social desirability. Gough agrees that these are all desirable qualities. He simply maintains that if he must choose between practical usefulness and psychometric elegance, he prefers the former.

Of course, we might object to this as a false alternative. Assume we have an item that correlates highly with a criterion, but we find it is also included on other CPI scales measuring different traits or that it correlates highly with SD. Why not devise another item that measures the criterion just as well, but which doesn't have these drawbacks—thus having our cake and eating it too.

There are two problems with this approach. If one were to eliminate overlapping items, then one must either have fewer scales, fewer items per scale, or a much lengthier inventory. Gough obviously felt item overlap and redundancy were lesser evils than having shorter, less reliable scales.

The second problem is that the more stringent the criteria for item selection, the more items one must evaluate. If high speed electronic computers are available, this does not present too much of a problem. However, this was not the case when the CPI scales were being derived in the late 1940s. Gough noted in a personal communication:

> "The actual early work was done with no money (I was a graduate student), and the item counts were carried out on the kitchen table of a three-room apartment where my wife read out the trues and I jotted them down. We used to take a quota of ten protocols a night, and work for two hours; after that we would have the screaming meemies and would need to go out into the cruel Minneapolis nights and pace the streets until our nerves calmed down. Even when I got to Berkeley there wasn't any money to finish the scale development, and the entire work was done on a shoestring and by ancient handcrafting methods."

Of course, with the resources now at his command, Gough could go back and refine the scales if he felt these criticisms reflected serious drawbacks. However, he does not feel this is the case and, like most test authors, he is reluctant to tinker with a completed scale once it has been published. As Starke Hathaway (1964) has pointed out with reference to the MMPI, changing a word can alter an item in an unknown fashion, and changing an item alters the scales and the norms. Unless one is willing to undertake a full scale revision of an inventory it is better to leave it alone. Given these alternatives, most test authors choose to leave the instrument as is. After completion of a major personality inventory, the typical test construction goes into a life-long refractory phase; the suggestion that he should go back and do it all over again is well calculated to arouse any latent homicidal impulses.

PART **II**

On an empirically de-
rived test such as the CPI, knowledge of how each scale was derived is essential
to its understanding. Knowing that the Tolerance (To) scale was based on correlations with the Anti-Semitism (A-S) scale clarifies many otherwise mysterious
aspects of the measure. When the name of a scale is ambiguous or misleading,
as in the case of the Psychological Mindedness scale, the developmental details
are particularly important. In this section, detailed descriptions are given of the
procedures followed in constructing each of the eighteen CPI scales along with
several others. The derivation of some of the scales however, has not been reported completely in the literature. Some scales were originally constructed as
MMPI scales and later revised for inclusion in the CPI. While there are good
accounts of the original derivations, the guidelines used in revising them are
often obscure. The writer had assumed that those items found only on the MMPI
were simply deleted, but close examination of the item lists indicated that a more
complex procedure was used. For some of these scales, items from the CPI pool
were apparently added to replace the lost MMPI items. Where that is so, the
criteria for selecting such items have not been described in the literature.

There are even a few scales which appeared on the CPI as if by magic,
with no derivation reports on them prior to the publication of the CPI. Recently,

36

CONSTRUCTION AND VALI-DATION OF THE BASIC SCALES

~~~~~~

Gough (1968a) did briefly describe the derivation of some of these measures, but the accounts are sketchy. All that is known about the construction of the Self-control (Sc) scale, for example, is contained in the following terse sentence: "The thirty-item Sc scale was constructed rationally, by gathering items that appeared to relate to expression of impulse and management of aggression, and then correlating each with a total score based on the complete initial set" (Gough, 1968a, p. 66). How was this experimental item pool generated? What samples were used in calculating the item-total correlations? What guidelines governed the item selection? Fortunately, Sc is an extreme example and there is more complete information for most of the other scales.

Along with the derivation of the various scales, the nature of the item content for each will be described. Different groups of items will be described, including a sample item or two. Some of these item clusters are based on Gough's originally published groupings. When no such reports were available, the present writer examined the item lists and generated his own item groups. In either case, the clusters are based on inspection and rational description of the manifest content and not on their statistical relationships or intercorrelations.

After the above descriptions, studies relevant to the validity of each scale are reviewed. These validational studies are limited to investigations exploring the relationship of the scale to observations of relevant overt behavior. With the exception of a few scales such as Intellectual Efficiency (Ie) for which correlations with test measures are peculiarly relevant, no studies using other test measures as criteria are included. (Detailed information on the relation of all CPI scales to other personality tests is contained in the CPI Manual. Some broad trends in that connection are summarized in Chapter Ten.) Studies reporting the relationship of CPI scales to behavior not directly relevant to their validity are also excluded. For example, dozens of studies have correlated all eighteen CPI scales to measures of scholastic achievement. The overall findings of these studies are reviewed in Chapter Twelve, but in this section such data are discussed only when directly relevant to the convergent validity of a particular scale. The correlation of grade point averages (GPA) with scales designed to assess academic achievement is reported, but correlations with scales designed to assess other variables are not. If a study found significant correlations between GPA and the Dominance and Achievement via Conformance scales, it will not be mentioned in the description of Do but will be included in the evidence for the validity of Ac. The guiding principle for inclusion of a study has been whether negative results would cast doubt on the scale's validity. If Do was not found to relate to academic achievement, it would not be noteworthy; similarly a zero order correlation between Do and some other scale of dominance is not conclusive since it could be that it is the other scale rather than Do that is invalid. As far as the order of presentation of scales is concerned, the simplest procedure was adopted: each scale is discussed in order of its placement on the profile sheet, with a chapter for each class of scales.

CHAPTER 4

Class I Scales:

Measures of Poise, Ascendancy, Self-Assurance, and Interpersonal Adequacy

Gough's first cluster consists of six scales, Dominance, Capacity for Status, Sociability, Social Presence, Self-Acceptance, and Sense of Well-Being, scales which, according to Gough, measure poise, ascendancy, self-assurance, and interpersonal adequacy. Factor analytic research has shown that the first five scales form a single factor. Well-Being loads on a different factor but is grouped with the other five on the profile sheet because Gough feels that the characteristics it assesses should be considered in describing an individual's effectiveness in interpersonal relations.

Dominance (*Do*)

PURPOSE

The Dominance scale was originally derived in connection with a project on political participation (Gough, McClosky, and Meehl, 1951) to identify strong, dominant, influential, and ascendant individuals who are able to take the initiative and exercise leadership.

CONSTRUCTION

Fifty fraternity and fifty sorority members at the University of Minnesota were given a description of the dominant person; each group was then asked to nominate ten fellow members who were high and ten who were low in dominance and also to rate their own dominance. From these ratings, eight high dominance men and eight high dominance women were selected. They were given the MMPI plus one hundred specially written items. Their responses were then contrasted with those of eight men and eight women rated low in dominance. The one hundred most discriminating MMPI items were selected and administered along with the one hundred specially written items to twenty-four high and twenty-four low dominance high school students. They were balanced in sex and had also been selected by peer ratings. From these item analyses, sixty items were selected, twenty-eight from the MMPI and thirty-two from the special pool.

ITEM CHARACTERISTICS

The present Dominance scale consists of only forty-six items, twenty-three keyed true and twenty-three false. (The reasons for the reduction of sixty items to forty-six and the criteria by which this selection was made have not been reported.) Of these items, twenty-five are "pure items" (that is, they are not scored on any other CPI scales); the principal item overlap is with the Responsibility (*Re*), Self-Acceptance (*Sa*) (six items each and Sociability (*Sy*) (four items) scales. (See Table 3 for item overlap on the CPI scales.)

Many of the *Do* scale items deal with poise and confidence. People who are high in dominance describe themselves as take-charge people who are willing to be leaders, and characteristically endorse the following items in the manner indicated here: "I think I would enjoy having authority over other people"—True. They indicate they are verbally fluent and persuasive: "I am a better talker than listener"—T; "I have a natural talent for influencing people"—T. There is also an element of dogged persistence and a sense of duty: "I sometimes keep on at a thing until others lose patience with me"—T; "People should not have to pay taxes for the schools if they do not have children"—F. In addition, there is a tendency in them to face reality even if it is distasteful: "There are times when I act like a coward"—T.

VALIDITY

The *Do* scale is one of the better-validated CPI scales. Several studies have tested its concurrent validity and *Do* is one of the few personality scales for which predictive validity has been established.

One of the most popular and appropriate research strategies has been to compare the *Do* scores of leaders and nonleaders. Gough (1969a, 1969b) has reported two studies using high school students. In the first study fifty-two boys and fifty-one girls nominated by their high school principals as being the most dominant students were contrasted with fifty boys and fifty-one girls nominated as least dominant. The differences were statistically significant, as indeed they should be with such extreme groups. The absolute scores were somewhat disappointing, however. The low dominance *S*s had mean *T*-scores of about forty, which is appropriate, but the mean *Do* scores of the most dominant *S*s were only near .52. Gough (1969b) reported similar results when he compared ninety boys and eighty-nine girls nominated as outstanding leaders by their high school principals to the national norms. As might be expected with such large Ns, statistically significant differences were obtained, but the magnitude of the differences was small; the T-scores for the leaders were about 52 for the boys and 54 for the girls, whereas the unselected high school students had T-scores of 43 and 46 for boys and girls, respectively.

Carson and Parker (1966) classified 356 entering college freshmen as leaders (top 25 per cent), average leaders (middle 50 per cent), and nonleaders (bottom 25 per cent) on the basis of their election to office in high school extracurricular activities. The results were similar to those obtained by Gough; the mean T-scores for the three groups were 55, 51 and 46 respectively, and an overall analysis of variance was statistically significant. Johnson and Frandsen (1962) reported more impressive findings. Their sample of fifty student leaders, all of whom had been elected to the presidency of a college organization having at least twenty members, had a mean Do T-score of about 62 while fifty nonleaders had a mean T-score of only 44.

In nonstudent samples, Knapp (1960) found that Marine Corps officers had significantly higher Do scores than enlisted men. Knapp's use of the shorter MMPI version of the Do makes it impossible to report T-scores, but the fact that 88 per cent of the enlisted men fell below the officers' mean indicates good discrimination was achieved. However, Olmstead and Monachesi (1956) failed to find significant differences between twenty-five fire department captains and 262 regular firemen. Although they concluded that such results cast doubt on the validity of the scale, it should be considered in evaluating their findings that they also used only the Do items common to the MMPI and that such a shortened form of the scale contains only 30 per cent of the Do scale items; also Megargee (1966b) has determined that the short scale correlation with the full scale is only .67.

Rawls and Rawls (1968) reported that Do significantly differentiated the thirty most successful from the thirty least successful of the 150 executives employed by a medium-sized utilities firm. However, they failed to report the magnitude of the differences between groups. The Do scores of seventy-five managerial personnel who were ranked by their supervisors as being in the top third in managerial effectiveness were compared with the Do scores of those falling in the lowest third by Mahoney, Jerdee, and Nash (1961). (Data from the middle group were discarded.) Statistically significant differences were found; the median Do score of the more effective managers was 60 while the less effective group scored 54. These two studies showed that the Do scale is able to make discriminations within fairly homogeneous occupational groups. Of course both studies would have been more powerful had the entire range, and not just the extremes of executive talent been represented.

Bogard (1960) reported that groups of labor and management trainees selected for their leadership potential had mean Do T-scores in the mid-60s. Although these T-scores are above the national norms, it cannot be said whether they would have exceeded those of trainees not highly regarded for leadership potential since no such contrast groups were studied. (These studies are reviewed in further detail in Chapter Twelve.)

Other concurrent validation studies have used ratings of leadership or dominance as their criteria. Such ratings are probably less adequate a criterion

Table 3. NUMBER OF ITEMS SHARED BY THE EIGHTEEN CPI SCALES

Scale	No.	No. Pure	Do	Cs	Sy	Sp	Sa	Wb	Re	So	Sc	To	Gi	Cm	Ac	Ai	Ie	Py	Fx	Fe
Do	46	25	X	3	4	2	6	1	6	2	1	2			1	1	2	2		1
Cs	32	15		X	4	7	4		2	2	1	3	1		1	2	5			
Sy	36	9			X	8	8		4		3	3			4	5	10	1		
Sp	56	6				X	8	3		3	10	2	3			2	7	4		1
Sa	34	3					X		3	2	8	1	3		2	2	3	1		1
Wb	44	29						X		1		3	1		2		1	1		
Re	42	16				1	1		X	3	4	4	1		5	5	6	1		3
So	54	28			1	3	1		3	X	5	3			3	3	3	1		2
Sc	50	2	3		3	10	8		4	5	X	5	13		5	3	2	3		3
To	32	9					1		4	3	5	X			1	8	6	1		
Gi	40	18	1			4	3						X							2
Cm	28	28												X						
Ac	38	18				1									X	5	6	1		1
Ai	32	11													5	X	8	1		
Ie	52	22				1							1				X			
Py	22	10					1						1					X		
Fx	22	22																	X	
Fe	38	22			1	3			3	1	3							1		X

NOTE: Common items scored in the same manner appear above the diagonal; those scored in the opposite manner are below the diagonal.

than the fact that one actually achieved a position of leadership. However, since the comparisons are based on more homogeneous groups, they often pose a more severe test of validity since the scale must detect smaller differences.

Several such studies have been conducted at the Institute of Personality Assessment and Research (IPAR) at the University of California where groups are often studied and tested over a two- or three-day period. In these studies, the *Do* scores of military officers, student engineers, and medical school applicants have been found to correlate significantly with pooled dominance ratings made by the IPAR staff (Dicken, 1963a; Gough, 1969b). Correlations ranged from .40 to .56. Dicken failed to find a significant correlation ($r = .16$) in a sample of research scientists, however. In a sample of sixty-six freshman women, Vingoe (1968) found *Do* scores correlated significantly with peer ratings ($r = .37$) and self ratings ($r = .64$) of dominance based on the trait description in the CPI *Manual*. Similarly, Hase and Goldberg (1967) reported a correlation of .38 between *Do* scores and peer ratings of dominance in a sample of 190 freshman women. Less direct evidence of construct validity was afforded by Zuckerman, Levitt, and Lubin (1961), who found a significant negative correlation ($r = -.33$) between *Do* scores and peer ratings of dependency in a sample of seventy-eight student nurses. However, Bohn (1965) found no difference in the directiveness of high and low *Do* counselors. Two of these studies (Dicken, 1963; Hase and Goldberg, 1967) included tests of discriminant validity in their design and both obtained data supporting the discriminant validity of the *Do* scale.

Thus far, the focus has been on the upper end of the *Do* scale to determine whether people with higher Dominance scale scores manifest more leadership. There are also data available regarding whether people with low *Do* scores are more submissive. Some information relevant to this question can be gleaned from studies on conformity. In each of these studies, Ss were placed in the Asch situation in which they were required to judge the length of a line after hearing erroneous judgments from four fellow subjects, all of whom were in fact confederates of the experimenter. One would expect a negative correlation between *Do* scale scores and the degree to which Ss yielded to the majority opinion. Studies of the CPI correlates of yielding to a distorted group norm have been performed by Crutchfield (1955), Tuddenham (1959), Appley and Moeller (1963), and Harper (1964). In all, these investigators examined three samples of college students, one sample of student nurses, and three samples of adult men and women. In the four student samples, no significant correlations between *Do* and yielding were noted. In two of the three adult samples, significant negative correlations were reported (Tuddenham, 1959). (See Chapter Fourteen, Table 1.)

The *Do* scale was also used in two other investigations (Altrocchi, 1959; Smelser, 1961) to select Ss high and low in dominance who then interacted in a mutual problem-solving situation. Although the validity of the *Do* scale was not the subject of investigation, it was noted in both studies that the high *Do* Ss behaved dominantly and the low *Do* Ss submissively.

Meehl (1959) and Myers (1950) have both stressed the importance of establishing the predictive validity of tests. Such studies are difficult to carry out, not only because of the time that must elapse to determine the accuracy of the prediction, but also because of the numerous situational factors that can cause

to go awry those predictions based solely on personality data. Several studies by
the present writer and his students of the predictive validity of the *Do* scale illustrate the last point. The basic design in each of those studies was to administer
the *Do* scale to large groups of college or high school students;[1] pairs of *S*s would
then be selected, each consisting of one high *Do S* and one low *Do S*. They would
then be given appointments to return to the laboratory and told to work together
on a task in which one *S* had to be the leader and the other the follower. It was
predicted that the high *Do S* would usually assume the leader role.

In the first study in the series, the instructions did not stress leadership
and only 56 per cent of the high *Do S*s adopted the dominant role. In the next
study, however, the importance of leadership was stressed, and when dominance
was thus made salient, 90 per cent of the high *Do S*s became the leaders of the
two-man groups (Megargee, Bogart and Anderson, 1966, p. 295). The results
of the study indicated "that the CPI *Do* scale is capable of predicting leadership. However, the conditions under which leadership is to be exercised are as
important as the personality trait of dominance in determining whether or not
dominant behavior will be manifested."

Subsequent studies explored the ramifications of particular contexts by
pairing high *Do S*s with low *Do S*s when it would be culturally appropriate for
the high *Do S* to be the leader, as opposed to situations where cultural-role stereotypes would oppose this. For example, Megargee (1969b) paired: 1) high and
low *Do* men, 2) high and low *Do* women, 3) high *Do* men and low *Do*
women, and 4) high *Do* women and low *Do* men. In the first three conditions
the assumption of leadership by the high *Do S* was in harmony with cultural
roles and, as expected, the high *Do S*s usually became leaders. However, in the
last condition, only 20 per cent of the high *Do* women assumed leadership over
the low *Do* men, probably because of cultural mores stressing masculine dominance. Replication of the experiment using a different task and different experimenter produced identical results. In the replication, a careful record of the de-
cision-making process was made and it was found that under condition 4, although the high *Do* girls did not actually assume the formal leader role, it was
they who chose the leader in 69 per cent of the teams, and appointed a male
partner to be leader 91 per cent of the time. They thus exercised their dominance
in a culturally approved manner.

Subsequent studies by Fenelon and Megargee (1971), and Rubinroit
(1970), have explored the effects of race, ethnic background, and socioeconomic
status on leadership assumption by high *Do S*s. The results have consistently
shown a high degree of predictive validity for the *Do* scale when dominance is
stressed but the assumption of leadership does not violate cultural mores. When
potential conflict is involved, however, the results have been more variable. In
evaluating this research, it should be pointed out that at least 20 *T*-score points

---

[1] To save time, the *Do* scale was abstracted and administered separately in these
studies. This widespread practice is rather questionable because one never knows how the
overall context influences the responses to the items. The writer is not aware of any research
investigating the extent to which scores on the *Do* and other CPI scales are altered by separate administration, but it is a question that should be investigated.

separated the two partners. Considerably less predictive accuracy would be expected if the differences in dominance were smaller.

Armilla (1967) used a somewhat different strategy. Rather than actually making predictions in advance, he rated the leadership manifested by seventy-five Peace Corps volunteers in Latin America; he then correlated these ratings with *Do* scores obtained during training. Considering the fact that Armilla had only MMPI protocols available and was therefore limited to scoring the fourteen common items, the fact that he obtained a significant correlation is noteworthy, even though the absolute magnitude of the relation was low ($r = .21$).

Overall, the *Do* scale is one of the best-validated of the eighteen CPI scales, and almost all of the evidence available supports its concurrent and construct validity. Indeed, Butt and Fiske (1968), in their broad comparison of dominance scales from a variety of personality inventories, concluded that the CPI *Do* scale was the most appropriate for assessing leadership and peer ratings. In addition, the *Do* scale is one of the few scales for which predictive (as opposed to postdictive or concurrent) validity has been established.

Capacity for Status (*Cs*)

Status is certainly a good folk culture variable, despite occasional protests to the contrary since status differentiations exist in most locales and cultures. The initial derivation of the *Cs* scale represented a straightforward attempt to construct a personality scale that correlated significantly with external criteria of status, which are defined as the relative level of income, education, prestige, and power attained in one's social-cultural milieu (Gough, 1968a).

However, as with many CPI scales, the *Cs* scale is also treated as a trait measure. Gough (1968a, p. 61) has written that the *Cs* scale "attempts to appraise those qualities of ambition and self-assurance that underlie, and lead to, status" [rather than measuring actual or achieved status (1969a)]. Some of this ambivalence is reflected in the fact that the scale was originally named Status, but has now been renamed Capacity for Status.

The Sims Score-Card for Socioeconomic Status and the MMPI were administered to 223 high school seniors from a Minnesota town of 25,000. The MMPI responses of thirty-eight students (twenty girls and eighteen boys) who were one standard deviation above the group's mean on the SES measure were compared with those of thirty-eight *S*s who were one SD below the mean. In addition to differing in SES, the criterion groups also differed significantly in IQ (109 vs. 99) and in grade point average (2.5 vs. 2.0) (Gough, 1948a).

Phi coefficients were computed for all the MMPI items. Those that were significant at the .02 level were retained to form the Status (*St*) scale. This *St* scale and the American Home Index, another SES measure, were administered to a cross-validating sample of 263 high school students. A correlation of .50 was obtained (Gough, 1948a). The *St* scale also had a correlation of .28 with the

Gough Home Index in a sample of fifty-five college students (Gough, 1949b). Some construct validity was also provided by a study showing St and the Sims Score-Card displayed a similar pattern of correlations with other personality and achievement measures (Gough, 1948b).

Upon formal publication of the CPI, Gough retained nineteen of the thirty-four MMPI items and replaced thirteen with items from the CPI item pool. This revised scale made use of additional Ss as well as new criterion data that had not been available at the time of the initial derivation. Conceptual analyses of the revised scale suggested that it assessed factors underlying or leading to social status rather than status itself. Accordingly, Gough renamed it Capacity for Status.

ITEM CHARACTERISTICS

Of the thirty-two Cs items, eleven are keyed true and twenty-one false; fifteen of the items are pure items. The rest are also scored on other scales, the principal overlap being with $Sp, Ie,$ and $Sa.$

Many of the items on the Cs scale reflect social poise and self-confidence: "I usually don't like to talk much unless I am with people I know very well"—F; security and an absence of fears or anxieties: "I get very nervous if I think that someone is watching me"—F; and literary and aesthetic interests: "I would like to hear a great singer in an opera"—T. There are also items reflecting social conscience: "Only a fool would ever vote to increase his own taxes"—F; and an interest in belonging to various groups: "I think I would like to belong to a singing club"—T.

VALIDITY

Gough has correlated the Cs scale with scores on his Gough Home Index, a measure of SES based on certain kinds of objects such as books, phonographs, and similar things present in the individual's home. In four samples ranging in size from 152 to 238, Gough reported correlations ranging from .38 to .48 (1957, p. 23 and p. 37).

Bogard (1960) compared the Cs scores of executive trainees from a labor union and a shipping line. Despite the fact that the social class identification of the management group was significantly higher than that of the union group, there were no significant differences on Cs. This could be because both groups were ambitious and upwardly mobile.

Other studies have addressed themselves directly to the question of whether the scale assesses *capacity* for status as opposed to actually achieved status. According to Gough, discrepancies between actual status and Cs scores should be predictive of upward social mobility if Cs is higher, or downward mobility if it is lower. Gough (1949a) tested this hypothesis using groups of high school students that were 1) high on both St and the American Home Scale, 2) high Cs and low AHS, 3) low on Cs and high on the AHS, and 4) low on both. The high school principal of the students was then asked to describe each S and predict his eventual salary level; using this estimate as a criterion, Gough (1949a) obtained support for the hypothesis that discrepancies indicated status mobility and that the Cs scale assessed potential for status.

Somewhat less direct evidence was afforded by a recent study showing that in three of four large samples of highly qualified high school students, those who went on to college had significantly higher *Cs* scores than those who did not (Gough, 1968b). The magnitude of the mean differences ranged from three to nine *T*-score points, with the four groups that matriculated having mean *Cs* *T*-scores from 45 to 50, while the four groups who did not continue their education had mean scores ranging from 39 to 42.

In general, the evidence collected by Gough supports the validity of the *Cs* scale as a measure of potential status; further research in other laboratories is needed, however.

Sociability (*Sy*)

PURPOSE

Originally designated the *Sp* or Social Participation scale, the *Sy* scale was devised to differentiate people with an outgoing, sociable, participative temperament from those who shun involvement and avoid social visibility (Gough, 1952c, 1968a, 1969b).

CONSTRUCTION

The Sy scale was constructed by means of external criterion analysis, the criterion of social participation being the number of extracurricular activities that students engaged in. One hundred selected items were administered to three samples of high school seniors who ranked in the top and bottom quarters of their classes in participation in extracurricular activities; the forty-two items that significantly differentiated the high and low groups in all three samples were selected. When applied to the total pool of the 450 students from which the criterion groups had been selected, a correlation of .42 between the scale scores and the number of extracurricular activities the *S*s had engaged in was obtained (Gough, 1952c). Despite the undistributed middle, this validity coefficient appears to be rather low considering the fact that it is based in part on the original derivation samples.

Although it was originally designed to predict participation in social activities, subsequent research with the scale convinced Gough that it assessed sociability more than participation, and he renamed the scale accordingly (Gough, personal communication, 1971).

ITEM CHARACTERISTICS

The current *Sy* scale has been shortened to thirty-six items, of which twenty-two are keyed true and fourteen false. *Sy* has considerable overlap with other scales, sharing ten items with *Ie*, eight items each with *Sp* and *Sa*, and four or more items with *Ai, Do, Cs,* and *Ac*. Only nine of the thirty-six items are pure. (See Table 3.)

The manifest content of the scale is appropriate for a scale of sociability. Many of the items deal with enjoyment of social interactions: "I should like to belong to several clubs or lodges"—T; and feelings of poise and self-assurance in dealing with others: "I am a good mixer"—T; "I like to be the center of attention"—T. Other items reflect intellectual and cultural interests: "I like science" —T; and tolerance toward others coupled with stricter standards for oneself: "I can be friendly with people who do things which I consider wrong"—T.

The validation studies that have been conducted on Sy can be divided roughly into two groups: those that have assessed its effectiveness in predicting social participation, and those that have tested its validity as a measure of sociability or outgoingness. The pattern of the data indicates that Gough was correct in changing the name of the scale.

Several studies have used participation in extracurricular activities and the joining of social fraternities or societies as criteria. Gough (1969b) had the principals of five high schools nominate the fifty-two boys and fifty-one girls who were most active in extracurricular activities and contrasted their Sy scores with the fifty-two boys and fifty-one girls who participated the least. The socially active boys and girls had mean Sy T-scores of 52; the inactive boys had a mean of 42 and the inactive girls, 36. Those differences were statistically significant; however, considering the fact that extreme groups were used, and considering the existence of the relatively low mean scores for the most active Ss, those differences do not provide impressive evidence for the validity of the Sy scale.

Carson and Parker (1966) used the extent of participation and election to offices in church and school activities as an index of leadership. The groups differing on this leadership index differed on Do, but not Sy, thus supporting the distinction between Dominance and Sociability.

The data from studies comparing members of social fraternities and sororities with independents are also less than totally convincing of validity. Hase and Goldberg (1967), in a sample of 174 freshman women, found a modest but statistically significant correlation ($r = .24$) between Sy scores and sorority-joining. The present investigator found seventy-two fraternity members had significantly higher Sy scores than 203 non-members, but the magnitude of difference was trivial (2.43 T-score points); less than one T-score point separated the mean Sy score of sixty-four sorority women from 140 independents, a difference not statistically significant. Thus, for various academic settings the data indicate that Sy is not a particularly good predictor of participation in group activities.

Another form of "extracurricular" activity is participation in gang delinquency. Two studies have compared the Sy scores of delinquents who commit most of their offenses as part of a group, with those of delinquents who mostly commit offenses when alone. Mizushima and DeVos (1967) did find significant differences using Japanese delinquents, but Richardson and Roebuck (1965)' found none in a sample of American delinquents. Wilcock (1964) reported a non-significant trend for offenders who had committed solitary crimes of violence to have lower scores than those who committed property offenses, some with the aid of an accomplice. Hirt and Cook (1962) found that psychologically withdrawn military offenders did not have significantly lower Sy scores than offenders who acted out or who showed no signs of disorder. Thus, overall, Sy has not discriminated among these deviant groups very well.

The evidence for Sy's validity as a measure of sociability (as opposed to participation) is much more convincing. Hase and Goldberg (1967), in a sample of 190 freshman women, found significant correlations between their Sy scores and their peer ratings of sociability ($r = .44$) as well as with a measurement of how well each girl was known ($r = .31$); they also reported Sy correlated significantly ($r = .29$) with the number of dates a girl had per month. Moreover, Sy correlated higher with those criteria than did any of the ten other CPI scales they investigated. Hase and Goldberg's findings were replicated by Vingoe (1968) who obtained a correlation of .42 between Sy scores and peer ratings of sociability in a sample of sixty-six freshman women; Vingoe also reported a correlation of .68 with self-ratings on sociability.

Studies such as these, which use the entire range of Sy scores in relatively homogeneous samples (young women in their first year of college) provide more convincing data than studies using extreme groups and vast samples. Gough (1969b), for example, reported that 87 girls and 90 boys nominated by the principals of fifteen high schools as being the most popular, had Sy scores significantly higher than the national normative sample. However, the mean T-score was only 49 for the most popular boys and only 53 for the most popular girls.

Bouchard (1969) studied the relationship of the CPI to effectiveness in various types of group problem-solving situations. Sy was the only CPI scale that correlated consistently with this criterion in a variety of situations.

Social Presence (Sp)

PURPOSE

The Sp scale (once designated as the Sr scale) was constructed to assess poise, self-confidence, verve, and spontaneity in social interactions (Gough, 1968a, 1969b). Thus it is closely related to Sociability, which is supposed to identify outgoing, gregarious people. According to Gough, "there is more verve, more verbal aggression, more sarcasm, more irritability in Sp than in Sy. The high-scorer on Sy, if average on Sp, just plain likes people and their company. The high-scorer on Sp likes to be in the presence of others, but uses them, manipulates them, and takes pleasure in clever onslaughts against their defenses and self-deceptions" (Gough, personal communication, 1971).

CONSTRUCTION

The Sp scale was constructed rationally by means of internal consistency analyses; eighty-five items that appeared to be related to social poise, verve, and spontaneity were administered to several samples of males and females, the exact compositions of which have never been specified (Gough, 1968a, p. 62). For each subject, a score on the eighty-five items was computed; item-total correlations were calculated and the fifty-six items with the highest correlations were selected.

ITEM CHARACTERISTICS

The Sp scale is comprised of fifty-six items of which twenty-five are keyed true and thirty-one false. Item overlap, both positive and negative, is high. The principle positive overlap is with Sy and Sa (eight items each), Cs and Ie (seven items each), and Py (four items). In addition, there is negative overlap (common items but keyed opposite) with Sc (ten items) and Gi (four items). (See Table 3)ᐟ.

Like the Sy scale (with which it shares eight items), many of the items on the Sp scale deal with poise and enjoyment of social interactions: "I like to go to parties and other affairs where there is lots of loud fun"—T. There is also a strong element of self-assurance: "Criticism or scolding makes me very uncomfortable"—F. Sp goes somewhat farther than Sy in its inclusion of items indicating broadminded, unstuffy attitudes about social rules and prohibitions: "I would disapprove of anyone drinking to intoxication at a party"—F; and has some items in which there is an outright rejection of the Protestant ethic with its emphasis on duty, conformity, and moderation: "I always follow the rule of business before pleasure"—F; "Sometimes I rather enjoy going against the rules and doing things I'm not supposed to"—T. It is these latter clusters which account for most of the negative overlap with Sc and Gi.

VALIDITY

Evidence for the validity of Sp is relatively sparse. In the CPI *Manual,* Gough (1969b) reports that fifty-two boys and fifty-one girls in five high schools nominated by their principals as being highest in social presence obtained Sp scores significantly higher than those of the fifty-two boys and fifty-one girls who were lowest. The Ss high in the dimension did not have elevated scores (T-scores $= 53$ and 52) but the Ss lacking the trait did score low ($T = 42$ and 43). In a sample of seventy medical students Gough also reports data from IPAR indicating a significant correlation ($r = .43$) between Sp and staff ratings of social presence. Hase and Goldberg (1967) found that Sp correlated significantly with peer ratings of sociability ($r = .35$), ratings of how well known a girl was ($r = .21$), and the number of dates she had ($r = .37$). (Sy also correlated significantly with these measures.)

The data from the studies performed by Mizushima and DeVos (1967), Richardson and Roebuck (1965) and Wilcock (1964), indicate that Sp discriminates differences among "social" and "lone wolf" delinquents and criminals better than Sy. The magnitudes of the reported mean differences were larger, and attained statistical significance in all three investigations.

Further research on Sp is needed, particularly studies aimed at sharpening the distinction between Sp and Sy.

Self-Acceptance (Sa)

PURPOSE

In the CPI *Manual,* Gough states that the Sa scale goal is to "assess factors such as sense of personal worth, self-acceptance, and capacity for independent thinking and action" (1969b, p. 10). Later (1968a, p. 63), he emphasizes the first of these characteristics, indicating its purpose is to "identify individuals who would manifest a comfortable and imperturbable sense of personal worth, and who would be seen as secure and sure of themselves whether active or inactive in social behavior."

CONSTRUCTION

The *Sa* scale was rationally constructed through internal consistency analyses. The sample used and the nature of the initial item pool have not been reported nor have the criteria for item selection.

ITEM CHARACTERISTICS

The *Sa* scale consists of thirty-four items balanced between true and false keying. Of the thirty-four items, only three are pure. The pattern of overlap is similar to those of the *Sy* and *Sp* scales—with which *Sa* is closely related. The principal positive overlap is with *Sy* and *Sp* (eight items, *Do* (six items), and *Cs* (four items). As was the case with *Sp,* there is negative overlap with *Sc* (eight items) and *Gi* (three items).

The primary resemblance of *Sa* to *Sy* and *Sp* exists in a number of items dealing with social poise and self-confidence: "I am certainly lacking in self-confidence"—F; and a broadminded attitude toward social prohibitions: "Once in a while I laugh at a dirty joke"—T. However, in contrast to *Sp,* a cluster of items emphasizes the value of hard work, attention to duty, and consideration of others: "I often do whatever makes me feel cheerful here and now even at the cost of some distant goal"—F; "Before I do something I try to consider how my friends will react to it"—T. Another group expresses a candid acceptance of human frailties: "I looked up to my father as an ideal man"—F; "When a man is with a woman he is usually thinking about things related to her sex"—T.

VALIDITY

Gough (1969b) had the principals of five high schools nominate the fifty-two boys and fifty-three girls they regarded as most self-accepting, and fifty-two boys and forty-nine girls least self-accepting. The results were similar to those already reported on other scales: statistically significant, but with modest differences on the order of eight *T*-score points, with the high boys and girls having mean *T*-scores of 53 and 52 respectively, while the lows scored 45 and 44. One might question how well a principal is able to judge self acceptance in his students, particularly since the trait is not supposed to be related to participation in social activity.

More convincing data come from correlational studies. In a study at *IPAR,* in a sample of seventy medical school applicants, Gough (1969b) obtained a positive correlation ($r = .32$) with staff ratings of self-acceptance, and in a sample of forty college seniors, a negative correlation ($r = -.57$) with the staff's judgment of the seniors' "readiness to feel guilty." In a sample of sixty-six freshman women, Vingoe (1968) found *Sa* correlated significantly with peer ratings (.44) and self ratings (.49) of self-acceptance based on the *Manual's* description. However, Rosenberg (1962) did not find a significant correlation between *Sa* and a measure of the magnitude of self-ideal discrepancy in a sample of 144 enlisted men.

Lazarus, Speisman, Mordkoff, and Davison (1962) investigated the relationship between CPI scores and autonomic nervous system reactivity to stress. Individuals with high *Sa* scores manifested significantly less autonomic disturbance, supporting Gough's hypothesis that such people are less likely to become upset or perturbed.

Frankel (1969) classified undergraduate women and female alumnae as goal oriented or non-goal oriented. Analyzing their CPI scores, she found the goal oriented women to be significantly higher on *Sa,* as one would expect.

Since the *Sa* scale is supposed to identify individuals who are secure and self-confident, it seems reasonable to expect that neurotics and other disturbed individuals would score low on the scale. Gough disagrees with the writer on this point, stating in a personal communication, "*Sa* is not intended to relate to psychiatric pathology of the kind psychiatrists would see." Whether the writer's position is valid, the data do indicate disturbed individuals can not be detected adequately on the basis of low *Sa* scores. Stewart (1962) found no differences in the *Sa* scores of psychosomatic and symptom-free adults. Hirt and Cook (1962) found that *Sa* did not distinguish military offenders with no psychiatric disorder from those who were withdrawn or who acted out. Corotto's (1963) alcoholic samples had mean scores in the normal range ($T = 49$). Canter (1963) did report alcoholics had *Sa* scores significantly lower than psychiatric aides, but their mean T-score of 45 was not particularly low on an absolute basis, and the differences on *Sa* were eliminated when the alcoholics tried to fake good. Goodstein, Crites, Heilbrun and Rempel (1961) did find significant differences between a sample of nonclients and students who applied for help at a university counseling center. However, this was because the well-adjusted students had unusually high *Sa* scores (mean T-score = 61.4)—not because the personal adjustment clients ($T = 55.6$) or the vocational-educational clients ($T = 56.8$) had low scores. Thus the data indicate that the Self-Acceptance scale can not be regarded as a measure of adjustment.

Sense of Well-Being (*Wb*)

PURPOSE

Originally called the Dissimulation (*Ds*) scale, *Wb* was derived to discriminate individuals feigning neurosis from normals and psychiatric patients responding truthfully. Gough (1968a, 1969b) states, that in addition to its implications for validity, interpretation is possible in *Wb*—with high scores indicating health and verve, and low scores suggesting diminished vitality and inability to meet the demands of everyday life. Because interpersonal effectiveness derives in part from feelings of physical and psychological well-being, Gough placed the *Wb* scales in Class I, despite the fact that factor analytic results show *Wb* loads on a different factor from the other five Class I scales.

CONSTRUCTION

The Dissimulation scale was derived through external criterion analyses comparing the MMPI responses of actual neurotics with those of normals asked to feign neurosis (Gough, 1954). The neurotic *S*s included three male samples with a total N = 125, as well as women. The dissimulated records were obtained from fifty men and fifty women who were students in an abnormal psychology class and eleven male professional workers in an Army hospital. Three item analyses were carried out comparing the different criterion samples, and the seventy-four MMPI items showing similar and significant differences in all three were retained for the *Ds* scale.

The *Ds* scale was extensively cross-validated: eight samples of clinical patients and two samples of high school students took the test under standard instructions. Three samples of normals responded under fake bad conditions. The distributions of *Ds* scores in the three samples which were requested to malinger were much higher than those in either the two normal or eight clinical samples. The overall mean *Ds* score of the 354 fake bad *Ss* was 54.13, compared with mean scores of 15.94 for the 915 clinical cases and 15.88 for the 507 normals. This clearly showed that high *Ds* scores reflected attempts to simulate pathology and not psychopathology itself.

When the CPI was formed, the *Ds* scale was revised for inclusion as a validity scale. The scale was reduced in length and some of the MMPI items were replaced with items from the CPI pool. The keying was reversed so that low scores reflect dissimulation while high scores were said to indicate well-being.

ITEM CHARACTERISTICS

The Sense of Well-Being scale consists of forty-four items of which five are keyed true and thirty-nine false. With twenty-nine pure items, item overlap is very low; the only scale sharing four or more items in *Sc*. In this respect *Wb* differs from the other Class I scales, and, as we shall see, the difference is reflected in the factorial structure of the CPI, for *Wb* loads on an entirely different factor from the other scales discussed thus far.

The content of the *Wb* scale consists primarily of denials of various physical and mental symptoms: "I am troubled by attacks of nausea and vomiting"—F; "I am afraid to be alone in the dark"—F. The high scorer on *Wb* denies any major family problems: "I have felt embarrassed over the type of work one or more of my family members have done"—F; also, he denies sexual conflicts or preoccupations: "I wish I were not bothered by thoughts about sex"—F; and indicates he is not particularly tense, anxious or fearful: "Several times a week I feel as if something dreadful is about to happen"—F. Instead he endorses items reflecting independence and self-sufficiency: "Any man who is able and willing to work has a good chance of success"—T; and indicates confidence in the future: "I usually feel that life is worthwhile"—T.

VALIDITY

As we have seen, the purpose of the original *Ds* scale was to detect dissembled records. Normal groups and disturbed groups were supposed to obtain similar mean scores if they responded truthfully. When the MMPI *Ds* scale was converted to the CPI *Wb* scale, the goals also changed somewhat. People faking bad were still supposed to obtain the most deviant scores. However, psychiatric patients were no longer supposed to have scores equal to those of normals (indicating no efforts to distort the test); instead they were supposed to obtain scores lower than normals, indicating a lower sense of well-being and diminished verve and vigor.

Gough (1969b) has compared the mean *Wb* scores of the 915 psychiatric patients and 354 dissemblers tested in connection with the cross-validation of Ds with those Wb scores of 2,800 college students tested in the standardization of the CPI. As was the case with Ds, the fake bad records are quite different from the valid protocols, but unlike Ds, Gough found a significant difference between the scores of the psychiatric cases and the normal students. Reflecting the changed purpose of the scale, he states, "The lower score among patients is . . . in support of the scale's validity" (1969b, p. 21). It should be pointed out, however, that the mean difference of about five T-score points, although statistically significant (with 3713 degrees of freedom), is not substantial. Aside from this study, there are few, if any, data on the validity of Wb as a measure of malingering—perhaps because the primary focus in recent years of research in dissembling has shifted from faking bad to faking good.

A number of studies have investigated the relationship between the CPI and psychological adjustment. Different criteria of adjustment have been used and most have shown the expected relations with Wb. Hirt and Cook (1962) in their study of military offenders found those with no psychiatric disorder significantly higher on Wb scores than those who were withdrawn or who acted out; the absolute magnitude of the differences was not reported. Canter (1963) found psychiatric aides had significantly higher Wb scores (mean T-score $= 58$) than their alcoholic patients (mean T-score $= 44$), and that under fake good instructions, the better-adjusted alcoholics still had higher Wb scores than the poorer-adjusted ones. Corotto (1963) reported that among alcoholics committed to a state hospital, those who wanted to be released immediately after they had been "dried out" had higher Wb scores (mean $= 41$) than those who volunteered to remain for further psychiatric treatment (mean $= 35$). In those studies, some of which employed relatively small and rather homogeneous samples, the magnitude of the differences and the absolute value of the mean scores all lend further support to the construct validity of the Wb scale.

Goodstein, Crites, Heilbrun, and Rempel (1961) found that a group of students who had never sought help at a university counseling center had higher Wb scores ($T = 50.8$) than a group which had sought assistance with vocational or educational problems ($T = 46.1$), and that the latter group in turn scored higher than a group counseled for difficulties in personal adjustment ($T = 39.9$). Stewart (1962) reported that a group of eleven normal men tested in connection with the Oakland Growth Study had significantly higher Wb scores (mean $T = 60$) than another group of ten Ss from the same study with a history of psychosomatic illness (mean $T = 53$). The differences for similar groups of women were smaller ($T = 52$ vs $T = 47$) and not significant. A trend of the symptom-free groups to score higher than groups with behavior disorders also did not prove to be statistically reliable. Rosenberg (1962) found a significant negative correlation between Wb and magnitude of self-ideal discrepancy in a military sample; however, he failed to report the magnitude of the association and with an N of 144, an r as low as .17 could be significant. Gough (1969b) obtained a significant correlation ($r = .26$) between Wb scores and ratings of health and vitality made by IPAR observers on a sample of one hundred military officers. However, Lorei (1964) reported that within a sample of released psychiatric patients, he was unable to find any relation between Wb scores obtained prior to release and the length of stay outside the hospital. In commenting on this study, Gough notes in a personal communication (1971), "A patient might have a sense of well-being at release sufficient to send him on his way, but this does not guarantee that he will stay happy. Wb is not a scale for ego strength, in other words." The present writer would infer from this comment that Gough regards Wb as a "state" scale, that is, a scale which varies or fluctuates as a function of the patient's mood, as opposed to a trait scale. The writer questions Gough's position on this issue because of the high test-retest correlation noted for Wb. However, it would be interesting to explore the question further by determining the relation between Wb and the scales of trait and state anxiety in Spielberger's State-Trait Anxiety Inventory (Spielberger, Gorsuch, and Lushene, 1968).

Although not all studies found significant or substantial relationships, the general finding from a number of investigations is that Wb reliably reflects differences in adjustment as defined by a number of criteria. As we shall see in Chapter Thirteen, the Wb scale shares this distinction with a number of other CPI scales. However, that reflects on the discriminant validity of those other scales and does not diminish the convergent validity of Wb.

CHAPTER 5

Class II Scales:

Measures of Responsibility, Socialization, Maturity, and Intrapersonal Structuring of Values

꿈꿈꿈꿈꿈꿈꿈꿈꿈꿈꿈꿈꿈꿈꿈꿈꿈꿈꿈꿈

Class II, like Class I, includes six scales: Responsibility, Socialization, Self-control, Tolerance, Good Impression, and Communality. Gough grouped these six measures together because he felt that all assessed some aspect of socialization, maturity, responsibility, and intrapersonal structuring of values. Of these six scales, the first four were originally devised as trait measures, and the last two were designed as validity scales. As we shall see in Chapter Nine, most of these Class II scales have their principal factor loading on the same factor; however, several of them also have substantial secondary loadings on other factors.

Responsibility (*Re*)

PURPOSE

The Responsibility scale was developed as part of a study on political behavior by Gough, McClosky and Meehl (1952) to identify people who were conscientious, responsible, dependable, articulate about rules and order, and who believe that life should be governed by reason (Gough, 1968a, 1969b). It differs from the related *So* and *Sc* scales in that *Re* emphasizes the degree to which values and controls are conceptualized and understood (Gough, 1965a).

The *Re* scale was derived in conjunction with the *Do* scale and the same basic peer rating procedures were used to select the criterion groups from University of Minnesota fraternal organizations and a Minneapolis high school. For the *Re* scale, additional criterion groups were selected from a St. Cloud high school and junior high school based on ratings made by the principal and the teachers, respectively. As with *Do*, the MMPI item pool was used in conjunction with other specially devised items. After external criterion analyses were carried out, fifty-six items were selected, of which thirty-two were from the MMPI and 24 from the special pool.

The scale was then administered as part of an IPAR assessment battery to two samples of fourth-year graduate students at the University of California and to one sample of fourth-year medical students. There were forty *S*s in each sample. The *Re* scale scores correlated .22 (n.s.), .33 ($p < .05$), and .38 ($p < .05$) with staff ratings of responsibility. The authors suggested that the homogeneity of the samples might have been a factor contributing to these rather unimpressive results.

As with many CPI scales, *Re* has been shortened from fifty-six to forty-two items, of which seventeen are keyed true and twenty-five false. While sixteen of the items are pure, there is broad positive overlap, *Re* sharing four or more items with scales *Do, Sy, Sc, To, Ac, Ai,* and *Ie.* (See Table 3.)

The manifest content includes a number of items indicating a concern for social, civic and moral obligations: "Every citizen should take the time to find out about national affairs, even if it means giving up personal pleasures"—T; an emphasis on duty and self-discipline: "If I get too much change in a store, I always give it back"—T; and disapproval of any special privileges or favoritism: "Maybe some minority groups do get rough treatment, but it's no concern of mine"—F. In addition to these ethical attitudes, *Re* items reflect poise and self-confidence: "When I work on a committee, I like to take charge of things"—T; trust and confidence in others: "There is no use in doing things for people; you only find that you get it in the neck in the long run"—F; and a denial of impulsivity or rebelliousness: "I have never done anything dangerous just for the thrill of it"—T.

The validational research for the *Re* scale shows a mixed pattern. Studies using ratings for criteria have generally failed to support the scale's validity. Dicken (1963a), in three samples, correlated *Re* scores with IPAR observers' ratings of responsibility; in two of the samples he failed to get significant convergent validity, and the overall correlation for all 181 *S*s was only .09. Similarly Vingoe (1968), in his sample of sixty-six freshman women, failed to obtain significant correlations with peer or self ratings based on the *Manual*'s description of the trait. Hase and Goldberg (1967) found *Re* correlated significantly ($r = .29$) with peer ratings of responsibility in a sample of 190 freshman women.

However, the *So* scale correlated higher ($r = .39$) with this criterion, thus demonstrating difficulties with discriminant, and thereby trait, validity. All three of the above studies included their entire samples. In a comparison of extreme groups with an undistributed middle, Gough (1969b) found fifty-two high school boys and fifty-one girls nominated by their principals as the most responsible had significantly higher *Re* scores than a similar number nominated as least responsible. The differences were fairly substantial, reaching 16–18 *T*-score points, with the least responsible groups having quite low *T*-scores (32–37) and the most responsible having average *T*-scores (50–53). The pattern of these studies suggests that the *Re* scale discriminates better at the lower end in a manner reminiscent of Fisher's (1959) "twisted pear" pattern.

Several studies have tested the validity of the *Re* scale by examining the scores of people in occupations in which responsibility and attention to duty are demanded. Using the abbreviated eighteen-item MMPI version of the *Re* scale, Knapp (1960) found that United States Marine Corps officers scored significantly higher than enlisted men, while Olmsted and Monachesi (1956) reported a nonsignificant trend in twenty-five fire captains obtaining higher scores than 262 regular firemen. The scores of the firemen, however, were significantly higher than those of high school students, thus lending some support to the scale's construct validity. Similarly, Collins (1967) found a significant correlation ($r = -.34$) between *Re* scores and class standing in an Army drill-sergeant training program.

Two studies have investigated the relation between *Re* scores and performance on tedious tasks when a strong sense of duty is one of the primary motivating factors. Kohlfield and Weitzel (1969) had soldiers walk a treadmill under conditions of social facilitation—a group of other soldiers was watching and evaluating their performance—and in a solitary condition because "it was good for them." Although instructed to walk as fast as possible, most soldiers were slower when they felt they were not being evaluated. The difference in speed in the two conditions served as the criterion of responsibility; the lower the difference, the greater the attention to duty. *Re* scores had a significant negative correlation ($r = -.51$) in one sample of forty-seven men, and the finding was repeated ($r = -.29$) in a second sample of thirty-eight men.

Similar evidence can be shown in a study of performance in a Federal Aviation Agency course on air traffic control. In a sample of 338 trainees, *Re* was found to correlate significantly ($r = .24$) with performance in training. The fact that this was limited to *Ss* who graduated from the training program makes the measurement more impressive. *Re* scores failed to correlate significantly with various indices of job performance collected a year later for that subgroup still employed at the time (ca. 244) (Trites, Kurek and Cobb, 1967). Gough reports that Gendre (1966) found *Re* predicted levels of performance of watchmakers.

The most consistent findings have come from studies of delinquent and antisocial groups. Reckless and his associates did a series of studies on the personality factors that influence whether boys from high delinquency areas come into contact with the law (Reckless, Dinitz, and Kay, 1957; Dinitz, Kay and Reckless, 1957; Dinitz, Reckless, and Kay, 1958). The data they collected provide evidence of the predictive validity of the *Re* and *So* scales. They first asked sixth-grade teachers to nominate boys felt to be potential delinquents, and compared their scores with boys nominated as immune to the influence of environmental pressures toward delinquency. The 125 boys "insulated" from delinquency were found to have a mean *Re* *T*-score of 46; the 101 "potential" delinquents a mean *T*-score of 36—a difference that was highly significant. Later the potential delinquents were divided into those who actually had court contact and those without it. The seventy-seven not known to the courts had a mean *Re* *T*-score of 38 while the twenty-four who were had a mean *T*-score of 31, thus demonstrating that *Re* could discriminate differences significantly within a fairly homogeneous sample. Further, a study by Richardson and Roebuck (1965), who compared delinquents with their nondelinquent brothers, showed significantly higher *Re* scores among the nondelinquents. Vincent (1961) learned that single girls from intact homes who had never been pregnant obtained higher *Re* scores than unwed mothers. Gough (1969b) found high school students regarded by their principals as best citizens had significantly higher scores than students considered disciplinary problems. Hogan, Mankin, Conway, and Fox (1970) found the *Re* scores of university students who smoked marijuana occasionally were higher than those who did so regularly, that those who had never smoked pot were higher than those who had done so occasionally, and that those who had never smoked had the highest *Re* scores of all.

Summing up the evidence, it is clear that groups characterized by antisocial behavior obtain low scores on the *Re* scale. There are also indications that occupational groups for whom responsible behavior is required may have above average scores, and that *Re* correlates with performance on tasks emphasizing attention to duty. However, the general failure of the *Re* scale to relate closely to ratings of responsibility indicates that further research is needed to clarify its meaning.

Socialization (*So*)

PURPOSE

Gough's original goal was to construct a delinquency scale based on his role-taking theory of sociopathy (Gough, 1948c); Gough and Peterson, 1952). Subsequent research indicated that the scale reflected not just delinquency, but a full range of socialization. In more recent writings, Gough (1965a, 1968a, 1969b) has indicated that the scale reflects the degree of social maturity, integrity, and rectitude the individual has attained. It orders individuals along a continuum from asocial to social behavior and forecasts the likelihood that they will transgress the mores established by their particular cultures (Gough, 1965b). In contrast to *Re* and *Sc,* the *So* scale thus measures the extent to which values are internalized and made useful in the life of the individual (Gough, 1965a).

CONSTRUCTION

The Socialization scale, or, as it was originally called, the Delinquency scale, was constructed through external criterion analyses comparing the responses of delinquents and nondelinquents. Nine samples of adolescents were used in deriving the scale. The five male samples included forty-three high school boys from a small Minnesota town, 125 high school boys from two Minneapolis schools, nineteen boys with behavior problems from Minneapolis schools, 243 young delinquents committed to the Minnesota Youth Commission, and 698 inmates of the Minnesota Reformatory for Men. Female samples included forty-four high school girls from the same small town as above, 134 Minneapolis high school girls, nineteen girls with behavior problems from the same high schools, and 105 inmates of the Minnesota Reformatory for Women.

The item pool consisted of "personality test items which would incorporate the salient features of the role-taking theory, as well as items believed on intuitive grounds to hold promise for the differentiation of delinquents from nondelinquents" (Gough and Peterson, 1952). Empirical item analyses of all the control samples versus all the delinquent samples were made one at a time and separately by sex, and sixty-four items showing "good differentiating power" were retained. On cross-validation, forty-two of the sixty-four items, chosen randomly, were administered to 1,092 Army recruits and ninety-nine stockade prisoners. It was found that the prisoners obtained significantly higher scores than the recruits. The optimal cutting score was determined on the basis of the samples. Next, a fifty-eight-item version of the *So* scale was administered to 253 stockade prisoners at Lackland Air Force Base. It was found that 64 per cent of the prisoners scored above the pro-rated cutting score. These prisoners were then subdivided into first offenders and recidivists; the recidivists scored higher than first offenders. The scale was published as the Delinquency (*De*) scale in 1952; when included on the CPI the keying was reversed and it was renamed Socialization.

ITEM CHARACTERISTICS

The present *So* scale consists of fifty-four items of which twenty-two are keyed true and thirty-two false. Twenty-eight items are pure and *So* shares relatively few items with any other scale except *Sc*, which has five items in common with it.

The manifest content of the *So* items, while not always obvious, is consistent with delinquency theory and research. A number of studies (cf., Glueck and Glueck, 1950; Rosenquist and Megargee, 1969) have demonstrated a relationship between delinquency and a lack of cohesiveness in the family. It is hardly surprising to find a cluster of items dealing with feelings of warmth, satisfaction, and family stability as opposed to resentment and alienation in the family milieu: "The members of my family were always close to one another"—T; "My parents never really understood me"—F. Similarly, a negative world view has been found to characterize delinquents in this and other cultures (Rosenquist and Megargee, 1969), and a cluster of *So* items reflect optimism and self-confidence, in contrast to feelings of despondency, alienation or inferiority: "With things going as they are it is pretty hard to keep up hope of amounting to something"—F. As noted above, one purpose in deriving the *So* scale was to test Gough's theory that sociopathy results from an egocentric inability to perceive the effects of one's behavior on others. A number of items reflect social sensitivity and empathy as opposed to ignorance of one's own stimulus value: "I often think about how I look and what impression I am making on others"—T. The final and most obvious group of items refer to scholastic and familial adjustment as opposed to waywardness and rebellion: "As a youngster in school I used to give the teachers lots of trouble"—F; "I sometimes wanted to run away from home"—F.

These groups of items, based on inspection of the manifest content by Gough and Peterson (1952), have been largely validated through a cluster analysis of the *So* items by Stein, Sarbin, and Gough (1966), which yielded four clusters: the three that were interpretable closely resembled those above.

VALIDITY

The similarity of the relationship between an inventory and its author to that of the child and its parent(s) was discussed earlier. If that simile is authentic, the seventeen other scales would have just cause to harbor strong feelings of sibling rivalry toward *So,* for that scale is clearly its creator's favorite, and has received a disproportionate share of his attention. As a result, the *So* scale has been far more thoroughly researched than any of the others, and one of the first bits of evidence that Gough will adduce to support the cross-cultural validity of the CPI is the work on the *So* scale.

Surveying the extensive literature on this scale, it is possible to divide the studies into groups according to population and design.

Comparison of delinquents and nondelinquents in the United States. The basic design in these studies has been to compare adjudicated juvenile delinquents with a control group that has been matched for various environmental factors. Such studies have consistently found both male and female delinquents to have significantly lower *So* scores (Gough, 1965b, 1969b; Peterson, Quay and Anderson, 1959; Richardson and Roebuck, 1965; Tonra, 1963). As can be seen in Table 4, delinquent groups rarely have mean *T*-scores over 40. Other groups have mean scores ranging from the low 40s to the upper 60s (depending on their degree of socialization). Gough (1965b) reported point-biserial correlations between *So* and the dichotomous criterion of delinquent versus nondelinquent for 11,795 boys and 10,724 girls. The correlation for the boys was .39, that for the girls .46.

This writer knows of only one published investigation that failed to find significant differences. Rusk (1969) selected fifty delinquent and fifty nondelinquent Mexican-American youths. Both groups were equivalent in age, SES, IQ, and geographical origin, and both came from urban, deprived backgrounds and had histories of family upheaval, hostility, and emotional disturbance. In this study, the nondelinquent youths from this chaotic background were found to have *So* scores as low as the delinquent youngsters.

A series of studies by Reckless and his colleagues at Ohio State University has shown that the *So* scale has predictive as well as concurrent validity. In this investigation, teachers nominated 101 sixth-grade white boys in high delinquency neighborhoods whom they felt were potential delinquents and 125 others unlikely to get into trouble. The "good" boys were found to have significantly higher *So* scores than the "bad" boys (Reckless, Dinitz, and Kay, 1957). Of the bad boys, those who were already known to the police had the lower *So* scores (Dinitz, Reckless, and Kay, 1958). Four years later a follow-up of the bad boys showed that twenty-seven of the seventy that could be traced had had continuing and serious delinquency. In contrast, of the 101 good boys that were traced, only four were known to the police. Retesting showed that the *So* scores of the two groups had not changed (Dinitz, Scarpitti, and Reckless, 1962; Scarpitti, Murray, Dinitz, and Reckless, 1960).

Comparison of delinquents and nondelinquents in other countries. The *So* scale has been translated into a number of languages and administered to adjudicated offenders and nonoffenders (usually students) in a number of countries, including Austria, Costa Rica, France, Germany, India, Israel, Italy, Japan, Puerto Rico, South Africa, Switzerland, and Taiwan. In every nation tested thus far, significant differences have been found ($p < .001$). Moreover, the mean raw scores are remarkably similar from one country to the next. The highest mean score obtained by any delinquent group (a sample from India that included some very minor offenders) was still significantly lower than the lowest score obtained by any nondelinquent group (members of an Austrian boys club, many of whom had disturbed family backgrounds) (Adis-Castro, 1957; Gough, 1965b, 1968c; Gough and Sandhu, 1964; Mizushima and DeVos, 1967).

The differences obtained in those foreign studies are not only statistically significant, but also large enough to be of practical importance. The mean *T*-score differences between the male delinquents and nondelinquents in the various countries ranged from about 9 (Puerto Rico) to 21 (Japan), with a median of 14. For girls, the range was from 13 (Switzerland) to 21 (France), with a median of 17. Overall, Gough (1965b) has reported a point-biserial correlation of *So* and delinquency of .43 for 3,209 males and .56 for 1099 females both tested cross-culturally. In short, the cross-cultural data, like the domestic data, give consistent evidence of the discriminating power of the *So* scale.

Offenders and nonoffenders: military samples. Several studies have compared military offenders with military nonoffenders, or with published norms, and found the offenders to have significantly lower *So* scores (Datel, 1962; Knapp, 1963, 1964). The mean scores of the offenders in these studies were all consistent with the research reviewed thus far.

Differentiation of socialization levels within delinquent samples. Most studies, with the exception of one by Thorne (1963) show the *So* scale can reflect different levels of socialization within samples of offenders. Donald (1960) and Peterson, Quay, and Anderson (1958), both found recidivists to have lower *So* scores than first offenders; but Thorne (1963) failed to find such differences. Knapp (1963) and Peterson, Quay and Anderson (1959) both found significant associations between *So* and indices of offense frequency. Hirt and Cook (1962) found that military offenders who were classified as acting out differed significantly from those with no psychiatric disorder. (Hirt and Cook reportedly failed to find significant *So* scale differences between withdrawn and acting-out offenders, a finding which caused them to question the sensitivity of the *So* scale. However, one might question the appropriateness of their criterion.)

Data published by Gough (1969b, p. 22) on the mean *So* scores of various groups of offenders show a systematic decrease in mean *So* scores as one moves from high school disciplinary cases to inmates of various correctional institutions. (See Table 4.)

Several studies have also attempted to determine whether the *So* scale

Table 4. So Scores of Male and Female Groups
Differing in Socialization

MALE SAMPLES:	N	M	SD
1. High school "best citizens"	90	39.44	4.95
2. Medical school applicants	70	39.27	4.82
3. Bank officers	71	39.06	4.61
4. City school superintendents	200	37.58	4.19
5. Business executives	116	37.47	4.72
6. College students	1,745	37.41	5.28
7. Electronic technicians	55	36.93	5.66
8. Correctional officers	620	36.72	5.47
9. Skilled and semi-skilled workers	108	36.62	5.17
10. High school students	4,474	36.46	5.56
11. Social work graduate students	182	36.40	4.62
12. Military officers	495	36.38	4.74
13. Machine operators	105	35.99	4.98
14. Psychology graduate students	89	34.24	4.23
15. Selective service inductees	139	32.83	6.71
16. High school "disciplinary problems"	91	31.25	5.40
17. County jail inmates	177	29.27	6.44
18. Young delinquents, California	206	28.66	5.86
19. Prison inmates, New York	94	28.28	5.80
20. Prison inmates, California	177	27.76	6.03
21. Training school inmates, New York	100	26.53	4.89
Total, samples 1–15	8,559	36.70	5.65
Total, samples 16–21	845	28.58	5.98

diff. = 8.12
C.R. = 10.55
$p <$ .01

FEMALE SAMPLES:	N	M	SD
1. High school "best citizens"	90	41.51	4.55
2. High school students	5,295	39.69	5.57
3. College students	3,452	39.37	5.05
4. Factory workers	291	38.99	4.76
5. Nurses	142	38.24	4.89
6. Airline hostesses	60	38.07	4.51
7. Social work graduate students	320	37.99	4.38
8. Psychology graduate students	37	36.65	3.59
9. High school "disciplinary problems"	87	34.79	7.00
10. Unmarried mothers	213	32.92	6.24
11. County jail inmates	51	29.61	5.86
12. Prison inmates, Indiana	127	28.37	6.24
13. Prison inmates, California	135	28.36	5.68
14. Prison inmates, Wisconsin	76	26.83	7.04
15. Youth authority cases, California	47	25.79	5.30
Total, samples 1–8	9,687	39.48	5.33
Total, samples 9–15	736	30.21	6.92

diff. = 9.27
C.R. = 11.24
$p <$ .01

Source: Gough, 1969b

can discriminate differences between offenders convicted of different kinds of offenses. In one well-thought-out investigation, Donald (1960) reasoned that federal reformatory inmates convicted of moonshining are better socialized than those incarcerated for other offenses, and he obtained the expected differences in *So* scores.

Sarbin, Wenk and Sherwood (1968) found that *So* used in conjunction with the Hand Test significantly discriminated assaultive from nonviolent offenders.

Two studies (Megargee, 1964; Wilcock, 1964) comparing assaultive and nonassaultive criminals have reported higher *So* scores among the more violent offenders. At first glance this would appear to be a reversal from the expected pattern; however, these findings are consistent with Megargee's (1964, 1965, 1966d, 1970, 1971) theory that some assaultive offenders are characterized by excessive inhibitions and controls, which might well be reflected in part by higher *So* scores than are found for most criminals. The inclusion of overcontrolled *S*s in the sample might also account for Thorne's (1963) failure to find a significant correlation between *So* scores and a scale rating the severity of delinquent acts: some of the crimes such as arson, assault, and rape committed by Megargee's overcontrolled types were grouped at the upper end of the scale.

Differences in socialization within nondelinquent samples. Gough's data, reproduced in Table 4, show a progressive decrease in mean *So* scores as one moves from high school best citizens at the upper end down toward psychology graduate students at the lower end, a finding he feels supports the construct validity of the scale.[1] Peterson, Quay, and Anderson (1959) also found significant differences between high school good citizens, unselected high school students, and disciplinary cases.

Hogan, Mankin, Conway, and Fox (1970) administered a questionnaire concerning drug use to 148 students at Lehigh and Johns Hopkins. On the basis of the responses, they divided the *S*s into 1) frequent marijuana users, 2) occasional marijuana users, 3) nonusers, and 4) principled nonusers (those who said they had not and never would smoke marijuana). They found a regular and significant increase in *So* scores from the first group to the last group. In another questionnaire study, Siegman (1962) found a significant negative correlation ($r = -.30$) between *So* scores and the amount of criminal behavior in which Israeli students admitted participation.

Datel (1962) hypothesized that young soldiers in the stockade would have lower *So* scores than draftees, who in turn would have lower scores than men who enlisted, and that enlisted men would be lower than Reservists serving on six-month active duty (who presumably fit military service into a large range program of goals). The mean *So* scores fell into the predicted pattern and all differences were highly significant except that between the enlistees and draftees.

Vincent (1961) found that unwed mothers had lower scores than single girls who were never pregnant. Moreover, among unwed mothers, *So* scores de-

---

[1] When the writer was in graduate school he used to question this conclusion. Now that he is no longer a student he is inclined to agree, reserving, of course, the right to excoriate Gough should he ever become foolish or unsocialized enough to publish his data on the mean *So* scores of psychology professors.

creased as the number of illegitimate pregnancies increased (Vincent, 1961, p. 246). The *So* scale has also discriminated between college students who cheat and those who do not; students who facilitated class discussions from those who were disruptive (Kipnis, 1968); and high school dropouts from graduates (Hase and Goldberg, 1967; Gough, 1966c). Wernick (1955) reported that a New York department store found half the temporary employees it hired during the Christmas rush, who had low *So* scores, had to be fired or jailed for stealing; also that none of those with low scores proved to be satisfactory workers (Wernick, 1955).

Construct validity. In addition to the many studies demonstrating the ability of the *So* scale to differentiate groups characterized by different levels of socialization, other investigators have obtained data supporting its construct validity. One approach has been to investigate the familial and social backgrounds of college *S*s falling at different points on the scale. Studies by Hill (1967) and Megargee, Parker, and Levine (1971) have demonstrated striking differences in family composition and milieu, differences consistent with the notion that *So* measures socialization. For example, Megargee, Parker, and Levine (1971) found almost linear negative relationship between incidence of parental divorce and children's *So* scores.

Others have used the *So* scale to test Gough's role-taking theory of sociopathy. Two studies (Reed and Cuadra, 1957; Baker as cited by Gough, 1965a) have found that the higher the *So,* the better an individual is able to predict how others will describe him.

Another approach has been to study "diagnostic errors" on the *So* scale, as might exist in the case of delinquents with high scores or nondelinquents with low scores. Two recent studies of this type have shown that such *So* scale "misses" are not the products of random error but instead stem from stable groups with distinctive characteristics (Kurtines and Hogan, 1971; Stein, Vadum, and Sarbin, 1970).

In short, an impressive array of data have accumulated demonstrating the concurrent, predictive and construct validity of the CPI socialization scale in the United States and elsewhere. There seems to be little doubt that the *So* scale is one of the best-validated and most powerful personality scales available; and as with any personality test score, reliable discrimination will even be improved by using *So* in conjunction with other data, particularly case history material. As one does research on personality assessment devices, one becomes aware of inherent limits on the degree to which any single scale score can correlate with overt behavior. However, the data indicate that few scales approach these limits as closely as does *So*.

Self-control (*Sc*)

PURPOSE

The Self-control scale was designed to assess the adequacy of self-regulation, self-control, and the degree of freedom from impulsivity and self-centeredness (Gough 1968a, 1969b). It thus resembles the Responsibility and Socialization scales. According to Gough (1965a, p. 296) the distinction among them is that while *Re* measures the degree to which controls are understood, and *So* the extent to which they influence the individual's behavior, *Sc* stresses "the

degree to which the individual approves of and espouses such regulatory dispositions." Very high scorers on *Sc* are thought to be overcontrolled, and therefore
potentially volatile; low scorers are considered undercontrolled, impulsive and
aggressive. These negative implications of high *Sc* scores also distinguish the scale
from *Re* and *So*.

CONSTRUCTION

The *Sc* scale was rationally constructed through internal consistency analyses. The item pool, subject samples, and criteria for item selection have not
been specified. It was originally constructed as the Impulsivity scale and was later
rekeyed and renamed Self-control.

ITEM CHARACTERISTICS

The *Sc* scale consists of fifty items, six true and forty-four false. All but
two of the *Sc* items are also scored on other scales. The principal positive overlap
is with *Gi*, which has thirteen items in common with *Sc;* four or more items are
also shared with *Wb, Re, So, To,* and *Ac. Sc* has more negative overlap than any
other CPI scale. Ten *Sc* items are keyed in the opposite fashion on *Sp* and eight
on *Sa,* apparently indicating that social poise and self-confidence are associated
with impulsivity.

The content of the *Sc* items deals with generalized restraint of irrational
behavior in general: "I must admit I have a bad temper once I get angry"—F;
and aggression in particular: "I think I would like to fight in a boxing match"—
F. Instead, thought and reason are seen as the best solution to problems: "I
consider a matter from every standpoint before I make a decision"—T; and the
respondent indicates he shuns impulsive or antisocial behavior: "I keep out of
trouble at all cost"—T; "I would do almost anything on a dare"—F. Other *Sc*
items reflect a self-effacing modesty: "I used to like it very much when one of my
papers was read to my class at school"—F; and social inhibitions: "I like to go
to parties where there is lots of loud fun"—F.

VALIDITY

There is much less evidence for the validity of the *Sc* scale than for *So*.
Gough (1969b) found significant differences between the *Sc* scores of extreme
groups of boys and girls rated as most impulsive and least impulsive by their high
school principals. The mean differences were on the order of 10 *T*-score points.
In three IPAR assessment samples he has also demonstrated low but statistically
significant ($r = .21$ to $.34$) correlations between *Sc* scores and staff ratings of
impulsivity. In Hirt and Cook's (1962) study of military offenders, *Sc* differentiated the no disease sample from the acting out and withdrawn groups, but
did not discriminate between the latter two.

Megargee and Mendelsohn (1962) compared the *Sc* scores of extremely
assaultive, moderately assaultive, and nonviolent criminals with one another
as well as with the scores of a sample of noncriminals. The only difference that
reached statistical significance was the tendency of moderately assaultive criminals
to be more controlled than the noncriminals. Although they used only the twenty-
one *Sc* items common to the MMPI, subsequent research has indicated this abbreviated scale correlates .79 with the full CPI version (Megargee, 1966b). Later,

in a test of his typology of assaultive offenders, Megargee (1966d) predicted that an extremely assaultive group (which would characteristically contain some chronically overcontrolled individuals) would have higher Sc scores than groups of delinquents detained for other offenses. The data were in the predicted direction but fell short of statistical significance. More research is needed on the Sc scale, particularly studies exploring the implications of above average scores.

Tolerance (To)

PURPOSE

Studies of social intolerance in general and anti-Semitism stimulated by World War II in particular received considerable impetus with the publication of the *Authoritarian Personality* in 1950 (Adorno, Frenkel-Brunswik, Levinson, and Sanford, 1950). In addition to the theoretical development of the construct of authoritarianism, this major work provides scales by which anti-Semitic attitudes can be measured. The following year, Gough published a series of studies on social intolerance which included accounts of the derivation and validation of an MMPI scale to assess the same constructs assessed by the California Anti-Semitism (A-S) scale (Gough, 1951b, 1951c, 1951d, 1951e). That scale, named the Prejudice (Pr) scale, was later rekeyed for inclusion on the CPI where it was named Tolerance. The purpose of this revised scale was the identification of permissive, accepting, and nonjudgmental social beliefs and attitudes (Gough, 1969b).

CONSTRUCTION

The Levinson-Sanford Anti-Semitism scale had been administered to 271 high school seniors in a Midwestern town. On the basis of their scores the forty highest and forty lowest students were selected. The MMPI was administered and an item analysis carried out in which the forty-seven items that discriminated the two samples at the .05 level of confidence were retained. The California scales were then administered to a new sample of 263 students and the new MMPI scale was given to thirty-eight highest and thirty-eight lowest Ss. After a second item analysis, thirty-two items were left which differentiated the new samples. In a subsequent validational study the new Pr scale was found to correlate $-.28$ with the Purdue Attitude-Toward Jews scale. Later the scale was rekeyed for inclusion on the CPI and four of the MMPI items were discarded and replaced by CPI items.

ITEM CHARACTERISTICS

The To scale consists of thirty-two items of which three are keyed true and twenty-nine false. Thus it has the same imbalance in keying that characterizes the California F scale. Principal positive item overlap is with Ai (eight items), Ie (six items), Sc (five items), and Re (four items).

The manifest content of the items reflects openness and flexibility as opposed to rigidity or dogmatism: "I feel sure that there is only one true religion" —F; and an interest in aesthetic or intellectual pursuits: "I like poetry"—T. High scores reflect trust and confidence as opposed to cynicism and suspicion: "Most people are honest chiefly through fear of getting caught"—F; "The future is too uncertain for a person to make serious plans"—F. The high scorer denies any misanthropic resentment or hostility against others: "I feel that I have often been punished without cause"—F; "Sometimes I feel I must injure either myself or someone else"—F. He also denies anxiety, isolation and alienation: "I have strange and peculiar thoughts"—F; and indicates he is poised and self-assured: "I refuse to play some games because I am not good at them"—F.

VALIDITY

Most of the evidence for the validity of the To scale comes from studies in which it has been correlated with various test measures of prejudice. Several investigators have correlated To with the California F scale. Gough (1969b) reported a correlation of −.46 in a sample of one hundred military officers and one of −.48 in a sample of 419 college students. Jensen (1957), using the MMPI version, obtained a correlation of −.27 in a sample of 826 college students; the present writer in an unpublished study found correlations of −.22 in a sample of 293 college men and −.40 in a sample of 210 college women.

In addition to these correlations with the F scale, Gough (1969b) has reported a correlation of .34 between To and the Chicago Inventory of Social Beliefs; and the present investigator has found a significant correlation between To and scores on the Young Desegregation scale (Young, Benson, and Holtzman, 1960) in a sample of 210 women ($r = -.24$), but failed to obtain a significant association among their 293 male classmates ($r = -.10$). The latter correlations are noteworthy primarily because the Desegregation scale focuses specifically on attitudes toward Negroes while To was constructed to reflect anti-Semitism.

Apart from these studies correlating To with other paper and pencil measures (such studies are particularly suspect in view of the large role that common methods variance such as response sets may play in the covariation) there is little evidence of the To scale's validity. Unpublished data collected by the present investigator show that fraternity members ($N = 72$) had significantly lower To scores than independents ($N = 203$); the difference was small, however, and a similar trend for sorority members failed to attain significance.

It is clear that additional research using more overt behavioral criteria must be done on the To scale. In particular it must be determined if the scale is truly bimodal. Do high scores reflect tolerance, or do low scores simply indicate prejudice? What is the role of response sets? How general are the attitudes reflected by the scale? Does the scale identify only anti-Semites, or does it also identify people who are anti-black, anti-brown, anti-white, anti-red, and so on? Does it indicate tolerance toward people, or toward ideas, or both? Research on intergroup attitudes has shown all those factors to be important; such parameters must be explored throughly if the exact role and utility of the To scale are to be determined.

Good Impression (Gi)

PURPOSE

The original purpose of the Good Impression scale was to identify dissimulated records for which the normative data did not apply (Gough, 1952b,

1968a). It is also used to identify people who are able to create favorable impressions and who are concerned about how others react to them (Gough, 1969b).

CONSTRUCTION

The *Gi* scale was constructed through external criterion analyses of the responses of high school students to 150 specially devised items. The questionnaire was first administered using standard instructions and later with instructions to respond as if one were applying for a very important job or trying to make an especially favorable impression. Those items which changed significantly from the first to the second administration were selected (Gough, 1952b). *Gi* was thus one of the first scales constructed to assess what came to be called social desirability.

ITEM CHARACTERISTICS

The *Gi* scale consists of forty items, eight of which are keyed true and thirty-two false. The scale has eighteen pure items. There is very high positive overlap with the rationally constructed *Sc* scale, thirteen items being common to both. Principal negative overlap is with *Sp* (four items).

As might be expected on a social desirability scale, most of the item content consists of rather obvious claims to good functioning, virtue, and a denial of antisocial behavior, complaints, or human failings. The high scorer "accentuates the positive and eliminates the negative." The items reflect confidence and self-assurance, mixed with some modesty: "I like to boast about my achievements every now and then"—F. There is a denial of any tendency to be aggressive: "Sometimes I feel like smashing things"—F; or to engage in any unethical behavior: "I have never deliberately told a lie"—T. The high scorer on *Gi* denies that he is plagued by any anxieties or insecurities: "I get pretty discouraged sometimes"—F; he indicates instead that he is stable and able to withstand adversity; "Criticism makes me very uncomfortable"—F. The high scorer indicates that he does all the socially approved things: "I always follow the rule of business before pleasure"—T; "I like to listen to symphony concerts on the radio"—T; that he is able to get along well with others: "I do not mind taking orders and being told what to do"—T; and that he has a high opinion of his fellow man: "There are a few people who just cannot be trusted"—F.

VALIDITY

Gi is first and foremost a validity scale, and it is appropriate that most of the validational research has focused on its ability to discriminate dissimulated records. Gough (1969b) found that 179 high school students told to respond so as to present the best possible impression scored significantly higher than the high school norms (mean T score = 57). Canter (1963) administered the CPI to alcoholic patients and hospital aides under standard and fake good instructions and found a *Gi* peak in the faked records. (He also found that the more well-adjusted the respondent, the better his ability to improve his profile.)

The most thorough study of the validity of the *Gi* scale was undertaken by Dicken (1960), who administered the CPI to five groups, each consisting of twenty students. After taking the test in the usual manner, each group took the test a second time, one group being told to role-play a person high in dominance, the second a person high in responsibility, the third intellectual efficiency, and the fourth flexibility. The fifth group was simply asked to create a favorable impression. The role-playing instructions had a pronounced effect, the profiles in general and the particular scale in question rising considerably in each group. However, in every group save one it was the Gi scale that had the greatest increase; by using a cutting score of $T = 60$ it was possible to identify 79 per cent of the simulated records, while falsely classifying only 3 per cent of the unsimulated profiles. When applied to a sophisticated, "test-wise" clientele, Gi is less successful. Psychologists were able to increase their Fx and Do scores substantially without increasing Gi significantly (Dicken, 1960).

In a later study, Dicken (1963b) investigated whether Gi could be used as a suppressor scale to improve the validity of other CPI scales, as is done with the K scale on the MMPI. He found that the addition of Gi, or other measures of validity or response bias did not improve their validity. On the basis of these findings, Dicken (1963, p. 716) concluded that "the available evidence supports Gough's position that social desirability variance need not and perhaps should not be removed from scales designed to measure personality traits of the type studied here."

In addition to its utility as a validity scale, a study by Heilbrun, Daniel, Goodstein, Stephenson, and Crites (1962) indicates that Gi scores can be of interpretive significance; this study is of particular interest because it is one of the few efforts to validate the configural interpretation of CPI scales. Heilbrun, et al. constituted four groups on the basis of their Do and Gi scale scores: high Do-high Gi, high Do-low Gi, low Do-high Gi, low Do-low Gi. As expected, the two high Do groups manifested greater leadership, but in the high Do-high Gi group leadership was tempered with concern for others while the high Do-low Gi group was argumentative, egotistical and domineering. The low Do groups were more passive, but in the low Do-high Gi group this was manifested through a shyly sought approval from others, while the low-low group was withdrawn, socially inept, and resentful. The data thus supported the construct validity of both scales.

Communality (Cm)

PURPOSE

Another validity scale, Communality (Cm), was originally designed to detect protocols on which the respondent had answered in a random fashion. It thus served a purpose similar to that of the MMPI F scale.

CONSTRUCTION

Originally designated as the Infrequency (In) scale, its items were chosen by surveying the response frequencies obtained in a number of samples. Those items answered in a particular direction by no more than 5 per cent of the respondents were selected for the scale. When the CPI was published and the decision made that high scores would reflect positive traits, the keying was reversed and the scale was designated as Communality. Thus in its present form, it consists of items answered in the keyed direction by 95 per cent or more of the Ss in the normative samples.

The present Cm scale consists of twenty-eight items, fourteen keyed true and fourteen false. Despite the fact that the Cm scale items are answered in the keyed direction by almost everyone, they are not platitudes. For example, "I would fight if someone tried to take my rights away," is answered "true" by practically everyone, yet CPI respondents do not regard it as an absurd item.

Cm items appear to fall into the following groups: 1) items reflecting good socialization: "If I am driving a car I try to keep others from passing me"—F; 2) denial of neurotic tendencies: "I can't do anything well"—F; 3) items reflecting conventional behavior and attitudes: "There have been times when I have been very angry"—T; 4) items reflecting conformity: "I usually try to do what is expected of me to avoid criticism"—T; and 5) items reflecting optimism: "I doubt if anyone is really happy"—F.

Only one study has investigated the usefulness of Cm as a validity scale. In that investigation, thirty CPI answer sheets were completed using a table of random numbers, with the even numbers classed as true and odd numbers false. According to Gough (1969b, p. 17), "The highest individual score on Cm in the sample of thirty records was twenty; this value is in the lowest one-half of one percent of scores on the Cm scale for all CPI cases in our files. The *mean* value of 13.83 is lower than any individual score we have observed under ordinary conditions of testing. This would seem to suggest that any record produced by scrambling or randomizing of responses is detectable by low scores on the Cm scale."

Gough (1969b) has also found low Cm scores on the profiles of students asked to fake bad, although, as we have seen, it is the Wb scale that is primarily used to detect such malingering.

High Cm scores are interpreted clinically as reflecting an overly conventional attitude. Some evidence to support that interpretation can be found in the adjectival analyses summarized in Chapter Ten. On the other hand, the research on conformity reported in Chapter Fourteen shows Cm bears no relation to yielding in Asch-type experiments. Until there are more data, it appears best to use Cm simply as an indicator of improperly answered protocols.

CHAPTER 6

Class III Scales:

Measures of Intellectual Efficiency
and Achievement Potential

ᔑᔑᔑᔑᔑᔑᔑᔑᔑᔑᔑᔑᔑᔑᔑᔑᔑᔑᔑᔑᔑᔑᔑᔑᔑᔑ

The third cluster of scales to appear on the profile sheet are ones designed to assess achievement potential and intellectual efficiency: *Ac, Ai,* and *Ie*. Despite the fact that these scales load on different factors, they are grouped together to make it easy for the interpreter. The level of these scales indicates whether an individual has the personality traits associated with academic success; differences between the scales can be interpreted configurally to predict different types or patterns of achievement.

Achievement via Conformance (*Ac*)

PURPOSE

The original goal of the *Ac* scale was to assess the motivational and personality factors associated with academic achievement in high school settings (Gough, 1953c). It was originally named *Achievement,* but "Gradually, through working with the scale and through individual acquaintance with high scorers, it became clear that the basic theme of the measure was one of a strong need for achievement coupled with a deeply internalized appreciation of structure and organization. The term 'conformance' was chosen to reflect this channeling of the need for achievement as 'conformity' would be too strong and would also connote a kind of unproductive stereotypy that is in fact not strongly embodied in the scale" (Gough, 1968a, p. 69).

CONSTRUCTION

The *Ac* scale was constructed by the external criterion method. After reviewing the literature on academic achievement, Gough (1953c) made up an item pool consisting of the best items from previous studies and over a hundred specially written items based on earlier research. For example, such early work showed poorer students tending to rebel against traditions and conventions, so Gough included items such as "I must admit I find it very hard to work under strict rules and regulations." The item pool was administered to Minnesota high school students matched for intelligence and sex but differing widely in academic achievement. The sixty-four items that differentiated between the criterion groups in all three samples used were retained for the scale; it was then shortened to thirty-eight items and found to correlate .44 with grade point average in a sample of 234 Illinois high school students.

ITEM CHARACTERISTICS

The present *Ac* scale consists of thirty-eight items of which twelve are keyed true and twenty-six false. There are eighteen pure items, of the shared items, six overlap with *Ie*, five each with *Re, Sc,* and *Ai*, and four with *Sy*.

In manifest content, some items deal straightforwardly with enjoyment of school work and effectiveness in academic settings: "I was a slow learner in school"—F; others refer to vitality and efficiency outside school: "I wake up fresh and rested most mornings"—T. The high scorer endorses items indicating that he regards himself as a diligent worker who plans ahead: "I like to plan my activities in advance"—T; "I always try to do at least a little better than what is expected of me"—T. As might be expected in a scale that stresses achievement through conformance, the high scorer also indicates that he accepts rules and regulations and rejects frivolous or nonconformist behavior: "I must admit I find it very hard to work under strict rules and regulations"—F; "I think I would like to belong to a motorcycle club"—F; and he is even-tempered: "I am sometimes cross and grouchy without any good reason"—F; and confident of his own abilities: "If given the chance I would be a good leader of people"—T.

VALIDITY

In surveying the assessment literature, it appears the scales receiving the most attention are those that 1) assess behavior many investigators, particularly those in educational settings, regard as important, such as dominance and socialization, and 2) those for which adequate criterion measures are readily available. The Achievement via Conformance scale combines both qualities so it is not surprising that *Ac* and its stablemate *Ai* are among the most thoroughly researched CPI scales.

The basic design of most of these studies is simple: The CPI is administered to a sample and the relation of the various scales to some criterion of achievement is determined. Within such a broad framework, the studies vary in several dimensions:

The first variation exists in regard to samples. Most studies focus on academic achievement by using samples of students, not only because they are an available "captive" population but also because it is academic achievement that the Ac and Ai scales were developed to assess. Such investigations vary according to whether high school students, college undergraduates, graduate students, or students in specialized training programs were used. In addition to academic levels, samples also vary according to the national or cultural group studied.

Group composition also creates variations. Some studies use extreme groups such as over-achievers and under-achievers. In such investigations the CPI scale is usually treated as the dependent variable and tests of mean difference are used to analyze the data. Given the differences between these groups, the demonstration of significant differences is not too impressive, particularly in studies using large samples; however, *any* failure to find a significant difference is damaging.

Other investigators use all the Ss including those in the middle; such data are typically analyzed by correlating the CPI scale with a measure of achievement such as grade point average (GPA). Such studies present the test with a more difficult task but provide better indications of the usefulness of the test in the field.

Variations exist because of differences in IQ. Both the CPI achievement scales correlate significantly with intelligence, despite the fact that the criterion groups used in the derivation of Ac were matched for IQ. In some studies the investigators have attempted to determine whether these scales can discriminate differences in achievement when IQ is controlled; such research is particularly relevant for those who are concerned with over-achievement and under-achievement. In others, IQ has been left free to vary; this greater heterogeneity should result in higher validity coefficients.

Criteria of achievement also vary. Most studies use the overall GPA of the students as the criterion. Some use performance during a single year, usually the freshman year. Others use the grade achieved in a single course, typically, introductory psychology. Obviously the more limited the criterion, the less reliable it is. While grades are the most common criterion, other yardsticks have also been employed, such as completion of a degree program, volunteering for honors, admission to college, and so on.

A survey of the literature on the Ac scale follows, with the studies grouped on the basis of the above variables.

Studies of Anglo-American high school students.   Several have examined the relationship between achievement in high school and Ac. Gough (1963) and Pierce (1961) compared high and low achievers, all with high ability, Gough and Fink (1964) compared high and low achievers of average intelligence, and Gough (1964a, 1964c) has reports on the association between Ac and school achievement in large heterogeneous samples of high school students. Fink (1962) reported Jack Block's previously unpublished results of a comparison of over- and underachievers. In addition, Keimowitz and Ansbacher (1960) have reported comparisons of overachievers and underachievers in the area of mathematics, Gough (1966c) compared the Ac scores of four large samples of high school students with those of dropouts, and Gough (1968b) reported the differences between the CPI scores of four samples of able high school graduates who went on to college with those who did not. With the exception of one of Gough's (1966c) four samples, all these studies found significant associations between Ac and the various criteria of achievement. The correlations between Ac and grades have been quite consistent, ranging from .35 to .40 in most samples. (See Chapter Twelve.)

Cross-cultural studies of high school achievement. Snider and Linton (1964) compared the CPI scores of forty-seven over- and forty-seven under-achievers in a Canadian high school and found a significant difference on Ac. Gill and Spilka (1962) had similar results with Mexican-American high school students as did Benjamin (1970) with black ghetto youths. Gough (1964c) has reported significant correlations in the low 30s between Ac scores and the grades of Italian high school students.

Studies in college settings. The data indicate that Ac relates much less closely to indices of achievement in college than it does in high schools. Although a few studies have reported significant results using Ac in college settings, many more have found mixed, marginal, or nonsignificant relationships. Gough believes that that is because secondary school grades reflect the more structured approach to learning, which is in turn reflected by the Ac scale, while college is more likely to emphasize originality, creativity and intellectual independence. Gough (1963) found positive results by comparing the grades of pairs of Ss matched for IQ. Griffin and Flaherty (1964) and Flaherty and Reutzel (1963) also found positive results, but did not control for intelligence. Moving away from overall GPA, Gough (1964b), in four large samples ranging in size from 867 to 1773 Ss, found low but significant correlations ranging from .13 to .18 with grades in introductory psychology; Aiken (1963) found Ac correlated positively with attitude toward mathematics. Holland (1959) correlated the Ac scores of four large samples of National Merit Scholars with their freshman GPAs and found a low but significant correlation ($r = .19$) in only one sample. A number of other investigators have determined the relationships between Ac and various criteria of college achievement, those criteria including GPA (Demos and Weijola, 1966; Hase and Goldberg, 1967; Winkelman, 1963); participation in honors programs (Capretta, Jones, Siegel and Siegel, 1963; Demos and Weijola, 1966; Mason, Adams and Blood, 1966); instructor's ratings of performance in independent study (Koenig and McKeachie, 1959); and degree programs (Swisdak and Flaherty, 1964). None of the investigations found a significant association with Ac. It can be concluded from the available evidence that Ac does not relate closely to college achievement.

Achievement in other educational programs. Ac has also been used to predict performance in other educational programs. Four studies have investigated its relationship to success in student teaching. Three (Durflinger, 1963a, 1963b; Hill, 1960) found no significant relationship; the fourth (Gough, Durflinger and Hill, 1968) found that in a female sample the better student teachers scored significantly higher than the poor ones, but found no difference in a male sample. Trites, Kurek and Cobb (1967) found a low but significant correlation ($r = .22$) between Ac and performance in an air traffic control training program. In military training programs, Datel, Hall, and Rufe (1965) found Ac unrelated to success in an Army language training program despite the structure and conformity entailed. Rosenberg, McHenry, Rosenberg, and Nichols (1962) found *Ac* unrelated to success in military courses in clinical psychology, social work, and neuropsychiatric procedures. However, Kohlfield and Weitzel (1969) found *Ac* correlated significantly ($r = -.33$) with the discrepancy in speed of walking a treadmill with and without external social facilitation.

    Construct validity. Although the bulk of the research has focused on concurrent and predictive validity, some data have been reported, regarding *Ac*'s construct validity. MacKinnon (1964) found a significant negative correlation ($r = -.24$) between *Ac* and measures of creativity in architects. That finding belongs in the nomological net because if a significant positive correlation had been observed, it would have cast doubt in the hypothesis that *Ac* measures achievement via *conformance*. The chief evidence for the construct validity of both the *Ac* and the *Ai* scales has been provided by a study in which 348 college juniors were administered both scales after being divided into four groups: high *Ac*-high *Ai,* high *Ac*-low *Ai,* low *Ac*-high *Ai,* low *Ac*-low *Ai* (Domino, 1968). The *Ss'* grades for their last four semesters were then obtained and, on the basis of interviews with the instructors, the courses were classified according to whether conformity or independence was rewarded. As expected, the hgh *Ac*-high *Ai* group had the best grades in all courses and the low *Ac*-low *Ai* group the poorest. The high *Ac*-low *Ai* group did better in the courses calling for conformity, the low *Ac*-high *Ai* groups did better in courses emphasizing independence. This last study is important not only for the information it provides on the validity of the two scales, but also because it presents cogent evidence on the importance of *configural* interpretation of the CPI—that is, a modification of the interpretation of a high score on one scale in the light of the score on another. (Goldberg reports in a recent personal communication [1970] an attempt to replicate Domino's study, an attempt which failed because in a sample of 350 male students, only ten met Domino's criteria for inclusion in the high *Ai*-low *Ac* cell while none met the criteria for the low *Ai*-high *Ac* scale. Out of 430 women, Goldberg could find only seventeen for the first cell and three for the second. He consequently warned that the findings of the Domino study might not apply to *Ss* with less extreme discrepancies between their *Ai* and *Ac* scores.)

    Ac thus emerges as another thoroughly investigated CPI scale and one that has consistently correlated with achievement in high school settings. In other settings it has proven less useful.

Achievement via Independence (*Ai*)

PURPOSE

    While the *Ac* scale was devised to predict academic achievement in high school, the *Ai* scale was constructed to predict achievement in college undergraduate courses, particularly undergraduate courses in psychology (Gough, 1953b). As data accumulated on the CPI, it appeared that the *Ai* scale predicted achievement in settings where independence of thought, creativity and self-actualization were rewarded. Hence, *Ai,* which had initially been dubbed Honor Point Ratio

(*Hr*), was renamed Achievement via Independence. (The evolution of the *Ac* and *Ai* scales demonstrates how Gough's conceptual analysis of a scale is used to refine its original meaning and interpretation. In the process, of course, the scale may drift away somewhat from the original folk concept that inspired it. Whereas achievement is certainly a folk concept, the distinction between achievement via conformance and independence is not as firmly rooted in the popular ethos, although Gough's data show it to be a useful one.)

CONSTRUCTION

The procedures used to develop the *Ai* scale were quite similar to those used for *Ac* (Gough, 1953b). An initial item pool of 150 items was assembled based on previous research, theories about academic motivation and achievement, and hunches about contributory factors. The item pool was administered to four large classes in introductory psychology, one at the University of California, two at the University of Minnesota, and one at Vanderbilt. The procedure differed in two respects from that used for *Ac:* 1) the samples were not matched for IQ, and 2) the higher and lower groups consisted of those falling above and below the median for the class—not those at the extremes.

Not all of the 150 items were administered to all four criterion samples; however, every item was given to at least three. Those items discriminating significantly in three of the samples were selected for the preliminary scale. This thirty-six-item scale, dubbed *Hr* for Honor Ratio, was then administered to four cross-validating samples totaling 336 *S*s. In these samples the correlations with course grades ranged from .26 to .58 with a median of .33. Four of the items dealing directly with school attendance and study habits were deleted to decrease the obviousness of the scale. The remaining thirty-two items were administered to seven cross-validating samples totaling 917 *S*s. In those seven samples the correlations with course grades ranged from .26 to .60 with a median of .32. In addition, the 32-item scale was given to six high school samples totaling 1,108 *S*s. There the correlations with grade point average ranged from .26 to .42 with a median of .38.

In the course of the development of the *Ai* scale, Gough sought to determine whether *Ai* was simply an inefficient measure of intelligence or whether it measured achievement. Accordingly, he correlated *Ai* with IQ in six high school samples and found it correlated less with IQ than it did with GPA in each sample. Other studies using college students and military officers yielded the same finding. From these data Gough concluded that *Ai* in itself is a partial predictor of grades without depending too heavily on intellectual factors. This suggested that *Ai* would be useful in multiple regression equations, contributing variance not sampled by conventional intelligence measures.

ITEM CHARACTERISTICS

The *Ai* scale includes thirty-two items of which three are keyed true and twenty-nine false. There is positive overlap with *To* and *Ie* (eight items), and with *Sy, Re,* and *Ac* (five items each).

Many of the items suggest a high tolerance for ambiguity and a rejection of simple dogmatic or authoritarian attitudes: "For most questions there is one right answer, once a person is able to get all the facts"—F; there are also items indicating the respondent is willing to reject conventional answers and think for himself, even if it involves holding an unpopular or controversial opinion: "Only a fool would try to change our American way of life"—F; "I looked up to my father as an ideal man"—F. In addition to those items, which have a clear relation to independent thought, there are others reflecting an enjoyment of intellectual activities even if they are not necessarily utilitarian: "I like poetry"—T; "I liked 'Alice in Wonderland' by Lewis Carroll"—T. The high scorer on *Ai* also indicates that he thinks well of others although he is not a social butterfly: "People pretend to care more about one another than they really do"—F; "I usually take an active part in the entertainment at parties"—F. In addition, the manifest content suggests positive adjustment: "I am bothered by people outside, on the street cars, in stores, etc. watching me"—F; and well developed moral values: "I don't blame anyone for trying to grab all he can in this world"—F.

VALIDITY

The validational literature in *Ai* is very similar to that of *Ac;* indeed most of the studies reviewed above also examine the relation of *Ai* to whatever criterion of achievement was used, although there are a few investigations in which only *Ai* was validated. Given its derivation, *Ai* should do better than *Ac* in predicting achievement in college, particularly in introductory psychology and independent study programs. Since differences in intelligence were not controlled in the criterion groups, we might also anticipate *Ai* doing best in studies in which groups differing in achievement have not been matched for IQ.

Studies of achievement in college settings. Most of the validational work on the *Ai* scale has been done in college settings. A number of studies have related *Ai* scores to GPA when no attempt was made to partial out IQ in the samples. Studies of this type have been performed by Barnette (1961), Bendig (1958), Bendig and Klugh (1956), Goldberg and Hase (1967), Gough (1969b), Griffin and Flaherty (1964), and Flaherty and Reutzel, 1965). Without exception they have reported significant associations between *Ai* and GPA. The actual correlations ranged from .19 to .44. Gough (1964b, 1969b), in several large samples, reports significant correlations between *Ai* and grades for introductory psychology courses. The correlations ranged from .29 to .38. Several other studies have reported on the differences between undergraduates electing to take honors programs and those who are eligible but do not volunteer. In such studies IQ is roughly controlled in that the brighter students are the only ones eligible to participate. Demos and Weijola (1966) found those who agreed to take honors were significantly higher on *Ai*, but Capretta, Jones, Siegel, and Siegel (1963), and Mason, Adams, and Blood (1966) failed to obtain significant differences. Koenig and McKeachie (1959) failed to find a significant relationship between *Ai* and instructors' ratings of achievement in an independent studies program. Thus, most studies indicate *Ai* fails to predict achievement well in samples whose members are uniformly bright.

The final criterion of achievement in college level investigations has been completion of a degree program. In some ways this is the most meaningful criterion, although it is also the sloppiest since many factors such as the draft, financial support and the like can influence the outcome. Hill (1966) found a significant association between Ai and graduation for a sample of University of Texas women, but failed to find it for men. It should be noted that this sex difference is not reliable; Swisdak and Flaherty (1964) failed to find a significant association with graduation in their exclusively female sample.

Studies of validity in high school settings. Both studies relating Ai to high school GPA conducted on Anglo-American samples which did not partial out intelligence reported significant associations (Bendig and Klugh, 1956; Gough, 1964a). In addition, Gough has reported positive results in an Italian sample (1964c). The correlations in these studies are generally in the .30s. (See Table 11, Chapter Twelve.)

While the investigations in college settings showed a consistent difference in the results, depending on whether or not intelligence had been controlled, the same is not true for studies of high school achievement. Several studies have used groups matched for intelligence and still found significant differences on Ai (Gough, 1963, Gough and Fink, 1964; Keimowitz and Ansbacher, 1960; Pierce, 1961). However, the magnitude of the correlations tends to be lower. Less positive results have been obtained in cross-cultural samples in which IQ has been controlled. Snider and Linton (1964) found significant differences between achievers and underachievers in a sample of Canadian high school girls, but not in a sample of boys, while Gill and Spilka (1962) failed to find such a difference in a Mexican-American sample.

Gough (1966c) compared high school graduates with high school dropouts; he found small but statistically significant differences in two of the four large samples he studied. He also compared the scores of four samples of high school graduates who chose to enter college with those of students who did not seek higher education and failed to find any significant differences (Gough, 1968b). Thus while Ai appears to be related to high school grades, it does not relate closely to those other criteria of achievement at the high school level.

The relation of Ai to achievement in other training programs. Durflinger (1963b) found significant negative correlations between Ai and grades in student teaching, but other studies have failed to find any significant association, positive or negative (Durflinger, 1963a; Gough, Durflinger, and Hill, 1968).

Trites, et al. (1967) found a small but significant correlation between Ai and grades in an air traffic control training program ($r = .18$). In military training programs, Datel, Hall, and Rufe (1965) found soldiers who completed an Army language training program had higher Ai scores than those who dropped out, and Rosenberg, McHenry, Rosenberg, and Nichols (1962) found significant correlations with course grades in clinical psychology and social work ($r = .46$), and neuropsychiatric procedures ($r = .47$). Kohlfield and Weitzel (1969) also reported a significant correlation ($r = -.32$) with their treadmill measures.

Construct validity. Most of the evidence for the construct validity of the Ai scale, as with the Ac, rests on its ability to predict achievement in various academic settings. However, Ai is not supposed to assess simply achievement, but achievement *via independence*. Several studies have focused on that aspect of the scale; the most direct support for the notion came from the study by Domino (1968), already reviewed under Ac, in which Ai was found to be better at predicting achievement in courses stressing independent thought than in those emphasizing rote learning.

Several studies have investigated the relation between the CPI and conformity or "yielding to an erroneous group judgment" in the familiar Asch experimental situation. Insofar as Ai stresses independence, a negative relationship with conformity would be expected, even though the Asch paradigm is not directly related to achievement in the usual sense. Significant and substantial negative relations between Ai and yielding were reported by Tuddenham (1959), and Harper (1964) also found a low but significant negative correlation. Similar studies, however, by Crutchfield (1955) and Appley and Moeller (1963) failed to replicate these findings.

Since creativity involves achievement through independence, it is to be expected that Ai, in contrast to Ac, should relate to measures of creativeness. MacKinnon (1961b) compared the CPI scores of three groups of architects, all of whom were productive, but who differed in the originality of their work. He found that all three groups were uniformly high on Ai; thus the scale reflected the differences in creativity to be found between successful architects and the population at-large, but failed to discriminate the differences in creativity within the occupational group.

Five years after a group of creative college seniors had graduated from college, Helson (1967a) conducted a follow-up study and on the basis of the post-college careers of those graduates classified them as 1) creative single, 2) creative married, 3) non-creative married. She found the creative single women, most of whom worked with single-minded determination at their careers, had significantly higher Ai scores than the other two groups.

The final evidence regarding construct validity comes from a study of autobiographical material on college students differing in Ai (Hill, 1967). Hill found that high Ai students were apt to be first-born or only-children with well-educated fathers. They fitted the stereotype of the solitary scholar in that they tended to be loners who were not very popular, did not date much, and manifested lower social adjustment.

The Ai scale thus emerges as another of the more thoroughly investigated CPI scales. The evidence collected shows that Ai correlates significantly with GPA in college and high school samples when IQ is not restricted. However, the magnitude of the correlations is generally lower than would be desirable for individual prediction. There is also evidence to support Gough's claim that Ai assesses achievement best in settings where originality or independence is rewarded.

Studies relating Ai to measures of independence (as opposed to *achievement* through independence) have had mixed results; in general they can be interpreted as offering some support for the scale's construct validity, but the evidence does not suggest that Ai can be used as a predictor of independent behavior in the individual case.

Intellectual Efficiency (Ie)

PURPOSE

Originally referred to as a "nonintellectual intelligence test" the Ie scale was constructed to provide a set of personality items that would correlate significantly with accepted measures of intelligence.

A pool of MMPI items supplemented by specially written items was administered to senior high school students in four Minnesota high schools; in each school, students in the top 25 per cent on conventional intelligence tests were compared with those in the bottom quarter. The seventy-six items which consistently differentiated the criterion groups significantly were retained for the scale (Gough, 1953a).

The initial cross-validation was done in two phases. The first consisted of administering the full seventy-six-item preliminary scale to thirty psychology graduate students for whom Miller Analogies Test scores were available; the scale correlated .44 with the MAT scores. The second phase made use of five samples totaling 815 Ss, for whom MMPI protocols and IQ scores were available. For these Ss only the fifty-nine items that also appeared on the MMPI could be used. The correlations in these five samples ranged from .36 to .53. Further analysis led to the elimination of twenty-four of the seventy-six items that were contributing only slightly to the correlations. Additional cross-validational research was conducted on the fifty-two-item revised scale. In two high school samples, correlations of .49 and .50 were obtained between Ie scale scores and IQs; in a university sample the correlation was .42 (Gough, 1953a).

The Ie scale in its present form consists of fifty-two items, of which nineteen are keyed true and thirty-three false. There is considerable positive item overlap, which is not too surprising in a scale that is supposed to assess intelligence, or at least co-vary with it. Ie shares ten items with Sy, eight with Ai, seven with Sp, six each with Re, To, and Ac, and five with Cs. The manifest content reflects an interest and enjoyment in intellectual pursuits: "I like to read about history"—T; and self-confidence and assurance: "I seem to be as capable and smart as most others around me"—T. The high scorer indicates that he is free from physical complaints and ailments: "I seldom worry about my health"—T; and from worries and apprehensions: "I've had more than my share of things to worry about"—F. He also gets along well with others without being overly suspicious, hostile or sensitive: "I am quite often not in on the gossip and talk of the group I belong to"—F.

Like the other Class III measures, Ie has been thoroughly studied. Data regarding its convergent validity stems from several sources, including correlations with conventional intelligence tests, studies of its relation to achievement in various academic settings, investigations of its relation to creativity, and studies of its construct validity.

Relation of Ie *to conventional measures of intelligence.* Gough reports in the CPI *Manual* (1969b) the results of several studies in which Ie was correlated to various measures of intellectual functioning. In all of the studies significant correlations were obtained: .58 with scores on the Terman Concept Mastery Test in a sample of one hundred military officers, .44 with the Miller Analogies

Test in a sample of seventy psychology graduate students, .50 with the Kuhl-mann-Anderson in a sample of 691 high school students, and .49 with the General Information Survey in a sample of one hundred men. Aiken (1963) reported a lower but still significant correlation (r = .23) with the SAT Mathematics Apti-tude score.

Comparisons of gifted and average individuals have also shown significant differences on *Ie*. Lessinger and Martinson (1961) reported a comparison of gifted high school students and gifted eighth-graders with a random sample of eighth graders. The students were tested as part of the California Study of Gifted Pupils; the samples used were stratified to be representative of the entire state. Among the boys, the gifted high school students had a mean *T*-score of 52, the gifted eighth graders a mean of 48, and the random eighth-grade sample a mean of 21. For the girls, the comparable means were 55, 52, and 32. The extraordi-narily low *Ie* scores of the random sample is a cause for concern. The investigators speculated that differences in reading ability might have contributed to the result of the randomly selected eighth-graders having significantly lower scores on *Ie* and thirteen other scales.

Purkey (1966) found students whose SAT scores were in the gifted range scored higher on *Ie* than did average students. The mean difference was about 20 *T*-score points. Southern and Plant (1968) reported an *Ie* *T*-score of fifty-six for members of MENSA, a score significantly higher than the national norms. (Some problems in discriminant validity were evident in that study, since the MENSA members scored even higher on *Ai* [*T* = 65 for men and 61 for women] than they did on *Ie*.) Plant and Minium (1967) tested students about to enter jun-ior college and again after two years there. The *Ie* scores of the gifted students significantly exceeded those of the students with less ability, the difference being about 12 *T*-score points. They also found that the difference increased after two years of college, which could mean that college increases the intellectual efficiency of bright students more than it does that of duller ones.

Relationship of Ie *to academic achievement.* If *Ie* does assess intelli-gence, it should relate to achievement in academic settings, particularly when a sample representing a wide range of ability is being investigated. A number of studies have tested this hypothesis in different academic situations using a variety of criteria of achievement. Studies conducted in high school settings have reported uniformly significant results, not only when samples using a range of ability levels were used (Bendig and Klugh, 1956; Gough, 1964a, 1964c), but also when some controls for IQ or roughly homogeneously intelligent groups were employed (Gill and Spilka, 1962; Gough, 1963; Gough and Fink, 1964; Keimowitz and Ans-bacher, 1960; Pierce, 1961; Snider and Linton, 1964). The studies included inves-tigations carried out using Canadian (Snider and Linton, 1964), Italian (Gough, 1964a), and Mexican-American (Gill and Spilka, 1962) students as well as An-glo-American samples. The correlations reported ranged from .25 to .45. While GPA has been the typical criterion in such research, Gough (1966c) has also found that *Ie* discriminates between high school dropouts and those who remain in school, although in his later study of entry into college (Gough, 1968b) he found significant differences in *Ie* in only one of the four samples studied.

In achievement at the college level—which of course restricts the range of variation among those who are intelligent enough to gain admission—mixed findings have been the rule. Two studies (Flaherty and Reutzel, 1965; Griffin and Flaherty, 1964) investigated the relationship of Ie to GPA without restricting the range of IQ variation in their Ss; both reported significant positive relationships. For studies in which the variation in IQ was controlled to some extent, positive results were reported by Gough (1963) and by Morgan (1952), but no significant differences were found by Demos and Weijola (1966), Holland (1959), or Winkelman (1963).

The interpretation of a study presents problems when the influence of IQ is controlled or partialled out. If the scale measures intelligence, as it was originally designed to do, there should be no differences between groups differing in achievement but equivalent in intelligence. One could argue that *failure* to find differences supports the Ie scale's construct validity. Significant associations, however, would mean that either 1) the IQ matching was not done adequately, or 2) the scale measures something other than intelligence. However, if the Ie scale measures not merely intelligence, but the *efficiency* with which the intellectual endowment is utilized, then one could reasonably expect the scale to relate to achievement whether IQ was controlled or not. Given the overlap, redundancy, and general random variation to be found in personality measurement, efforts to determine whether the scale assesses intellectual ability or intellectual efficiency are probably impractical, amount to semantic quibbling, and most likely will never be resolved empirically. The important point is that sufficient ambiguity exists concerning what the Ie scale is supposed to measure to make it impossible to invalidate on the basis of a failure to find significant correlations with achievement in samples where IQ variation is limited. In other measures of college achievement, Hill (1966b), and Swisdak and Flaherty (1964) found no differences between students who graduated and those who failed to complete their degree programs. Koenig (1959) and McKeachie (1959) found no relation between Ie scores and achievement, although Gough (1964b) did find low but significant correlations in four large samples between Ie and grades in introductory psychology, with rs ranging from .19 to .27.

Mixed results have also been found in other academic programs. Their interpretation is made difficult because the relation of the various criteria to intelligence is not always clear. That is especially true in studies on Ie in elementary education programs. Gough, Durflinger, and Hill (1968) found that women with high grades in student teaching had significantly higher Ie scores than did those with low grades; however, they found no significant difference for men, and Durflinger (1963b) failed to find any significant relationship with various criteria of success in student teaching. Durflinger (1963a) compared the Ie scores of those who received their elementary education credentials with those who either quit or flunked out of the program. He found the people completing the program to have significantly *lower* Ie scores than those who failed to finish. This could be interpreted as showing the Ie scale to be thoroughly untrustworthy or that brighter individuals withdraw from elementary education.

Trites et al. (1967) in their study of the relationship of CPI scores to the performance of members of an FAA air traffic control course, showed Ie with the highest correlation ($r = .34$) to course performance of the eighteen CPI scales. Studies of military and police training programs have shown Ie to be one of the CPI scales most consistently related with achievement in such courses (Collins, 1967; Hogan, 1970; Rosenberg, et al., 1962). (See Table 21, Chapter Twelve.)

   Relationship of Ie *to creativity.* As with achievement, the relationship between intelligence and creativity has been a matter of some debate. (See MacKinnon, 1962, 1964; McNemar, 1964). Intelligence clearly does not guarantee creativity; at the same time a certain minimal level of intelligence is required for creative achievement in most fields. Thus, while there is a relationship between intelligence and creativity, it appears that the relationship is not linear; instead it falls into what Fisher (1959) has termed a "twisted pear" pattern, low intelligence being reliably associated with low creativity, but high intelligence having no relation to creativity. Given this state of affairs, it is clear that the relationship to be expected between Ie and creativity is a function of the samples employed. In a broad, heterogeneous population there should be a positive relation between Ie and measures of creativity, but this relation should decrease as the overall ability level of the sample that is studied increases. MacKinnon (1964) reported no differences in the Ie scores of three groups of architects differing in creativity; however, he also found no relationship between scores on the Concept Mastery Test and the ratings of creativity in these samples. Garwood (1964) administered a battery of creativity tests to 105 undergraduate science majors and compared the CPI scores of the twenty who scored highest with those of the twenty-four who scored lowest. Garwood's prediction that the high creative group would have higher Ie scores fell just short of statistical significance ($p = .055$, one tail). The fact that Garwood used extreme groups and that her criteria of creativity included verbal tests probably accounts for her finding a stronger association with creativity than MacKinnon reported.

   Construct validity. Another approach to the validation of the Ie scale has been to correlate Ie scores with ratings of intellectual competence made by observers. Studies have been carried out on four samples at IPAR. The first, by Gough (1969b), revealed that the Ie scores of one hundred military officers correlated .41 with the staff ratings. Dicken (1963a) studied samples of student engineers, medical school applicants, and research scientists and found significant correlations with staff ratings in each, with rs ranging from .23 to .41. Dicken employed the multitrait-multimethod matrix of Campbell and Fiske (1959) to ascertain the discriminant validity and learned that of the five scales studied, Ie best met the criteria for discriminant validity.

   In the *Manual*, Gough (1969b) points out that Ie is supposed to assess, "the adequacy and effectiveness with which a subject employs his intellectual resources." He suggested that the Witkin rod-and-frame task would be a good criterion measure, stating, "Our prediction is that accuracy in setting the rod at true verticle would be significantly and positively correlated with scores on the Ie scale" (Gough, 1969b, p. 26). However, the suggested experiment was carried out by Lipp, Erickson, and Skeen (1968), and they found no such correlation ($r = .03$). They concluded that Ie is probably related more to the existence of intelligence than to its effective use.

   A third approach was taken by Hill (1967), who studied autobiographical material on Ss differing in Ie. Results indicated that, in general, people high in Ie are well organized, efficient, and committed to intellectual and cultural pursuits. Hill concluded that the description presented in the *Manual* was confirmed. His data are consistent with Frankel's (1970) report that Ie discriminates significantly between goal-oriented and non goal-oriented women.

Overall, it appears that Gough was successful in producing a personality scale that correlated significantly with conventional tests of verbal intelligence. It is difficult to say on the basis of the available evidence whether the scale assesses ability or, as Gough has suggested, the efficient utilization of whatever ability the individual has. It is likely that it is responsive to both factors, but more to intelligence than to efficiency in its use. Use of the scale as a predictor of achievement, creativity and the like is difficult because the relationship of intelligence to those factors is not yet adequately understood.

CHAPTER 7

Class IV Variables:

Measures of Intellectual and Interest Modes

ฅฅฅฅฅฅฅฅฅฅฅฅฅฅฅฅฅฅฅฅฅฅฅ

The final cluster of scales comprises leftovers that did not fit into the first three classes. Loosely designated as assessing intellectual and interest modes, Class IV includes Psychological Mindedness, Flexibility, and Femininity. *Py* and *Fx* co-vary and have their principal loadings on the same factor, but *Fe* is independent of the other seventeen scales, defining a factor of its own.

Psychological Mindedness (*Py*)

PURPOSE

In his discussions of folk culture theory, Gough has not indicated how one determines what variables qualify as folk concepts, but with the exception of the three validity scales, and perhaps *Ac* and *Ai*, there are probably few who would argue about the folk nature of the scales. However, Psychological Mindedness often causes some raised eyebrows. According to Gough (1968a) the purpose of the *Py* scale is to "identify individuals who are psychologically oriented and insightful concerning others." In another context Gough (1969b) indicates the scale measures "the degree to which the individual is interested in, and responsive to, the inner needs, motives, and experiences of others." By this, Gough does not mean that *Py* is a measure of sympathy, empathy, kindness, or nurturance, but instead that the high scorer has a knack for figuring out how people feel

86

and think. Whether these insights will be used to help or hurt others must be determined from other characteristics of the CPI profile.

During the late 1940s and early 1950s, a pool of three hundred experimental items was given to twenty-five outstanding young psychologists. The responses of this elite group were contrasted with those of subjects in other fields and training programs. The items that distinguished these groups were then correlated with instructors' ratings of the competence and potential of fifty graduate students in psychology. Those items that correlated with this second criterion were retained. The degree of correlation required in this second analysis has not been specified (Gough, 1968a).

Follow-up data on the later careers of the criterion group indicated that their initial promise was fulfilled. By 1967 three of the individuals has been presidents of the American Psychological Association, three had won awards from national professional organizations for outstanding service, and ten had been elected president of APA divisions or of regional or state psychological associations. Their scholarly output had been extensive (Gough, 1968a).

The Py scale consists of twenty-two items of which six are keyed true and sixteen false. Item overlap is relatively low; ten of the twenty-two items are pure and there is only one scale (Sp) sharing items with Py.

The item content suggests that the person who scores high on Py indicates he can summon his resources to concentrate tenaciously on a problem: "I have a tendency to give up easily when I meet with difficult problems"—F. He is able to tolerate ambiguity and disorder: "I always like to keep my things neat and tidy and in good order"—F; but is not likely to change his mind easily: "People can pretty easily change me even though I thought that my mind was already made up on a subject"—F. He endorses items indicating he enjoys his work in general: "I often feel that I made a wrong choice of occupation"—F; and research in particular: "The idea of doing research appeals to me"—T; and he is willing to sacrifice immediate need gratification to achieve long range goals or ambitions: "I often do whatever makes me feel cheerful here and now, even at the cost of some distant goal"—F. While laymen might expect the psychologically minded individual to have a taste for abstruse abstractions, it will come as no surprise to scientists to learn that Py items instead reflect a greater concern for practicality: "I have frequently found myself, when alone, pondering such abstract problems as free will, evil, etc."—F. A final cluster of items consists of frank, liberated, or unconventional opinions and attitudes: "One of my aims in life is to accomplish something that will make my mother proud of me"—F; "I believe we are made better by the trials and hardships of life"—F.

The derivation of the Py scale suggests that it should be a practical predictor of achievement in psychology as manifested through high research productivity and attainment of national recognition. Although CPI data have been collected on generations of Berkeley graduate students, no studies have been published on the ability of Py to predict later eminence.

As we have seen, a number of studies have examined the relationship between the CPI and measures of overall college achievement such as GPA. Those measures have generally not been found to correlate significantly with Py. Py has been found to relate to achievement in psychology courses, however. Gough (1964b) correlated Py with course grades in four large samples of introductory psychology students, two male and two female, with Ns ranging from 867 to 1773; the correlations ranged from .21 to .26. In an earlier study, Gough (1963) studied the differences in the CPI scores of twenty pairs of men matched for IQ but differing markedly in their introductory psychology grades. No significant difference on Py was obtained. However, Rosenberg, McHenry, Rosenberg, and Nichols (1962) did obtain significant correlations ($r = .37$) between Py and military courses in clinical psychology procedures. Holland and Astin (1962) reported that Py was the only CPI scale that correlated significantly with scientific achievement in a sample of 681 National Merit finalists. The correlation was quite low ($r = .13$), however. Other studies have provided less direct evidence for the validity of Py. Capretta, Jones, Siegel, and Siegel (1963) found that students who took honors work and succeeded were higher on Py than those who could have successfully pursued an honors course but chose not to do so. Aiken (1963) found Py correlated significantly ($r = .22$) with a positive attitude toward mathematics, and Helson (1967a) reported that Mills College seniors nominated by the faculty as unusually creative were significantly higher on Py than were their less creative classmates.

From these data, as well as from the derivation of the scale and inspection of the item content, the present writer is convinced that Py reflects characteristics or behavior associated with success in scientific psychology more than "the degree to which the individual is interested in, and responsive to the inner needs, motives, and experiences of others." This conviction was strengthened by the results obtained by Goldberg and Hase (1967), who found a small but significant negative correlation ($r = -.18$) between Py and peer ratings of psychological-mindedness in a sample of 152 freshman women. Vingoe (1968) reported negative but nonsignificant correlations with peer ratings.

Gough (1969b) has adduced two sorts of data to demonstrate that Py measures psychological-mindedness. The first is significant correlations (ranging from .40 to .44) between Py and the Psychologist scale of the Strong Vocational Interest Blank. The second is that graduate students in psychology and allied professions score higher than people in other less psychologically oriented occupations. These data indicate that Py does assess traits peculiar to psychologists; however, it does not establish whether these traits are associated with the psychologist as a scientist or as a clinician. The fact that the CPI *Manual* lists somewhat higher correlations between Py and some scientific occupations such as physicist ($r = .23$), mathematician ($r = .25$), and chemist ($r = .26$) than for "helping" occupations such as physician ($r = .16$), osteopath ($r = .05$), veterinarian ($r = -.12$), dentist ($r = .02$), mortician ($r = -.30$), or minister ($r = .18$) could be used to support the writer's position.

Flexibility (*Fx*)

The Flexibility scale was designed to identify people who are flexible, adaptable and even somewhat changeable in their thinking, behavior, and temperament (Gough, 1968a, 1969b).

Fx was originally developed as a scale of rigidity by Gough and Nevitt Sanford. A list of forty-five items that appeared to the authors to embody inflexibility of thought and manner and resistance to change were administered to four hundred introductory psychology students. The one hundred highest scoring students (fifty of each sex) and the one hundred lowest scoring students (fifty of each sex) on this preliminary scale were identified. An item analysis was conducted to identify those items which differentiated the high scoring and low scoring students on the basis of which twenty-two items were selected. This twenty-two-item scale was then administered to two subsequent psychology classes and the correlations of the individual items of the total score were checked. In subsequent research on the scale, it was found that graduate students and medical students obtained scores lower than those of introductory psychology students. In a sample of forty senior medical students and another sample of forty University of California Ph.D. candidates, correlations of .36 and .46 were obtained with observer ratings of *rigidity*. Moreover, significant correlations ranging from .34 to .46 were obtained with the California Ethnocentricism Scale and correlations ranging from .21 to .64 were found with the California *F* scale (both of which scales were used in the derivation to the *To* scale). When it was included on the CPI, the Rigidity scale was renamed Flexibility, and the direction of the keying was changed accordingly (Gough, 1951a).

The *Fx* scale consists of twenty-two items of which one is keyed true and twenty-one false. Thus, like the *To* scale, it has a strong naysaying bias. This is noteworthy since the *Fx* and *To* scales are designed to measure similar constructs —flexibility and tolerance on the positive end, rigidity and authoritarianism on the negative. None of the twenty-two items is scored on any other scale.

A large proportion of the manifest item content consists of a rejection of the sorts of simple dogmatic assertions that characterize the authoritarian personality: "Our thinking would be a lot better off if we would just forget about words like probably, approximately, and perhaps"—F; coupled with a high tolerance for uncertainty and ambiguity: "I don't like things to be uncertain and unpredictable"—F. The high scorer on *Fx* indicates that he is impulsive: "I often start things that I never finish"—T; untidy and disorganized: "I like to have a place for everything and everything in its place"—F; and has a relaxed, nonjudgmental view regarding moral standards and ethical proscriptions: "I set high standards for myself and I feel that others should do the same"—F.

In his initial report of the Fx scale, Gough (1951a) reported significant conditions between the Fx scale and ratings of rigidity as well as significant correlations with the California F and E scales. Dicken (1963a) correlated Fx scores with IPAR observers' ratings of flexibility in three samples; none of the three correlations was statistically significant. By pooling the data from all three samples to make a total N of 181, Dicken was able to obtain a validity coefficient which, while low ($r = .18$), did manage to attain statistical significance. These studies thus provide some evidence that low Fx scores reflect rigidity, but little support for the notion that high scorers are flexible.

Other studies of the Fx scale have been less direct. Hills (1960) took students in the top and bottom quarters on Fx and administered two performance tasks thought to be related to rigidity: mirror-tracing and the Stroop color-naming test. The more flexible students did not perform better than the rigid ones on these two tasks.

One might also expect a positive relationship between flexibility and creativity, since research has shown the creative person to be innovative, adaptable, and able to break away from past patterns and perceive new relationships. The evidence on the relationship between Fx and creativity is mixed. Garwood (1964) found no differences in Fx between young scientists nominated as being high or low in creativity. Helson (1967a), who compared with their classmates Mills College women nominated as highly creative by the faculty, found no significant differences in their Fx scores obtained during the senior year, but did find the creative women scored higher on a follow-up conducted five years later ($p < .05$). However, the fact that Helson obtained statistical significance on only about 5 per cent of her CPI significance tests makes the reliability of that last finding questionable.

It appears that the Fx scales does correlate negatively with measures of rigidity, but that it fails to relate positively to criteria of flexibility. Gough (1968a) states that Fx is curvilinear with moderate elevations reflecting adaptability, but very high scores ($T > 75$) indicating instability. This may account for the mixed evidence. Nevertheless, the data presently available indicate Fx is one of the least valid CPI scales.

Femininity (Fe)

Gough apparently had several purposes in mind when he derived the Fe scale. Noting that previous femininity scales had been too long, too obvious, and too related to intellectual ability and interests, Gough originally set out "to develop an instrument that is brief, easy to administer, relatively subtle and unthreatening in content, and which will, at the same time, differentiate men from women and sexual deviates from normals" (Gough, 1952a, p. 427). In the CPI *Manual* Gough indicated that the purpose of the scale was to assess masculinity or femininity of interests. Later he expands on that, stating, "the purpose of the Fe scale was not merely to distinguish between men and women but to define a psychological continuum which may probably be conceptualized as masculine versus feminine" (Gough, Chun, and Chung, 1968, p. 155). Thus the purpose of the scale appears to have evolved from the original goal of distinguishing between men and women, toward defining a continuum of *psychological* femininity; moreover, there has been a decrease in emphasis in *Fe* to detect sexual psychopathology.

CONSTRUCTION

The *Fe* scale was derived by external criterion analyses in which the responses of men and women were compared to a specially constructed item pool. Items that had originally been written for the Gough, McClosky, and Meehl investigations of political participation were used as a nucleus; in addition, a large pool of items was assembled which appeared on empirical or intuitive grounds to have some relationship to psychological femininity. The pool was then administered to successive samples of high school and college subjects. On the basis of the resulting data the pool was reduced to 112 items. The 112-item pool was presented as a personality scale to a high school sample consisting of 188 girls and 176 boys and a college sample consisting of 270 women and 301 men. Item analyses were carried out and fifty-eight items that had shown significant differences between the sexes in both samples were selected to make up the final scale. For cross-validation, the scale was administered to one sample of sixty-two college men and sixty-two college women and a second sample of 404 high school boys and 408 high school girls. Significant mean differences between the sexes were obtained in both samples (Gough, 1952a).

Thirty-two of the fifty-eight items had also been included in an item pool used in a study of crime and delinquency. For those inmates whose records indicated homosexual problems, the scores on the thirty-two items were computed and compared with the scores of a control sample of inmates, matched for education and IQ, who were known to be exclusively heterosexual. Highly significant mean differences were again obtained.

The fifty-eight-item scale was published in 1952; it was later included in the CPI (Gough, 1966a) after elimination of the twenty weakest items.

ITEM CHARACTERISTICS

The present *Fe* scale consists of thirty-eight items of which seventeen are keyed true and twenty-one false. High scores reflect femininity and low scores indicate masculinity. Item overlap is low; there are twenty-two pure items and no scales with more than three common items.

Some of the *Fe* items are fairly obvious, dealing with a preference for conventional female as opposed to masculine roles; "I would like to be a nurse"—T; "I very much like hunting"—F. However, most items are subtler. If one knows an item appears on the Femininity scale, one can see social stereotypes at work, but the items themselves do not deal directly with sex differences or sex-related behavior. Several clusters of items deal with emotionality and interpersonal sensitivity, with the direction of the scoring indicating that the more feminine individuals state that they are more responsive to the general emotional atmosphere: "I get very tense and anxious when I think other people are disapproving of me"—T. High scoring individuals indicate that they are restrained, modest, and less likely to be boisterous or impulsive: "I like to be with a crowd who play jokes on one another"—F; "I like to boast about my achievements every now and then"—F. There is also less emphasis on achievement and less interest in politics and current affairs: "I'm pretty sure I know how we can settle the international problems we face today"—F.

VALIDITY

Studies comparing Fe *scores of men and women in the United States.* Scales that have natural, easily assessed criteria tend to have the most validity research done on them, and *Fe* is no exception. The first requirement of a femininity scale is that women should obtain higher scores than men; nothing could be simpler than administering a test to a mixed group and comparing the scores of the men and women. Gough tested large numbers of people in standardizing the CPI, and reports in the *Manual* (1969b) on the differences among high school students (4,056 girls and 3,512 boys), college students (803 women and 787 men) and psychology graduate students (46 women and 113 men). The mean differences were all highly significant and point-biserial correlations ranged from .64 to .78. Gough apparently felt that further calculations of this sort would have been redundant, for the norms in the *Manual* would have permitted similar comparisons of male and female social work graduate students, medical school students, white collar workers, young delinquents, and prison inmates. However, it can be seen in these populations that the mean differences between *Fe* scores of the men and women range from 1.7 to 2 times the standard deviations of the samples. Gough (1966a) did report an overall comparison of 5,647 women and 6,419 men based on the normative data. The mean difference of seven raw score points was twice the standard deviation (r p.bis $= .71$). Similar results have been reported for college samples by Bielauskas, Miranda, and Lansky (1968); Gough (1966a); McCarthy, Anthony, and Domino (1970); Nichols (1962); and on high school students by Leton and Walter (1962). Webster (1953) even managed to differentiate males from females significantly using only ten of the thirty-eight items.

Studies comparing Fe *scores of men and women in other countries.* As *So* does, *Fe* lends itself to cross-national research because of the ready availability of a criterion measure. Gough (1966a) compared the *Fe* scores of men and women in France, Italy, Turkey, and Venezuela and obtained significant mean differences in each study. Point-biserial correlations between *Fe* scores and sex ranged from .47 to .58. He also cited a study of Norwegians by Von der Lippe in which a r p.bis $= .62$ was reported. Later in a study of Korean youths, Gough, Chun, and Chung (1968) again found a significant difference. According to the investigators, the smaller correlation (r p.bis $= .37$) might have been because the Korean sample was younger than those used in the other cross-national studies.

Studies using other tests or ratings as criteria. Obviously the *Fe* scale was designed to do more than merely sort out men and women, although as the sexes merge in dress, hair styles, and behavior it may become increasingly necessary to replace the more conventional inspection techniques with tests such as *Fe*. Still if the sole purpose was to identify the sex of a respondent, it is likely that the thirty-eight *Fe* items could be replaced with one item such as "Are you a female?" (Yes, No, Cannot Say).

However, as we have noted, *Fe* is supposed to measure a continuum of psychological femininity. More than mere physical sex differences is needed to establish its validity for that purpose. Nichols (1962) correlated *Fe* with a number of other measures of the masculinity-femininity dimension. Using a sample of one hundred male and one hundred female college students, he reported correlations of .39 with the MMPI *Mf* scale, .36 with the Guilford-Martin M-F scale, .28 with the Heston M-F scale, and .43 with the Webster Feminine Sensitivity scale. La Grone (1969) reported a correlation of −.75 between *Fe* and the Guilford-Zimmerman Masculinity scale. For subsamples of one hundred men and 171 women the correlations were −.41 and −.40, respectively. Similar evidence is to be found in the CPI *Manual* in which correlations of .44 with the MMPI *Mf* scale and −.41 with the SVIB Masculinity scale are reported for large all-male samples. McCarthy, Anthony, and Domino (1970) obtained a significant correlation ($r = .45$) between *Fe* and the MMPI *Mf* scale, but reported that *Fe* failed in a college sample of thirty-one men and twenty-nine women to correlate significantly with the M-F score of the Franck Drawing Completion Test or the WAIS M-F Index.

Gough (1966a) administered the CPI to forty-one fraternity and forty-five sorority members. He also had them rate one another on masculinity or femininity and respond to his Adjective Check List. He found the *Fe* scores correlated significantly ($r = .38$) with the girls' ratings on femininity and also with the mens' ratings on masculinity ($r = −.48$). For the men, he found *Fe* correlated .37 with the number of raters who described them as feminine and −.31 with the number marked masculine; for the girls *Fe* correlated .27 with feminine and −.34 with masculine. Hase and Goldberg (1967) found a correlation of .24 between *Fe* scores and peer ratings of femininity in a sample of 190 freshman women. The studies thus demonstrated that *Fe* can reflect differences in femininity within all-male and all-female samples.

Vitz and Johnston (1965) had obtained ratings of the masculinity of the image associated with each of the thirteen most popular brands of cigarettes. Forty male and forty female smokers then reported their cigarette preferences. The masculinity of the preferred brand correlated significantly with the *Ss Fe* scale scores in both the male ($r = −.35$) and female ($r = −.33$) samples.

Somewhat more tangential evidence is provided by Webb's (1963) finding that high *Fe* scores are correlated with good attendance and low *Fe* with absenteeism in a junior high school. Insofar as "playing hookey" is a more masculine form of behavior, these data are consistent with the *Fe* scale's construct validity.

Thus there is considerable evidence to support the notion that *Fe* reflects psychological femininity and not simply physical sex differences. A third goal was the detection of homosexuals; all studies reviewed, with the exception of the original cross-validation of the longer fifty-eight-item scale, have employed normal rather than clinical samples. Therefore the *Fe* scale's usefulness in the detection of sexual psychopathology is yet to be established.

CHAPTER 8

New Scales

$\text{\large I\!\$\!U\!\$\!U\!\$\!U\!\$\!U\!\$\!U\!\$\!U\!\$\!U\!\$\!U\!\$\!U\!\$\!U\!\$\!U\!\$\!U\!\$\!U\!\$\!U\!\$\!U\!\$\!U\!\$\!U\!\$\!U\!\$\!U\!\$}$

Gough originally regarded the CPI as an "open" inventory to which new scales could be added as the need arose. More recently he has come to feel that to predict or assess most forms of socially relevant behavior among normal individuals the eighteen basic scales are sufficient, either alone or in combination. (Indeed, Crites, Bechtoldt, Goodstein and Heilbrun, 1961, have suggested that six scales would be enough to account for most of the reliable variance.) Nevertheless, some individuals, perhaps inspired by the example of the MMPI—for which well over 200 scales have been developed—have proceeded to derive additional CPI scales. The writer has not attempted to ferret out all the CPI scales that have been devised. (At the Oregon Research Institute no less than 299 CPI scales are routinely scored [Goldberg, personal communication].) However, in the course of the research for this book, some new scales were found that may be of interest. They are described briefly in this chapter. (Item lists for many of these scales, as well as for the standard scales, will be found in Appendix One). Further details regarding those scales can be learned in the original reports or by writing the authors.

Abbreviated MMPI Scales

Given the item overlap between the MMPI and CPI, it was perhaps inevitable that individuals unwilling or unable to administer both inventories would use their common items to estimate the scores of the scales on the other inventory. Dahlstrom and Welsh in their MMPI *Handbook* listed abbreviated MMPI-based versions of a number of CPI scales which have, as we have seen, been used in several validity studies. In evaluating such a practice, Megargee (1966b) concluded that using the MMPI, one could estimate the scores on scales *Do, Cs, Sy,*

Wb, Re, To, Ac, and *Ai* accurately enough for between-group comparisons, but only *Wb* and *To* were approximated well enough for individual interpretation. The parallel procedure of using the CPI to estimate MMPI scale scores is also possible, and Megargee was busily analyzing his data to determine the feasibility of that procedure when he opened a journal and learned that David Rodgers, in whose seminar he had first been exposed to the CPI, had just published a paper on the subject (1966).

The proportion of common items on the thirteen MMPI scales ranges from 22 per cent to 60 per cent with a median of 43 per cent. Using a sample of sixty neurotic outpatients who had taken both the CPI and the MMPI, Rodgers prepared special scoring stencils and scored the CPI for the abbreviated MMPI scales. He reported correlations ranging from .59 to .90 with a median of .81 between the MMPI subscales scored from the CPI answer sheet and the full scales scored from the MMPI answer sheet. Rodgers went on to develop regression weights to estimate the full MMPI, and cross-validated those formulas in six normal and clinical samples. Rodgers (1966, p. 89) concluded that when using these weights the correlations between the estimated and actual MMPI scores "closely approached test-retest reliability of the MMPI itself, with a median correlation of all scales across each group and each sex of .74. The estimated mean profiles closely duplicated the actual means in the neurotic groups, slightly overestimated the pathology in the normal samples, and slightly underestimated the pathology in the predominantly psychotic sample."

The item composition and the regression weights are presented in Appendix One.

Hase Experimental Inventory Scales

Harold Hase and Lewis Goldberg of the Oregon Research Institute have been engaging in a program of research to determine the best strategy of constructing a structured psychological inventory. Holding constant the item pool, the subject population, and the criterion measures, they have varied the method of item selection to determine what procedure, if any, yields scales having the highest relations with the criteria (Hase and Goldberg, 1967; Goldberg and Hase, 1967; Goldberg, Rorer, and Greene, 1970; Goldberg, 1971). In such research, they have compared eleven scales constructed from the CPI item pool by each of the following strategies: external, internal, theoretical, rational, stylistic, and random. For scales representing the external approach, they used the eleven scales empirically derived by Gough. (That placed the "external" strategy at a disadvantage since the other scales were designed for this project using local *Ss.*) For the remaining strategies the scales had to be specially constructed. The net result was a series of eleven scale inventories, each representing a different item-selection strategy.

INTERNAL (FACTOR ANALYTIC) SCALES

Hase developed eleven factor scales on the basis of factor analyses of the item data from 179 University of Oregon freshman girls. The inability of the the computer to digest a 179 x 480 matrix necessitated a sequential series of analyses on various subpools of items. This procedure, which is described in detail elsewhere (Hase and Goldberg, 1967), eventually yielded eleven factor scales provisionally named, (1) Extraversion-Introversion, (2) Harmonious Childhood, (3) Surgency, (4) Conformity-Rebelliousness, (5) Ascendence-Submission, (6) Neuroticism, (7) Orthodoxy-Flexibility, (8) Self-Confidence, (9) Amiability-Irritability, (10) Serenity-Depression, and (11) Psychoticism. The number of items per scale ranged from nine to twenty-seven. (Item listings appear in Appendix One.)

To illustrate intuitive item selection on the basis of psychological theory, Hase chose to construct eleven scales to measure concepts postulated by Murray. Three advanced graduate students in clinical psychology read Murray's description of eleven psychological needs. Referring to it continuously, they selected CPI items which tapped each of the needs. Items on which at least two of the three judges concurred were retained. In that manner items were selected for the need scales of (1) Achievement, (2) Affiliation, (3) Autonomy, (4) Deference, (5) Dominance, (6) Exhibition, (7) Infravoidance, (8) Nurturance, (9) Order, (10) Play, and (11) Understanding. The number of items per scale ranged from eleven to twenty.

Hase and Goldberg used the term *rational* to delineate scales derived by what has been referred to here as internal criterion analysis. It will be recalled that this involves selection on intuitive or rational grounds of a preliminary item pool designed to measure a particular construct. The items are then administered to a sample and correlations between each item and the total score computed. The items correlating highest are then retained in the final scale.

Hase felt constrained to build only seven scales of that type, using the four scales constructed by Gough to round out the group. Preliminary pools ranging from fifty-two to sixty-six items were selected for each of seven constructs from the CPI item pool. These preliminary scales were then scored on a sample of 108 female college sophomores and juniors. Items correlating significantly were retained, yielding from twenty-seven to forty-five items per scale. The traits purportedly measured by these seven scales were (1) Dominance, (2) Sociability, (3) Responsibility, (4) Psychological Mindedness, (5) Femininity, (6) Academic Achievement, and (7) Conformity. In addition to those scales, Hase also used eleven stylistic scales devised to assess various response styles, and eleven scales composed of randomly selected items to provide a base-line measure for comparison.

Goldberg, Hase, and their associates have engaged in extensive research comparing the validity of those groups of scales for predicting various types of behavior in a sample of 190 University of Oregon freshman women. The first-order correlations of the scales with such criterion have been compared along with the multiple correlations of the various inventories. A detailed review of the results is beyond the scope of this chapter, but the earlier reports generally indicated that the validity of the scales produced by the various methods was quite comparable. Later reports have suggested that the rational method has an edge.

(In evaluating the above findings, however, it should be borne in mind that by using that 468 CPI items, Hase was taking advantage of the lengthy research that went into their selection. The empirical strategy by which the item pool was reduced from 3500 provisional items to 468 best-discriminating ones thus contributed to the success of *all* the strategies tested. A more rigorous comparison would be that of the current CPI scales versus scales chosen by various means from the original, more massive pool.) Further research on different populations are required before any definite conclusions can be reached.

Amenability Scale

The Amenability scale (Rudoff, 1959) was developed by the staff of the California Youth Authority Pilot Intensive Counseling Organization (PICO) to predict juvenile delinquents' responsiveness to intensive counseling. The scale was devised by external criterion analyses. To select their criterion groups, the staff surveyed the records of inmates who had had CPIs administered on intake then readministered just prior to parole. These "before-and-after" profiles were submitted to three judges who then rated on a five point scale the amount of improvement or deterioration. Eighteen inmates rated "markedly improved" by two out of three judges were contrasted with 120 cases who had not demonstrated such improvement. Preliminary analysis of the CPI data showed that the *Sy, Wb, So, Sc,* and *Ac* scales best differentiated the two groups. An item analysis was carried out using the 193 items making up those scales; forty were found to significantly differentiate the two criterion groups. A split-half reliability coefficient of .78 was obtained on the scale.

The validity of the scale was first tested by applying the items back to the original derivation samples. As might be expected, they differentiated the two groups significantly. It was next applied to a larger sample of 216 which included the 138 derivation cases. That test also showed significant differences between the groups, as could have been expected with the criterion *S*s included in the sample. Since anxiety is considered essential to progress in counseling, the construct validity of the new scale was tested by correlating it with the Taylor Manifest Anxiety scale. A correlation of .59 was obtained for a sample of 210 inmates.

Anxiety Scale

Leventhal (1966) constructed an anxiety scale for the CPI by selecting 110 students who had sought assistance at the University of Maryland Counseling Center for emotional or social problems rated by the counselors as of moderate to extreme severity. For each of those students, he selected four additional ones of the same sex who had had no contact with the counseling center. All of these students had had the CPI administered to them during freshman orientation, approximately twelve months earlier. Thus the procedures were designed to emphasize predictive validity. Leventhal divided the two samples in half and performed an item analysis, comparing half the client sample with half the control sample. Twenty-four items were found to significantly differentiate the two groups. Those items were then cross-validated on the remaining *S*s. The twenty-two items that survived were formed into a twenty-two-item scale he named "Anxiety." A check on a new sample revealed the scale had no sex differences.

The test-retest reliability of the scale was found to be .66 for males and .65 for females. Initial validation research showed that students scoring one standard deviation above the mean required approximately three times as many counseling interviews before termination of treatment than those scoring one sigma below the mean.

In a subsequent study Leventhal (1968) reported norms based on samples of 2,047 men and 2,032 women. He also reported correlations between his Anxiety scale and other scales on the CPI and MMPI. In general, the pattern supported the validity of the scale, with significant positive correlations reported between his Anxiety scale and the MMPI *F, D, Pt,* and *Si* scales, as well as the Taylor Manifest Anxiety Scale and the Welch *A* Scale. In addition Leventhal also reported a significant positive correlation with the IPAT Anxiety Scale. Ratings by the counseling center staff gave further evidence that students with high scores on the scale had more severe problems and required more sessions before terminating counseling.

Empathy Scale

Hogan (1969) adopted a mixed rational and empirical approach to devise an Empathy Scale using the combined CPI and MMPI item pools. To secure a criterion measure of empathy, he first had seven psychologists describe their conceptions of a highly empathic man using the California Q-Sort. A composite Q-sort description was then constructed based on those data. Hogan then went to the IPAR files and obtained observers' Q-sort descriptions of the *Ss* in two IPAR samples. These individual Q-sort descriptions were then correlated with the composite criterion Q-sort, and the magnitude of the resulting correlations served as a measure of the degree of empathy for each individual. On the basis of those measures, the *Ss* in the top and bottom 27 per cent on empathy were selected. An item analysis was performed on their responses to the 957 items on the CPI, MMPI, and a special IPAR item pool. From those analyses, sixty-four items, were selected for the final scale, thirty-one of which were from the CPI. Hogan pointed out, however, that the item selection was not purely empirical. In addition to the items that significantly differentiated the two samples in the same direction on both analyses, he also included seventeen other items that had not attained significance but whose content seemed relevant. He also selected additional items to balance the true-false keying of the scale. The test-retest reliability of the scale was .84 and the internal consistency as determined by K-R Formula 21 was .71. Validational data were then collected. In a sample of medical school applicants, a correlation of .39 was found between Empathy scale scores and Q-sort-derived empathy ratings. On the same sample the Empathy scale was found to correlate .42 with rated social acuity. Significant differences were also found in a high school sample between students nominated as being very high and very low on social acuity.

In recent years, Hogan has advanced a theory of moral development in which empathy, as operationally defined by his CPI scale, is a key construct (Hogan, 1970). In the course of testing predictions from his theory, Hogan has obtained data relevant to the construct validity of the Empathy scale. Hogan,

Mankin, Conway, and Fox (1970) reported that Empathy scale scores correlated significantly with the extent of marijuana usage in a college population, with frequent users recording high scores and principled nonusers the lowest. Hogan and Dickstein (1971) found a significant correlation ($r = .48$) between Empathy and a measure of the maturity of moral judgments. Following up on Megargee, Parker, and Levine's (1971) study of socialization in college students, Kurtines and Hogan (in press) predicted that college students with low Socialization scores would be found to have high Empathy scores. This prediction was confirmed. All of those findings were consistent with Hogan's theories of the role of empathy in moral behavior; the confirmation of these predictions lent support to the construct validity of the Empathy scale as well as to his theoretical position.

Factor P and V Scales

The factor P and V scales (Nichols and Schnell, 1963) were designed to measure the two principal factors that are commonly isolated in factor analyses of the eighteen CPI scales. The factor V (Value Orientation) scale was derived to measure what the present writer arbitrarily designates as CPI Factor 1. That is the factor typically defined by high loadings from scales *Wb, Re, So, Sc, To, Gi,* and *Ac.* (See Chapter Nine.) The scale was constructed by administering the CPI to a sample of three hundred undergraduates and computing factor scores on the first factor. Item scores were then correlated with the factor scores; items were selected for inclusion on the factor V scale which correlated significantly with factor V ($p < .01$), but did *not* correlate significantly with factor P ($p > .05$). By that means 110 items were selected. The internal consistency as estimated by KR-21 was .88. The factor V scale was correlated with scales from the MMPI, EPPS, GZTS, and SVIB, and was found to correlate positively with "a variety of other scales and behavior ratings indicating psychological stability, control, and good interpersonal relations. It correlated negatively with indices of maladjustment and emotionality" (Nichols and Schnell, 1963, p. 232).

The same procedures were used to derive a scale to measure CPI factor 2. This 55-item scale, called "Factor P" for "Person Orientation," assesses the variance common to the *Do, Cs, Sy, Sp,* and *Sa* scales. KR-21 was found to be .81. "The P scale correlated with other scales and behavior ratings which suggested activity and outgoingness" (Nichols and Schnell, 1963, p. 232).

Managerial Scale

Goodstein and Schrader (1963) used the external criterion method to derive a managerial key by contrasting the responses of 603 managers and supervisors with those of 1748 general employees. They found that 206 of the 480 items were able to differentiate the two groups. They also found that people in top management scored significantly higher than those involved in line supervision. When applied back to the 603 managers from whom the scale had derived, a correlation of .23 was found between the scores and the individual ratings of success. In a subsequent study Zdep (1969) reported that Ss with high scores on this scale exhibited more leadership than Ss low on the score in four-person problem-solving groups.

Sociality Scale

For a study of political participation, Milbrath and Klein (1962) constructed a twenty-two-item CPI scale they called Sociality. They first experimented with reducing the number of items in various CPI scales and devised shortened subscales of *Sc, Sp, Sa,* and *So* that they felt were satisfactory substitutes for the full-length scales. They also intercorrelated those scales and decided that the *So, Sp,* and *Sa* subscales all measured the same general characteristics, and that low scores on *Sc* also reflected that trait. They combined those four subscales to form the twenty-two-item Sociality scale. It showed a corrected Kuder-Richardson reliability coefficient of .67. In their subsequent work they found it correlated significantly with a number of different indices of participation in political activity. (See Chapter Fourteen.)

Underachievement Scale

Fink (1962a, 1963) performed two item analyses of the CPI to select items for his Underachievement scale. In the first study, the CPI protocols of forty-four high achievers were contrasted with those of forty-four low achievers. In the second study, Fink administered the CPI to 590 high school students. Separating the results for the boys and girls, he placed the Ss into four groups on the basis of their IQs: 89 and below; 90–110; 111–120; 121 and above. In each range, the boys and girls in the top and bottom quartiles on achievement were selected. This led to the identification of seventy-two high and seventy-two low achieving boys, and seventy-three high and seventy-three low achieving girls. Their CPIs were then item analyzed and Fink selected for his scale the sixty-nine items that differentiated in both item analyses the high and low achievers at .10 or better.

Item lists and scoring keys for most of the scales described in this chapter can be found in Appendix One. Since most of such scales are only in the earliest stages of development, it would be advisable to use them for research purposes only. Until normative data are collected and their reliability and validity have been established, it would be inappropriate to use them in clinical assessment or selection.

PART **III**

The correlates of the scales are described in this section. In Chapter Nine the interrelationships and factorial structure of the inventory are examined; Chapter Ten presents the relation of the scales on the five CPI factors to other test and demographic measures, along with the adjectives describing people high and low on the scales; and Chapter Eleven discusses, with examples, the interpretation of the CPI in the individual case.

CONCEPTUAL ANALYSIS
AND INTERPRETATION

CHAPTER 9

Factorial Structure

$$\text{\textipa{∫∗∬∗∫∗∬∗∫∗∬∗∫∗∬∗∫∗∬∗∫∗∬∗∫∗∬∗∫∗∬∗∫∗∬∗}}$$

Although the CPI has eighteen separate scales, many of them are related to each other both statistically and conceptually. Social Presence is obviously related to Sociability, just as Responsibility is related to Socialization and Self-Control, and Achievement via Conformance and Achievement via Independence have much in common. Rogers and Shure (1965) have estimated that on the average CPI scale, 55 per cent of the items overlap with other scales. Such a lack of independence or significant amount of redundancy is a sore point with those who prefer to have independent scales. Gough maintains that convergent validity and usefulness are more important than factorial purity. A study such as that by Domino (1968), which demonstrated that *Ac* is best for assessing achievement in courses requiring conformity while *Ai* is better for courses emphasizing independent thought, justifies the inclusion in the CPI of both scales, despite the fact that they correlate significantly with one another. Obviously the interrelatedness of CPI scales is a matter on which test users will continue to disagree because of their particular orientations and values. The purpose of the present chapter is not to debate the pros and cons of interrelated inventory measures but to describe how the scales co-vary.

Gough (1969b) has provided a complete correlation matrix for all eighteen scales based on data collected on more than nine thousand *S*s from many sources; the correlations vary from $-.28$ to $+.78$. As might be expected, the vast majority of the coefficients is positive. (Levin and Karni (1970) recently compared that matrix with a similar one obtained on 550 Israeli medical school applicants. The correlations proved to have a great deal of cross-cultural invariance. A smallest space analysis of proximities yielded a correlation of .92 between the two matrices.) The first-order relationship between any two CPI scales can be found in Table 5.

While a correlation coefficient is the best measure of the relationship between a given pair of scales, the interrelatedness of all the elements in the test as a whole is summarized better by factor analyses, since they indicate which groups of scales co-vary in a similar fashion. Gough divided the eighteen scales into four groups or classes to increase the ease of interpretation of the profile. In the *Manual,* Gough (1969b, p. 5) stated, "no claims are advanced that these four categories represent psychometric factors." Consequently it has often been assumed that this grouping was based solely on rational or intuitive analyses. For example, Crites, Bechtoldt, Goodstein, and Heilbrun (1961, p. 408) state, "The groupings were not based upon factor analysis, but rather on inspection of intertercorrelations among scales," while Pierce-Jones, Mitchell, and King (1962, p. 65) write, "it should be understood that (Gough) has not proposed that the four classes into which the CPI scales are grouped have anything to do with empirically defined factors." Gough (1964c, p. 194) later took issue with those remarks:

> In several reports on the CPI, it has been said that the grouping of scales on the profile sheet was done by subjective inspection only. This statement is incorrect. Prior to the publication of the *Manual* in 1957, five factor and/or cluster analyses were conducted (three on samples of males, two on samples of females), and the clusters on the profile sheet were defined so as to emphasize the common pattern obtained among these analyses. Clusters I and II on the profile sheet are largely factorially determined. Cluster III (the achievement cluster) was defined for the convenience of counselors and others who might find it useful to have the achievement indices grouped together. Cluster IV included variables having only slight loadings on the earlier factors.

Given that clarification of the origin of the four classes, it is appropriate to inquire how closely they correspond to the factor analytic groupings reported by other investigators.

Factor Analytic Methods

Factor analysis is not a single unitary method but instead a name given to a family of related statistical techniques. Different methods can be used to extract factors, to determine when further extraction is unrewarding and, to rotate the factors extracted. The results naturally vary according to the methods used; the most obvious difference is in the number of factors extracted, but the loadings of the rotated factors will also differ depending on the procedures adopted.

Even more important sources of variation in the results of factor analytic investigations are the samples selected and the variables included in the correlation matrix. It would not be surprising for the factorial structure of a test to vary as a function of the age, sex, or condition of the respondents. In the case of the CPI, somewhat different results have been obtained in analyses of male and female samples. Most studies have analyzed only the eighteen CPI scales, but some investigators have analyzed the CPI in conjunction with variables

Table 5. SCALE INTERCORRELATION MATRIX

		Do	Cs	Sy	Sp	Sa	Wb	Re	So	Sc	To	Gi	Cm	Ac	Ai	Ie	Py	Fx	Fe
De	M:	—	.49	.61	.35	.48	.23	.35	.11	.01	.25	.24	.12	.40	.08	.41	.21	−.14	−.05
	F:	—	.60	.67	.46	.60	.31	.36	.11	.05	.36	.28	.13	.46	.21	.44	.36	−.08	−.13
Cs	M:	.49	—	.57	.47	.43	.33	.31	.16	.15	.44	.32	.06	.39	.37	.53	.29	.19	−.01
	F:	.60	—	.66	.60	.54	.43	.38	.13	.15	.57	.36	.08	.46	.45	.60	.45	.19	−.12
Sy	M:	.61	.57	—	.55	.57	.31	.24	.13	−.03	.25	.22	.15	.37	.02	.48	.17	−.13	−.19
	F:	.67	.66	—	.63	.60	.46	.33	.18	.11	.47	.34	.21	.50	.27	.58	.31	−.03	−.14
Sp	M:	.35	.47	.55	—	.48	.28	.00	−.06	−.16	.23	−.03	.04	.08	.18	.42	.23	.25	−.30
	F:	.46	.60	.63	—	.57	.35	.06	−.02	−.14	.39	.06	.07	.20	.32	.51	.33	.32	−.26
Sa	M:	.48	.43	.57	.48	—	.10	.04	−.03	−.28	.03	−.13	.15	.06	.03	.29	.00	−.07	−.09
	F:	.60	.54	.60	.57	—	.12	.09	−.05	−.26	.22	−.01	.10	.20	.17	.34	.18	.06	−.10
Wb	M:	.23	.33	.31	.28	.10	—	.43	.39	.57	.63	.52	.25	.58	.34	.58	.39	.04	−.07
	F:	.31	.43	.46	.35	.12	—	.49	.49	.66	.67	.61	.27	.66	.40	.66	.43	.01	−.07
Re	M:	.35	.31	.24	.00	.04	.43	—	.45	.45	.51	.43	.25	.55	.35	.47	.22	−.06	.21
	F:	.36	.38	.33	.06	.09	.49	—	.45	.51	.58	.45	.31	.60	.43	.54	.36	−.06	.18
So	M:	.11	.16	.13	−.06	−.03	.39	.45	—	.45	.32	.39	.26	.48	.12	.27	.13	−.17	.09
	F:	.11	.13	.18	−.02	−.05	.49	.45	—	.52	.35	.39	.34	.52	.16	.35	.12	−.20	.19
Sc	M:	.01	.15	−.03	−.16	−.28	.57	.45	.45	—	.54	.72	.08	.60	.36	.34	.41	.01	.18
	F:	.05	.15	.11	−.14	−.26	.66	.51	.52	—	.51	.78	.14	.62	.33	.40	.37	−.13	.12

To M:	.25	.44	.25	.23	.03	.63	.51	.32	.54	—	.50	.10	.57	.61	.63	.46	.21	−.04
F:	.36	.57	.47	.39	.22	.67	.58	.35	.51	—	.50	.21	.58	.63	.70	.47	.19	.03
Gi M:	.24	.32	.22	−.03	−.13	.52	.43	.39	.72	.50	—	−.04	.61	.27	.31	.38	−.04	.01
F:	.28	.36	.34	.06	−.01	.61	.45	.39	.78	.50	—	.03	.64	.29	.41	.39	−.13	.03
Cm M:	.12	.06	.15	.04	.15	.25	.25	.26	.08	.10	−.04	—	.22	−.10	.21	−.10	−.24	−.04
F:	.13	.08	.21	.07	.10	.27	.31	.34	.14	.21	.03	—	.29	.01	.24	−.01	−.21	.18
Ac M:	.40	.39	.37	.08	.06	.58	.55	.48	.60	.57	.61	.22	—	.39	.57	.34	−.08	.14
F:	.46	.46	.50	.20	.20	.66	.60	.52	.62	.58	.64	.29	—	.38	.60	.42	−.18	.06
Ai M:	.08	.37	.02	.18	.03	.34	.35	.12	.36	.61	.27	−.10	.39	—	.52	.40	.48	.11
F:	.21	.45	.27	.32	.17	.40	.43	.16	.33	.63	.29	.01	.38	—	.60	.46	.40	−.04
Ie M:	.41	.53	.48	.42	.29	.58	.47	.27	.34	.63	.31	.21	.57	.52	—	.36	.11	−.06
F:	.44	.60	.58	.51	.34	.66	.54	.35	.40	.70	.41	.24	.60	.60	—	.50	.16	−.09
Py M:	.21	.29	.17	.23	.00	.39	.22	.13	.41	.46	.38	−.10	.34	.40	.36	—	.22	.02
F:	.36	.45	.31	.33	.18	.43	.36	.12	.37	.47	.39	−.01	.42	.46	.50	—	.18	−.14
Fx M:	−.14	.19	−.13	.25	−.07	.04	−.06	−.17	.01	.21	−.04	−.24	−.08	.48	.11	.22	—	.04
F:	−.08	.19	−.03	.32	.06	.01	−.06	−.20	−.13	.19	−.13	−.21	−.18	.40	.16	.18	—	−.10
Fe M:	−.05	−.01	−.19	−.30	−.09	−.07	.21	.09	.18	−.04	.01	−.04	.14	.11	−.06	.02	.04	—
F:	−.13	−.12	−.14	−.26	−.10	−.07	.18	.19	.12	.03	.03	.18	.06	−.04	−.09	−.14	−.10	—

Source: Gough, 1969b

Table 6. SUMMARY OF METHODS USED WITH FACTOR ANALYSES OF THE CPI

Analysis No.	Authors	Sample	Tests Analyzed	Extraction Method	No. Factors	Rotation Method
1	Bouchard (1969)	194 male college students	CPI only	not reported	5	normalized varimax
2	Crites, Bechtoldt, Goodstein and Heilbrun (1961)	62 male and female counseling center clients with personal problems	CPI only	complete centroid	5	analytic and graphic to oblique simple structure
3	Crites, Bechtoldt, Goodstein and Heilbrun (1961)	62 male and 62 female counseling center clients with vocational-educational problems	CPI only	complete centroid	5	analytic and graphic to oblique simple structure
4	Crites, Bechtoldt, Goodstein and Heilbrun (1961)	62 males and 62 females non-clients	CPI only	complete centroid	5	analytic and graphic to oblique simple structure
5	Mitchell and Pierce-Jones (1960)	213 female and 45 male teacher trainees	CPI only	centroid	4	varimax
6	Nichols and Schnell (1963)	4098 men (matrix in CPI Manual)	CPI only	principal components	3	normalized varimax
7	Nichols and Schnell (1963)	3572 women (matrix in CPI Manual)	CPI only	principal components	3	normalized varimax
8	Pierce-Jones, Mitchell, and King (1962)	56 male school superintendents	CPI only	centroid	4	varimax
9	Shure and Rogers (1963)	100 college fresh-men, IQ 133–183	CPI only	principal axes	5	varimax

10	Shure and Rogers (1963)	100 college freshmen, IQ 117–133	CPI only	principal axes	5	varimax
11	Shure and Rogers (1963)	100 college freshmen, IQ 76–117	CPI only	principal axes	5	varimax
12	Springob and Struening (1964)	226 male high school juniors and seniors	CPI only	centroid	5	quartimax
13	Veldman and Pierce-Jones (1964)	266 men in teacher education project	CPI only	principal axes	5	normalized varimax
14	Veldman and Pierce-Jones (1964)	1049 women in teacher education project	CPI only	principal axes	4	normalized varimax
15	Parloff, Datta, Kleman, and Handlon (1968)	938 creative high school students	CPI only	principal components	4	varimax
16	Parloff, Datta, Kleman, and Handlon (1968)	101 more creative and 99 less creative adults	CPI only	principal components	4	varimax
17	Cook (personal communication)	29 female and 28 male psychology undergraduates	CPI and CAS[a]	principal components	8 (3 CAS)	varimax
18	Leton and Walter (1962)	150 boys and 114 girls in ninth grade	CPI and MCI[b]	principal components	5	quartimax
19	Mitchell (1963)	226 female and 65 male college sophomores	CPI and 16 PF	centroid	6 (1 PF)	varimax
20	Gendre (1966)	410 skilled Swiss tradesmen, engineers, and technicians	23 CPI scales, age, and IQ	principal components	7 (1 new scale and 1 age/IQ)	varimax

[a] Community Adaptation Schedule
[b] Minnesota Counseling Inventory

from other tests. Such analyses typically yield more factors since there are usually more sources of variance in two tests than in one.

Factor Analyses

Table 6 lists twenty factor analyses of the CPI. Almost all were performed in a relatively brief period from 1960 to 1964. For each analysis, the table presents the basic data regarding the samples and tests employed, and the method of analysis. While most investigators used fairly heterogeneous samples, one team (Shure and Rogers, 1963) stratified their samples by IQ level. Another investigation analyzed samples of counseling center clients with personal, vocational, or educational problems, as well as nonclients (Crites, Bechtoldt, Goodstein, and Heilbrun, 1961). One study was done using a sample of Swiss employees (Gendre, 1966). The studies are about evenly divided between those that used one sex and those that used both sexes. Analyses 1–16 were based on the CPI only; analyses 17, 18, and 19 employed the CPI in conjunction with some other instrument, and analysis 20 factored the eighteen regular CPI scales in conjunction with five new scales as well as measures of age and IQ.

Results of Factor Analyses

Despite the diversity evident in such studies, as listed in Table 6, there is considerable uniformity in the number of factors extracted. Of the sixteen CPI-only analyses, nine reported the extraction of five factors, five extracted four factors, and two extracted only three. The analyses of the CPI and other tests often yielded more factors, but in each there were five clearly identifiable CPI factors. In general the same basic factors were found in most of the analyses. Tables 7, 8, 9, and 10 show the scales with noteworthy loadings on each of the five factors. (Noteworthy means here that a scale had loadings of .45 or better in at least three of the twenty factor analyses.)

A word about notation. Every investigator labels his factors arbitrarily; some use letters, others Roman numerals, and a few employ arabic numbers. For the purposes of this book, it has been necessary to adopt a uniform way of designating the factors lest a reader become mired in attempting to recall whether one investigator's factor I is the same as some other's factor II or yet another's factor C. Since most investigators have used Roman numerals or letters, I have selected arabic numbers to emphasize the fact that my notation is a uniform system peculiar to the present work. Number "1" (one) was used to designate the factor which accounts for the largest proportion of the variance in most of the twenty analyses; number "2" to the next largest factor, and so on down to number "5" which designates the smallest factor. In the analyses of the CPI in conjunction with other tests, only the readily identifiable CPI factors have been reported and numbered.

FACTOR 1

Factor 1 is the largest factor extracted in most analyses, in terms of both the percent of the total variance for which it accounts, as well as the number of scales which have high loadings on it. The pattern of loadings varies from one analysis to the next. *Sc* and *Gi* invariably have high loadings on factor 1; in many analyses *Sc* provides almost a pure measure of factor 1 and shows loadings as high as .93. *Wb, To,* and *Ac* also have high loadings in every analysis except those carried out by Crites et al. (1961). *Re* is also prominent. In addition *So, Ai, Ie,* and *Py* have high loadings in most analyses. By and large, factor 1 bears a strong resemblance to Gough's Class II with the addition of some measures included in Class III plus the *Wb* scale from Class I.

Table 7. SCALES HAVING NOTEWORTHY LOADINGS ON FACTOR 1
IN TWENTY FACTOR ANALYSES

Analysis Number	SCALES									
	Wb	Re	So	Sc	To	Gi	Ac	Ai	Ie	Py
1	.67	.70	.48	.83	.56	.87	.72			
2				.50		.61	.45			
3				.65		.69				
4				.58		.67				
5	.79	.58		.92	.67	.83	.80	.47	.46	.47
6	.70	.68	.58	.83	.71	.77	.79	.48	.58	.45
7	.78	.67	.55	.87	.74	.75	.75	.55	.66	.49
8	.67			.78	.60	.75	.57		.58	.45
9	.81	.65	.53	.87	.78	.80	.77	.50	.61	.58
10	.77	.60	.57	.91	.67	.83	.76	.46		
11	.64	.48	.47	.86	.50	.85	.62			
12	.78	.70	.70	.91	.81	.77	.79	.62	.66	.55
13	.71	.72	.61	.93	.76	.83	.84	.56	.64	.56
14	.70	.63	.50	.91	.64	.86	.79		.52	.47
15	.83	.63	.55	.89	.78	.83	.75	.50	.59	
16	.82	.46	.58	.85	.62	.86	.72			
17	.72	.66	.63	.87	.76	.71	.79	.59	.60	.51
18	.82	.70	.72	.79	.85	.63	.82	.77	.79	.69
19	.62			.84	.60	.86	.61		.45	
20	.79	.57	.63	.81	.51	.74	.70		.53	

Inspection of Table 7 shows how the pattern of high loading scales varies somewhat between analyses. These variations account for the manner in which different investigators have labeled factor 1. All agree that it measures some form of positive adjustment; however, different test analysts have emphasized different facets of such a measure. Crites et al. (1961) name this factor "good impression-adjustment by adapting self to reality," probably because the principal loadings in their analysis were from the *Gi* scale. However, in most analyses, other Class II scales such as *Sc* have been more prominent and the names assigned to reflect that prominence: *adjustment by social conformity* (Mitchell and Pierce-Jones, 1960; Pierce-Jones, Mitchell, and King, 1962), *value orientation* (Nichols and Schnell, 1963), *self-control* (Springob and Struening, 1964), *conformity and value orientation*[1] (Gendre, 1966). Parloff et al. (1968), who performed their analyses as part of research on creativity, called it *disciplined effectiveness*. Other investigators, particularly those who have analyzed the CPI in conjunction with other instruments, have regarded factor 1 as a general adjustment scale. Bouchard (1969) called it *adjustment,* Shure and Rogers (1963) labeled factor 1 *personal integrity and mental health,* Mitchell (1963) named it *general adjustment,* and Leton and Walter (1962) called it *mental health and personal efficiency.*

FACTOR 2

This factor is extremely stable and appears in all analyses, usually as the second largest factor extracted. Almost invariably it has high loadings from all Gough's Class I variables except *Wb.* However, while *Do, Cs, Sy, Sp,* and *Sa* all load highly on this factor, it is rare for any of the other CPI scales to have high loadings on it.

Factor 2 has been given a variety of names by different investigators. Since the structure of this factor has been quite invariant, the labels generally reflect the different emphases of the investigators more than different loading patterns. A number of investigators have labelled it *social poise or extraversion* (Mitchell and Pierce-Jones, 1960; Pierce-Jones, Mitchell, and King, 1962; Shure and Rogers, 1963). Leton and Walter (1962) referred to it as *social confidence and drive,* Gendre termed it *extraversion,* Springob and Struening (1964) called it *self acceptance and outgoingism,* Bouchard referred to it as *interpersonal effectiveness* and Parloff et al. (1968) named it *assertive self-assurance,* while Nichols and Schnell (1963) labeled it *person orientation.* The only major deviation from this emphasis on social poise and extraversion was on the part of Crites, Bechtoldt, Goodstein, and Heilbrun (1961) who referred to it as *dominance-adjustment by control of external reality,* because in their analyses, the *Do* scale had the highest loadings on this factor. (See Table 8.)

FACTOR 3

Factors 3, 4, and 5 are all considerably smaller than factors 1 and 2. Not only do they account for less variance, but they are also defined by fewer variables and are less stable. Indeed, in some analyses they do not appear at all.

Factor 3 is defined by high loadings from *Ai* and *Fx* and often has strong secondary loadings from *To* and *Ie* and occasionally from *Py.* All of those scales except *Fx* in most analyses also have noteworthy loadings on factor 1. Those who favor interpretation of personality scales in terms of response sets and biases will undoubtedly be interested in the fact that three of the scales (*To, Ai,* and *Fx*) have over 90 per cent of their items keyed false. Although some might regard factor 3 as a naysaying-yeasaying factor, most of the factor analysts have preferred to interpret it in terms of independent thought. Thus it has received such names as *capacity for independent thought and action* (Mitchell and Pierce-

---

[1] "Hypercommunalite ou orientation vers la valeurs."

Table 8. SCALES HAVING NOTEWORTHY LOADINGS ON FACTOR 2
IN TWENTY FACTOR ANALYSES

Analysis Number	SCALES				
	Do	Cs	Sy	Sp	Sa
1	.83	.74	.89	.79	.88
2	.74		.62		.64
3	.72	.66	.77	.66	.69
4	.76	.48	.50		.57
5	.76	.59	.78	.62	.77
6	.63	.60	.78	.71	.74
7	.74	.68	.79	.73	.77
8	.63	.56	.71	.69	.66
9	.74	.69	.84	.72	.85
10	.83	.66	.79	.64	.81
11	.81	.63	.74	.55	.79
12	.71	.61	.82	.60	.82
13	.75	.67	.83	.73	.86
14	.78	.69	.86	.75	.85
15	.79	.68	.87	.79	.86
16	.80	.64	.87	.77	.83
17	.86	.59	.77	.64	.85
18	.63	.50	.70	.61	.78
19	.64	.48	.80	.69	.79
20	.71	.69	.84	.66	.85

Jones, 1960; Gendre, 1966;[2] Shure and Rogers, 1963), *responsibility independent, nonauthoritarian attitudes* (Pierce-Jones, Mitchell, and King, 1962), *intellectual functioning* (Bouchard, 1969), *adaptive autonomy* (Parloff, et al., 1968), and *flexibility* (Crites, Bechtoldt, Goodstein, and Heilbrun, 1961; Springob and Struening, 1964). Analysts who have included other tests in the battery have emphasized slightly different factors. Leton and Walter (1962) regarded factor 3 as a measure of social dependence and personal independence, while Mitchell (1963) labeled this factor as one measuring intellectual resourcefulness.

FACTOR 4

Factor 4 is defined by high loadings from *Cm* and *So. Cm* almost always has its principal loading on factor 4 but *So* as often as not has its primary loading there. In the four analyses in which only four factors were extracted, *Fe,* the scale that defines factor 5, turned up on factor 4. However, *Fe* should not be considered a factor 4 scale since it always appears on factor 5 when five factors are extracted.

Because of the high loading of *Cm,* several analysts regard factor 4 as re-

[2] ("Independance au capacite de pensée et d'action independante.)

Table 9. SCALES HAVING NOTEWORTHY LOADINGS ON FACTOR 3
IN TWENTY FACTOR ANALYSES

Analysis Number	SCALES				
	To	Ai	Ie	Py	Fx
1	.61	.77	.50	.50	.78
2	.51	.70	.51		.59
3		.70			
4	.48	.65	.50		.55
5	.54	.67	.53		.56
6		.65			.71
7		.49			.67
8	.45	.54			
9		.62			.74
10		.66			.70
11	.69	.79	.62		.60
12		.56			.61
13		.68			.86
14	.55	.76	.51		.81
15		.64		.51	.84
16		.85	.54	.65	.79
17		.53	.46		.85
18					
19	.63	.65	.70	.50	
20	.62	.81		.58	.56

flecting test-taking attitudes or sets. Thus it has been labeled *modal response* (Springob and Struening, 1964), *communality* (Gendre, 1966), and *communality test-taking set* by Crites et al. (1961). Others have emphasized the conventionality implicit in factor 4. Bouchard called it *conventionality;* Pierce-Jones, Mitchell, and King (1962) labeled it *inflexible conformity to conventional standards,* while Shure and Rogers (1963) regarded it as a measure of *contented normativism.* Other investigators have emphasized the Socialization scale more than the Communality aspects. Thus Mitchell and Pierce-Jones (1960) labeled the scale *super-ego strength.* (Mitchell [1963] found some support for this designation in his joint analysis of the CPI and the 16 PF, for he found the 16 PF Super-Ego scale also loaded highly on this factor.) (See Table 10.) Unlike other investigators, Leton and Walter (1962) obtained a high loading from the *Gi* scale on this factor and thus labeled it *attempt to look good and impress others.* Parloff et al. (1968), who obtained high loadings from *Fe* as well as *Cm,* called it *humanitarian conscience.*

FACTOR 5

Factor 5, the smallest of the CPI factors, does not appear in all analyses. Where it does appear, it is quite stable, being invariably defined by a high loading

Table 10. SCALES HAVING NOTEWORTHY LOADINGS ON FACTORS 4 AND 5
IN TWENTY FACTOR ANALYSES

| Analysis Number | FACTOR 4 SCALES | | | Analysis Number | FACTOR 5 SCALE |
	So	Cm	Fe		Fe
1	.69	.86		1	.92
2				2	.51
3	.53	.58		3	.58
4				4	.46
5	.57	.58	.45	5	ne[b]
6	ne[a]	ne		6	ne
7	ne	ne		7	ne
8	.63			8	ne
9		.51		9	.61
10		.58		10	.53
11	.55	.52		11	.56
12		.47		12	.56
13	.48	.90		13	.94
14	.54	.78	.65	14	ne
15			.84	15	ne
16		.62	.49	16	ne
17				17	.83
18		.56		18	.77
19	.52			19	.69
20			.76	20	.83

[a]ne: no fourth factor extracted   [b] ne: no fifth factor extracted

from the *Fe* scale. (See Table 10.) Given this loading pattern it is not surprising that there is relative unanimity in labeling factor 5. The major difference of opinion seems to be whether it is best to call it *masculine-feminine, feminine-masculine,* or simply *femininity.* The only originality displayed in labeling the factor was by Mitchell (1963) who largely on the basis of the 16 PF loadings called it, *emotional sensitivity versus masculine toughness.*

Implications of Factor Analyses

Despite the variety of samples and methods used, the results of the twenty different factor analyses are remarkably similar. Indeed, the results are so stable from one study to the next that little need exists for further factor analyses of the test. (A favorite project for students in a cluster analyses course at Berkeley was to perform such an analysis of the CPI using the matrix in Table 5 or some other supplied by Gough. Over a ten-year period, Gough estimates he saw seventy-five to one hundred of such analyses which invariably showed the same clusters [Gough, personal communication, 1971].) Aside from procedural differences, the only variable that seems to systematically influence the results is the sex of the sample; studies using male samples seem to obtain a slightly different pattern of loadings from those found in female samples (Mitchell and Pierce-Jones, 1960; Mitchell, 1963; Pierce-Jones, Mitchell, and King, 1962).

Two of the five factors, factor 2 and factor 5, are quite reliable and self-contained. They are always defined by the same scales and those scales never have significant loadings on any other factors. The interpretation of the remaining three factors is more complex since there are several scales that have high loadings on more than one of them. That demonstrates the factorial complexity of some CPI scales.

Such factor analytic results confirm Thorndike's (1959) impression that considerable overlap exists between many CPI scales, a fact that is evident from a glance at the first order correlations between the scales presented in Table 5. Like Thorndike, many of the factor analytic investigators deplore such redundancy. Mitchell and Pierce-Jones (1960, p. 555) conclude, "It seems quite apparent from the results of this research that the CPI cannot be regarded with real justification as measuring the eighteen relatively independent personality dimensions that it is purported to measure." Crites (1964b, p. 202) states, "Not the least of (the CPI's) shortcomings has been the excessive number of scales in the CPI, which has made it difficult to interpret conceptually, and cumbersome to use in counseling."[3] Those investigators maintained the CPI should be reduced to a set of five or six relatively independent scales which would account for most of the reliable variance. Crites, Bechtoldt, Goodstein, and Heilbrun (1961) suggested that Do, Gi, Ie, Fx, Fe and Cm would be the best set; Mitchell and Pierce-Jones (1960) suggested Sc be used to assess factor 1; Do, Sy, or Sa to measure factor 2; and Cm, Fx, and Fe to account for the remaining three factors. However, since the various CPI scales were not devised as factorially pure measures, such use of existing scales must be regarded only as a stopgap measure if one really seeks to eliminate redundancy. The tables of factor loadings suggest that a few of the suggested scales load highly enough on their respective factors to be considered pure factor scales. A better approach would be to use specially devised factor scales such as those of Nichols and Schnell (1963).

Campbell's (1960) distinction between trait validity and practical validity is central to the above issue. For those who feel the CPI scales should define independent traits, evidence of redundancy and low discriminant validity is cause

_____

[3] The CPI is not uniquely redundant. It will be recalled that the intercorrelations of the eighteen CPI scales range from −.28 to +.78 and that five factors accounted for most of the common variance. Intercorrelations among the regular MMPI scales among normal Ss range from −.74 to +.80 and two factors account for most of the common variance (Dahlstrom and Welsh, 1960). On the Adjective Check List, interscale correlations range from −.65 to +.70 (Gough and Heilbrun, 1965), and Parker and Megargee (1967) found that four factors accounted for most of the common variance. Although the 16 Personality Factor questionnaire was constructed using factor analytic methods, its sixteen scales also correlate significantly with one another, the magnitude of the correlations ranging from −.69 to +.75; second order factor analysis typically yields eight secondary factors (Cattell, Eber, and Tatsuoka, 1970).

for alarm. From such a standpoint, the relationships among the eighteen scales are the primary yardsticks of their usefulness. If two or more scales correlate highly they must be assessing the same trait, in which case the most efficient and valid of such trait measures should be retained, and the rest discarded. One can quarrel with that position by asking (rhetorically) if human traits are totally unrelated to one another. If so, there would be little, if any, consistency and predictability in human personality and behavior. However, insofar as the test is used to define traits for research purposes, a good case can be made for the elimination of redundant scales.

Those who feel that practical validity or usefulness are of primary importance disagree strongly with the position that the intercorrelations among scales should be the primary evidence of their usefulness. They would maintain that it is the correlation of each scale with behavior that is of paramount importance. Crites, et al. (1961) suggest that *Gi* be used to estimate factor 1, while Mitchell and Pierce-Jones (1960) advise the *Sc* be used for this purpose. Both would eliminate *Ac* on the grounds that it correlates too highly with those scales (*Gi* and *Sc*), which both have higher loadings on factor 1. However, the literature clearly shows *Ac* is a better predictor than *Sc* or *Gi* of academic achievement in high school. From the standpoint of practical validity, *Ac* should be retained because it is a better predictor of behavior. Similarly, the psychologst who is primarily concerned with practical prediction of behavior would object to the elimination of the well-validated *So* scale—unless it could be demonstrated that the scales that are retained predict delinquency as well or better.

The present writer's position is that *both* redundancy and correlations with external criteria should be used as yardsticks. Any scale that does not adequately predict nontest behavior should be eliminated. *Sp* is a good example of a scale whose value has not yet been adequately demonstrated. If two scales are highly correlated and assess the same behavior, then the more efficient one should be retained. Until recently, evidence for the validity of *Re,* for example, rested almost entirely on its ability to predict delinquency. However, it does not do this as well as *So.* The *Re* scale thus appeared to add little to the test while making it longer and more difficult to learn; but recent findings suggest that it may predict performance on tedious tasks requiring a strong sense of duty (Kohlfield and Weitzel, 1969; Trites et al., 1967). If that proves true, then *Re* has unique value and should be retained. In making a decision to retain a scale, one should look beyond the first-order correlations with criteria. Some scales may be valuable not because they are good predictors of behavior on their own, but because they contribute otherwise untapped variance to a multiple regression equation.

The factor analyses also have implications for the interpretation of the individual profile. As we have noted, Gough divided the eighteen scales into four classes on the basis of clinical as well as factor analytic considerations. As a first step in profile interpretation, Gough recommends comparing the elevations on the four groups of scales. However, another mode of attack, and one favored by the present writer, is to examine the relative elevation on the five factors. This will be discussed in Chapter Eleven.

CHAPTER 10

Relationship of Scales to Other Variables

¡ª¡ª¡ª¡ª¡ª¡ª¡ª¡ª¡ª¡ª¡ª¡ª¡ª¡ª

The correlation between a scale and another test is less important than the relationship of a scale to "real" (that is, non-test) behavior. However, correlations between tests help one understand the constructs a scale assesses as well as the degree of similarity between measures of logically related traits. Moreover, such correlations can indicate the discriminant as opposed to the convergent validity (Campbell and Fiske, 1959). For example, upon learning that the CPI Sociability scale correlates more closely with the Need Dominance scale ($r = .56$) (of the Edwards Personal Preference Scale [EPPS]) than it does with EPPS Need Affiliation scale ($r = .07$), one wonders if Sy identifies outgoing, sociable people (as it is supposed to) or assertive, socially ascendant individuals. Of course such questions must be resolved through further research, for the problem could lie with the EPPS rather than the CPI.

The CPI *Manual* reports the correlations between the eighteen scales and the MMPI, the EPPS, the Guilford-Zimmerman Temperament Schedule (GZTS), the 16 PF and the SVIB. In addition, correlations with measures of socioeconomic status, intelligence, and the like are included. Over 2,200 coefficients are listed in all. In addition, inferences regarding the influence of age, education, and so on, can be drawn from normative data collected on a variety of samples differing in those dimensions.

118

Relationship to Demographic and Test Variables

A few of the major trends evident in such a mass of data are summarized below. To make the task manageable, we will not examine the full array of correlations for each of the eighteen scales; instead, the pattern of statistically significant correlations for each of the five CPI factors identified in the preceding chapter are briefly described. The patterns for the scales loading on each factor are sufficiently similar so that such a procedure will not result in any serious distortion. (However, this summary does not replace a first-hand study of the actual correlation tables for ascertaining all the quirks and vagaries of any particular scale.) The relationships of the scales loading on each factor with demographic variables such as socioeconomic status, sex, and intelligence are also described. Indicated next are the correlations between the scales and measures of response sets such as Social Desirability. Then the pattern of the statistically significant correlations with scales on the MMPI, GZTS, 16 PF, EPPS, and SVIB reported in the *Manual* is summarized.

FACTOR 1

Factor 1 is defined by high loadings from *Wb, Re, Sc, Gi,* and *Ac,* with *Sc* being almost a pure measure of the factor. Other scales such as *So, To, Ai, Ie,* and *Py* also have high loadings on factor 1 in most analyses, although some also load high on other factors as well. Factor 1 is generally interpreted as reflecting intrapersonal values and social conformity.

Demographic variables. The factor 1 scales have negligible correlations with SES and IQ among male *S*s; however, some of the scales show low but significant correlations with SES for women. That may reflect shifts in values as a function of status for women. Women usually score two or three raw score points higher than men on the factor 1 scales—which is not surprising since women tend to be better-controlled and more conforming in American society.

Response sets. As might be expected in a cluster of scales assessing social conformity and value orientation, the correlations with both the Edwards and the Marlowe-Crowne Social Desirability scales are generally significant, ranging as high as .76 for the *Gi* scale, which was, of course, designed to assess response set (Lichtenstein and Bryan, 1966). For most scales the proportion of items keyed false ranges from 60 per cent to 70 per cent, although it sometimes ranges as high as 89 per cent.

Correlations with other tests. There are substantial positive correlations (.30 to .65) between the factor 1 scales and the MMPI scales, as well as significant positive correlations as high as .50 with the Welsh *R* (Repression) scale. The principal negative correlations are with the *F* scale, the F-K index, and with Block's Undercontrol scale. That MMPI pattern supports the interpretation of factor 1 as reflecting good adjustment through social conformity and making a good impression. That interpretation finds additional support in the correlations with GZTS and 16 PF. Factor 1 scales consistently correlate with the GZTS Emotional Stability, Objectivity, and Personal Relations measures and with 16 PF Factor *G,* Super-Ego Strength. The correlations with the EPPS and SVIB are negligible, however. The person scoring high on those scales thus appears to be a stable, well-socialized, controlled individual with a conventional value system who is sensitive to social demands and tries to behave so as not to offend others.

Factor 2 invariably included scales *Do, Cs, Sy, Sp,* and *Sa.* Gough regards these scales as measures of social poise, ascendancy, self-assurance and interpersonal adequacy. The labels supplied by the various factor analysts are not too dissimilar from his description.

Demographic variables. The factor 2 variables correlate higher with measures of socioeconomic status than the other CPI scales, several of the former having correlations in the .30s and .40s with such measures of status as the Gough Home Index. There are also significant correlations (in the high .20s and .30s) with measures of verbal intelligence. There are no noteworthy sex differences in the raw score means for the factor 2 scales. This pattern is consistent with the notion that the individual who is high on such scales is upwardly mobile, ascendant, and verbally fluent.

Response sets. The factor 2 scales have moderate correlations (in the upper .30s and .40s) with the Edwards Social Desirability (*SD*) scale, but not with the Marlowe-Crowne *SD* scale (Lichtenstein and Bryan, 1966). The keying of the scales is well balanced, the proportion of true responses ranging from 34 per cent to 61 per cent.

Correlations with other tests. The pattern of correlations with the MMPI suggests that the person who scores high on the factor 2 scales is a well-adjusted, happy, outgoing person who is rarely withdrawn or depressed. Almost all the scales have positive correlations with the MMPI, *K, Es,* and *Ma* scales, coupled with negative correlations with such measures of anxiety and depression as *D, Pt,* and *MAS;* there are also negative correlations (ranging from $-.44$ to $-.78$) with the *Si* scale. People high on the factor 2 scales obtain low scores on the Welsh factor *A* and *R* measures and the Welsh Internalization Ratio, suggesting freedom from neurotic conflicts and anxieties. Similarly, on the GZTS, significant correlations with the Ascendancy and Sociability scales are the rule, with correlations ranging from .21 to .56. The principal correlations with the 16 PF are with the scales for Factors *A, E, F,* and *H.* The *Handbook* for the 16 PF (Cattell and Eber, 1957) suggests that such a test pattern is found in an outgoing, spontaneous, socially participative individual who is good-natured but also assertive and ascendant in his interpersonal relations; he is cheerful, talkative, and often elected the leader of a group. That pattern is consistent with the CPI scale labels. The factor 2 scales also correlate significantly with the EPPS Dominance scale, but the correlations with the EPPS *n* achievement and *n* Affiliation scales do not approach significance. In the SVIB, the principal correlations are with the scales for personnel director, public administrator, Army officer and city school superintendent. There are moderate correlations with Interest Maturity, but those for Occupational Level are not as high. The common denominator for those occupations (and for others that a few factor 2 scales relate to), is an interest in a position with some authority in which one works with others. That interest in working directly with others apparently takes precedence over status or power since the correlations are negligible with such high-prestige positions as banker, or the presidency of a manufacturing concern. Likewise there is a negative correlation with the arts in which one is isolated and independent of others. By the same token, however, there is relatively little interest in low-status jobs such as high school teaching, despite the fact that they involve working with others.

Thus the pattern of correlations between the factor 2 scales and other test measures indicates that such scales reflect characteristics shared by well-adjusted, outgoing, ascendant, socially active, verbally fluent people who move up to positions of leadership.

FACTOR 3

Factor 3 is defined by high loadings from *Ai* and *Fx* and, to a somewhat lesser extent, *To*, *Ie*, and *Py*. It is interpreted as reflecting independent thought and rejection of authoritarian attitudes. All of those scales except *Fx* also have high loadings on factor 1 in many analyses. To some extent the pattern of correlations reflects that, with *Fx* having a pattern that differs from those of the other scales.

Demographic variables.   The correlations with SES are on the order of zero for *Ai* and *Fx*, but *To* and *Ie* resemble the factor 1 pattern with negligible *r*s for men but significant correlations for women. Of all the CPI scales, the factor 3 scales have the highest correlations with IQ, *r* ranging from .28 to .58 (*Ie*, of course, was designed to assess intelligence.) Women tend to score about one point higher than men on the above scales.

Response sets.   *Ai* and *Fx* have negligible correlations with Edwards' *SD* scale, but *To* and *Ie* resemble the factor 2 pattern with correlations in the .40s. The correlations with the Marlowe-Crowne *SD* scale are miniscule for *Ai* and *Ie*, low but significant in the positive direction for *To*, and negative for *Fx*. There is a heavy imbalance in the keying with over 90 per cent of the items on the *To*, *Ai*, and *Fx* scales keyed false. That suggests that the person who scores high on factor 3 is not only bright, but rejects standardized, conventional, dogmatic solutions to problems. The low scorer however appears to be more rigid and stereotyped in his thinking.

Correlations with other tests.   Compared with other CPI scales, the factor 3 scales have few significant correlations with other personality tests, suggesting that they occupy a somewhat different "factorial space." Most personality scales are designed to assess some aspect of adjustment or interpersonal relations. However, the factor 3 variables seem to tap a somewhat different area of functioning, one that is not reflected in most instruments: an attitude of intellectual independence versus authoritarianism.

Some people in reading such findings gain the impression that the two major CPI factors are the same as the two major MMPI factors. That is not the case. Judging from correlations between Welsh's MMPI factor scales *A* and *R*, and Nichols and Schnell's CPI factor scales *P* and *V* (supplied by Lewis Goldberg), it appears that the two major CPI factors are displaced about 45 degrees from the two major MMPI factors.

Two factor 3 scales correlated with the MMPI *Mf* scale, perhaps reflecting some covariation with intelligence or artistic interests. There are also positive correlations with the K and R scales, on which all the items are also keyed false. There is no consistent pattern of negative correlations with the MMPI.

In the factor analytic personality tests, the principal correlations are with the GZTS Friendliness scale and the 16 PF Factor Q-1 measure. Factor Q-1 is labeled as *conservative versus experimenting.* The high Q-1 individual is described as being interested in intellectual matters and fundamental issues and ideas; he is well informed and inclined to experiment but unlikely to moralize or to value tradition for the sake of tradition (Cattell, 1962).

While there are no significant correlations with the EPPS, the relationships with the SVIB are interesting. The pattern is one of positive correlations with occupations requiring originality and independent achievement: artist, architect, psychologist, mathematician, musician, author and so on. There are negative correlations with more mundane or routine occupations such as sales, construction, and small business operation. That pattern is also consistent with this writer's interpretation of factor 3 as an indication of independent thought.

FACTOR 4

Factor 4 is defined by Cm and, to a lesser extent, So. With only two scales, one of which also loads highly on another factor, interpretations based on inspection of correlational patterns are necessarily more speculative and less reliable.

Demographic variables. There is no significant correlation with SES; the correlation with IQ is significantly negative for Cm and zero order for So. Women tend to score higher than men.

Response sets. The influence of response sets is negligible. The correlations with SD, while statistically significant, are low; and there is no appreciable imbalance in the keying of the items.

Correlations with other tests. Many factor analytic investigators have suggested that factor 4 assesses a broad test-taking set. One might anticipate from this a number of significant correlations. However, that is not the case. The MMPI is the only test in the present battery to which the factor 4 scales relate. As might be expected there are significant negative correlations with the F scale, although the rs ($-.31$ and $-.35$) are less than one would expect. So also has negative correlations with Pd and Ma, the MMPI scales most closely associated with delinquent behavior, but those correlations are not shared by Cm. In short, examination of the correlations with other personality tests contributes little to our conceptual analysis of factor 4.

FACTOR 5

The final CPI factor is defined by and consists of the Fe scale.

Demographic variables. Fe has negligible correlations with SES and IQ. Women of course score much higher than men.

Response sets. Fe has a slight but significant negative correlation with Edwards' SD scale ($r = .17$), but not with the Marlowe-Crowne measure; there is no particular bias in the true-false keying.

Relations with other tests. As expected, the major correlation with the MMPI is with the Mf scale ($+.44$); Fe also correlates positively with D and R, suggesting that *Fe* also reflects a pattern of internalizing and worrying about problems. The GZTS fits into the same pattern, the principal correlations being with the Restraint and Friendliness scales. So is this the case with the 16 PF where *Fe* correlates positively with factor 1 (Toughness versus Sensitivity), and negatively with the factor *Q-1* (Conservative versus Experimenting). That suggests that factor 5 reflects cautious conformity to traditional patterns and an opposition to change, coupled with a tender-minded, artistic, emotional attitude. Individuals with such a pattern are inclined to be fastidious, disliking rough or crude behavior, impractical, and sometimes demanding (Cattell, 1962). A pattern of passivity and conformity was indicated by the EPPS on which the only significant correlation was with Need Deference.

On the SVIB there were positive correlations with occupations stressing artistic interests or work with abstractions: artist, musician, author. As might be expected, there were negative correlations with traditionally masculine occupations such as Army officer, policeman, aviator, forest service man and production manager. The correlation with the Masculinity Index was −.41. All of those data are added evidence that *Fe* assesses psychological femininity.

Characteristics of People with Differing Scale Scores

A major step in Gough's (1965a) recommended procedures for conceptual analysis is the systematic study of individuals whose scales scores differ. Informal observations of that sort are a taproot for the growth of clinical lore, and were quite important in the development of the MMPI. Over the years, clinical experience modified the interpretation of various scales; the MMPI *Pt* scale, for example, is now regarded primarily as a measure of anxiety rather than of the obsessive compulsive tendencies it was originally designed to assess.

Given his Minnesota background, it is not surprising that Harrison Gough formalized and accelerated the process of accumulating clinical lore about people with high and low scores on the various CPI scales. His primary technique for accomplishing this has been through Adjective Check List analyses. The method consists of having a group of people who are acquainted with an individual check off all those descriptions they feel characterize him on the Gough-Heilbrun Adjective Check List. Those adjectives agreed upon by several members of the assessment group are considered to be descriptive of him. When ACL descriptions are collected for a large number of individuals who have also taken the CPI, the stage is set for the ACL analysis. The distribution of scores on the first CPI scale, *Do,* is divided at some arbitrary point (such as at the median or the quartiles) and then for the first adjective, *absent-minded,* the number of high and low *Do* Ss so described is determined. The differences are tested by chi square, then the process is repeated for the next adjective, *active,* and so on through the list to the three hundredth adjective, *zany.* The same is done for each of the eighteen CPI scales for a grand total of 5,400 significance tests. Such a method of performing ACL analyses was used to generate the high and low adjective descriptions of people on each of the scales included in the CPI *Manual.* More recently, Gough has turned to correlating with scores on the scale in question the number of times a word is checked by different observers. That procedure, which employs the entire sample rather than arbitrarily selected extreme groups, is a much sounder procedure. Not only are the results more general, but the resulting correlation coefficient provides much more information about the strength of the association.

There are obvious problems with adjective analyses. The problem of multiple significance tests can be handled by cross validating, but still it is not uncommon to have forty to fifty adjectives significantly associated with a scale. The user must be wary of generalizing too far beyond the original samples. The fact that college students high in the *Do* scale are described as ambitious does not necessarily mean that the same term could be applied to psychiatric patients with similar *Do* scores; moreover, it is not always clear what is meant by *high* scores. Are high scores in the range from 50 to 59, 60 to 69, 70 to 79, or higher? Is a low *T*-score in the 40s, 30s, or 20s? The problem is significant for, as Gough often points out, interpretation of elevated scores is not a simple monotonic process. For example, moderate elevations on *Fx* indicate adaptability, but very high scores suggest instability (Gough, 1968a). One of the novice's common problems in CPI interpretations is a tendency to apply the descriptive adjectives slavishly, without considering how the absolute level of the individual's scores or the total profile configuration may modify the modal interpretation. However, when used as directed, adjectival analyses can be valuable, not only because they can give the test user a "feel" for the measure, but also because they provide data relevant to the construct validity of the scale. Formal validational studies predict that a certain relationship will be found; those studies then seek to test their predictions. Adjectival analyses suggest relationships not previously suspected. For example, the narcissistic component involved in high Self-Acceptance scores was first revealed by the Adjective Check List data. Adjective analyses are also particularly helpful in giving meaning to low scores. By examining the descriptions of *S*s with low Dominance scale scores, one can learn to interpret such scores by themselves as indicating a detached, unpredictable, somewhat hostile and alienated individual rather than someone who simply lacks the leadership ability of high *Do S*s.

The best known and most widely used adjective analysis of the CPI is that published in the *Manual*. It is based on the comparison of high and low scoring *S*s as described by professional observers during the live-in assessment programs at IPAR. Unfortunately the *Manual* fails to describe the nature of the sample or samples that provided that data, the distribution of the various scale scores, or the procedural details of the analysis. More recently Gough has published an analysis using the correlational method and peer descriptions (Gough, 1968a). His study relied on ACL descriptions made by five fraternity brothers or sorority sisters of the 101 male and ninety-two female students who were *S*s. Each adjective was weighted according to the number of times it was checked as descriptive of an *S*. The adjective scores were then correlated with the CPI scale scores, thereby including data from the *S*s in the midrange as well as the extremes. From the fifty to seventy-five adjectives found to correlate significantly with each scale score, Gough selected the ten with the highest positive and the ten with the highest negative correlations for each sex. The actual magnitude of these correlations is not reported. The adjectives are presented in Appendices Two and Three. Gough (1968a) has discussed the pattern for each scale; only a few of the evident trends will be mentioned.

The adjectives associated with factor 1 scales stress the triumph of reason over emotion; high scorers are seen as calm, mature, dependable people who are warm and responsive to others but in good control of their own feelings. Low scorers are volatile, impulsive, and likely to step on people's toes in their heedless pursuit of pleasure. That is true for both sexes. It is not surprising that the factor 1 scales have been found to discriminate delinquents from non-delinquents as well as those who do well in school from those who do not.

Some of the redundancy to be found in the factor 1 scales is evident in the adjectival descriptions. One would be hard put to differentiate from one another those individuals high on *Re, So,* and *Sc.*

While there are no marked sex differences in the adjectives associated with the factor 1 scales, sexual stereotypes do appear to influence the descriptions of high-scoring men and women on the factor 2 scales. High scorers of both sexes are seen as outgoing, assertive, and ascendant. However, with this pattern, more favorable adjectives are used to describe the men. The high *Do* male is seen as self-confident, his female counterpart as conceited. It is impossible to say whether the behavior of the women high on these scales is in fact more abrasive or whether such negative reactions stem from the greater cultural approval given to ascendancy in men. The mirror image of such a finding is found in the data for the low-scoring men and women. Passivity is a more culturally approved trait in women than in men (Megargee, 1969b), and it is not surprising that the terms used to describe the low-scoring women are generally more favorable than those used for the low-scoring men. It may be that these women, who are not particularly outgoing or assertive, have found a comfortable social niche and are not particularly alienated or bitter, while the men, who are not living up to social expectations, do exhibit greater signs of distress. However, it may simply reflect the fact that sorority women are more tolerant of quiet, unassuming sisters than fraternity men are of their equally passive and retiring brothers.

The adjectival analyses also suggest the different emphasis of each of the scales, at least for the men. The description of the man who scores high on *Do* emphasizes a more forceful, dynamic person than the typical high scorer on *Cs;* and the man who scores high on *Cs* seems to be an easier fellow to get along with than the high-scorer on *Sa.* Women who are high or low on the various factor 2 scales, however, seem to be described in much more similar terms than their male counterparts. That may be because there is less common and more specific variance for men than for women among those scales; those similarities may also reflect a greater "halo effect" in the ratings made by the sorority women.

In interpreting ACL data, it is important to remember the socio-cultural context is relevant and that adjectival wording is relative. The low scoring girls, for example, are frequently described as withdrawn; however, they could not be too withdrawn if they are all members of social sororities. Relative to schizoid psychiatric patients, such withdrawn girls might be described as outgoing, or even effervescent.

Factor 3 is more difficult to characterize because only four scales load heavily on it, two of which also have high loadings on factor 1. Those latter scales are primarily responsible for the fact that terms similar to those used for factor 1 are also applied to people scoring high on the factor 3 scales. The adjectives are generally consistent with the notion that high scorers on those scales share a tendency to think for themselves. The adjective appearing most frequently for men is *independent;* for women, *logical.* Low scorers appear to others as immature.

There is less similarity in the ACL descriptions associated with factor 3 than in the other factors. The Flexibility scale in particular has little in common with the other three. That reflects the fact that Fx has twice as much specific variance as any other CPI scales (Springob and Struening, 1964).

These factors are both quite small, each in essence being defined by one scale, factor 4 by Communality and factor 5 by Femininity. The reader who consults Appendices 2 and 3 will find that the adjectival pattern associated with Cm supports Gough's interpretation of it as being akin to F per cent on the Rorschach, a reflection of the degree to which the S reflects the modal attitudes and behavior of his peers.

The adjectives used to describe people high and low on the Femininity scale also support its construct validity. As on factor 2, there is a sex difference in the connotations of the adjectives: the feminine woman is described in more favorable terms than the feminine man. She is seen as a strong, warm, mature person while he is described as a rather weak, neurotic sort of individual. The converse is true of low scorers; masculine men are described more favorably than masculine women. In evaluating such patterns, it should be remembered that the ACL descriptions were made by peers of the same sex. It is possible that women would describe feminine men somewhat more favorably than other men would; similarly, men might find more admirable qualities in the more masculine women.

CHAPTER 11

Interpretation of Individual Profiles

𝕽𝕸𝕽𝕸𝕽𝕸𝕽𝕸𝕽𝕸𝕽𝕸𝕽𝕸𝕽𝕸𝕽𝕸𝕽𝕸𝕽𝕸𝕽𝕸𝕽𝕸𝕽𝕸𝕽𝕸𝕽𝕸

This chapter moves beyond established empirical findings into the realm of clinical folklore and speculation. Many of the assertions made in it are not yet supported by data. Because of that, some might consider it easy to regard as unscientific. But that is not the case; there is a perfectly good niche for such assertions in science. They are called *hypotheses*. Hopefully they will inspire the design and performance of empirical studies to test them.

No violence is being done to Gough's philosophy of testing or to his conception of CPI utilization by advocating nonactuarial (individual) CPI interpretation. Gough (1965c, p. 1) states, "To me, the first and cardinal principle is that tests are made to be used, and a subsidiary principle is that they are to be used in the analysis and conceptualization of the individual case." He deplores the fact that books and courses on psychological testing focus primarily on test construction and minimize test interpretation. That, he maintains, is as absurd as if schools of music offered myriad courses on how to build pianos but none on how to play them, then raised to eminence those who could write rulebooks for piano construction while looking down upon the artists who merely wish to use the piano to make music.

If we accept for a moment this radical thought, that a structured test (or any other test) is an instrument to be played, a tool to be used, we encounter at once a series of consequences. The first is that playing the instrument is an art or skill in and of itself, and is not to be learned simply by studying the methods for building and verifying the tool. Thus we must recognize in our training programs that seminars in diagnostic interpretation of profiles have their own justification, and are not to be replaced by seminars in methodological psychometrics and multivariate design [Gough, 1965c, p. 2].

Basic Principles

The basic principles governing CPI interpretation are no different from those governing the usage of other personality tests, structured or projective. Two important points are that the CPI must be interpreted by a well-trained, skilled psychologist who is thoroughly versed in the research literature, and that interpretations must be made in the context of other data if they are to be accurate. It is easy to lose sight of these points if one's knowledge of the CPI comes exclusively from the research literature, because little empirical research deals with the CPI as it is used in clinical practice. Most CPI investigations explore quantitative relationships between a given scale and some criterion measure, leaving other scales, the clinical acumen of the interpreter, and environmental factors completely out of the picture. Because of that, and because the CPI appears on first inspection to invite "cookbook" usage, many psychologists fail to realize that the CPI—no less than the Rorschach, the TAT, or the MMPI—must be interpreted, and that such interpretations should be based not on the CPI profile alone, but also on conditions under which it was administered, the respondent's basic characteristics (age, race, marital status, sex, education, and so on), and other relevant case history, interview, and test data. Blind interpretation is fun, and the interpretation of CPI profiles out of context is often instructive; but in a professional setting the client's interests dictate that the appraisal be as accurate as possible—and accurate appraisal cannot be consistently achieved on the basis of test data alone, because the meaning of test patterns varies as a function of the context.

An example demonstrates how the context can modify the interpretation of a particular score pattern: Virginia Grazio was a twenty-year-old junior college graduate who was in training to be a hospital technician in a foreign country. (This and other case names are fictitious.) In general her CPI profile was quite adequate. Her scores closely approximated the college mean and she scored 7 to 10 T-score points above the mean on such important scales as Tolerance, Intellectual Efficiency, and Flexibility. However, she had low scores on Socialization ($T = 30$) and Self-control ($T = 33$). These latter scores were cause for concern because this job was no place for an impulsive, amoral, or undependable person.

The case history showed that Virginia had come from an extremely unstable home with an alcoholic mother and a withdrawn father. Throughout her adolescence she had to cope with severe stress and assume much of the responsibility of caring for her younger siblings. Finally, she left home, got a job, and worked her way through junior college.

Given that background, it is not surprising that many of her statements and attitudes, particularly regarding her family, resembled those expressed by delinquents. That would lead to lower So and Sc scores. However, her mature, constructive response to this stressful home situation, as well as her responsible behavior during the training program indicated that the antisocial attitudes and rebellious behavior usually implied by her CPI scores were not applicable to her. (Her high scores on *Ie, Ai,* and *To* suggest that her independence was expressed intellectually rather than behaviorally.) She was selected for the overseas project and performed outstandingly there.

Such an example shows how extra-test data can influence interpretation and modify the behavioral implications of a given score pattern. Megargee's studies of the Dominance scale further demonstrated how situational factors such as the sex or race of a task partner interact with *Do* scale scores and modify predictions (Megargee, 1969b; Megargee, Bogart, and Anderson, 1966; Fenelon and Megargee, 1971). It is frustrating for the novice to be told that a certain test sign suggests a certain pattern of behavior—except for certain circumstances when it does not. Because of its apparent simplicity, the CPI appears to offer a shortcut to assessment, in contrast to instruments such as the Rorschach. However, just as with the Rorschach, if the interpreter is to interpret data accurately, he must learn the subtle meanings of the various scale configurations and their contraindications.

Learning to Interpret

The fledgling test-interpreter who learns that *CF* on the Rorschach means the number of "color-form" responses generally realizes that he still has a long way to go before he can use the score to make valid inferences about behavior. However, when he learns that *Sc* on the CPI stands for self-control, he is apt to assume falsely that he is ready to begin interpretation. Learning the scale names is not enough. The would-be interpreter must first develop a thorough understanding of the constructs each scale defines; he must study their construction as well as content, and read the validational literature and conceptual analyses. Only then is he ready to begin learning to interpret the individual profile.

Gough has stated that the best way to learn such an art is by studying with a virtuoso and using his behavior as a model. In his interpretive seminars, that process is formalized. Gough engages in free-wheeling clinical interpretations of MMPI and CPI profiles, specifying whenever possible the test cues to which he is responding. Later the students interpret CPIs by sorting Q-decks; they get immediate feedback about how closely their interpretations correlate with the criterion Q-sort. Both modeling and feedback are essential to the learning process. Unfortunately, there are few places where this type of training is available.

Even with the best training, not every student can expect to master the interpretational art any more than everyone who studies music can expect to become a concert pianist. Gough recalled in 1965 (1965c, p. 3):

> I have been teaching a graduate seminar since 1949 which is addressed entirely to the interpretation of the profiles of structured tests and have observed perhaps 200 students in this seminar. Of these, no more than twenty or thirty have shown any real flair for this interpretational art. All of these students were bona fide, certified, grade A Ph.D. candidates, but this is not tantamount to saying that they had the interpretational talent needed to learn how to use tests in a manner befitting the virtuoso.

But the talented student can learn much on his own if he is conscientious in maximizing the feedback. Once he has read the relevant literature, including the CPI *Manual,* Gough's *Interpreter's Syllabus for the CPI* (1968a), and the present text, he must seek actual experience using the test. Ideally he should practice interpreting CPIs under the supervision of a psychologist who is experienced in its use. If such supervision is not available, there are two ways of getting experience if one has access to a suitable population. The first is by consulting the records of the school or agency and pulling the folders of people who have taken the CPI. By doing blind analyses of such records, and checking the interpretations against the rest of the case record, it is possible to gain valuable experience. One advantage in reinterpreting old records is that by checking subsequent developments in a given case one can quickly determine the accuracy of one's predictions.

If one has access to a suitable population he should also take every opportunity to administer the CPI and observe how the profile patterns vary from one individual to the next. He should observe the similarities between people with common problems and backgrounds and the differences in the test patterns that reflect the unique characteristic of each individual. At that stage he should administer the CPI in addition to, rather than in place of, his customary battery. The tentative CPI interpretations and predictions can then be checked against those derived from the more familiar instruments. Later, such cases should be followed up and the relative accuracy of the CPI-based predictions determined.

The literature is not encouraging on the ability of psychologists to profit from experience. Studies by Chapman and Chapman (1967, 1969) and by Goldberg (1968, 1969), among others, have shown a distressing tendency for clinicians to seize upon false but plausible interpretative principles while overlooking valid relationships. If Gough is correct in his estimate that only 20 per cent of the candidates for the Ph.D. in clinical psychology have the potential to become expert interpreters, it could account for these findings.

In the process of making tentative interpretations, it will be necessary to refer frequently to the *Manual* and to the relevant sections in this book in order to review what each scale is supposed to assess, its validity and reliability, and the modal characteristics of individuals with high and low scores on each measure. The most important learning will come about through the analysis of errors. One lesson that will soon be learned is that some scales appear to have a curvilinear relationship with behavior. In the prediction of aggression, for example, a moderate elevation on the Self-control scale can be taken as contraindicating aggressive acting out. However, an extremely high Sc score may indicate a potentially unstable conflict between strong aggressive impulses and rigid controls that can result in episodic lashing out (Gough, 1968a, p. 66; Megargee, 1966d). Moderate elevations on Flexibility indicate adaptability, but T scores over .80 "seem to presage a mercurial, too-volatile temperament" (Gough, 1968a, p. 73).

The second important principle is that the interpretation of some scales depends on the altitude of other scales. The study by Heilbrun, Daniel, Goodstein, Stephenson, and Crites (1962) demonstrated how the interpretation of the Do scale varies as a function of the elevation of Gi. From a large sample of students who had taken the CPI, four groups were selected: 1) high on both,

2) high *Do*-low *Gi*, 3) low *Do*-high *Gi*, and 4) low on both. The characteristics of each group were then investigated using self-descriptions on the ACL. The results showed that students high on the *Do* scale indicated they were more outgoing and concerned with leadership; however, those who were also high on *Gi* indicated they exercised this leadership in a way that demonstrated their concern with and respect for others, while those who were low on *Gi* indicated they were domineering, bossy, and egotistical. The students low on *Do* described themselves as avoiding positions of responsibility and authority; however, the low *Do*-high *Gi* group did this in a way that indicated that while avoiding social responsibilities, they nevertheless sought social approval, while those who were also low on *Gi* reported they were withdrawn, socially inept, and rather resentful. More research using better criteria is needed to demonstrate the validity of configural approaches to CPI interpretation. Good starts at that can be found in the studies by Domino (1968) on the *Ac* and *Ai* scales, and Kurtines and Hogan (1971) on the *So* and Empathy scales.

Steps in Interpretation

PREPARATION

Prior to interpretation, the CPI must be scored on all standard scales and a profile sheet drawn up. It is often helpful to pencil in the average profile for the most appropriate reference group, or to have such a profile available for ready reference. In addition, it may also be helpful to compute some of the various special scoring formulas that have been devised for the CPI. As we shall see in Chapters Twelve to Fourteen, multiple regression equations have been devised for the assessment of a number of characteristics such as social maturity, high school achievement, and parole success. Those that are relevant in a particular setting should be routinely scored and the results added to the profile sheet. This should be done by clerical personnel or electronic computers without the expenditure of valuable clinical time.

When he is using the CPI in actual clinical or counseling practice, the psychologist will approach the test somewhat differently from the manner in which he used it during his training. In training, he probably blindly analyzed the CPI to test his skills and see how much valid data he could extract on the basis of the CPI alone. In actual use, however, the welfare of the client is more important than the education of the psychologist. Before examining the profile the psychologist should review the specific referral questions he seeks to answer and the hypotheses he is testing through the CPI. (If there are no particular questions to be answered by the CPI, then he might question the reason for taking the time to administer it.) Before starting his CPI interpretation, the psychologist should also review the case history along with any special circumstances that may have influenced the testing situation. Such factors as education, race, reading level, and client-examiner relations should be checked, and hypotheses about the client's most likely mode of approach formulated before examining the actual protocol. If the protocol is in the expected pattern, he can usually feel more confident that the interpretation is not merely after-the-fact rationalization. However, deviations from the expected pattern should be closely examined.

No matter what the referral problem, the first question to be answered by the interpreter is whether the profile is valid or has been distorted by some test-taking set. The three basic causes of invalidity are non-responsive answering, faking bad, and faking good.

Non-responsive answering. Non-responsive answering means that the subject marks his answer sheet true or false without regard to the content of the question. That can come about for several reasons. The respondent could have failed to understand or to follow the directions. He may have placed the answer for one item into the space on the answer sheet reserved for another; if such an error is not caught and corrected he may go on and place many or even all the subsequent answers in the wrong spots. This will result in a random response pattern.

Inadequate reading ability is another common cause of non-responsive answering. Many Ss who are unable to read well enough will go ahead and do their best without mentioning their problem. Some will answer responsively to those items they can read, and guess on those they can't figure out. Others will give up and attempt to conceal their reading deficiency by marking their answers randomly or in some pattern such as all true, all false, two true-one false, and so on. Those problems can be avoided in individual administrations if the clinician has the client read the first few items aloud. A person who can read and understand item number 5 ("Our thinking would be a lot better off if we would just forget about words like probably, approximately, and perhaps,") should be able to read well enough to produce a valid profile.

The Cm scale is the key to the identification of the non-responsive answer patterns. Figures 1 and 2 show the profiles stemming from all-true, all-false, and random response patterns in men and women. (The random profile used in this example was obtained by dividing the number of items on each scale by two, on the supposition that random answers should hit keyed and unkeyed alternatives equally often.) In each, an extremely low Cm score exists. Gough (1969b), in a study of thirty computer-generated random profiles, has reported that in none was a Cm T-score as high as 30 found. Given a low Cm score, a low Wb score suggests that the profile was from random or all-true responses. (Such a pattern could also stem from faking bad. See below.) A high Fx peak identifies the all-false pattern.

A mixture of non-responsive and responsive answers is more difficult to detect. Gough wisely placed all the Cm scale items in the last third of the test so that the respondent who struggles along for a hundred items or so before giving up and answering non-responsively will be identified as surely as one who answers erroneously from the start. Inspection of the twelve repeated items for inconsistent responses also aids in detecting the mixed response pattern as well as the random one.

Another source of invalidity is the omission of a large number of items.

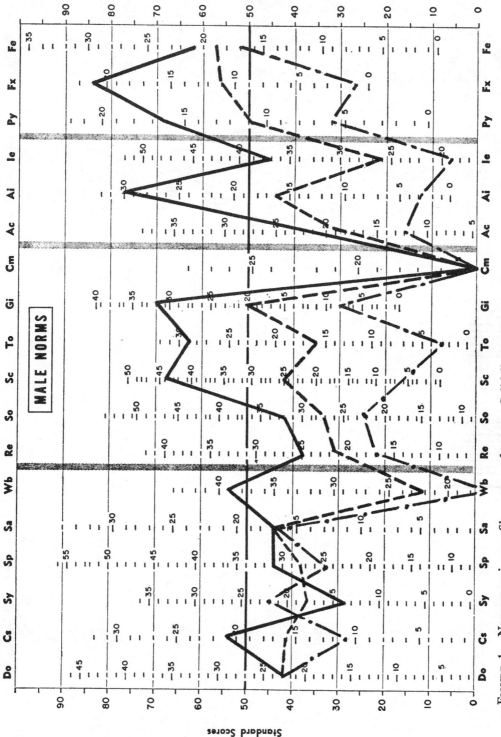

Standard Scores

FIGURE 1.   Nonresponsive profile patterns for men. Solid line: all false. Broken line: random. Dot-dash line: all true.

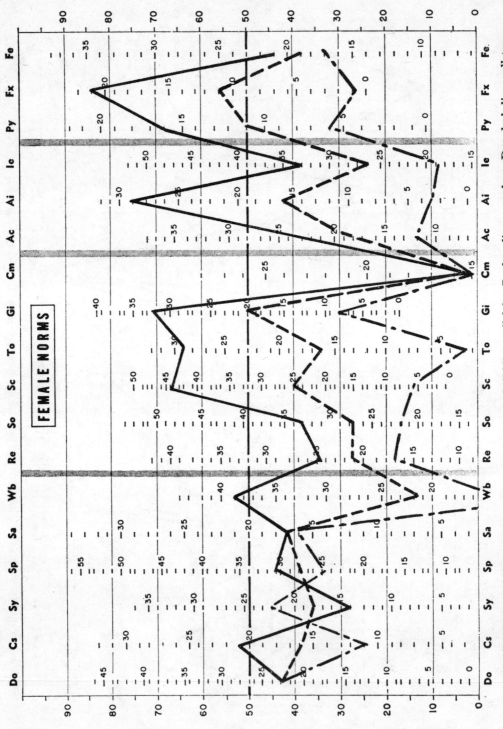

FIGURE 2. Nonresponsive profile patterns for women. Solid line: all false. Broken line: random. Dot-dash line: all true.

While some respondents guess when they are not certain how to answer an item, others simply skip it. This may be because they can not understand the item or because they can not decide on an answer. A large number of unanswered items will lower the validity of the overall profile.

Double-checking is another test-taking strategy. Unable to make up his mind, a test taker sometimes checks both true and false, and thereby increases the overall elevation of his profile.

If the interpreter has relied on a clerk to score the protocol and prepare the profile, he should check the answer sheet when the profile suggests non-responsive answering. Sometimes the problem will be found to be the result of scoring or clerical errors. Visual examination of the answer sheet will reveal if many items have been omitted or double checked, or if the respondent has adopted a systematic pattern in answering such as all true, one true-one false, and so on.

Faking bad.   Gough (1969b) administered the CPI to twenty-two college students (eight men and fourteen women) with instructions to fake bad. The means of these dissimulated protocols are reported in the *Manual*. Profiles plotted from these data are presented in Figures 3 and 4. The key to the fake bad profile is a low score on *Wb*. *Cm*, too, is depressed well below normal.

To distinguish the fake bad from the all-true response pattern, the interpreter should examine the scales that have 85 per cent or more of their items keyed false: *Wb, Sc, To, Ai,* and *Fx*. Usually the scores on those scales will be lower if the all-true response pattern has been used. This occurred less often among the men in Gough's study than the women. *Gi* is the primary scale that distinguishes the fake bad from the random profile. The random profiles usually have *Gi* T-scores of 50, while the *Gi* scores of malingerers are characteristically lower. Once again, that sign is more valid when applied to men than women.

Even if a profile is invalid, it is important to determine the reason for its invalidity. In some cases that can be done through analysis of the profile and the answer sheet; in others, additional data are needed. Consider these case histories:

Mary Stewart was a sixteen-year-old high school junior referred for evaluation because she had become angry and slashed some of the clothing in her mother's closet. In the course of a brief interview Mary was cooperative, but could offer no explanation for her behavior. She was given a CPI to fill out and an appointment was made with her for more extensive evaluation the following week. When her CPI was scored and plotted, it was obvious the profile was invalid. (See broken line, Figure 5). While it could not be diagnosed conclusively, the profile suggested a non-responsive or partial non-responsive pattern with a predominance of true answers. That was consistent with her interview behavior, during which Mary had not made the complaints one would expect from a malingerer. Although no school difficulties had been mentioned in the initial referral, her CPI results made it imperative that Mary's reading ability be checked to determine if she had been unable or merely unwilling to respond appropriately.

A reading test showed approximately third-grade reading skills, and the WAIS indicated a Verbal IQ of 63, a Performance IQ of 76, and a Full Scale IQ of 65. Inquiries at her school revealed that Mary had received passing grades

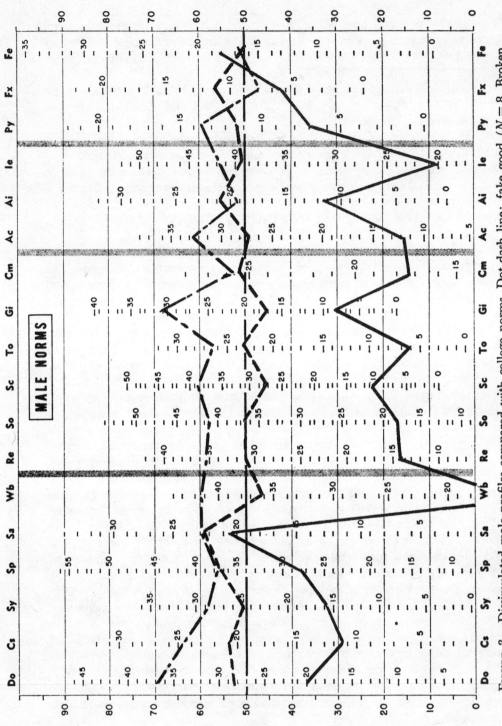

FIGURE 3. Dissimulated male profiles compared with college norms. Dot-dash line: fake good (N = 8). Broken line: college norms (N = 1137). Solid line: fake bad (N = 6). Data from Gough (1969b).

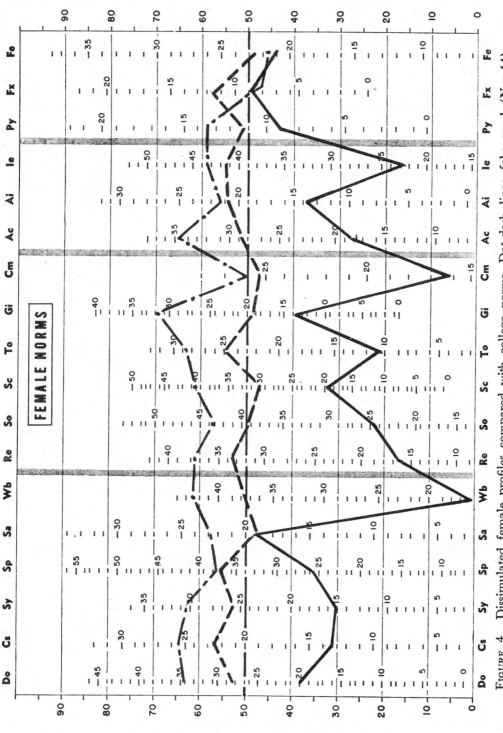

FIGURE 4. Dissimulated female profiles compared with college norms. Dot-dash line: fake good (N = 14). Broken line: college norms (N = 2120). Solid line: fake bad (N = 13). Data from Gough (1969b).

because of her generally amiable disposition. Her biology teacher, for example, let her wash test tubes rather than do experiments. Consequently, Mary had been promoted regularly. Her counselor, who did not believe in tests, had never administered any intelligence or achievement tests that might have revealed her deficits. By age sixteen Mary was a junior enrolled in a totally unsuitable academic program, with her parents planning on sending her to junior college. The frustration engendered by her meaningless school existence and constant exposure to a situation in which she was unable to compete with her peers had been a major factor in her acting out. Her parents were counseled and she was guided into classes and extracurricular activities that better suited her needs.

To illustrate with another case, Victoria Romelia, a fourteen-year-old Mexican-American girl, ran away from home and was taken into custody by juvenile authorities. While in custody she reportedly took forty-five antacid pills in what appeared to be a suicide attempt.

The CPI profile, reproduced in the solid line on Figure 5 indicated an invalid protocol. However, her Cm raw score of 21 contraindicated non-responsive answering because it was higher than any of the computer-generated random profiles reported by Gough (1969b). Instead, the low Wb score and the general profile pattern suggested that Victoria was answering the test in such a way as to emphasize her personal problems and difficulties.

In interview, Victoria reported that she had made several suicide attempts since her mother's then recent divorce and remarriage. She said she might well try to kill herself again and asked to be kept at the juvenile detention center rather than being sent home to her mother and new stepfather. The reported suicide attempts appeared to be manipulative efforts to effect her removal from the home and punish her mother more than genuine efforts to kill herself. Her negative dissimulation or faking bad on the CPI was part of that same pattern of behavior.

Some readers may object that the profile was not invalid because Victoria was in fact disturbed. The fake bad label does not imply that Victoria was actually normal. She was not; in fact, she was eventually committed to the state hospital with a diagnosis of personality trait disturbance, emotionally unstable personality. The invalidity of the profile means that it cannot be used to assess her relative strengths and weaknesses or to evaluate her dynamics and conflicts because her response pattern was too strongly influenced by her desire to impress the examiner with the seriousness of her problems.

Faking good. The fake good profile has generally elevated scores on all scales with a peak on Gi. It is this Gi peak and the relatively slight interscale variability that distinguishes the positively dissimulated record from those obtained by individuals with superior adjustment. Figures 3 and 4 contrast the scores obtained by college men and women asked to fake good with those obtained under normal conditions.

Success in altering a CPI record in the positive direction depends on the adjustment and the test sophistication of the respondent. Canter (1963) found alcoholic patients could significantly improve their CPI scores when told to do so; the better-adjusted patients were able to dissimulate better than the poorer-adjusted ones, but in both groups there was a peak on Gi. In neither group was

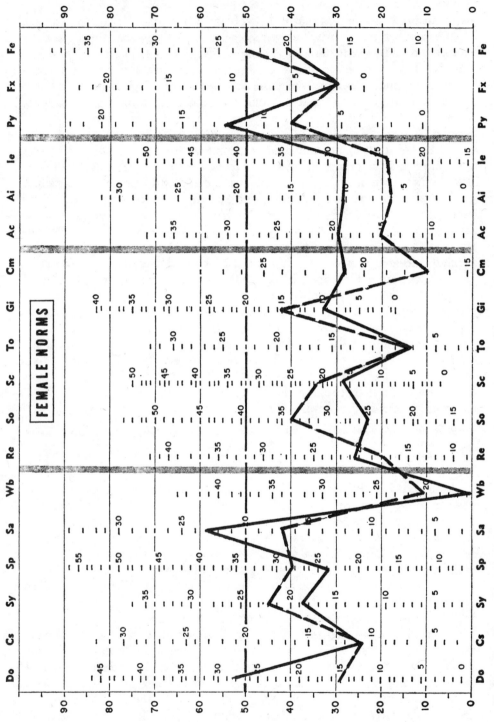

FIGURE 5. Examples of nonresponsive and fake bad profiles. Solid line: Victoria Romelia. Broken line: Mary Stewart.

the mean profile as high as that usually obtained by normals asked to fake good. That is another reason why the psychologist must know something about the background and current status of the respondent if he is to interpret a profile accurately. The mean dissimulated profiles of the poorly adjusted alcoholics in Figure 6 are quite different from those obtained from college students in Figures 3 and 4. Being unaware that a profile was obtained from a poorly adjusted alcoholic might cause the CPI interpreter to miss the dissimulation, despite the peak on *Gi*.

Dicken (1960) attempted to determine whether the CPI could be selectively altered. Four groups of twenty students were administered the CPI in the usual fashion, then again under instructions to role-play dominance, responsibility, intellectual efficiency, and flexibility. The first three groups were able to significantly increase their scores on *Do, Re,* and *Ie* scales, but in the process, they also raised their scores on other scales so that generally favorable, total profiles emerged. A fifth group told to make the best possible impression also produced generally elevated profiles. In every case, *Gi* increased substantially, and in every group except one (flexibility), it was *Gi* that had the greatest increase of all the eighteen CPI scales. By applying a cutting score of $T = 60$ on *Gi*, Dicken was able to detect 79 per cent of the dissimulated records while misclassifying only 3 per cent of those obtained with the standard administration.

Dicken also had two groups of ten psychologists take the CPI under standard and role-playing conditions. Those more sophisticated *S*s were able to alter their relevant scores successfully without significantly increasing their *Gi* scores. Such data indicate that sophisticated, experienced clinicians can successfully distort their profiles in the healthy direction.

PROFILE INTERPRETATION

Assuming the test is valid, the interpreter next notes the overall profile height. Generally, scores above the mean ($T = 50$) indicate positive adjustment, while those below the mean indicate problem areas. It is best to make this gross determination in reference to the norms established for the most appropriate reference group. A male high school student with a T-score of 40 on the *Ie* scale is actually a little above average when evaluated on the basis of high school norms. On the other hand, a graduate student in psychology with a T-score of 60 is below the average for psychology graduate students.

The next step is to look at the average elevation of different homogeneous groups of scales. Gough (1969b) naturally recommends looking at the differences in the elevation of the four classes of scales that he has isolated. Those clusters were specifically designed to facilitate profile interpretation and for this reason they are placed together on the profile sheet. Gough's first class includes scales supposed to relate to interpersonal effectiveness, style, and adequacy (*Do, Cs, Sy, Sp, Sa,* and *Wb*); the second consists of scales stressing intrapersonal controls, values, styles, and beliefs (*Re, So, Sc, To, Gi, Cm*); the third cluster is composed of the scales most useful in academic counseling (*Ac, Ai,* and *Ie*). "The final grouping of three (*Py, Fx,* and *Fe*) on the profile sheet includes measures that ordinarily fall out as residuals in factor analysis, and which, if placed earlier in the series, would interfere with visual recognition of recurrent and diagnosti-

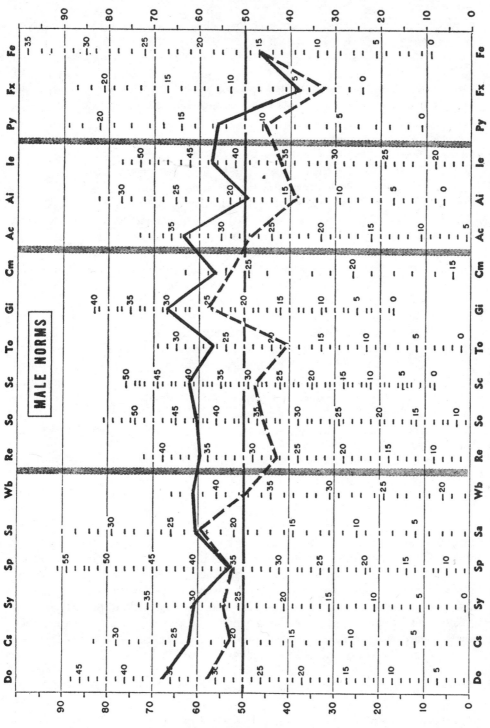

FIGURE 6. Alcoholic patient profiles under fake good instructions. Broken line: fifteen poorly adjusted alcoholics. Solid line: fifteen better adjusted alcoholics.

cally meaningful configurations. Psychologically, these scales reflect broad and far-reaching attitudes toward life" (Gough, 1968a, p. 76).

The present writer prefers to group the scales somewhat differently and instead examines each of the five factors identified in Chapter Nine. Factor 1 is the most general and includes *Wb, Re, So, Sc, To, Gi,* and *Ac.* Scale *Sc* is the best single index of this factor unless Nichols and Schnell's factor V scale has been scored. That factor is an index of mental health, adjustment, and social conformity. Factor 2, consisting of scales *Do, Cs, Sy, Sp, Sa,* is virtually identical to Gough's first class except for the exclusion of *Wb.* (Gough prefers to interpret *Wb* in conjunction with those scales since he feels that one's sense of well-being, vigor, and vitality is an important part of how the individual presents himself to the world.) Those scales give a general indication of the individual's social poise and interpersonal effectiveness. Because of their placement on the profile sheet, it is easiest to interpret them first. The third cluster includes *Ai* and *Fx,* as well as *To, Ie,* and *Py.* Their common denominator is an emphasis on independence of thought and action, as opposed to rigid conformity with authority. The fourth and fifth factors, consisting of *Cm, So,* and *Fe,* respectively, are residual. They should be examined, however, lest the important specific variance contributed by them be overlooked.

The usefulness of profile cluster interpretations can be illustrated by comparing the profiles of a pair of volunteers training for two years of overseas service to an underdeveloped nation. The first candidate, Miss Parsons, was a thirty-eight-year-old single woman with a high school diploma. She had been a professional night club entertainer who applied for the service project after deciding that her prolonged but discreetly conducted affair with a married man was leading nowhere. Warm and outgoing, she was very popular with the group and quickly assumed a position of leadership. Because she was older, more mature, and had considerable poise as well as administrative skills, she was assigned to a central coordinating position within the group.

The second candidate, Mr. Wilson, was a twenty-year-old single man with an A.A. degree. The son of an alcoholic father and a warm, overprotective mother, he was a lone wolf whose principal recreational activities were reading and listening to classical music. His major reason in applying for the service program was to escape from the stress of his family situation. Upon completion of the project he wanted to study abroad, then return to the United States to study library science. In the group, his pattern of withdrawal and his rather feminine identification pattern made him a social isolate. He responded to counseling, and by the end of his training period had started making tentative overtures toward other members of the group.

The similarities and differences between Mr. Wilson and Miss Parsons are well-reflected in their CPI profiles, plotted together in Figure 7. On the factor 2 scales (*Do, Cs, Sy, Sp,* and *Sa*) Miss Parsons (dotted line) typically scored 20 to 30 *T*-score points higher than Mr. Wilson (solid line). With the exception of *Cs,* his factor 2 scores were all below average, reflecting his social ineptness and passivity, while her scores were all high, consistent with her social poise, spontaneity and ability to influence others by winning their loyalty and trust. On factor 1 scales, however, the two candidates had virtually identical scores on *Wb, Re, So,* and *Ac.*

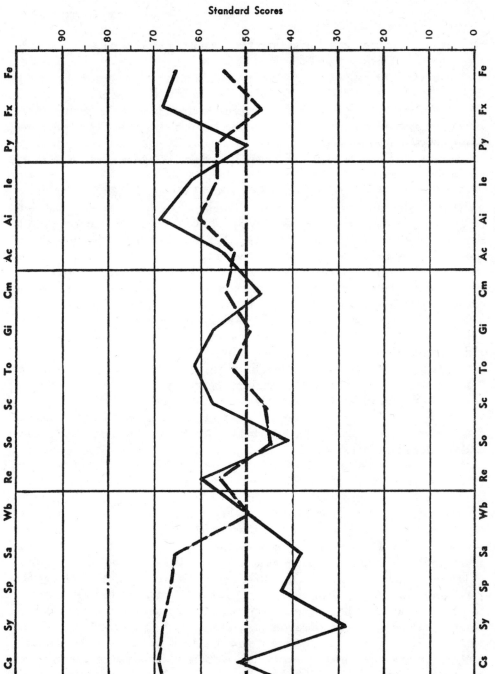

Figure 7. CPI profiles of Miss Parsons and Mr. Wilson. Broken line: Miss Parsons. Solid line: Mr. Wilson. Each profile based on appropriate sex norms.

Such a similarity in scales reflecting basic values and general adjustment is consistent with the fact that both were highly motivated to devote two years of their lives to the service of others. While their decision was influenced by family problems in both cases (which may be one reason why the absolute elevation of these scales was not higher), they nevertheless were able to make mature, long-range plans, and both worked hard in the training program, taking their responsibilities quite seriously. Mr. Wilson's somewhat higher scores on Sc were consistent with his more inhibited sexual life, while his higher Gi score reflected his passive dependence on the approval of others.

On the factor 3 scales ($To, Ai, Ie, Py,$ and Fx)', both had average or higher scores, reflecting not only that they were bright and achievement-oriented, but also their willingness to step outside their cultures and commit themselves to a new way of life for two years. Of the two, Mr. Wilson had the higher scores on those scales, reflecting his greater independence of thought and his superior imagination. A better-educated and more widely read individual, he liked to reflect on and discuss abstract intellectual issues. (His Rorschach was full of references to obscure Assyrian mythological creatures and caricatures drawn by a seventeenth century English humorist.) Miss Parsons was more conventional in her thinking and opinions. She was somewhat higher on $Py,$ however, perhaps reflecting her greater interest in others.

On factor 4, they had almost identical average scores on Cm and $So.$ That serves as a reminder that both were essentially normal, well-functioning people. While they differed considerably in their interpersonal effectiveness (factor 2)', the differences were in the normal range of variation. Miss Parsons was extroverted and ascendant but not hypomanic; Mr. Wilson was somewhat passive and withdrawn but not schizoid.

The scores on factor 5, Femininity, showed Mr. Wilson to have more psychological femininity than Miss Parsons. Her scores were average; she was able to lead and influence others without masculinizing herself. Instead of being bossy, she led by example and suggestion. Mr. Wilson was quite high on the Fe scale. This is consistent with the fact that he felt closer to his mother than his father. (On the Draw-A-Person he started to draw a man first, then erased it and found it easier to draw a large head of a strong-looking, middle-aged woman. When the examiner requested a male picture the result was a drawing of a rather fragile, immature young man of eighteen.) His social behavior was also observed to be somewhat feminine (but not effeminate) in that he was rather shy and retiring. However, that identification pattern appeared to be in the process of changing. He had joined the project despite his mother's wishes to the contrary, and, as already noted, he planned to stay overseas and study even after his tour of duty had ended. His desire to break loose and establish his own identity had much to do with such plans. Some of that ambivalence is suggested by the fact that although he drew the woman first (omitting the body), upon looking at the square-jawed, tight-lipped face he had produced, he commented, "I'm sure *she's* not my dream girl."

SCALE INTERPRETATION

The individual CPI scales are considered next. Gough (1969b) recommends listing the highest and lowest scales. The present writer agrees, but also suggests noting the highest and lowest scales within each of the major scale clusters. The interpreter then spells out the behavioral and dynamic implications of the high and low scales, adjusting his interpretation on the basis of his conceptual understanding of the individual scales and the meaning of the degree of elevation or depression. This procedure enables him to fill in some of the finer details missing from the broadly outlined portrait provided by the interpretation of factor groupings.

It is in this stage of analysis that an intimate conceptual knowledge of each scale becomes of paramount importance. Drawing on his knowledge of the validational literature and the adjective analyses, the interpreter must first consider the implications of the *absolute* elevation of each scale, bearing in mind that some scales may bear a curvilinear relationship with behavior. Next, he must consider the *relative* elevations. There are two aspects of relative elevation: 1) deviation from the norms of the most appropriate reference group, and 2) deviation of a scale from the general level established for the profile as a whole. It is quite possible for a score to be high (for example, $T > 50$) on an absolute basis, but still be low relative to the rest of the profile or to some set of norms. This enables the interpreter to identify weak spots in a basically strong profile and areas of strength in a generally maladjusted profile. This technique is particularly valuable when there are indications of attempts at dissimulation in one direction or the other.

PATTERN ANALYSIS

The next step is to integrate the above data into an overall CPI portrait. Here configural analysis of scale interactions is of primary importance. Once a trend has been established, the elevation on other scales will often provide clues about how that trend will be manifested. The interaction of *Do* and *Gi*, described above, is a good example. If a teenage boy has low scores on *Re, So,* and *Sc,* one would infer alienation from family and authority figures. If that pattern is coupled with high scores on *Do* and *Sy*, it might suggest that he would be active in instigating group activities that are displeasing to authorities. If *Ai* and *Ie* are also high, such activities could take the form of writing critical editorials and organizing social protests while underachieving in class. If his intellectual scales are low, however, more physical expressions of hostility might be expected and a delinquent pattern found. However, if a low *So* score is accompanied by low scores on *Do* and *Sy,* then a more passive pattern may be expected; there could easily be delinquent behavior, but it might be more likely to take the form of running away or passively participating in delinquent activities initiated by others. In girls, a pattern of being sexually exploited would be predicted. Some young people with such a scoring pattern, particularly those with low *Wb* scores, might drift into the dreamy world of drug dropouts.

Learning the implications of different configurations is a time-consuming process that is never completed. Some of the learning proceeds inductively as the psychologist observes the repeated association of certain test configurations with particular behavior patterns; however, when configurations not previously encountered occur, the interpreter must resort to deductive inferences based on his understanding of the scales in question. Whenever possible, of course, he should make note of the hypotheses he has thus formulated and attempt to verify them by following up the cases in question and by designing objective empirical investigations to test them.

Scale configuration patterns are thus part of the psychological folklore, one step beyond the realm of well-validated test-behavior relationships. A few pioneering studies, like those of Crites (1964b), Domino (1968), Goodstein, et al. (1961) Heilbrun, et al. (1962), and Kurtines and Hogan (1971) have examined two-scale interaction patterns, and Gough (1968a, 1969b) has examined the adjectival correlates of others. However, only a miniscule percentage of the 153 possible pairs of CPI scales has been investigated; no studies to the writer's knowledge have attempted systematic validation of triads or larger combinations of scales. Even if such research were undertaken, many of the findings would be peculiar to particular subject populations.

While a discussion of the interpretive meaning of the most common interaction patterns is beyond the scope of this chapter, the following example illustrates how certain aspects of a profile may modify the behavioral implication of other scales: In Figure 8, the profiles of two teenage boys are plotted together, Tim Williams with a solid line and Mickey Krupp with a dotted line. Their scores are remarkably similar on a number of scales; however, on a few, particularly *So,* there are noteworthy differences. A comparison of the two cases will provide insight about how the interpretation of scales on which they had similar scores is modified by other scales on which their scores diverged.

Tim, a seventeen-year-old middle class white boy, was referred by his family physician because of difficulty in school. A boy with an IQ of 113, Tim attributed his problem to severe test anxiety. However, his mother indicated that Tim rarely studied unless she nagged him considerably. His poor performance had become a matter of concern to everyone in his milieu, including not only his parents, but also his older siblings, his cousin, and his girl friend, all of whom had brilliant academic records. Tim's parents had even sent him to a boarding school where he could get tutoring and develop better study habits, but he had contracted mononucleosis and returned home.

The clinical examination indicated that Tim's behavior was a covert, passive-aggressive form of adolescent rebellion against parental pressures. The whole issue of dependence versus independence had become focused on his school performance. Rather than overtly rebelling, he took the path of least resistance and spent his evenings watching television or reading magazines. If his parents' pleadings and polemics became intolerable, he would make perfunctory attempts to study. It was his lack of preparation that was primarily responsible for both his test anxiety and his poor performance. Before final exams he would engage in crash study programs and on such tests, for which he was better prepared, he felt less anxious and obtained higher grades.

Mickey, a fourteen-year-old middle class white boy, was referred by his probation officer after he had come to the attention of the juvenile court for violating the compulsory school-attendance laws. The son of a rejecting, inflexible, German-born father and a weak, permissive, overprotective mother, Mickey's behavior was part of a pattern several years old. At the age of eleven he had been sent for a year to a relative in a distant state. From ages twelve to fourteen he had been placed in a private boarding school, but several months before the

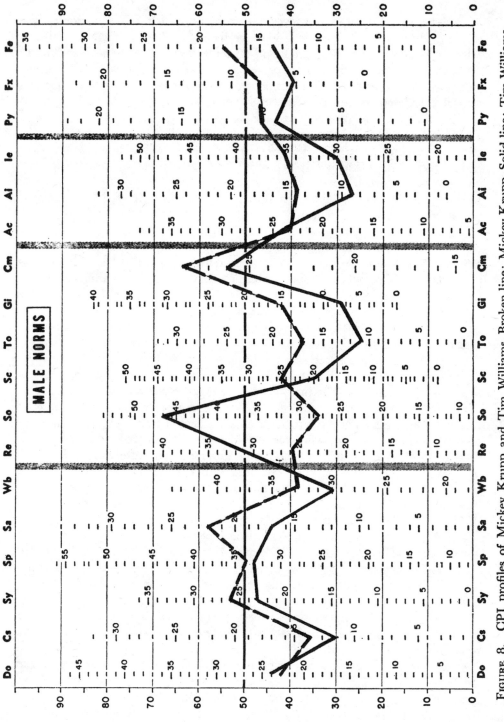

FIGURE 8. CPI profiles of Mickey Krupp and Tim Williams. Broken line: Mickey Krupp. Solid line: Tim Williams.

referral his father abruptly removed him because he felt Mickey's grades were too low. He enrolled Mickey in a local junior high school but Mickey failed to attend classes regularly. The probation officer making the referral described his situation as "beyond parental control, refuses to attend school, sleeps all morning, and runs around all night with troublemakers and homosexuals." Such behavior seemed calculated to infuriate Mickey's father, and in that it succeeded so admirably that their relationship became as warm and friendly as that between Sitting Bull and General Custer.

Thus both Tim and Mickey were rebelling against home atmospheres they perceived as being overly repressive, and in both cases their school performances were casualties of family tensions. However, while Tim protested passively, never acknowledging any hostility against his parents, Mickey resorted to outright defiance and rebellion.

On the CPI, the pattern of scores on most of the scales is similar and consistent with maladjustment, underachievement, and problems in interpersonal relations. The low scores on Cs, Ac, and Ai reflect a lack of drive and ambition, particularly in Tim, whose problems were focused on his school adjustment. The low Wb scores suggest anxiety, but the peaks on Cm indicate that neither boy would be considered cut off from reality or psychotic. The average scores on Sy and Sp indicate adequate peer group relations and are consistent with the fact that the problems in interpersonal relations are confined to authority figures.

It is the contrasts between the profiles that are most interesting however, because they reflect the marked difference in the behavioral manifestations of such authority conflicts. The most striking divergence was on the So scale. While Tim's So T-score of 68 was well above average and higher than that usually attained by high school best citizens, Mickey's T-score of 35 was lower than that of most delinquents. Tim, who was also higher on Re, scored below Mickey on most of the factor 3 scales as well. Those differences indicate Tim had a much stronger superego—that he was more rigid and repressed and less likely to rebel overtly. They are consistent with the fact that Tim manifested a pattern of covert rebellion through underachievement while Mickey was overtly defiant. The difference on the Sa score is also consistent with the divergent behavioral patterns. Mickey's above average score is typical of a person who is, "outspoken, sharp-witted, demanding, aggressive, self-centered, persuasive, and verbally fluent," while Tim's below average score suggests a person who is, "quiet, self-abasing, given to feelings of guilt and self-blame, passive in action, and narrow in interests" (Gough, 1969b, p. 10).

Turning to the interaction of specific pairs of scales, we can use those two cases to examine some of Gough's hypotheses regarding pair-wise interaction patterns. According to Gough (1968a, p. 75), individuals who, like Mickey, have low scores on both Do and Re are typically described as "irresponsible, suggestible, careless, foolish, unstable, pleasure-seeking, apathetic, changeable, confused, and lazy." However, a low Do score coupled with a high Re score, as in the case of Tim, suggests a person who is "quiet, calm, peaceable, mild, modest, gentle, reserved, thoughtful, cooperative and honest." These descriptions are quite apt. Gough (1969b, p. 9) also suggests that a person low on both Sc and So as Mickey was, would be "aggressive, demanding, excitable, and refractory," while a low *Sc*-high *So* individual such as Tim would be "counter-active, critical, dominant, and persistent." While the pattern suggested for Mickey fits his behavior, the adjectives hypothesized for Tim do not apply.

Once the interpreter has completed his analysis of the CPI, he must integrate these data with the rest of the test battery and case history. A useful procedure is to write on the left side of a sheet of paper the major hypotheses about the individual along with test characteristics on which they are based. On the right, opposite each hypothesis, the psychologist can then note whether the hypothesis is supported or contradicted by other material in the respondent's file. For example, in the case of Tim Williams, the interpreter might note, "lacking in imaginativeness and creativity (low *Ai* and *Ie* scores)." If a Rorschach was also given, he could then indicate the degree to which the Rorschach analysis supported his observation: "confirmed by Rorschach (low M, high F per cent, no originals)"; or, "contradicted by Rorschach (many rich and original responses)."

Such a procedure has two advantages. First, it provides the interpreter with a concise list of the complementary and contradictory test findings that he must discuss and integrate in his report and, second, it preserves a systematic record of the reason for each of the various interpretations. Later, when he follows up the case, his written record will enable the interpreter to determine the basis for his correct and incorrect inferences and improve his test analyses in the future.

Specialized Applications

Usually the CPI is administered along with other tests to provide information about on individual's current level of interpersonal functioning. However, in certain cases psychologists may find one of the following specialized approaches of value:

Much of the writer's clinical work has been with adolescents who have various types of behavior disorders. In outpatient clinics, youths are frequently brought in by one or both parents who describe the problem from their point of view, then wait while the child is interviewed and tested. Whenever possible, the writer has the parents occupy their time by taking a CPI, explaining that since most problems are family problems, he can get a better picture of the total situation by understanding every family member. That procedure in itself is useful in establishing rapport, for it demonstrates the psychologist has not automatically assumed that the child or any other family member is the "guilty party."

Adolescents are usually seen in the late afternoon, after school, and time is limited. That time is best spent interviewing and administering individual projective or intelligence tests, so the youth is given a CPI booklet and answer sheet to take home, along with a stamped envelope with which he can mail them back to the clinic. If the father has not accompanied the family to the clinic, the mother is given another booklet and answer sheet for him to use. Having already completed the test herself, the mother usually sees to it that the other members of the family, including siblings (if it seems desirable), complete and return their inventories. That procedure enables the clinician to get valuable data about significant family members who would otherwise be "missing persons," and also involves the whole family in the problem from the outset, thereby paving the way for family-centered treatment if that seems necessary. Of course, not all family members are willing to cooperate to the extent of taking a test. However, refusals constitute valuable data, for those individuals who do refuse are the ones most likely to resist any plans for family-centered therapy.

The value of family testing can be seen in the case of Benny Simmons, age sixteen, and his parents, Clay, forty-four, and Maude, forty-one. Benny was referred by the juvenile court for a series of antisocial acts which included three auto thefts, a burglary, several runaways, and a fight with a teacher. The last got him suspended from school. On examination, Benny presented a classic picture of an amoral, immature, egocentric delinquent, impulsively living for the pleasures of the moment. Polite, charming, and carefree when in control of the situation, he would lash out angrily if thwarted. Such a pattern is accurately reflected in his CPI profile, presented in Figure 9. On the factor 2 scales, he shows low scores on *Do* and *Cs*, indicating little in the way of persistence, ambition, or initiative. Along with the low scores on *Ac, Ai, Ie,* and *Py,* his pattern is consistent with his poor school achievement. However, he has high scores on *Sy, Sp,* and *Sa,* reflecting his sociopathic charm and poise. The factor 1 scales, which measure values and restraints, are uniformly low, consistent with his impulsive amoral hedonism. The factor 3 scales are also low, indicating a rigid, dogmatic outlook and a lack of creative or imaginative outlets. Factor 4, *Cm* and *So,* is high relative to the rest of the profile, showing that Benny was aware of societal conventions and not so alienated as to be out of contact with the culture. These scales, in conjunction with the rest of the profile, suggest that he was not driven to act out against society by dark, bitter feelings of hatred or rejection, but that he simply wanted to have fun, but in the process, heedlessly broke many rules and laws. The low score on factor 5, *Fe,* reinforces this tough, masculine image.

However, in his case, the referral question was not primarily concerned with Benny's current functioning; instead, it inquired about the origin of his pattern and the implications for treatment. To answer such questions, Mrs. Simmons, who had accompanied Benny to the court clinic, was interviewed and tested wtih the CPI. She also took a CPI home for Mr. Simmons to fill out. (Their profiles are presented in Figure 10.)

Mrs. Simmons, whose profile is indicated by the dotted line, was clearly the dominant figure in the family, not because she was particularly ascendant herself, but because Mr. Simmons was very passive and retiring. Her *Do* score is only average, yet it exceeds his by 30 *T*-score points. She reported that she was the one who had to administer what little discipline Benny had received in the course of his development. Her high Femininity scale score would indicate that that role was not what she wanted and that she would have been happier if Mr. Simmons had been more assertive. Both parents tend to be low on the other factor 2 scales, indicating social awkwardness and an inability to communicate effectively with their son, and that they strived for peaceful coexistence rather

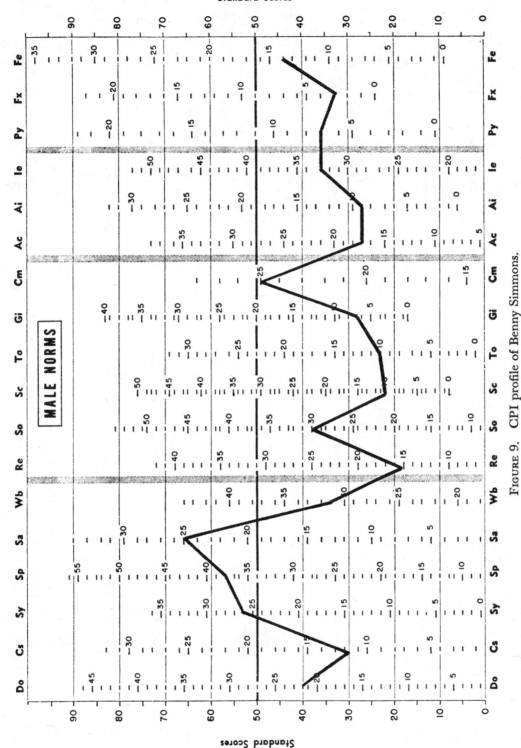

FIGURE 9. CPI profile of Benny Simmons.

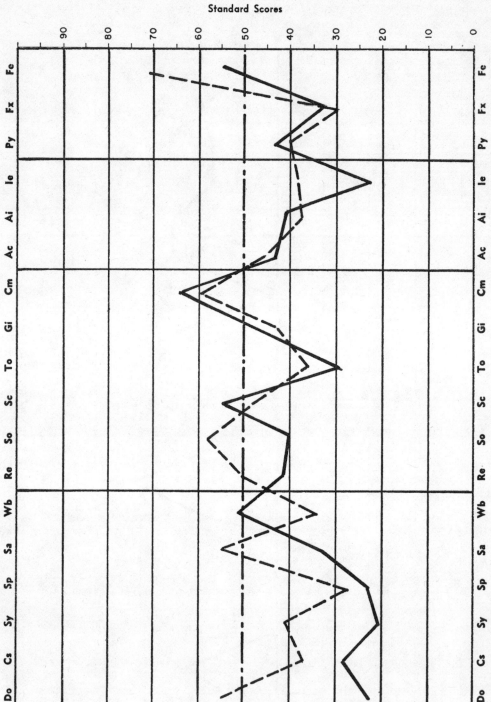

Standard Scores

FIGURE 10. CPI profiles of Mr. and Mrs. Simmons. Broken line: Maude Simmons. Solid line: Clay Simmons. Each profile based on appropriate sex norms.

than parental control. Such passivity had led to the abdication of their disciplinary role, so that Benny had grown up with few limits on him. Ostensibly this was because Benny had suffered from a childhood disease and was overprotected. However, the CPI profiles and the fact that controls had not been instituted once he had been cured, showed the parents' laissez faire style to be firmly rooted in their own personality patterns.

Such a parental vacuum and lack of discipline helped foster Benny's egocentric attitude, and the confusion of parental roles and lack of a clear fatherimage undoubtedly retarded the socialization process. Moreover, the CPIs indicate that the parents' values were not very dissimilar from their son's. Mr. Simmons' Socialization scale score was only one point higher than Benny's, and the father's scores relating to achievement suggest that he placed no great premium on intellectual pursuits and school achievement, besides being rather narrow and judgmental in his outlook. Mrs. Simmons had a somewhat stronger sense of what is right and wrong, as is indicated by her *Re* and *So* scores (another difference that may have led to covert passive-aggressive parental conflicts), but her orientation toward academic achievement was no higher than her husband's. The parents' high *Cm* scores suggest that both could be expected to verbalize the conventional statements about the value of an education, but a boy seeking models would not find such values acted on in the Simmons' life style. Indeed, Mrs. Simmons blamed the school authorities for much of Benny's difficulties, reserving the rest of her censure for Benny's evil companions and the effects of the childhood disease.

The implications of such attitudes were that the supervising probation officer would have to spend as much time working with Benny's parents as with the boy himself, not only for Benny's sake, but also for the benefit of his younger siblings. Moreover, it could be anticipated that Benny would react angrily as firm limits came to be imposed. That proved to be the case. Several weeks after the referral, when Mrs. Simmons ventured to complain that Benny was playing his radio too loudly, he tore up household furnishings, threatened to hit her, and ran away from home. The court then told the family to enter treatment at a local clinic or Benny would be sent to a state juvenile institution. The family agreed to cooperate, but a serious illness contracted by Mr. Simmons made it appear unlikely he would be able to assume much more authority in the family.

Family testing is so prosaic a procedure that it hardly warrants being considered a specialized application. However, despite its high potential for gaining valuable data with minimal expenditure or professional time, it is employed only rarely, if at all, by most counselors or clinicians.

The other techniques described here are more specialized. Typically, they involve changing the instructions in various ways to help isolate certain salient data. These applications have not been formally described in the literature and there are no data available about their validity.

INSIGHT ANALYSIS

This procedure is most likely to be useful when interpersonal conflict exists between a husband and wife, although it can be used in other dyads as well. Each partner is administered the CPI in the standard fashion; next, he is asked to take the test, responding to each item as he feels his spouse would. Each individual's profile is then plotted along with the partner's perception of him. That highlights any discrepancies between how the individual sees himself and how he is perceived by his marital partner; it also reveals each person's empathy toward, and understanding of, his spouse's attitudes. Those data can be useful in counseling the couple, as well as in assessment. (A logical extension of that procedure would be to administer a third CPI on which the individual responds as he thinks his partner would role-play him. That might give some information on his awareness of his effect on others.)

This procedure involves having the individual respond both as he is and as he would like to be. The technique would be most useful with neurotics; however, it is likely that the approach would reveal little more than could be obtained in a good interview.

This procedure is probably more useful in therapy than in assessment. In cases being treated using insight-oriented verbal procedures, a "dry spell" may develop, during which there is little new material being generated. Sometimes it is helpful to tell the client to respond to the CPI as he would have at some critical period earlier in his life, such as at puberty. The choice of time will be dictated by the particular case and the associations the therapist is trying to stimulate. Sometimes just taking the test may be sufficient to start the therapeutic work; other times, the therapist, after scoring the test, may have to prime the pump with interpretive remarks based on the profile, such as, "You seem to have felt pretty lonely as a child," or, "Doing well in school was very important to you."

Psychological Folklore and Empirical Research

It was noted that this chapter ventured beyond the established empirical findings on the CPI into the realm of clinical folklore. There is little hard evidence for the validity of pattern analysis and configural interpretations aside from observations of the individual cases presented above.

Why this gulf between the established findings and the folklore? Actuarially oriented psychologists are inclined to believe that clinicians over-interpret and needlessly complicate essentially simple relationships. They maintain that configurations or interactions between scales are a fantasy, pointing to data showing the superiority in many settings of actuarial assessment based on simple linear models. (See articles by Goldberg, 1968, 1969; and papers in Megargee, 1966d.)

The present writer obviously believes in the configural approach. However, in the majority of cases, the CPI scales co-vary rather than interact. It is not unusual for a profile to have a two-scale interaction pattern. Indeed, Crites (1964b) reported 145 statistically significant two-scale interactions among three groups differing in pathology. However, the frequency of any *given* two-scale interaction is relatively rare. It was only after considerable searching through clinical files that the case of Tim Williams was found to illustrate the interaction between *So* and *Sc*. Because of such rarity, a linear judgmental model will often be satisfactory, as Goldberg (1968, 1969) points out. It is in the exceptional case that the psychologist must intervene and "use his head instead of the formula," as Meehl (1959) puts it.

The matter of curvilinear relations between CPI scale scores and behavior also has not been satisfactorily demonstrated because the changes in the meaning of the scales typically occur with extreme scores which are, of course, rare. In a correlational study using a normal group, such individuals are too few in number to influence the results.

The primary reason why empirical research has lagged behind personal observations on these issues is the difficulty in sampling. To investigate interaction patterns it is necessary to study groups of individuals with odd score patterns—the high *So*-low *Sc* and low *So*-high *Sc* people. But they are hard to locate. Similarly, to test Gough's assertion that *Fx* *T*-scores over 80 indicate a volatile temperament, one must get an adequate sample of such individuals. But only one person in a thousand has a *T*-score over 80. Given such sampling problems, it is inevitable that more time will pass between hypothesis formation and hypothesis test than is the case with more easily investigated questions. Nevertheless, the literature on clinical judgment clearly shows that many psychologists over-interpret their data by "using their heads" when they should have relied on the base rates. If one is to plead rarity as an excuse for delay in demonstrating the validity of configural and curvilinear patterns, one should also make certain he is consistent and does not invoke such principles more often than their frequency warrants.

PART **IV**

※※※※※※※※※※※※※※※※※※※※※※※※※※※※

The remainder of this book deals with the nomothetic use of the CPI. In idiographic interpretation the subject of the preceding chapters, the CPI is used to infer many different attributes about a single individual. Nomothetic analysis represents the converse: the measurement of a single dimension in a large group. Some of the modal assessment problems for which the CPI has been used are reviewed; specifically, those having received the greatest research attention or which seem to be among the more promising subjects for new research. (It was suggested earlier that the two major sources of variation in psychological tests are the choice of constructs to assess, and methods of constructing the scales to measure them. The modal areas of application for each test result from the interaction of those choices of what to measure and how to go about measuring.)

The usefulness of the CPI for various assessment and selection problems is not solely a function of the test. Many other external factors can influence its usefulness. Meehl and Rosen (1955) demonstrate the importance of the base rates for the occurrence of a characteristic within a particular population. Unless a measure is perfectly valid, or has a false positive rate of zero, it can be demonstrated that its use will increase errors if the rate of occurrence of that trait within the population is very low. For example, a large university was shocked when it

156

APPLICATION IN ASSESSMENT
AND RESEARCH

◊◊◊◊◊◊◊◊◊◊◊◊◊◊◊◊◊◊◊◊◊◊◊◊◊◊◊◊◊◊◊

was found that a student had brutally slain two coeds. The writer was appointed to a committee charged with determining what steps, if any, could be taken to prevent another such tragedy. Among the data reviewed was the murderer's CPI profile. When it was pointed out that he had a low So scale score (approximately T = 40), *it was suggested by some that the So scale could be used as a device for screening new students, with individuals having scores of 40 or below excluded. Given the fact that 16 per cent of the normal student population would have such scores and that the apparent base rate for murderers was only .005 per cent (one murderer among twenty thousand students), use of that formula would have meant denying admission to 3,200 nonhomicidal students in order to avoid admitting one potential murderer.*

Externally imposed selection ratios can also increase or decrease the usefulness of a test. Most selection studies are predicated on the assumption that the user can apply the optimal cut-off point. A test may be used to determine which patients in a neuropsychiatric inpatient facility are ready for release. However, the need of the hospital to maintain a certain average daily census may at times lead the administration to delay releasing some patients that the test indicates are ready to go home. At other times the pressure of an increased rate of admissions might force premature discharge of others the test classifies as not yet ready.

157

Values also enter into these decisions. In the case of a marginal applicant to college, it might be decided to admit the student and give him a chance to try, even though the odds are against his completing the program successfully; a similar candidate would be rejected from admission to pilot training or the astronaut program where the consequences of his failure are much more hazardous.

Those and other extra-test considerations are important, well known, and are discussed in detail in most texts on clinical assessment and inference (c.f., Cronbach and Glaser, 1965). The purpose of raising them in the present discussion is simply to remind the reader that the validity of a test alone is not the sole determinant of its usefulness. In reading the research literature on the nomothetic use of the CPI, as well as other tests, he should remain aware of how external factors can influence the usefulness of the test.

Some of the studies that are reviewed in the last three chapters have already been discussed. However, there is a difference in approach to them here. Thus far we have asked, "What are the implications of a study's findings for the validity of the CPI? The emphasis was thus on determining convergent validity; the issue of discriminant validity was put aside. Here we will examine a particular attribute or set of behaviors and ask, "What CPI scales relate to these behavior patterns?" And since the goal is no longer the conceptual analysis of particular scales, one can also ask "Is there a combination of scales that will enable us to predict such attributes more accurately than is possible with a single scale?"

In answering such questions one must keep in mind Shneidman's (1959) injunction to examine "validity for whom," "validity for when," "validity for which," and "validity for what." In short, one must determine whether the findings reported in a particular study are generalizable to different situations, examiners or populations. Because of the special appropriateness of cross-cultural research to the validation of the CPI, we shall also discuss a further question Shneidman overlooked: "validity for where."

In Chapter Twelve there is a discussion of the use of the CPI in educational and vocational assessment. Since Gough designed the test to measure the social functioning of "normal" people, it is not surprising that the CPI should be used most frequently in schools, colleges, and industrial settings. The CPI has also been used in clinical settings where disturbed people are treated for various emotional problems. That application of the test is reviewed in Chapter Thirteen. The final use of the CPI is as a measure of various personality attributes in research settings. Research using the CPI to investigate creativity, conformity and other attributes are described in Chapter Fourteen.

Tables are presented in this section in order to avoid having to repeat the lists of scales for which significant results were reported. In the case of correlational studies, only the coefficients which are significant (p < .05) for each scale in each study are listed. The researcher needing the complete results for a given study can consult the original report.

For studies in which the difference between the means of two or three groups were tested, the magnitude of the statistically significant differences (p < .05) between the means in raw score units is reported. The group first named has the higher score in every comparison in which the difference was positive; a minus sign indicates the second group had the higher score. That *method of summarizing was done for economy; unfortunately, it does not convey the absolute elevation of the group profiles. In a few cases figures have been included as examples to provide a "feel" for the typical elevation, but for the others the original reports will have to be consulted.*

CHAPTER 12

Educational and
Vocational Assessment

֍֍֍֍֍֍֍֍֍֍֍֍֍֍֍֍֍֍֍֍֍֍֍֍

In this book the importance of the individual has been emphasized by tracing many of the characteristics of the CPI to Gough's philosophy and personal values (see Chapter Two). However, as E. G. Boring pointed out in his classic histories of psychology, one must never underestimate the importance of the prevailing intellectual atmosphere, which not only influenced Gough in devising the inventory but also shaped the direction the newly developed test took once it was published.

The CPI was first published in 1957. On October 4, of that year, the USSR launched the first successful earth satellite. Sputnik I had a tremendous impact on American education in general and science education in particular, inspiring a massive infusion of federal and state funds into science education at all levels. The rapid increase in funds for research and training continued unabated for over a decade—until the success of the US space program, inflation, domestic violence, and protracted involvement in Vietnam resulted in a shift in national priorities and a deceleration of support for education during the Nixon administration (Boffey, 1970).

One of the first concerns of educators in the post-Sputnik era was to nurture academic achievement. Projects were established to locate talented, highly motivated youths who could be placed in special programs or awarded scholarships for advanced education. Underachievement by intellectually gifted students was viewed not simply as a personal problem but as a wasteful squandering of a valuable national resource.

How was such talent to be discovered? How could underachievement be eliminated? It was clear from the outset that measures of intellectual ability were not enough. Achievement depended on personality factors as well as sheer brainpower. Projective tests, which had their heyday in the decade immediately following World War II, were clearly not suited to the mass testing programs required. The MMPI, to which a number of investigators turned, proved to be overly oriented toward psychopathology. The CPI could not have come on stage at a more propitious time. It is a group test precisely designed to measure inexpensively and efficiently the necessary variables.

The CPI was introduced not only at the right time, but in the right place. In 1957, California, under the administration of Governor Edmund G. Brown, was the home of many of the chief aerospace and electronics industries. Unprecedented population growth following World War II had forced rapid expansion of the educational system at all levels and such growth attracted talented, innovative educators. Thus the CPI had fertile soil in which to grow.

Given these circumstances of time and place, it comes as no small surprise that the ability of the CPI to identify the personality factors associated with achievement has been the subject of intensive and extensive investigation using a variety of research designs. One of the most important discoveries to emerge from such research is that different personality characteristics are associated with different levels of achievement. For that reason, the different academic levels are discussed separately, first elementary school, then high school, college, and postgraduate studies respectively.

Different findings emerge when the CPI is used alone, as opposed to its use in conjunction with an intelligence test; similarly, in a CPI-only study, somewhat different patterns are found in samples heterogeneous with respect to IQ than in those which are homogeneous. In those studies in which there is considerable variability in IQ and no intelligence tests are included, the CPI scales (such as Ie) reflecting intellectual ability typically emerge as more powerful predictors. When IQ does not vary or when it is otherwise assessed, those scales assume less importance.

Intelligence level is also important in another respect. Studies of the personality factors associated with achievement have shown that the bright underachiever differs from the underachiever of average intelligence. The underachiever of normal IQ is likely to have a CPI pattern reflecting an apathetic or lackadaisical attitude, while the bright underachiever is more likely to be rebellious and antisocial (Gough, 1963).

Not only academic and intellectual levels are relevant in such studies; sex differences in the factors associated with achievement are also important. In addition, the criterion of achievement must be considered. Most studies use the overall GPA as the criterion. In those, the longer the period over which the average is calculated, the more reliable the criterion. GPAs based on four years of college work are much more stable and satisfactory measures than those obtained after the first quarter of the freshman year. Other studies use grades in a particular course—introductory psychology is a favorite—or a particular area, such as mathematics. As Domino (1968) has demonstrated, courses of study that emphasize rote learning and memory will show a different pattern of correlations than those requiring independent thought. Some investigators have used completion of a degree program or dropping out of school as criteria of achievement. Since so many situational factors such as marriage, military service, and finances can influence those latter criteria, a weaker relationship with the CPI is to be expected.

Achievement in Elementary School

Studies of young subjects on the CPI are always somewhat suspect because reading problems can seriously influence the results. This is probably one reason why there are few studies relating the CPI to academic achievement in elementary school students. Keimowitz and Ansbacher (1960) compared the CPI scores of twenty-nine boys who were overachievers in the area of mathematics with twenty-seven designated as underachievers (on the basis of discrepancies between their scores on the Otis and a standard mathematics achievement test). Using a covariance analysis to control for intelligence, they found the overachievers significantly higher on eleven scales (*Cs, Sy, Sp, Re, So, Sc, To, Gi, Ac, Ai, Ie,* and *Py*), and significantly lower on one (*Cm*).

Bennett (1970) divided underachieving eighth-grade boys into high and low achievers on the basis of discrepancies between Stanford Achievement Test scores and measures of intelligence. She found no significant differences on factor scores for the CPI. Given the probable homogeneity of the original sample as well as the reading difficulties likely in a population of underachieving eighth-graders, the failure to find reliable differences is not surprising.

Baron (1968) contrasted the CPI scores of boys and girls of normal intelligence who did well on a programmed English course with those who did poorly. The study was thus unusual in respect to both the subject population and criterion of achievement. Baron found three CPI scales differentiated the high from the low achieving boys: *Sa, Cm,* and *Fe,* while *To, Ac,* and *Fe* separated the high and low achieving girls. The direction and magnitude of the differences were not specified in the abstract, but it did indicate that Baron was not impressed with the usefulness of the CPI in predicting achievement in such a specialized area.

Achievement in Secondary School

Many studies, both in the United States and abroad, have investigated the relationship between the CPI and achievement in high school. Some investigators simply correlate the eighteen CPI scales with the students' GPAs. Others divide the students into high and low achieving groups some on an absolute basis, and others with respect to ability, then test the groups' mean differences on the various scales. The results of such studies are likely to be similar to those of the correlational investigations if the samples are split at the mean or median; however, if only the subjects at the extremes are compared, and those in the middle ignored, the investigation is much more likely to find statistically significant differences. The results are less applicable, however, to the problems of the high school adviser who must make decisions about every student.

GRADE POINT AVERAGE AS A CRITERION

Heterogeneous IQ. A study by Benjamin (1970) tested the validity of the CPI among black teenagers in a ghetto community. Benjamin selected the thirty highest-ranking and the forty lowest ranking black students in each high school class, from freshman to senior. (The size of the classes and the proportion of students in the midrange who were excluded were not reported in the abstract available to this writer.) The academically successful boys were significantly higher on six scales: *Re, So, Cm, Ac, Ie,* and *Wb;* the successful girls were significantly higher on *Re, So, Cm,* and *Ac.*

Gough (1964a, 1964c) performed two correlational studies of the relationships between the eighteen CPI scales and GPA using large samples of high school students. In the first study he tested 571 boys and 813 girls from fourteen high schools in eleven states. The results were then replicated using 649 boys and 722 girls from eight states. Gough reports the correlations for both sexes in each sample as well as for the combined sexes in each. These data are reproduced in Table 11. In the second study, Gough (1964c) administered the Italian version of the CPI to 204 boys and 137 girls from four Italian high schools. The correlations of the CPI scores with the grades for those samples are also reported in Table 11.

In those samples, Gough also calculated the correlation between conventional intelligence measures and GPA and found IQ correlated higher with GPA than did any of the CPI scales. However, when he computed multiple regression equations, he found the best predictions could be made using a combination of IQ and selected CPI scales. On cross-validation in the American study, for example, a combination of IQ and CPI scales correlated .68 with GPA, while IQ alone correlated .60 and the best CPI-only equation correlated .56.

Homogeneous IQ. Gough's primary purpose in the two above studies was to derive and cross-validate multiple regression equations that would yield the best possible prediction of high school achievement using a combination of ability and personality measures. Therefore, he left the intelligence level of his samples free to vary and included an IQ measure with the CPI as one of his predictor variables.

Investigators primarily concerned with determining the personality factors most closely associated with achievement have generally sought to eliminate the influence of ability by restricting the intelligence range of their Ss, or by comparing high and low achievers of equal ability. A study by Gough and Fink (1964), used a correlational approach, but most have chosen to compare the mean differences through *t* tests. Such studies are reviewed in this section and the results summarized in Table 12. Table 12 reports the significant correlation coefficients of the Gough and Fink study; for the studies of mean differences, the *p* value of the significant *t* tests is shown. In evaluating a study's results, one should keep in mind 1) The larger the sample size, the lower the magnitude of the mean difference or correlation coefficient required for statistical significance, and 2) those studies which eliminate the middle of the distribution and simply compare the extremes are more likely to report statistically significant findings. The studies in this section compare the CPI scores of high and low achievers of average intelligence; others have made similar comparisons among bright students. Thus far there has been no CPI research on the personality factors associated with differences in achievement level of dull normal or borderline high school students. Spe-

Table 11. STATISTICALLY SIGNIFICANT[a] CORRELATIONS OF THE CPI SCALES WITH GRADES IN SIX HIGH SCHOOL SAMPLES OF HETEROGENEOUS IQ

	Gough (1964a) U.S.						Gough (1964c) Italy	
Scale	Boys Original $N=571$	Boys Replication $N=649$	Girls Original $N=813$	Girls Replication $N=722$	Boys and Girls Original $N=1384$	Boys and Girls Replication $N=1371$	Boys $N=204$	Girls $N=137$
Do	.31	.26	.31	.32	.31	.28	.22	.19
Cs	.32	.28	.34	.36	.34	.33		.19
Sy								
Sp	.17	.11	.10	.18	.12	.09		
Sa	.25	.19	.21	.28	.23	.23		
Wb	.27	.26	.24	.26	.26	.25	.19	.32
Re	.43	.45	.37	.45	.41	.48	.33	.25
So	.30	.33	.31	.30	.33	.35	.25	
Sc	.13	.14	.15	.11	.15	.08	.19	.25
To	.30	.32	.36	.40	.34	.37	.18	.34
Gi			.16	.11	.13	.08	.17	.28
Cm	.25	.28	.11	.31	.19	.31	.27	.17
Ac	.35	.37	.35	.40	.36	.40	.32	.33
Ai	.30	.33	.35	.42	.34	.39	.35	.29
Ie	.41	.42	.38	.45	.40	.43	.26	.25
Py	.24	.18	.23	.23	.22	.17		
Fx							−.25	−.18
Fe					.10	.18	.17	

[a] $p < .05$

cial test procedures to compensate for deficient reading skills may be necessary, and the results would be of interest to many educators.

From a total pool of 1,763 students, Gough and Fink (1964) selected 288 from the center of the IQ distribution whose grades varied as widely as possible. The students' CPI scores were then correlated with their GPAs. The results for 104 boys, 114 girls, and the combined sample of 218 are reported in Table 12. Significant *r*s were obtained for the boys and for the girls on eleven scales; when the data from both sexes were combined the number of significant correlations rose to 14.

Fink (1962b) used a different approach in his study of high school freshmen with IQs from 90 to 110. Dividing the GPAs at the median, he formed twenty matched pairs of high and low achieving boys and twenty-four such pairs of girls. Their CPI profiles, along with a battery of other tests, were presented to three psychologists who then rated each *S* for adequacy of self-concept. The high achieving boys were rated as having significantly better self-concepts by each judge. Only one of the three judges rated the high achieving girls as significantly better. According to Fink (1962a), Jack Block subsequently performed *t* tests to determine the scales differentiating the pairs of high and low achieving girls and boys. Six scales differentiated the boys, four differentiated the girls, and the combined samples displayed significant differences on six scales. The magnitude and the direction of those differences between the means were not specified.

Gill and Spilka (1962) used thirty pairs of Mexican-American high school students matched for age, sex, grades, and IQ, which were all from 90 to 110. One student in each pair was above the seventieth percentile in grades and the other below the thirtieth. Only four CPI scales, *So, Ac, Ai,* and *Ie* were administered, and three significantly differentiated the two groups. (There are no data available to gauge the distortion introduced by administering only selected scales.)

The studies of average-ability students are fairly consistent: *Re* and *So* were significantly related to achievement in every sample in which they were included. *Wb, Ac,* and *Ie* had significant relations in every sample but one. Several other scales had significant correlations in several comparisons, usually those by Gough and Fink (1964) in which the large size of the initial subject pool (1,763) probably ensured great diversity on the achievement measure.

In studies of more gifted students, Pierce (1961) selected a sample of fifty-four bright tenth-graders whose mean IQs had all exceeded the seventieth percentile of their class when tested in the fourth grade. The use of an intelligence estimate based on not one, but four different tests, is commendable, but it is unfortunate Pierce did not have more recent data on which to make his selection. The criterion of achievement was a weighted average of grades in which college preparatory courses were weighted *three,* vocational training courses *two,* and extracurricular activities along with physical education weighted *one.* Dividing those weighted averages at the median, Pierce (1961) formed groups of high and low achievers equal in IQ, then compared their CPI scores; half of the eighteen scales showed significant differences.

From 1,105 male high school students (from thirteen communities in eight states) who had taken the CPI, Gough (1963) selected those whose IQs were in the top 15 per cent of their schools. From that sample, he chose sixty-five pairs of boys matched exactly for IQ but differing widely in GPA. From 1,433 girls tested in the same thirteen communities he took all whose IQs were in the top 9 per cent and selected sixty-three pairs whose IQs were equal but whose GPAs were quite divergent. He then contrasted their CPI scores. As in the Gough and Fink (1964) study in which selection from a large pool maximized the differences in achievement level, Gough found eleven scales differentiating his high and low achieving bright boys, and ten discriminating the girls (see Table 12).

Davids (1966) compared thirty-one boys enrolled in a National Science Foundation summer program, all of whom were in the top 10 per cent of their classes, with fifty-five boys who had been referred as underachievers. The mean IQ of the achievers was 134 and that of the underachievers was 128. (Davids also contrasted his underachieving boys with a sample of high achieving girls, with similar results; however, because of the sex difference, this comparison will not be discussed here.) Given such extreme groups, it is not surprising Davids found significant differences on fifteen of the eighteen scales.

In summary, seven scales differentiated the high and low achievers in all three samples of bright Ss: $Re, So, To, Ac, Ai, Ie,$ and $Py.$ Five others, $Do, Cs, Wb, Sc,$ and Fx reached significance in two out of three comparisons. They were generally the same scales that differentiated high and low achievers of average intelligence.

Overachievement and underachievement. The research in this section also examines achievement relative to ability. The design of studies differs somewhat from those above, however. The investigations just surveyed controlled for IQ by selecting pairs of Ss equal in tested intelligence but different in GPA. The investigations reviewed in this section, however, compute indices of achievement relative to ability for each individual subject. Students high on such indices are designated as overachievers, those in the midrange are considered average achievers, and those at the lower end are defined as underachievers.

Such an approach is attractive. It has an intuitive appeal and is much less wasteful of subjects than is a matching design. However, there are often problems associated with the interpretation of such index data. It is quite possible for an overachiever to have a lower GPA than an underachiever, because a dull student with a C average might be considered an overachiever while a bright student with a B average is designated as an underachiever. In some studies or settings that might present a problem. A more difficult situation arises when the sample shows much more variability on one measure than the other. Luttrell (1969), in a study of the relationship between the CPI and achievement in home economics courses, found significant negative correlations between the achievement index and several CPI scales that usually correlate positively with academic achievement. The achievement index was based on the difference between the GPA and the ability measure. (In fairness to Luttrell, it should be pointed out that this poorly considered index was devised by E. I. Megargee, a rather thickheaded member of her thesis committee who insisted she use it in her study.) Unfortunately her sample had little variability in achievement and great diversity in ability. Thus the differences between Ss on the achievement index were almost solely a function of the differences on the ability measure; the higher the ability, the lower the achievement index. Instead of correlating negatively with achievement, as it first appeared, the CPI scales were in effect correlating negatively with the reciprocal of IQ. Such problems must be considered in evaluating studies using index measures.

A more difficult procedure, but one which avoids some of the problems inherent in index scores, is to use residual scores, measures of achievement in which the influence of ability has been statistically partialled out. Of course, in that method, as with all procedures in which achievement relative to ability is considered, the investigator must worry about the reliability of both his test measures, and larger samples are often required.

Snider and Linton used an achievement index described as, "a deviation score . . . which took into consideration the individual's capacity and performance" (Snider and Linton, 1964, p. 109). Using that measure they formed twenty-eight pairs of adequately achieving and underachieving boys, and nineteen pairs of girls. The ability level of the groups was matched. They then compared the achievers and underachievers on the eighteen CPI scales. Their results, summarized in Table 13, show that three scales discriminated the achieving from the underachieving boys, four did so for the girls, while five differentiated the groups when the sexes were combined.

In the preceding section Pierce's (1961) study of achievement using matched samples of tenth graders was described. In that investigation, he also studied the relation between the CPI and achievement in a sample of twelfth-graders using a slightly different design. As in the study of the tenth-graders, the ability measure consisted of the average of four intelligence tests administered some years before, in this case in the sixth-grade. The achievement measure was a weighted average of high school grades emphasizing college preparatory courses. Pierce then used these data to derive an achievement index based on the difference between a student's rank on the achievement and ability measures. The twelfth-graders above the median on this index were then classified as high achievers and those below as low achievers; their scores on all of the CPI scales except *Sp, Gi, Py,* and *Fe*, which were not administered, were compared. Significant differences were obtained on eight of the fourteen scales (see Table 13).

Standridge (1968) administered the California Test of Mental Maturity, the Iowa Test of Educational Development, and the CPI to 840 eleventh- and twelfth-graders. After determining the regression of achievement on ability, he constituted groups of male and female overachievers, average achievers, and underachievers. Comparing the overachievers with the combined average and the underachievers, he found that nine scales significantly discriminated in the male sample and five in the female. When he compared the underachievers with the overachievers and average achievers, the number of scales discriminating significantly dropped to a chance level. He concluded that the CPI is more effective in detecting overachievement than underachievement.

The relationship between the CPI scales and those achievement indices resembles in certain respects the pattern noted for the other studies of the CPI and high school achievement, but there are some noteworthy differences. The *Ie* scale differentiated the overachievers and underachievers most consistently, followed closely by *Ai*. Those are the two CPI scales most closely correlated with intelligence; *Ai* has a correlation of .53 with the Concept Mastery Test and *Ie* an $r = .58$. Since ability-measures figure so heavily in the calculation of the vari-

Table 12. CPI Scales Significantly[a] Differentiating Achievement Levels in High School Samples with Homogeneous IQs

	Significant Correlations			Magnitude of Significant Differences Between Means							
	Average IQ Ss			Average IQ Ss				Bright Ss			
	Gough and Fink (1964)			Fink (1962a, b)			Gill and Spilka (1962)	Pierce (1961)	Gough (1963)		Davids (1966)
	Boys N = 104 r	Girls N = 114 r	Boys and Girls N = 218 r	Boys: 22 High versus 22 Low Achievers	Girls: 24 High versus 24 Low Achievers	Boys and Girls: 44 High versus 44 Low Achievers	30 High versus 30 Low Achievers Mexican-American Students	Boys: 27 High and 27 Low Achievers	Boys: 65 Achievers and 65 Underachievers	Girls: 63 Achievers and 63 Underachievers	Boys: 29 High and 29 Low Achievers
Do	.22	.25	.21				NA[b]		3.54		4.27
Cs		.23	.18				NA[b]		1.66	2.32	2.90
Sy	.22						NA[b]				3.29
Sp							NA[b]				5.43
Sa	.20						NA[b]				2.77
Wb	.29	.19	.19	+[c]	+[c]	+[c]	NA[b]		2.10	2.60	8.41

Re	.37	.33	.37	+	+	+	+	NA[b]	4.40	4.63	4.77	4.66
So	.41	.19	.34	+	+	+	+	3.75	6.50	4.71	4.93	6.95
Sc	.22		.18					NA[b]	3.70		3.25	3.24
To		.20	.19	+	+			NA[b]	2.70	1.91	4.22	4.41
Gi			.14					NA[b]			3.07	
Cm	.37	.26	.35	+	+	+		NA[b]				5.17
Ac	.37	.34	.35	+	+	+	+	4.35	3.00	3.71	4.06	6.20
Ai	.22	.27	.25					ns	2.60	1.73	3.58	4.65
Ie	.34	.30	.29	+	+	+	+	3.20	2.50	2.34	3.69	7.96
Py		.25	.16					NA[b]	1.25	0.98		2.59
Fx								NA[b]				
Fe		.19	.28					NA[b]	2.70	1.43		

[a] $p < .05$

[b] NA: Scale not administered

[c] High achievers significantly higher but magnitude of mean difference not reported.

Table 13. MAGNITUDE OF SIGNIFICANT[a] DIFFERENCES BETWEEN THE CPI SCORES OF HIGH AND LOW ACHIEVERS IN HIGH SCHOOL

| Sample Scale | Snider and Linton (1964) Canadian Achievers versus Underachievers | | | Pierce (1961) | Standridge (1968) BOYS | | | GIRLS | | |
	28 Pairs of Boys	19 Pairs of Girls	47 Pairs of Girls and Boys	25 High versus 25 Low Achievers Boys	35 Overachievers versus 30 Average Achievers	30 Average Achievers versus 28 Underachievers	35 Overachievers versus 28 Underachievers	44 Overachievers versus 31 Average Achievers	31 Average Achievers versus 23 Underachievers	44 Overachievers versus 23 Underachievers
Do					5.43		5.59			
Cs				4.10		1.98	3.23	2.98		3.86
Sy				4.00						
Sp				NA[b]						4.67
Sa										

Scale							
Wb	4.70						
Re	3.70	2.40	6.12	4.37	**5.40**	3.52	3.16
So	4.50	3.70	3.88	4.66			
Sc							
To	4.00	3.83	6.10	3.42	4.70		
Gi	3.10	2.70	NA[b]				
Cm	1.20						
Ac	2.50	4.90	3.48	4.13			
Ai	2.60	7.60	3.72	5.23	2.35	4.30	
Ie	3.80	2.30	3.70	4.12	6.46	3.07	4.15
Py	2.10	NA[b]	2.08	2.50			
Fx	1.82	2.26	4.08				
Fe	NA[b]						

[a] $p < .05$

[b] NA = Not administered

ous achievement indices, it is not surprising that the scales should assume greater importance. By the same token, some of the measures of values, notably *So,* were less likely to significantly discriminate achievement levels as operationally defined by index scores.

Overall, the pattern of significant differences varied more from study to study when indices were used as criteria. That may reflect their greater unreliability, the fact that different investigators used different measures, or the fact that less extreme contrast groups were used. Such differences, however, were outweighed by the similarities. As in the other studies it was the factor 1 and factor 3 scales on which the achieving groups were found to be significantly higher.

OTHER CRITERIA

All of the studies reviewed thus far have used high school grades or measures based on grades as their criteria. As students with poor grades frequently point out, GPA is not the only measure of success. Gough has performed studies of the relations between the CPI and two other criteria of achievement in high school: graduating from high school and going on to college.

Graduation from high school. In studying the differences between high school graduates and dropouts, Gough (1964c) followed his usual procedure of first comparing the groups on the standard scales, separately by sex, and then replicating his findings on a new sample before going on to derive and cross-validate a multivariate prediction equation. His initial sample was composed of 780 male and 881 female students from three high schools in different areas of the United States who had been tested with the CPI. Followup data showed that 124 boys and 160 girls dropped out before graduation. Their mean CPI scores were compared with those of the 656 boys and 721 girls who received their diplomas. The replication study used 406 boys, of whom 352 graduated and fifty-four did not, and 413 girls of whom 357 graduated and fifty-six did not. The magnitudes of the statistically significant differences are presented in Table 14. Five scales differentiated the graduates from the dropouts in all four comparisons: *Wb, Re, So, To,* and *Ie.* In addition, *Cs, Cm,* and *Ac* discriminated significantly in three of the four. In each significant comparison it was the graduates who had the higher scores. Given the relationship between grades and graduation, it is not surprising that the same basic scales should emerge as the primary discriminators.

College attendance. While dropping out of high school before graduation can be considered evidence of below average achievement, going on to college shows above average achievement motivation. Would the same CPI scales differentiate the graduates who went to college from others of equal ability who did not? (See Figure 11.) Gough (1968b) attacked this question by first reviewing the research files of 1,784 students who had taken the CPI in order to locate students with high IQs. From that select sample, fifty-five pairs of women and fifty-five pairs of men of equally high ability were formed. In each pair one member had gone to college and the other had not. Their CPI scores were contrasted. To replicate these findings, Gough surveyed the protocols of another 1,056 students to form fifty-four new female and fifty-two new male pairs. The results of those four comparisons are presented in Table 14.

Gough next sought to determine whether the same pattern of scales would

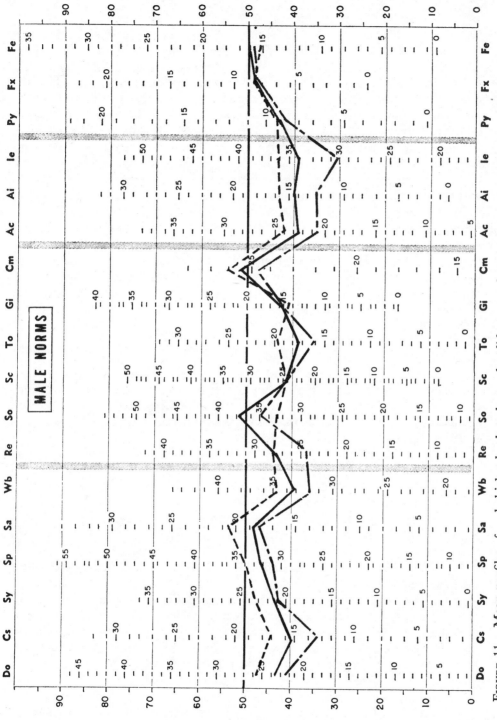

FIGURE 11. Mean profiles of male high school students who did not graduate, who graduated but did not go to college, and who graduated and did go to college. Broken line: went to college ($N = 227$). Solid line: graduated but did not go to college ($N = 124$). Dot-dash line: dropped out ($N = 189$). Data from Gough (1966c, 1968b).

relate to college attendance among students in general. He gathered the CPI scores of 416 high school boys (of whom 227 had gone to college and 189 had not) and from 483 high school girls (of whom 176 had matriculated at college and 307 had not). Because four complete high school classes had been used, Gough felt justified in calculating point-biserial correlations between each of the eighteen CPI scales and a dichotomous criterion of college attendance for both men and women. He found that for both sexes thirteen of the eighteen CPI scales correlated significantly with college-going. Moreover, the magnitude of many of these correlations equaled or exceeded the correlation between a measure of intelligence and college-going. (See Table 14.)

The results make an interesting contrast to the study on high school graduation. The data suggest that social interaction patterns are as important as values in the choice to seek higher education or not. As before, *Re* and *Ac* are among the primary predictors, and *Ie* is an important predictor when IQ is not held constant. However, in the college attendance study the factor 2 scales such as *Do, Cs, Sy,* and *Sa* assumed equal, if not greater importance, particularly among the women. On the other hand, the role of *So* as a predictor was considerably diminished. Apparently inadequate socialization can lead to dropping out of school, but above average socialization does not make it more likely that one will attend college.

WEIGHTED COMBINATION OF SCALES

Many CPI scales were found to relate to high school achievement. That is probably as much due to the complexity of the criterion as to the redundancy of the test. Indeed, scales loading on all five CPI factors were found to relate significantly to achievement in the studies just reviewed, although the most consistent performers were the factor 1 scales.

Another aspect of the data worth noting is that the absolute magnitudes of the differences between the means were rarely high enough to evoke confidence in the accuracy with which any given scale could forecast achievement in high school, particularly for those *S*s in the mid-range. Gough states that he designed the inventory so that if a given criterion could not be predicted adequately using a single scale, a weighted combination of scales might be employed. The pattern of results just surveyed, showing a large number of significant but relatively low-order relationships, inspired him and others to derive multivariate equations for the prediction of GPA.

The procedures for constructing such equations are straightforward, although the actual mechanics of computation and the equations that result can be quite complex. In many ways the procedure is similar to constructing an inventory scale except that the units involved are scale scores rather than item scores. Like scales, prediction equations can be put together rationally or empirically. When using a rational method, the investigator can combine whatever measures strike his fancy and weight them as he pleases. Once this is done, he must validate his formula by determining how closely the predicted GPAs correspond to the actual grades.

Most investigators prefer to use empirical methods to derive their equations. The first step is to obtain criterion data on a sample; in such studies cri-

Table 14. MAGNITUDE OF SIGNIFICANT RELATIONS* BETWEEN MEAN CPI SCORES OF HIGH SCHOOL GRADUATES AND DROPOUTS AND BETWEEN GRADUATES WHO CONTINUE AND TERMINATE THEIR EDUCATION

	Significant differences between means								Significant Correlations	
	Gough (1966c) (High School Graduation)				Gough (1968b) (College Attendance)				Gough (1968b)	
	Graduates (G) vs. Dropouts (DO)				College (C) vs. Noncollege (N)				.416 483	
	Male		Female		Male		Female		Men	Women
	656 G vs. 124 DO	352 G vs. 54 DO	721 G vs. 160 DO	357 G vs. 56 DO	55 C vs. 55 N	52 C vs. 52 N	55 C vs. 55 N	54 C vs. 54 N		
Do	1.21				5.55	5.63	3.42	3.16	.35	.42
Cs	1.62	3.60		4.66		2.69	3.03	2.87	.39	.54
Sy		5.04		5.95		2.39	4.18	2.30	.36	.37
Sp	1.27	5.32					2.27		.33	.31
Sa	0.88	3.68				3.15	2.09	1.61	.30	.37
Wb	1.18	6.98	2.04	6.94				2.29	.34	.17
Re	2.86	5.50	2.15	5.13	5.11	2.36	2.04		.44	.27
So	2.81	5.84	2.57	6.73	6.01				.29	
Sc			2.13							
To	1.57	5.18	2.51	6.09			2.62	2.79	.36	.32
Gi										
Cm	0.78	3.92	0.73						.30	
Ac	2.00		2.08	5.76	4.63	2.91	2.62	2.18	.34	.30
Ai	1.98		1.39				1.70		.28	.31
Ie	3.19	6.76	2.33	6.44			2.96		.45	.38
Py										.15
Fx										
Fe										−.21

* $p < .05$

teria typically consist of GPAs. Next, the relationship between each of the CPI scales and the criterion is determined. Those data have been presented in the preceding pages. Such correlations are then used in forming the equation. There are several alternative methods that can be used, but the goal of each is to find that weighted combination of scales that optimally predicts GPA. Some methods, which require the assistance of a high speed electronic computer, in essence survey all possible combinations of scales, and select the best one along with the optimal weight for each variable. Theoretically, all eighteen scales could be included in such an equation, but in practice there is usually little gain in accuracy beyond five or six variables (McNemar, 1962). A somewhat less demanding procedure, but one which is also less likely to give the best possible equation, is a step-wise technique in which the scale with the highest correlation is selected first. Next the other seventeen are surveyed; the one that most reduces the error is added and so on until no further error reduction can be achieved through the addition of more scales (Draper and Smith, 1966; Hicks, 1964; Nunnally, 1967). Of course, an investigator might not choose to use all eighteen scales. The more scales he includes as possible predictors, the more closely the derived equation will conform to the characteristics of the derivation samples. But because it is "tailor made" for the original samples, and conforms to all their unique quirks and peculiarities, there is a chance the equation might not hold up as well on cross-validation as would a more general equation derived using fewer predictors (Goldberg, 1971).

Just as in scale construction through empirical item analysis, the above methods capitalize on any chance factors that differentiate the criterion groups. It is therefore important that the groups be equivalent on all extraneous factors. Large samples are desirable, not only to minimize the chance of some random error being more prevalent in one group than the other, but also to maximize the reliability of the correlation coefficients that are the raw material of a multiple regression analysis. However, because chance factors can always enter in, it is essential that any multiple regression equation be cross-validated on a new sample.

There is often great temptation among some to examine a multiple regression equation and interpret it as evidence for or against the validity of the various scales that are included or excluded. It must be emphasized that *beta weights are not validity coefficients*. The fact that a scale is included or excluded has no direct bearing on its relation to the criterion because these programs are designed to minimize redundancy. For example, *Ac* might be excluded if the variance it shares with GPA is better assessed by a combination of other scales such as *So, Ai,* or *Ie,* despite the fact that *Ac* might have the highest first-order correlation with GPA. Moreover, a multiple regression equation may include so-called suppressor scales that are unrelated to the criterion, but which assess some unwanted variance so that it can be eliminated. For those reasons one must not infer that an excluded scale, or one included with a low weight, has a lower correlation with the criterion than one with a high weight.

The first equation proposed for the prediction of achievement in high school was rationally constructed. After comparing the CPI profiles of gifted male and female achievers and underachievers in both high school and college settings, Gough (1963) noted that four scales, *So, Re, Ac,* and *Ai,* consistently differentiated the two groups. He therefore proposed a simple, equally weighted sum of those four scales on a rational basis (see Table 15, equation 1), and demonstrated that that achievement index correlated significantly with the dichotomous criterion of whether an individual was an achiever or an underachiever in each sample; biserial rs ranged from .35 to .54. Since the index was validated using the data that had prompted Gough to construct it, that data was not a cross-validation, but simply a demonstration of how scales might be combined to improve the prediction possible with only one scale.

In 1964, Gough published three articles reporting the derivation and vali-

Table 15. EQUATIONS FOR CPI PREDICTION OF ACHIEVEMENT IN HIGH SCHOOL

Gough (1963)
  (1) $Ach = So + Re + Ac + Ai$

Gough (1964c, Italy)
  (2) $Ach = 35.92 + .92\,Ai + .18\,Ie - .81\,Fx$
  (3) $Ach = 34.77 + .33\,Ac + .85\,Ai - .56\,Fx$

Gough (1964a)
  (4) $Ach = 20.388 + .258\,Sa + .445\,Re - .346\,Gi + .230\,Ac + .181\,Ai + .180\,Ie$
       $+ .326\,Py$
  (5) $Ach = 24.737 + .175\,Do + .450\,Cs - .344\,Sp + .373\,So - .315\,Gi + .175\,Ac$
       $+ .328\,Ai + .158\,Ie$
  (6) $Ach = 20.116 + .317\,Re + .192\,So - .309\,Gi + .227\,Ac + .280\,Ai + .244\,Ie$
  (7) $Ach = -.786 + .195\,Re + .244\,So - .130\,Gi + .19\,Ac + .179\,Ai + .279\,IQ$

Gough and Fink (1964)
  (8) $Ach = 21.858 + .380\,Re + .338\,So - .332\,Gi + .256\,Ac + .353\,Ai$
  (9) $Ach = 28.149 + .460\,Do - .586\,Sa + .408\,So - .443\,Sc + .530\,Ac + .369\,Ai$
  (10) $Ach = 28.558 + .182\,Re + .248\,So - .387\,Gi + .370\,Ac + .457\,Ai - .337\,Fx$

Snider (1966)
  (11) $Ach = -11.98 - .201\,Sa + .088\,Wb - .027\,Re + .075\,So + .075\,Sc - .484\,To$
       $+ .116\,Gi + .120\,Ac + .361\,Ai + .130\,Py$

Gough (1966c)
  (12) High school graduation $= -4.513 + 1.027\,So - .210\,Sc - .448\,Gi + .461\,Ai$
       $+ .625\,Ie$

Gough (1968b)
  (13) College attendance $= 17.822 + .333\,Do + .539\,Cs - .189\,Gi + .740\,Ac$

Note: Constants chosen to fit different grading systems.

dation of multivariate equations to be used in predicting various criteria of high school achievement. The first (1964c) was a study conducted in Italy. Two stepwise multiple regression analyses were undertaken using 145 male and ninety female Italian high school students. On cross-validation with new samples of fifty-nine boys and forty-seven girls the equations correlated .42 and .37 with GPA. Using the data from those new samples, the equations were adjusted somewhat, and cross-validated using the opposite sex *Ss*' data. The validity coefficients for the final male and female equations were .40 and .45. They are presented as equations 2 and 3 in Table 15.

    In the next study, Gough (1964a) derived an equation to be used in predicting the achievement of American high school students. The derivation sample was composed of 571 boys and 813 girls from fourteen high schools in eleven states. Three equations were derived, one for males, one for females, and one for both sexes combined. (See equations 4, 5, and 6 in Table 15.) When applied to a new sample of 649 males and 722 females, the validity coefficients for those three equations ranged from .53 to .56. Of the three equations, the one based on the total data (no. 6) was recommended for use since it was shortest and had the highest correlations.

As personality test correlations with meaningful behavioral criteria go, such correlations are rather impressive; however, they are not as high as the correlations between GPA and a standard IQ measure. However, Gough derived another equation using both CPI and IQ (equation 7); on cross-validation the correlation of equation 7 with the criterion (.68) proved superior to the correlation of the IQ measure alone (.60). (A comparison of equation 6 with equation 7 demonstrates the effect of redundancy. The *Ie* scale, a somewhat inefficient measure of intelligence, is included in equation 6; however, it drops out of equation 7 when a better measure of IQ is available. Similarly, the weight attached to *Ai*, a scale on which some of the variance is associated with intelligence, dropped from .280 to .179.)

While the first two studies report equations to be used with any student of any intellectual level, the third (Gough and Fink, 1964) derived a formula for application to students in the average ability range. From a pool of 1,763 students, a sample of 288 who were in the center of the distribution but who differed widely in GPA were selected. Stepwise multiple regression analyses were used to compute three equations, one for males, one for females, and one for the total sample (see equations 8, 9, and 10 in Table 15). On cross-validation, equation 8 had a validity coefficient of .45, equation 9 of .33, and equation 10 of .44. Those data were, of course, based on a sample with a highly restricted range of ability, the total range in IQ being from 103 to 117. It is when ability is thus restricted that personality measures are likely to make their greatest contribution to assessment.

To determine how well those equations might predict performance in a sample representing the full range of intellectual ability, Gough and Fink (1964) also correlated their three equations with the GPAs of the 1,371 students in the Gough (1964a) study. The resulting correlations were .51, .54, and .55 for equations 8, 9, and 10, respectively. The results are thus virtually identical to those obtained with equations 4, 5, and 6.

Linton (1967) and Snider (1966a, 1966b) tested the relationship between equation 6 and academic achievement in samples of Canadian high school students. Each year, all the ninth-grade students are administered provincial examinations; those in the top two stanines are classified *honors* students and permitted to go to the university; the middle six stanines are considered *mediocres* and routed toward clerical and technical occupations, while those in the lowest stanine are designated *failures*. Linton administered the CPI to 124 honors, 164 mediocres, and eighty-nine failures, then computed the mean score of each group on equation 6. The mean score of the honors group was significantly higher than that of the mediocres, which in turn significantly exceeded that of the failures. Unfortunately, Linton failed to compute the correlation of predicted scores with GPA, which computation would have provided a better measure of the degree of association.

Snider (1966a, 1966b) computed achievement scores based on performance relative to capacity and formed groups of forty-seven achievers and forty-seven underachievers matched for IQ, age, grade, and sex. He maintained that that was a better measure of achievement motivation than GPA alone. Applying equation 6 to their CPIs, Snider obtained a tetrachoric $r = .47$ ($p < .005$) between the predicted and the actual achievement level. Despite the relatively small sample size, Snider then used a multiple linear regression analysis to derive his own equation (see equation 11, Table 15). That formula was not cross-validated.

Moving further away from GPAs, Gough also derived formulas to discriminate high school graduates from dropouts (equation 12), and bright high school graduates who went on to college from those who did not (equation 13). Equation 12 was derived from data on 1,661 students and cross-validated on 819 additional Ss. The first order correlations from males and females were so similar that only one equation was derived instead of the usual three; a step-wise iterative multiple regression solution arbitrarily limited to a maximum of five predictor variables were used. On cross-validation, a biserial $r = .33$ was obtained. According to Gough (1966c, p. 213), "This coefficient, although not high, is greater than the biserial values of +.17 and +.14 observed for intellectual ability and GPA, respectively."

In deriving equation 13, Gough (1968b) also restricted the number of terms in the equation. That formula was derived by comparing the CPI scores of 110 men and women who had gone on to college with 110 of equal intelligence who had not. The cross-validation sample was similarly composed of 106 pairs of men and women matched individually for ability and sex, half of whom had gone to college and half of whom had not. On cross-validation a biserial $r = .53$ was obtained for the fifty-two male pairs and a biserial $r = .37$ for the fifty-four female pairs. The equation was then applied to an unselected sample of 899 students of heterogeneous ability from four high schools. For the 416 males, the biserial r between equation 13 and college attendance was .51, which compared favorably with the biserial rs of .36 and .38 obtained from IQ and GPA respectively. For the 483 women, the biserial r with equation 13 was .52, which also exceeded the rs of .40 and .38 obtained from IQ and GPA.

Achievement in College

GPA AS A CRITERION

As Gough's (1968b) study demonstrated, only a select minority of high school students go on to college. This group is not only brighter but is also reliably higher on a number of CPI scales such as *Do, Cs, Sy, Re,* and *Ac.* That restriction on the range of variation makes prediction of college GPA more difficult.

Studies of college achievement are also complicated by the diversity in the curricula offered. Different courses of study reward different abilities and attributes; moreover, the university student typically has much greater freedom to select a course of study that is in harmony with his particular needs. That too can make prediction of GPA difficult, for in some instances the more achievement-oriented student who takes a higher load of more difficult courses may have a lower GPA than his more relaxed colleagues. Colleges and universities vary also in their admissions standards and in the level of performance demanded. The C student at one school might be an A scholar elsewhere. Prediction should be easier at a large state university with a heterogeneous student body than at a smaller, more select school having a smaller range of variation.

Most of the research reviewed in this section was performed before 1957 and reported in the early 1960's. The decade that has passed since those data were collected has been one of tremendous change on the nation's campuses. One such development is new admissions policies designed to end the exclusion of blacks and other minority group members who may have deprived backgrounds and lower College Board scores. As those policies take effect, the applicability of the CPI research of the 1960s to the student bodies of the 1970s will become increasingly questionable and many of such investigations will require replication.

Heterogeneous IQ. As noted above, the range of ability in a college is more restricted than in a high school. Thus the research in this section is not directly analogous to the secondary school studies that did not restrict the IQ range. However, those college studies do represent a greater range of IQ than is to be found in those college studies dealing only with the brightest students.

Griffin and Flaherty (1964) administered the CPI to 170 entering freshmen at Mount Mercy College; they correlated those scores with the Quality Point Ratios (QPR) of the 154 who remained at the end of the freshman year. Ten scales correlated significantly with QPR; however the magnitude of the largest correlation (.26) did not approach the correlation of the SAT verbal score with QPR (.63). Hase and Goldberg (1967) correlated eleven CPI scales with the GPAs of 190 freshman women and found significant correlations with three scales, *Re, So,* and *Ai.*

Gough (1946b) used the less reliable criterion of introductory psychology course grades in a large sample study of achievement. His original samples numbered 867 men and 1,330 women; the replication included 1,133 men and 1,733 women. All subjects were enrolled in introductory psychology courses at the University of California, Berkeley. Many statistically significant correlations were obtained, as might be expected with such large samples. The largest correlations (in the low .20s) were with the factor 3 scales, which assess independent thinking, and, with *Py,* which was designed to measure achievement in psychology (see Table 16).

Flaherty and Reutzel (1965) compared the mean CPI scores of women in the top and bottom 25 per cent of the freshman class at Mount Mercy College. The group with the higher GPA was significantly higher on eight scales and lower on one.

The results of those studies were in certain respects similar to the ones reported for high school students: *Re, Ac, Ai,* and *Ie* continued to relate to achievement, although the role of *Ac* was diminished somewhat relative to *Ai. So* was much less important, possibly because the low *So* students did not go to college. However, *Cs,* a scale relating to social mobility, assumed greater importance. Some sex differences were also apparent. For example, *Do* related to GPA significantly in every female sample but in neither male sample.

Homogeneous IQ. Although the range of ability in a college sample is already skewed toward the higher end of the distribution, some investigators have placed further restrictions on the intellectual range of their *S*s; in each of such investigations of samples with homogeneous IQs, the gifted student has been the

Table 16. CPI AND COLLEGE ACHIEVEMENT IN SAMPLES WITH HETEROGENEOUS IQs

	Significant[a] Correlations					Significant[a] Differences Between Means
	Griffin and Flaherty (1964)	Gough (1964b)				Flaherty and Reutzel (1965)
	170 Freshman Women	867 Men	1133 Men	1330 Women	1773 Women	149 Freshmen
Do	.23			.07	.12	4.52
Cs	.22	.08	.12	.11	.17	2.65
Sy	.23					3.18
Sp			.06		.08	
Sa	.26					
Wb		.09	.11	.08	.06	
Re	.23	.18	.19	.18	.17	
So				.07		
Sc			.10	.10		
To	.16	.20	.26	.18	.22	2.18
Gi				.06		
Cm				−.06	−.08	
Ac	.23	.18	.18	.13	.14	4.27
Ai	.23	.33	.36	.29	.35	1.90
Ie	.26	.23	.27	.19	.23	4.00
Py		.26	.21	.23	.25	
Fx		.13	.20	.11	.18	−1.45
Fe	.21	.08	.06			1.80

[a] $p < .05$

object of study. The primary question addressed by these studies is, "What causes the variations in performance among students who all have the ability to achieve at an A level?"

Two of such studies have used National Merit scholars as their *S*s. In the first, Holland (1959) correlated the SAT and CPI scores of four samples of Merit Scholars and Certificate of Merit winners with their freshman college grades. Like Gough, Holland studied the correlations in one sample (478 men and 185 women), then repeated his observations on a new sample (481 men and 179 women). The results are summarized in Table 17. As might be expected, the CPI scales correlating most highly with intelligence were not significantly related to differences in achievement among bright students. The factor 1 scales had the principal positive correlations, especially *Re, So,* and *Sc.* Most unusual were the significant negative correlations for the factor 2 scales *Cs, Sy, Sp,* and *Sa.* The most facile after the fact explanation for such a pattern would be that students high in those scales spend more of their time in extracurricular and social activities than at the library. However, it goes against the pattern found in the CPI studies of less able students and is not replicated by other studies.

One reason the present writer is inclined to distrust the negative correlations obtained by Holland for the factor 2 scales is the fact that those correlations failed to appear in a very similar subsequent study by Holland and Astin (1962). That study also used National Merit finalists; indeed from the report it seems quite possible that some *S*s from the Holland (1959) study might have participated in the Holland and Astin investigation. Holland and Astin related scores on various tests administered in the students' last year of high school with their achievement in four areas of college life: academic, social, artistic, and scientific. The relation of the CPI to academic achievement (defined as GPA after three years of college) in a sample of 681 men and 272 women will be discussed here. Given large sample sizes, even low correlations are statistically reliable. Therefore, significant correlations were obtained for a number of scales despite the three-year interval between administration of the test and collection of the criterion data. As before, several factor 2 scales showed significant correlations, but this time the relationships were positive rather than negative. One could engage in further after the fact speculations about the differences between freshman grades and those based on three years of college, but at this point a skeptical attitude toward the reliability of such patterns is probably the safest course.

The results of the third study on the relation between CPI scores and GPA among gifted students provides further reason for hesitating before speculating on the relation of the factor 2 scales. In this study Gough (1963) formed pairs of gifted achievers and underachievers matched on verbal ability but differing in their achievement. The thirty-two pairs of males selected from a population of 359 differed widely in their grades in introductory psychology; for the fifty pairs of women selected from a population of 1,199, overall freshman GPA was used as a criterion. The greater number of women available probably meant that the female pairs differed more in achievement than did the male; certainly GPA was a more reliable criterion. The results are summarized in Table 17. As would be expected with smaller samples, fewer significant differences were found. The factor 2 scales did not discriminate significantly in either sample; instead the familiar pattern of significant differences on the factor 1 and 3 scales was obtained. The women differed on more scales. This was probably a reflection of the sampling differences noted above, rather than a true sex difference. The mean profiles for the women are plotted in Figure 12. The magnitude of the differences is somewhat smaller than that found in the more heterogeneous high school samples. The profiles of both groups are elevated, as is typical among bright college students.

Some additional data can be gleaned from a study of the MMPI patterns associated with achievement (Morgan, 1952). Male sophomores who had ACE scores above the ninetieth percentile were classified as high, average, or low

Table 17. CPI Scores and Achievement in College Students of Superior Intelligence

| | Significant Correlations | | | | | | Significant Differences Between Means[b] | | |
| | Holland (1959) | | | | Holland and Astin (1962) | | Gough (1963) | | Morgan (1952) |
	476 Men	481 Men	185 Women	179 Women	681 Men	272 Women	Men: 32 Achievers 32 Under-achievers	Women: 59 Achievers 59 Under-achievers	Men: 40 Achievers 30 Under-achievers
Do					.22	.22			2.3
Cs	-.19	-.11		-.15	.12				NA[a]
Sy	-.21	-.12			.19	.17			NA[a]
Sp	-.26	-.18	-.19	-.24					NA[a]
Sa	-.15	-.12	-.15		.15	.17			NA[a]
Wb		.09			.08			1.98	NA[a]
Re	.16	.19	.25		.12		2.63	2.03	2.5
So	.22	.29	.22	.27	.12		2.72	4.39	NA[a]
Sc	.15	.24	.22			-.11			NA[a]
To								2.68	NA[a]
Gi		.19			.08				NA[a]
Cm					.13	.15			NA[a]
Ac		.19	.28		.14		2.31	2.06	NA[a]
Ai						-.09	1.90	3.30	NA[a]
Ie					.10				2.5
Py	-.10					-.12		2.87	NA[a]
Fx		-.14		-.22	-.13	-.19			NA[a]
Fe	.21	.21	.19						NA[a]

[a] Not administered
[b] $p < .05$

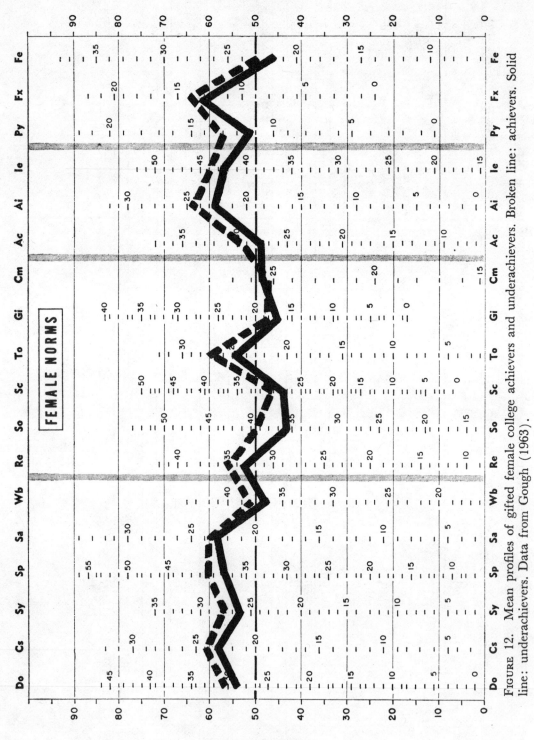

FIGURE 12. Mean profiles of gifted female college achievers and underachievers. Broken line: achievers. Solid line: underachievers. Data from Gough (1963).

achievers. The forty high achievers, who had at least B averages, were compared with the thirty low achievers, who all had GPAs below the class average. In addition to the regular clinical scales, their MMPIs were also scored for *Do, Re,* and *Ie* in their earlier incarnations. The achievers are found to be significantly higher on all three of those scales.

Overachievement and underachievement. Three studies examined the relationship between the CPI and indices of achievement relative to ability. Winkelman (1963) divided sixty male sophomores at the University of Maryland into groups of overachievers, average achievers, and underachievers, on the basis of the discrepancy between their GPA and their ACE scores. She found no significant differences between the CPI scores of the twenty underachievers and those of the other two groups.

Norfleet (1968) used GPA relative to SCAT scores as her index of achievement to constitute groups of high and low achieving women. The twenty-nine seniors in her high achiever group were significantly higher than the twenty-six seniors in her low achiever group on five scales: *Re, So, To, Ac,* and *Py.*

Hase and Goldberg (1967) also computed an achievement index based on actual GPA minus the GPA predicted by the college's admissions office on the basis of a college aptitude test plus high school grades. In a sample of 152 women, no significant correlations were obtained between that measure and the eighteen CPI scales.

OTHER CRITERIA

Graduation from college. Several studies have used completion of a degree program as their criterion of achievement. A person may withdraw from school for many reasons. Sex differences would appear likely in studies using this criterion. No girl ever left school because she was drafted and no boy ever dropped out because he was pregnant. (Whether the Women's Liberation Movement will be able to change this remains to be seen.) In any case, some investigators have refined the criterion to differentiate between those who left voluntarily and those who flunked out.

Swisdak and Flaherty (1964) did a followup study on 170 women who had taken the CPI upon entering Mount Mercy College. After five years, 102 had graduated and sixty-eight had not. None of the differences on the CPI reached acceptable levels of statistical significance although there were strong trends ($p < .10$) for the graduates to be higher on *Cs, Sy,* and *Ac.*

Astin (1964) reported on dropouts among 6,680 National Merit finalists. In that exceptionally able group, the overall dropout rate after three years was 10.4 per cent—8.7 per cent among the 4,472 men and 13.8 per cent among the 2,188 women. Astin calculated the point-biserial correlations between CPI scores and dropping out for the 502 boys and two hundred girls for whom CPI data were available. Significant negative point biserial correlations were obtained on scales *Sc, Ac,* and *Fe* in the male sample and on scales *Sc, Gi,* and *Ac* in the female. In addition, significant positive correlations were found on *Fx* for both sexes and on *Sp* for the girls. The absolute magnitudes of the significant correlations were modest, ranging from .12 to .28.

Hase and Goldberg (1967) correlated scores on eighteen CPI scales obtained when 152 women entered the university with their dropout rates in the first, second, and junior years. None of the scales correlated significantly with that measure.

Hill (1966) did a followup on sixty-two high aptitude students who had taken six scales of the CPI as part of the freshman orientation program at the University of Texas at Austin. Of the 308 men, 179 graduated, seventy withdrew voluntarily, and fifty-nine left involuntarily. Of the 320 women, 201 graduated, 178 left voluntarily, and eleven involuntarily. Hill performed analyses of variance, comparing the mean scores of each of the three groups, separately and by sex. Of the six CPI scales that had been administered (*Do, Re, So, Ac, Ai,* and *Ie*), two (*So* and *Ie*) differentiated among the men and one (*Ai*) did so among the women. On each of those significant comparisons the graduates obtained the highest mean scores and the involuntary withdrawals the lowest; the mean of the voluntary withdrawal group was in the middle. In general, the findings in regard to completion of degree programs are scattered and inconsistent. The magnitudes of the associations generally appear small, but the populations studied and the methods used are too diverse to permit any generalizations to be drawn without further research.

Participation in honors programs. Many schools offer voluntary honors programs for their more able students. Such programs typically involve a demanding course of independent research and study leading to a degree *cum laude.* Not all students who are academically qualified to participate in such programs accept such a challenge. Several investigators have used the CPI to study the differences between those students who volunteer to participate and those who decline.

Mason, Adams and Blood (1965, 1966) used analysis of variance to compare the mean scores of three groups: students who volunteered for the honors program, students who dropped out of the program, and students who were invited but declined. Significant differences were found, but when Mason and Blood (1966) replicated the study they found the order of the means was exactly reversed from the pattern originally obtained.

Demos and Weijola (1966) compared on six CPI scales (*Re, So, Gi, Ac, Ai,* and *Ie*) forty-two freshman honors participants with forty-four others who declined honors invitations. They found those who took honors were significantly higher on *Re, Ai,* and *Ie.* Unexpectedly, they also found the honors group significantly lower on *So.*

Capretta, Jones, Siegel, and Siegel (1963) administered four CPI scales, *Sa, Ai, Py,* and *Fx,* to three groups of students that had been invited to participate in honors: "AS," a group that had accepted and succeeded (N = 49); "AU," a group that had accepted but had been unsuccessful (N = 51); and "DS," a group that had declined but had been successful in their courses of study. The AS and the AU groups did not differ significantly on any of the four scales. The AS group was significantly higher than the DS group on *Fx* and *Py;* the AU group was also higher than the DS group on *Fx.* Interestingly, *Ai* did not significantly differentiate any of the groups.

As with the research on completion of degree programs, the data on participation in honors programs fall into what the writer calls a "George Wallace pattern"—that is, they defy all attempts at integration. Methodologically, the studies by Mason and her colleagues underline the importance of attempting to replicate research, while our inability to compare the results of the other two studies demonstrates the drawbacks associated with administering only a few CPI scales.

As with high school achievement, investigators have proposed a variety of weighted scoring formulas for the prediction of achievement at the college level. There is more diversity to be found in such proposed formulas than in the secondary school prediction equations. Two investigators have proposed formulas which use a combination of CPI and other data. Different equations have been proposed for use with different groups. Finally, a variety of criteria of achievement have been predicted, including achievement in psychology and an overall achievement orientation akin to McClelland's concept of need Achievement.

Gough (1963) proposed that the sum of the *T*-scores on *So, Re, Ac,* and *Ai* could be used as an achievement predictor at both the high school and college levels. When this rationally constructed equation was applied to the CPI scores of four samples of gifted achievers and underachievers, significant mean differences were found in each sample, and statistically significant biserial correlations ranging from .35 to .54 were obtained.

In a subsequent study, Gough (1964b) empirically derived three multiple regression equations for the prediction of grades in introductory psychology among men, women, and both sexes combined (see equations 2, 3, and 4, in Table 18). Those equations were cross-validated on samples of 1,133 men and 1,773 women. Equation 4 proved to be the best of the three; on cross-validation it correlated .41 with the grades of both the men and the women. Equation 2 correlated .39 with the grades of the men and .40 with the grades of the women, while equation 3 correlated .37 and .38 with the introductory psychology grades of the men and the women, respectively.

The last of the formulas involving only the CPI was proposed by Carney (1961), and has since been the object of considerable research by Carney and his coworkers (Carney, 1961, 1963, 1965, 1966, 1967; Carney and McKeachie, 1963, 1966; Carney, Mann, and McCormick, 1966). It is not a college achievement scale in the same sense as the formulas proposed for the prediction of GPA are. Instead it is purported to assess *achievement orientation,* a construct conceptually related to McClelland's need Achievement.

The achievement orientation measure was based on a cluster analysis of the CPI scales which resulted in two major clusters. The first of these was designated *achievement orientation* (AO), the second *social orientation* (SO). According to Carney, "AO indicates the degree to which a person describes himself as dominant, independent, and achievement motivated" (Carney and McKeachie, 1966, p. 137). The scales loading on this cluster were *Do, Cs, Sy, Sp,* and *Sa,* and the measure of AO adopted by Carney and his coworkers was the mean of the *T*-scores on those five scales.

AO is actually a measure of our old friend factor 2. The relation of the factor 2 scales to GPA and the other criteria of achievement typically employed in academic settings has, of course, been tenuous and inconsistent. Instead it is

Table 18. Equations for Prediction of College Achievement
using the CPI

Gough (1963)
(1) $Ach = So + Re + Ac + Ai$

Gough (1964b)
(2) Psychology
Achievement (Men) $= 34.468 - .495\,Sp - .334\,Sc + .263\,Ac + .635\,Ai$
$+ .353\,Ie + .750\,Py$

(3) Psychology
Achievement (Women) $= 37.477 - .224\,Sy + .333\,Re - .158\,Gi - .312\,Cm$
$+ .568\,Ai + .573\,Py$

(4) Psychology
Achievement (Combined) $= 35.958 - .294\,Sy - .180\,Sp + .185\,Re - .189\,Sc$
$- .152\,Gi - .210\,Cm + .275\,Ac + .523\,Ai$
$+ .241\,Ie + .657\,Py$

Carney (1961)
(5) Achievement Orientation $= \dfrac{Do + Cs + Sy + Sp + Sa}{5}$

Holland (1959)
(6) Male GPA $= .16\,$SAT-math$ + .11\,So - .19\,Sp + .17\,Fe$

(7) Female GPA $= .25\,$SAT-verbal$ - .14\,Sp + .06\,Re + .20\,Ac + .08\,Fe$

Demos and Weijola (1966)
(8) Frosh Honors Group: Honors GPA $= -3.077 + .071$(HS. A's)$ - .039$(H.S. B's)
$+ .087\,Re + .056\,So - .024\,Gi - .075\,Ac$
$- .020\,Ai + .069\,Ie$

(9) Frosh Honors Group: Over-all GPA $= -2.728 + .038$(H.S. A's)$ - .070$(H.S. B's)
$+ .101\,Re + .023\,So - .033\,Gi - .050$
$Ac + .001\,Ai + .065\,Ie$

(10) Frosh Honors Refused Group:
Overall GPA $= 1.781 + .042$ (H.S. A's)$ - .012$ (H.S. B's)$ + .001\,Re + .023\,So$
$- .020\,Gi + .021\,Ac + .022\,Ai - .035\,Ie$

Note: Constants chosen to fit different grading systems used.

the factor 1 scales, those which Carney identifies as reflecting social orientation, and the factor 3 scales that have correlated with academic achievement. Carney, however, had not set out to construct a practical utilitarian GPA predictor but to define a personality construct. In that regard his designation of the measure as achievement orientation is doubly unfortunate because 1) it obscures the relation of his data to other research on the factor 2 scales which are generally referred to as measures of social poise and extraversion rather than achievement, and 2) it leads to the erroneous assumption that AO and the research it has generated are conceptually related to the large body of CPI research on conventional academic achievement. While AO has not been used as a grade predictor, it has been related to a sometimes bewildering array of other variables, including a number of measures of physiological functioning, time estimation, perceptual behavior, preferences for different types of subject matter, religious beliefs, smoking behavior, and projective test data. Those studies will be reviewed in Chapter Fourteen on the research applications of the CPI.

The remaining two investigations used the CPI in conjunction with other data. Holland (1959) derived two equations for the prediction of GPA in his samples of National Merit scholars. Both used the CPI and the SAT (see equations 6 and 7 in Table 18). The equation for males was derived from a sample of 476, and cross-validated on a sample of 481 scholars representing 291 colleges. On cross-validation equation 6 correlated .32 with GPA. Equation 7 was derived using a sample of 185 women and cross-validated using a sample of 179. The correlation with grades in the cross-validation sample was .23. Those correlations, while significant, were low; however, they did represent an improvement on the predictions possible using the SAT alone in that sample of bright individuals.

Demos and Weijola (1966) derived three equations to predict GPA in their samples of students who had been invited to participate in an honors program. The first two equations were designed to predict GPA in honors courses (equation 8), and Overall GPA (equation 9) among the forty-two students who volunteered to take part in honors. The third, equation 10, was designed to predict overall GPA among the forty-four students who refused to participate in honors. All three equations used as predictors CPI scales and the number of A and B grades the individual earned in high school. When applied to the derivation samples, the correlations between predicted and actual grades ranged from .62 to .69. However, data based on cross-validational samples are required to assess the usefulness of those scales. Given the small size of the derivation samples, considerable shrinkage can be expected. Moreover, the weights attached to some variables are so small (for example, a weight of .001 for Ai in equation 9) that they could be shortened considerably.

Achievement in Specialized Educational and Vocational Training Programs

The research on prediction of academic achievement in college indicates that the CPI is more successful in predicting a relatively narrow criterion such as GPA than in assessing more general patterns such as leaving school. The studies in this discussion investigate the relationship between the CPI and achievement in a variety of specialized training programs. Since a narrower range of skills is required for achievement in a particular area, such as dentistry, it should be possible to detemine which areas the CPI is most and least effective in assessing.

The homogeneity of the subject population to which the test is applied will vary considerably from study to study. Postgraduate programs such as medicine and dentistry carefully select their students from among those who have completed a bachelor's degree and thus represent a narrow range of talent. A test can improve on the admission committee's decision only by identifying committee-admitted students who later failed; there is no way of determining which of the rejected students would have been successful if admitted. In such situations, where the amount of variation among candidates is relatively small, it is unlikely that the CPI will have a high correlation with the criterion. Never-theless, since admission is likely to be based primarily on ability, a personality measure may discriminate better among those admitted than ability measures will.

Other training programs, such as those for student teachers, are much less selective and consequently have a much more heterogeneous subject population. In these studies, the absolute magnitude of the correlation between the CPI and student success is likely to be higher; however, the correlation of ability with success is also likely to be higher, so while the CPI does better on an absolute basis, it may do more poorly relative to intellectual measures.

STUDENT TEACHING

Several studies have examined the relationship between CPI scales and success in student teaching. Durflinger (1963b) administered the CPI to twenty men and 130 women enrolled in two student teaching courses and correlated the scores with two criteria of success: supervisors' ratings and course grades. The CPI scales correlated more closely with the grades than with the supervisors' rat-ings (see Table 19). An interesting pattern of significant negative correlations with scales *Sa, Cm, Ai, Py,* and *Fx* was found. That pattern suggests that student teachers who are very self-assured, assertive, and verbal, got poor ratings in that setting. Other investigators have not obtained such a pattern.

Veldman and Kelly (1965) dichotomized a sample of thirty-four Uni-versity of Texas women into more and less effective groups on the basis of super-visory ratings and sentence completion data. The more effective teachers were significantly higher on nine of the eighteen scales, the major differences being on *Ac, Cs, Do, Gi,* and *Py.* The pattern had no similarity to that reported by Durflinger (1969b).

On the basis of supervisors' ratings of teaching effectiveness, Hill (1960) divided a sample of 204 student teachers into ninety-eight more effective and 196 less effective students. He then compared their scores on the *Do, Ac,* and *Py* scales. The means were virtually identical on *Do* and *Py,* but the more effective teachers were significantly higher on *Ac.*

In a subsequent study, Gough, Durflinger and Hill (1968) reported fur-ther analyses of the data for 202 of those 204 teachers. The overall sample was first divided by sex, and then the CPI scores of the twenty-five more effective and the forty-three less effective men were compared, as were the scores of the sixty-three more effective and the sixty-one less effective women. The results are summarized in Table 19. Few scales discriminated, and different scales dis-criminated in the male and female samples. The significant differences on *Re* and *Ac* for the women repeated the findings of Veldman and Kelly in their all-female sample. The data did not resemble Durflinger's.

Durflinger (1963a) contributed a study comparing women students who completed the elementary teaching credential program and those who did not. He compared 150 students who completed the program (group A) to three other groups who failed to do so: group B, which flunked out; group C, which trans-ferred to other majors; and group D, which withdrew from the university for personal reasons. The size of those subsamples was not reported, but the total number of *S*s in groups B, C, and D was 314. The results of those three compari-

Table 19. RELATION OF THE CPI TO ACHIEVEMENT IN STUDENT TEACHING

	Significant Correlations[b]			Significant Differences Between Means[a]				
	Durflinger (1963b)		Veldman and Kelly (1965)	Gough, Durflinger and Hill (1968)		Durflinger (1963a)		
						Students Who Completed the Program versus Those Who Did Not		
	130 Women: Significant Correlation with Ratings	20 Men: Significant Correlation with Grades	Women: 17 Effective versus 17 Ineffective	Men: 35 High Rated versus 43 Low Rated	Women: 63 High Rated versus 43 Low Rated	a) Failure	b) Transferred	c) Withdrew
Do			5.94					+[a]
Cs			3.70					
Sy		.26	4.59					
Sp								
Sa		−.24	2.35					
Wb								
Re			3.24		1.86			
So		.26						
Sc								−
To			3.17					
Gi			5.05					
Cm		−.24						
Ac			5.32		2.03			
Ai	−.22	−.31						
Ie			2.65		2.03			+
Py		−.47		1.72				
Fx	−.27	−.45		−0.48				
Fe						−[a]		

[a] Magnitude of significant differences not reported.

[b] $p < .05$

sons are summarized in Table 19. Of the fifty-four comparisons, only five attained statistical significance. The only consistent finding was that those who completed the program were significantly less feminine than those who failed or who left the university.

It is clear from the data reviewed that no CPI scales consistently differentiate successful from unsuccessful student teachers. Because of that, some investigators have turned to weighted combinations of those scales in an effort to improve prediction.

Hill (1960) performed a discriminant function analysis on the three scales he studied and derived the following formula: Teaching effectiveness $= -.003744$ $Do +.005057 Py +.026643 Ac$. Applied back to the original samples, that discriminant function did differentiate them significantly, but the proportion of misclassifications was so high that the formula was abandoned.

Gough, Durflinger, and Hill (1968) attempted to derive a multiple regression equation of teaching-effectiveness using the entire CPI. That study drew on data from all of the studies discussed thus far. The equation was derived by means of a stepwise multiple regression analysis applied to the supervisors' ratings of ninety-one of Durflinger's (1963b) female sample. That equation was cross-validated using Hill's samples. When applied to the male teachers, a significant biserial $r =. 37$ was obtained, but the correlation for the women was an insignificant .13. The Durflinger and the Hill data were then pooled and a sequential multiple regression analysis was performed, yielding this equation: Teaching effectiveness $= 14.743 + .334 So - .670 Gi + .997 Ac + .909 Py - .446 Fx$. That equation was then applied to Veldman and Kelly's data and a significant biserial $r = .44$ obtained. The equation correctly categorized 65 per cent of the thirty-four Ss in the sample. As the investigators point out, further validational work using larger samples is required.

PRACTICAL NURSING COURSES

Thomson (1969) tested the effectiveness of the CPI in predicting grades in practical nursing. His sample consisted of 179 students in practical nursing courses at Brigham Young University who had taken both the CPI and the Differential Aptitude Test (DAT). Although Thomson unfortunately did not include the first order correlations between the CPI scales and the various criteria, he did report in detail the results of a number of regression analyses performed using the CPI in conjunction with age as well as scores on the DAT.

The equation for courses in nursing theory was: Grades $= .0126$ DAT VR score $+.0063$ Age $+.0165 Ai -.0057 Fx -.0068 To$. Thomson's equation for applied nursing courses was: Grades $= .0043$ DAT VR $-.0025$ DAT AR $+.0073$ $Do -.0047 Sy +.0034$ Age. The best overall equation was Grades $= +.2000 Ai$ $-.1469 To -.0646 Fx -.0300$ Age $+.0364 Re -.0149$ DAT VR $+.0061$ DAT NA $-.00123 Cm$. Those equations were not cross-validated on a new sample, but the effectiveness of each in predicting grades on each of the three classes used in the overall study was determined. From those data, Thomson concluded that the equation for the prediction of grades in nursing theory was highly significant, but that overall grades and practical achievement could not be reliably predicted from the regression equations. Data on new samples are needed before those conclusions can be accepted.

The CPI has been used in several studies of effective medical students and practicing physicians. Gough and Hall (1964) administered the CPI to one hundred medical school applicants, thirty-four of whom entered medical school and graduated. Only one scale, *So,* discriminated significantly between those admitted and those rejected. Among those admitted, three scales were found to correlate significantly with overall GPA after four years of medical school (see Table 20). Despite the fact that they had only thirty-four *S*s, Gough and Hall (1964) went on to develop six multiple regression equations using different criteria. Deciding that overall ratings by the faculty were the most important criteria, they reported the following predictive equation: Medical promise = .794 *Sy* + .602 *To* + 1.114 *Cm* − .696 *Cs.* When cross-validated on a new sample of sixty-three, that equation was found to correlate .43 with four-year GPA.

In a subsequent study using the sixty-eight members of a medical school class, Korman, Stubblefield, and Martin (1968) correlated performance on the CPI administered before entering medical school with five factorially independent criteria of success obtained in the last year there. None of the CPI scales correlated significantly with three of these criteria: medical school GPA, ratings of internship success, and ratings of *humanism.* Significant positive correlations were obtained between *Ac, Ai,* and *Py,* and faculty ratings of *scientist potential.* Significant *negative* correlations were obtained between eight CPI scales and ratings of *peer esteem.*

It appears from those data that peers judge their fellows by different criteria from the faculty because the direction of those correlations is opposite to Korman's faculty ratings as well as the data on GPA and the faculty ratings reported by Gough and Hall. It can be seen from Table 20, for example, that *Py* correlated −.31 with peer ratings but +.30 with faculty ratings. Gough and Hall found in their study that *Py* correlated +.32 (ns) with four year GPA and +.22 (ns) with faculty ratings. Korman correlated Gough and Hall's (1964) equation for predicting medical school performance with each of the five criteria of success. The correlations ranged from −.06 to +.08; the most relevant correlation, that with GPA, was exactly .00. It is not immediately apparent why Korman's findings differed so from Gough and Hall's cross-validation. However, part of the reason might lie in the fact that a much larger period elapsed between taking the CPI and receiving the criterion measurement in Korman's study.

Howell (1966) used the efficiency ratings of USPHS physicians to select matched samples of 156 effective and 156 ineffective physicians. She compared their scores on the eighteen CPI scales, but unfortunately only reported whether or not the mean differences were significant at the .10 level (two tail). Given that large a sample and that high a significance level, even a small difference could be classified as significant. Howell reported the effective physicians were significantly higher on eleven of the eighteen scales. (Her report did not indicate which scales, if any, attained more conventionally accepted levels of statistical

Table 20. SIGNIFICANT RELATIONSHIPS BETWEEN CPI SCALES AND PERFORMANCE IN MEDICINE AND DENTISTRY

	MEDICINE				DENTISTRY	
	Significant[c] Correlations		Gough and Hall (1964)	*Significant[c] Differences Between Means* Howell (1966)	*Correlations* Kirk, Cummings, and Hackett (1963)	Gough and Kirk (1970)
	Korman et al. (1968[a])					
	68 Medical Students		34 Medical Students	156 Effective and 156 Ineffective Physicians	58 Dental Students	251 Dental Students
	Peer Ratings	Faculty Ratings				
Do						
Cs	−.24					
Sy			.35			
Sp				+		
Sa						
Wb				+	.30	.18
Re	−.27			+		.18
So				+	.41	.20
Sc	−.28			+		
To	−.23		.34	+		.15
Gi	−.23			+		
Cm						.15
Ac	−.24	.26		+		.28
Ai		.33		+		
Ie			.40	+	.28	.18
Py	−.31	.30				
Fx				+		−.13
Fe	−.25					

[a] Correlations with three other criteria all nonsignificant.

[b] Howell noted effective physicians "significantly higher" ($p < .10$) on these scales but magnitude of differences between means not reported.

[c] $p < .05$.

significance.) Howell also applied Gough and Hall's equation to her data and reported that it, too, discriminated the groups at the .10 level.

The CPI has been related to a variety of criteria of competence for dental students. Using a sample of 910 dental students and applicants, Kalis, Tocchini, and Thomassen (1962) report finding no differences between students rated high and low by faculty members, students high and low in class standing, students who stayed or who dropped out, and students accepted or rejected.

Kirk, Cummings, and Hackett (1963) found that three CPI scales correlated significantly with faculty ratings of fifty-eight students' personal qualifications (integrity, leadership, honesty, and so on). (See Table 20.)

Chen, Podshadley, and Shrock (1967) factor analyzed a matrix of data that included dental school GPA and a battery of personality-test data. Two factors emerged that by virtue of high GPA loadings could be identified as dental achievement factors. One CPI scale, Ac, had a significant loading on one of the two factors. Although the researchers did not report the first-order correlations between the CPI and dental GPA, they did conclude that "for this sample studied, the CPI and the dentist scale of the Kuder Preference Record are practically useless as predictors of student performance in dental school" (Chen, et al, 1967, p. 239). Gough and Kirk (1970) later reported that Chen's first-order correlations ranged from $-.26$ for Sp to $+.31$ for Ac. Given the size of the sample, an $r = .24$ would be statistically significant, although of little predictive value.

Gough and Kirk (1970) took Chen's data and derived two multiple regression equations, one using predental GPA, the Dental Aptitude Test (DAT) biology and carving scales, and Sp, Wb, and Re. Applied to the original data, this equation correlated .72 while a second one using GPA and five CPI scales correlated .66. Gough and Kirk next turned to the data obtained from the 251 dental students studied earlier by Kirk, Cummings, and Hackett (1963). They first correlated the eighteen CPI scales to the final cumulative GPA's. Significant correlations were obtained for eight scales, the highest being .28 for Ac (see Table 20). The second equation derived from Chen's data was applied and yielded an $r = .21$. Not satisfied with those results, Gough and Kirk (1970) used the data on the 251 students to derive three new equations, one based entirely on the CPI, one based entirely on DAT scores, and one based on both types of data. The CPI-only equation was: Dental performance $= 29.938 - .110\ Sp + .148\ Re - .262$ $Gi + .727\ Ac + .230\ Py$. Those three equations were first cross-validated using the Chen data. In that sample, the CPI-only equation correlated .38 with dental GPA. That correlation was higher than the aptitude-test equation (.29) and the combined equation (.35). Next, the CPI-only equation was applied to data made available by Kalis et al. (1962). In a sample of thirty-seven cases, a biserial correlation of $+.38$ was obtained between the CPI equation and the student's ranking relative to the class median. Using the optimal cutting score, the proportion of correct decisions, ("hit rate") would be 65 per cent as compared with a base rate expectation of 51 per cent. (Although such correlations are modest, it should be remembered that those discriminations were made among homogeneous samples of students who had satisfied all the requirements and had been admitted to dental school. Applied to a presumably more heterogeneous population of dental school applicants, it is possible that more impressive correlations might have been obtained.)

SEMINARIES

Query (1966) compared the CPI profiles of twenty-five seminarians who were ordained, with those of twenty-five seminarians who were advised to discontinue their studies. The successful candidates were significantly higher on *Cs, To,* and *Fx,* while the unsuccessful candidates were significantly higher on *Sy* and *Sa.*

POLICE AND MILITARY TRAINING

The CPI has been used in several studies of achievement in training programs by the police and in the armed services. The personnel in such programs are likely to vary more in education, intelligence, and personality than are the samples discussed on the prediction of success in graduate level professional schools.

Hogan (in press) administered the CPI to three classes of Maryland State Police cadets and to forty-three state troopers with one year of field experience. Ratings of cadets by instructors, and troopers by field commanders were used as criteria of effectiveness. Although eight scales correlated significantly with ratings of effectiveness in the first cadet class, only one of the thirty-six correlations in the next two classes was statistically reliable. Eight scales correlated significantly with the ratings of troopers' field performance. The magnitudes of some of these correlations were substantive for this type of study, ranging as high as .55. The pattern for the troopers emphasized intrapersonal values assessed by the factor 1 scales, while that of the first group of cadets stressed the social skills measured by the factor 2 scales. Overall, the *Ie* scale was most closely related to police effectiveness (see Table 21).

In an as yet unpublished subsequent study, Hogan administered the CPI to several Oakland, California police samples; twelve experienced police officers, thirty-one senior recruits, twenty-eight beginning recruits, and forty-two men who had applied for positions but were rejected after an interview and physical examination. Hogan first compared the CPI scores of unsuccessful applicants with all the cadets and officers. Although the unsuccessful applicants scored the same as or above the male adult mean on every scale except one *(To)*, their mean scores nevertheless were significantly lower than those of the successful applicants on eight scales: *Do, Cs, Sp, Sa, Ai, Ie, Py* and empathy. The unsuccessful applicants were significantly higher on *Fe.* Hogan concluded that "the police sample presents a picture of unusual personal soundness and effective social functioning." In a sample of fifty men who had completed recruit training, Hogan found significant correlations ($p < .05$) between class standing and four CPI scales: *To, Ai, Ie,* and *Py.* The results of that study of Oakland police were thus quite similar to those obtained on Maryland State Police.

Collins (1967) correlated the CPI scores of fifty-nine candidates in a drill-sergeant training program with four criteria of success: a test of leadership, academic grades, final class standing, and a field test of combat skills. The results

Table 21. STUDIES OF THE CPI AND CRITERIA OF POLICE EFFECTIVENESS

	Hogan (in press) Maryland State Police				Hogan (personal communication) Oakland Police	
	Significant[a] correlations with ratings of police effectiveness				50 police recruits	71 successful versus 42 unsuccessful police applicants (significant differences between means)[a]
	44 Police Cadets	51 Police Cadets	46 Police Cadets	42 Experienced Policemen	Significant[a] correlations with class standing	
Do	.39					2.0
Cs	.29					1.7
Sy	.45					
Sp						4.0
Sa	.38					1.1
Wb				.37		
Re				.30		
So						
Sc				.53		
To					.35	
Gi				.45		
Cm						
Ac	.31			.55		
Ai	.33			.32	.53	1.8
Ie	.40	.39		.51	.41	2.6
Py				.36	.36	0.9
Fx						
Fe	−.30					−1.7

[a] $p < .05$.

are presented in Table 21. The *Re, Sc, To, Ai,* and *Ie* scales related to all of the criteria except the combat test; only *Ie* correlated significantly with that. Contrary to the stereotype of the drill-sergeant as a rigid, authoritarian automaton, it was the factor 3 scales, which emphasize a nondogmatic imaginative approach, that related most closely to achievement. The *Ac* scale, stressing conformity, and the *Do* scale, assessing dominance, were notably absent from the list of significant scales (see Table 22).

Elliott (1960) administered the CPI to 1088 women entering Air Force basic training. The scores of the 858 who successfully completed the training program in the usual eight week period were compared with those of the 230 who

Table 22. CPI SCALES AND ACHIEVEMENT IN MILITARY TRAINING PROGRAMS

| | Collins (1967) 59 Drill-Sergeant Candidates Significant[b] Correlations with | | | | Elliott (1960) 858 Successful versus 230 Unsuccessful WAF Trainees | Rosenberg, McHenry, Rosenberg, and Nichols (1962) Significant Correlations[b] with Grades in Military Courses in | |
	Leadership	Academic Standing	Class Standing	Combat Proficiency	Significant Differences Between Means[b]	Clinical Psychology- Social Work ($N=98$)	Neuropsychiatric Procedures ($N=64$)
Do					1.7	.20	.31
Cs					1.1	.38	.44
Sy					1.5		
Sp						.32	
Sa					1.2	.35	
Wb					2.4	.24	
Re	.40		−.34		1.8	.25	
So					2.2		
Sc	.36		−.30		2.0		
To	.41	.39	−.41		1.5	.42	.23
Gi					1.2		
Cm							
Ac					2.2		
Ai	.37	.38	−.41		0.6	.46	.47
Ie	.29	.28	−.29	.30	1.7	.37	.31
Py						.21	
Fx					−0.2	.38	.34
Fe							

[a] Negative correlations because the best student had rank "1"; the poorest, rank "59."

[b] $p < .05$.

failed to finish training on schedule. Statistically significant differences between the groups were found on all scales except *Sc, Cm, Py,* and *Fe.* The unsuccessful group was lower on all of the significant scales except one, *Fx,* on which they were higher. In the large samples, differences as small as two *T*-score points are statistically significant and in no instance is a difference of more than six *T*-score points recorded.

The armed forces teaches service men specialized jobs in addition to combat skills. Datel, Hall, and Rufe (1965) administered the *Ac, Ai,* and *Ie* scales to 269 men who completed an Army language training program, and to twenty-one who dropped out; they found the graduates scored significantly higher on *Ai* and *Ie* but not *Ac.* The pattern suggests that intellectual ability may have accounted for much of the variance. Rosenberg, McHenry, Rosenberg, and Nichols (1962) attempted to predict grades for samples of enlisted men in advanced military courses in neuropsychiatric procedures and clinical psychology-social work. Six scales correlated with the course grades in neuropsychiatric procedures; eleven scales correlated with the social work-clinical psychology grades. In both samples the *Ai* scale had the highest correlation. A measure of intelligence correlated higher than any single CPI scale, but the best predictions were obtained using a combination of IQ and *Ai.* On cross-validation that combination correlated .56 with the neuropsychiatric grades and .61 with social work-psychology grades.

Generally, such studies of the use of the CPI in specialized training programs indicate that the inventory has considerable promise there. Given a heterogeneous population applying for a position in which a certain personality is most conducive to success, the CPI may be able to assist significantly in selection. In more homogeneous samples, such as medical school applicants, the CPI scales have been less useful, but still may improve on present selection procedures. The research suggests the CPI is most effective when a weighted combination of scales is used; no data have been collected on the accuracy with which a counseling psychologist can clinically (as opposed to actuarially) forecast success on the basis of a profile analysis.

Leadership

Most of the studies relevant to assessment in vocational and educational settings have dealt with the prediction of achievement. Some, however, have dealt with the equally important quality of leadership. In this discussion, the studies of leadership prediction using a full CPI scale profile are reviewed. (Those interested in the assessment of leadership should also review the material in Chapter Four dealing with the Dominance scale.)

The studies made in leadership have generally been arbitrarily divided by researchers into those that deal with *social leadership* and those dealing with *executive leadership.* Social leadership refers to situations in which a leader is chosen from below by members of the group; most of such studies are conducted in high schools and colleges, and compare student leaders with other students. Popularity and social skills often play a large role in such elections, a fact that should be reflected in the factor 2 scales. Executive leaders are more likely to be chosen from above rather than below. Their promotion is usually based on a record of sound administration and management at lower levels in a complex organization such as a business concern or military group. Social skills would probably be somewhat less important and achievement motivation a greater factor in their profiles.

Gough (1969a) used nominations by the principals of 15 high schools in which the CPI had been administered as criteria for the selection of ninety male and eighty-nine female leaders. Their CPI scores were compared with student body member scores at eight other high schools. The results, presented in Table 22, show the male leaders to be significantly higher on every scale except *Fx* and *Fe,* while female leaders are significantly higher on eleven of the eighteen scales.

Using fifty Utah State University leaders and fifty nonleaders, Johnson and Frandsen (1962) obtained virtually identical results: significant differences on every scale except *Fx* and *Fe.* Carson and Parker (1966), using less extreme groups, found fewer scales discriminated. They rated the leadership of 356 Brigham Young University freshmen on the basis of a questionnaire about their high school and church activities. The top 25 per cent were then classified as leaders, the middle 50 per cent as average leaders, the bottom 25 per cent as nonleaders, and the differences were tested among the three means by analyses of variance. Significant differences were found on three scales: *Do, Sa,* and *Ai* (see Table 23).

Correlational studies using the entire group have also shown lower correlations than one might expect after looking only at studies comparing extreme groups. Holland and Astin's (1962) study of the academic and scientific achievement of National Merit scholars who had taken the CPI in their senior year of high school and were then evaluated three years later has already been described. In that study, the leadership of those students was also assessed by means of questions relating to the number of elective offices held, student or social organizations founded, leadership awards received, or business enterprises initiated. In the sample of 681 boys, thirteen scales had low but statistically significant correlations with the criterion; two scales correlated negatively, the rest positively. In the smaller sample of 272 girls, a higher correlation was needed for statistical significance, and significant correlations were obtained on only seven scales. Of those, three were negative and the rest positive. Appropriately, the highest correlations in both samples ($r = .22$) were with the *Do* scale.

Armilla (1967) used as his criterion of social leadership an assessment of self-report questionnaires filled out by seventy-five Peace Corps volunteers assigned to Latin America. He then scored their MMPIs for several special scales which included abbreviated versions of four CPI scales: *Do, Sy, Sp,* and *Re.* All except *Sp* were scales for which Megargee (1966b) found the MMPI version to provide a reasonably good approximation. Two scales correlated significantly with the criterion, *Do* ($r = .21$), and *Sy* ($r = .30$).

In general, those studies showed that many CPI scales are sensitive to the differences between social leaders and nonleaders. However, in many of such studies, extreme differences and large samples have been used, so even small differences emerge as statistically significant. Of the eighteen CPI scales, the factor

Table 23. RESULTS OF STUDIES RELATING CPI SCALES TO SOCIAL LEADERSHIP

| | Significant Correlations[a] | | | Significant Differences Between Means[d] | | | | | |
| | Holland and Astin (1962) National Merit Finalists | | Armilla (1967) | High School Students — Gough, 1969a | | Johnson and Frandsen (1962) | College Students — Carson and Parker (1966) | | |
	681 Boys	272 Girls	75 Peace Corps Volunteers	Boys: 90 Leaders versus 1,121 Nonleaders	Girls: 89 Leaders versus 1,290 Nonleaders	50 Leaders versus 50 Nonleaders	48 Leaders versus 81 Average Leaders	81 Average Leaders versus 35 Nonleaders	48 Leaders versus 35 Nonleaders
Do	.22	.22	.21	4.75	4.53	9.0[a]		2.70	4.60
Cs	.12		NA[b]	3.10	4.76	6.0			
Sy	.19	.17	.30	3.93	4.56	6.5			
Sp			ns[c]	3.00	4.08	5.5			
Sa	.15	.17	NA[b]	2.52	3.97	4.3		1.90	3.50
Wb	.08		NA[b]	3.64	2.03	5.5			
Re	.12		ns[c]	4.04	1.63	5.0			
So	.12		NA[b]	2.88		2.5			
Sc		-.11	NA[b]	2.79					
To			NA[b]	3.44	2.67	7.0			
Gi	.08		NA[b]	1.79		5.5			
Cm	.13	.15	NA[b]	0.83		5.0			
Ac	.14		NA[b]	4.04	2.92	1.25			
Ai	-.09		NA[b]	2.42	1.55	7.0		1.90	2.05
Ie	.10		NA[b]	4.83	4.31	6.0			
Py		-.12	NA[b]	1.31		8.0			
Fx	-.13	-.19	NA[b]			2.7			

[a] Mean differences approximated from profile.
[b] NA: Not administered.
[c] ns: not significant.
[d] $p < .05$.

2 scales in general and the *Do* scale in particular seem to provide the best discrimination.

The second type of leadership to be considered is the actual ability to direct or to supervise others. Because it is less dependent on popularity than social leadership, it is likely that it may be associated with a somewhat different CPI pattern.

Several studies discussed in detail in Chapter Four reviewed the degree to which the CPI *Do* scale could assess such a quality. It will be recalled that those studies showed the *Do* scale could discriminate between officers and enlisted men, and that it related significantly to leadership ratings made by others. Megargee and his coworkers, using simulated industrial and clerical tasks, found *Do* could forecast which member of a team would emerge as a leader, but demonstrated the importance in making such predictions of situational factors such as the nature of the instructions, sex, or race of the team members. (Fenelon and Megargee, 1971; Megargee, 1969; Megargee, Bogart and Anderson, 1966).

In studies using the entire CPI, Rawls and Rawls (1968) used salary level, job title, and ratings of performance to select thirty highly successful and thirty less successful men from the 130 executives employed by a medium-sized utilities firm. They found the more successful executives were significantly higher on *Do, Cs, Sy, Sp, Sa, Ie, Py,* and *Fx,* and significantly lower on *Fe* and *Sc.* In a broad study involving executives from thirteen firms, Mahoney, Jerdee, and Nash (1961) identified seventy-five more effective and seventy-five less effective managers, excluding those in the middle. They compared those groups on a battery of tests which included thirteen of the eighteen CPI scales (*So, Cm, Ac, Ai,* and *Py* were deleted). Of the thirteen scales used, significant differences were obtained on two, *Do* ($p < .01$) and *Wb* ($p < .02$). *Do* was retained and used in a multivariable procedure for selecting effective managers; *Wb* was discarded because its relationship with the criterion was too irregular.

Bogard (1960) used the CPI to study the characteristics of union and management personnel selected for special executive training programs because they had impressed their superiors with their potential for leadership. The forty union trainees had graduated from a formal training institute while the forty management trainees had been screened by top business executives. Hodges hypothesized that the trainees from both management and labor would have high scores on the CPI *Do* and *Sa* scales. The mean *T*-scores for the two groups on the two scales ranged from .63 to .66, thus supporting his hypothesis.

As noted in Chapter Eight, Goodstein and Schrader (1963) derived a 206-item managerial scale for the CPI by comparing the responses of 603 managers and supervisors with a heterogeneous occupational sample of 1,748 men. Although items from all eighteen scales were included, several scales (*Do, Cs, Sa, To, Ac,* and *Ai*) had 50 per cent or more of their items selected for the scale. The *Fe* scale had 69 per cent of its items included, but scored in the opposite (masculine) direction. It can be assumed that of the regular CPI scales, those seven would have discriminated the managers most effectively. Leadership has also been studied in military settings. Collins (1967) found that *Re, Sc, To, Ai,* and *Ie* correlated significantly with scores on a leadership proficiency examination in a sample of fifty-nine drill-sergeant candidates (see Table 21).

The studies on executive leadership thus show fewer CPI scales correlating significantly with the criterion. The *Do* scale consistently differentiate leaders, but the pattern for the other scales is more variable. Compared with the studies of social leadership, there is less emphasis on the other factor 2 scales. As expected, the achievement scales seem more important relative to the other measures. *Fe,* the only scale which failed completely to relate to social leadership, emerges in two studies as a significantly discriminating measure, with managers and supervisors being assessed as more masculine.

WEIGHTED COMBINATION OF SCALES

On a rational basis, Liddle (1958) constructed three CPI summary scores. The first consisted of the mean of all Gough's Class I scales except *So;* the second of the mean of all the Class II scales except *Gi;* the third consisted of the mean on all ten of the above scales plus *Ie, Fx,* and a specially devised college attendance scale. He correlated the summary scores with ratings of leadership made by peers and teachers in a sample of 273 tenth-graders. (The leadership ratings were highly correlated with popularity, correlating .76 and .70 with friendship choices among the girls and boys, respectively.) For the 143 girls, the three summary scales correlated .53, .46, and .54 with the leadership ratings; for the 130 boys the corresponding correlations were .48, .43, and .48. Liddle also, with the influence of social class removed, computed partial correlations between leadership ratings and the CPI total score. That lowered the correlation for the girls from .54 to .43 and that for the boys from .48 to .45.

Gough (1969a) performed stepwise multiple regression analyses contrasting the scores of 179 high school students nominated by their principals as outstanding leaders with those of 2,411 other students. The equation was arbitrarily restricted to the best five or six variables. The best five-variable equation, based on raw scores, was found to be: $Leadership = 14.130 + .372\,Do + .696\,Sa + .345\,Wb - .133\,Gi + .274\,Ai$. To cross-validate that index, Gough applied the equation to the CPI scores of the high, average, and low leaders studied by Carson and Parker (1966). Gough (1969a, p. 287) reports, "The correlation ratio for the regression of the index on the criterion classifications was .34, and the *F* ratio across the three means was significant beyond the .01 level. That correlation, although statistically significant, is only of modest magnitude."

Employability. Virtually all of the studies applying the CPI to vocational problems have focused on the successful side of the continuum. A dissertation by Trimble (1969) is an exception because he set out to determine whether the CPI could discriminate a sample of fifty unemployed American Indians from a sample of eighty-four who had jobs. Trimble predicted that the gainfully employed sample would have higher CPI scores, and used one-tailed statistical tests to assess his hypotheses. He found the employed group to be significantly higher on eight scales: *Wb, Re, So, Sc, To, Cm, Ac,* and *Ie.* The magnitude of the differences ranged from three to nine *T*-score points. Trimble's study is noteworthy not only because it explores a different assessment problem, but also because members of a minority group were used as *S*s. The language difficulties Trimble had anticipated failed to materialize. However, even the employed

Indians had below average scores; on four scales they had mean scores below 40 and on thirteen others the mean was below 50. That indicates the need for special norms for such a population.

Schwartz, Dennerll, and Lin (1968) compared on the CPI and other personality and ability measures eighty-eight employed epileptics with ninety-three who were unemployed. They used multivariate procedures to isolate the combination of variables that best discriminated the groups, and reported optimal differentiation occurred when the CPI *Sp, Sa,* and *Cs* scales were used with three scales from the WAIS and one from the Halstead-Reitan battery. Unfortunately, they failed to cross-validate their equation on a new sample. First order biserial correlations with the dichotomous criterion of employed versus unemployed were reported only for the five variables with the highest correlations; among them were *Sa* ($r = .35$) and *So* ($r = .34$).

Concluding Remarks

In the CPI *Manual,* Gough (1969b, p. 5) states: "The inventory is intended primarily for use with 'normal' (nonpsychiatrically disturbed) subjects. Its scales are addressed principally to personality characteristics important for social living and social interaction. Thus, while it has been found to have special utility with a few problem groups (for example, persons of delinquent, asocial tendencies), it may be expected to find most general use in schools, colleges, business and industry, and in clinics and counseling agencies whose clientele consists mainly of socially functioning individuals."

The research reviewed in this lengthy chapter supports Gough's assertion that the primary usefulness of the CPI is in the assessment of behavior patterns relevant to functioning in educational and industrial settings. The first generation studies investigated the associations between the eighteen CPI scales and various criteria of achievement and leadership. A number of studies using different designs and criteria had been conducted so that it was possible to chart the differences in the patterns of relationships found in different academic levels and intelligence ranges. Although the patterns varied somewhat, the results generally show differences that are statistically significant, but of a magnitude too small to be of much use.

Those findings led to the second generation studies by Gough and others in which multiple regression equations were derived to improve on the predictions possible using any one scale. Many of those equations combined CPI data with other test scores or case history information. Although the usefulness of any psychometric device is as much a function of its base rates and selection ratios as it is of its validity coefficient, the data reported on many of those equations nevertheless indicated that in proper circumstances they could make significant and noteworthy improvements in hit rate over current assessment techniques.

The third generation studies have yet to appear. Those are the studies designed to answer Meehl's (1957) rhetorical question, "When shall we use our heads, instead of the formula?" Those, the third generation studies are the ones designed to identify which individuals or situations actuarial formulas cannot classify correctly, such as the interaction of high dominance women and low dominance men (Megargee, 1969b), in which the test-based prediction will be in error.

CHAPTER 13

Clinical Assessment

ᔕᔕᔕᔕᔕᔕᔕᔕᔕᔕᔕᔕᔕᔕᔕᔕᔕᔕᔕᔕᔕ

Despite the fact that the CPI was not primarily constructed to detect psychopathology or abnormality, it has often been used in clinical settings, sometimes as a diagnostic instrument and other times in connection with planning or evaluating treatment programs. In this chapter, some of the literature on the clinical applications of the CPI are reviewed. We shall first examine studies on the relation of the CPI to general maladjustment then others on the CPI patterns associated with more specific syndromes such as alcoholism, psychosomatic disorders, and delinquency. Lastly, studies of the CPI's applications to counseling and psychotherapy are surveyed.

Personal and Social Adustment

GENERAL PATTERNS OF MALADJUSTMENT

Several investigators have reported on CPI patterns associated with criteria of maladjustment globally defined. The typical procedure is to contrast a clinical sample with a normal group. The mean differences on the eighteen scales are then determined and tested for significance. A few investigators (notably, Goodstein, Crites, Heilbrun, and Rempel (1961) have performed more sophisticated multivariate comparisons of profile shape and scale interaction patterns. As those investigators soon discovered, the mass of data accumulating from even the most modest comparisons of the interaction patterns of eighteen partially correlated scales rapidly becomes overwhelming.)

Various criteria of maladjustment have been used. In the study by Goodstein et al. (1961), the files of a university counseling service provided CPI protocols of men and women who had sought counseling for personal adjustment or vocational-educational problems. Their scores were compared with those of students who were not clients but who were tested for research purposes. For both men and women, the mean scores on virtually all of the factor 1 and factor 2 scales fell into a neat progression, the nonclients (NC) having the highest scores, the personal adjustment (PA) referrals the lowest, and the vocational-educational (VE) clients falling in between. The VEs were generally closer to the PAs than to the NCs (see Figure 13). That progression would be expected if one assumes the PAs were most disturbed and the NCs the least. The differences for the most part were statistically significant. The progression from NC to PA was not found on the scales loading high on factors 3, 4, and 5. That is not surprising since those scales are less directly related to personal or social adjustment. On the factor 4 scales, which deal with independence of thought and achievement motivation, the VEs often had the lowest scores, while the PAs frequently had the highest. That might indicate more divergent thinking on the part of the PAs. The clients also had higher (more feminine) scores on the *Fe* scale than did the NCs. That is consistent with Tolor's (1957) report of elevated *Fe* scores among draftees with adjustment problems and with Webb's (1963) finding of a significant association between anxiety and *Fe* scores in junior high school girls. Webb (1963) also noted significant differences between the *Fe* scores of junior high school boys high and low in anxiety; however, in one grade the anxious boys were significantly higher while in the other they were significantly lower. That demonstrates how cautious one must be in making inferences regarding the adjustment of pubescent boys on the basis of their *Fe* scores. Those differences between the patterns found on the various groups of scales led to a number of significant interactions in Goodstein et al.'s study, (which are also discussed by Crites (1964b) but are too extensive to be presented here.

McCloud, in an unpublished dissertation, has compared PAs and VEs with NCs. The abstract of his study (McCloud, 1969) indicates that he also found the clients significantly lower on a number of scales. Leventhal (1966), however, selected 110 students who had sought help with emotional or social problems of moderate to extreme severity and forty who had never sought for counseling. He compared their scores on CPIs administered at freshman orientation a year earlier and found no significant differences.

Self-ideal discrepancy has been used as a criterion of adjustment in numerous studies, so Rosenberg (1962) correlated the CPI scores of 144 enlisted men enrolled in various military courses with their scores on a self-ideal discrepancy measure. He obtained statistically significant negative correlations, ranging from −.22 to −.33 with *Do, Cs, Sy, Wb, Sc, Gi,* and *Ac* (all of which are factor 1 or 2 scales), and a significant positive correlation with *Fx,* a factor 3 measure. That pattern is consistent with the studies already noted; since all of the *S*s were functioning normally, it is not surprising that fewer significant associations were found than in the comparisons of clients with NCs.

Because of the large number of partially correlated CPI scales, some investigators compute summary or total scores of various types and relate them to various criteria. In that procedure the scientist is combining maximally redundant measures, as opposed to the various multiple regression models in which the least redundant predictors are combined. Liddle (1958), after administering an ab-

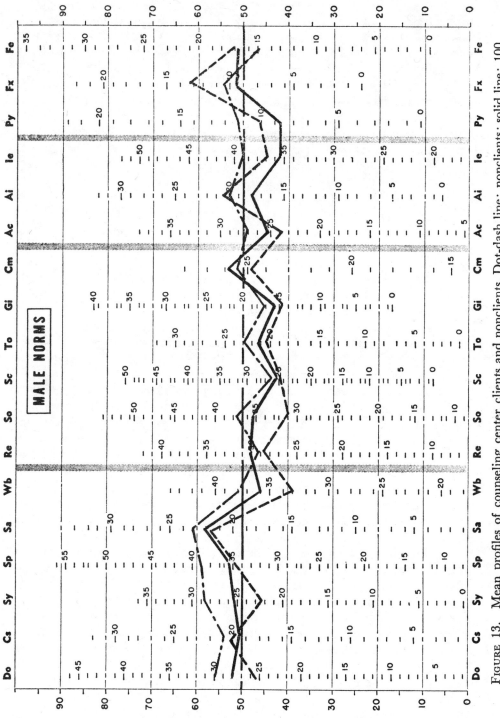

Standard Scores

FIGURE 13. Mean profiles of counseling center clients and nonclients. Dot-dash line: nonclients; solid line: 100 vocational educational clients; dashed line: 100 personal adjustment clients.

breviated CPI to 130 male and 143 female tenth-graders, computed three such summary scores. The first consisted of the mean on all Gough's Class I measures except *Sp*, which he had not administered; the second was the mean on all Class II measures except *Gi*; the third was the mean on all the above measures plus *Ie*, *Fx*, and a specially devised college attendance scale. Liddle correlated the scores with several sociometric ratings, three of which are relevant to social adjustment (friendship, withdrawnness, and aggressiveness). For both boys and girls, the friendship ratings were correlated significantly with all three summary scores; similarly, there were significant negative correlations between the measure of withdrawnness and all three scores for the girls, and with the Class I and total CPI scores for the boys. Both the friendship and withdrawnness ratings correlated higher (*rs* ranging from .39 to .56) with the Class I scores than with the other two. Unlike the other two sociometric measures, the ratings of aggressiveness did not correlate significantly with any of the CPI summary scores among the girls and did correlate significantly only with the Class II score ($r = -.26$) among the boys.

The results of those studies thus indicate that personal and social maladjustment, as defined by various global criteria, are reflected on the CPI by decreased scores on the factor 1 and factor 2 scales. The factor 2 scales are lower in the case of VE problems, but may be elevated in some individuals suffering from personal maladjustment. The latter finding should not be generalized beyond student samples, however, for Gough (1969b) has reported low scores on those scales among hospitalized psychiatric patients.

Little has been reported on the CPI patterns of more seriously disturbed individuals. In the *Manual*, Gough (1969b, p. 34) reports the mean scores of twenty-four male psychiatric hospital patients. However, there is no further information about the specific nature of their psychopathology. The mean scores of that sample, plotted in Figure 14, show a generally lowered profile with one peak on *Fe* and a second minor peak on *Gi*. The factor 2 and 3 scales are somewhat lower than in Goodstein's clients. However, the factor 1 scales are slightly higher, particularly Socialization and Self-control. Profiles based on mean scores are, of course, much smoother and less extreme than those obtained on individuals.

There is bias built into any study of a patient population, for one can never be certain how representative a group seeking or receiving treatment is of the general population of maladjusted individuals. A study by Stewart (1962) is relevant here. As part of the follow-up of the Oakland Growth Study (a longitudinal investigation of human development), 123 *Ss* who had been intensively studied in their adolescence were located twenty years later and reexamined on a number of medical and psychological measures. Since the group (comprising about 75 per cent of the original sample) was not self-selected, it was probably more representative of the general population than groups tested at clinics. On the basis of the follow-up, Stewart comprised three groups. Two will concern us here, the behaviorally maladjusted and the symptom-free. (The third, a psychosomatic group, will be discussed later.) The maladjusted group consisted of ten men and ten women who appeared to be having the most psychological difficulty in one or more areas. While none were psychotic, seven had a history of psycho-

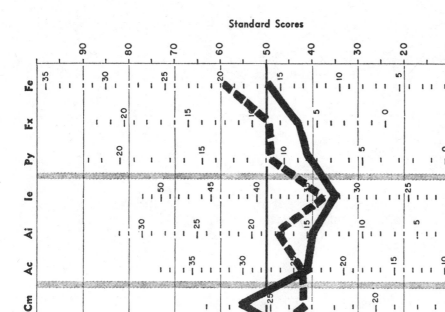

FIGURE 14. Mean profiles for twenty-six neuropsychiatric patients and fifty alcoholics. Broken line: neuropsychiatric patients. Solid line: alcoholics. Data from Carter (1963) and Gough (1969b).

therapy, two had had problems with alcoholism, six had poor vocational adjustment, and six had exceptional difficulties in heterosexual relationships. When compared with the symptom-free group, the maladjusted group was notably and often significantly lower on the factor 1 scales. The maladjusted men and women were significantly lower on *Re, So, Sc;* in addition, the men were significantly lower on *Ac* and *Ie.* There were also noteworthy trends ($p < .10$) for the men to be lower on *Wb, Gi,* and *Cm,* the women on *Gi, Cm,* and *Ac.*

SPECIFIC SYNDROMES

One would expect that studies of specific, well-delineated syndromes might be more productive than global comparisons of well-adjusted and poorly adjusted groups. To some extent that is true, but much of such literature is disappointing. That is so for several reasons. First, the CPI was not designed for differential diagnosis of psychopathology. Instead, it was constructed to discriminate differences in styles of interpersonal behavior within well-functioning groups. There is a strong tendency for different groups of disturbed individuals, whose life-styles are all ineffective, to look alike on the CPI, whether the label applied to their specific disorder is anxiety reaction, phobic reaction, alcoholism, inadequate personality, or whatever. Secondly, the research that has been done on disturbed groups has been relatively unsophisticated. The analysis of the data frequently consists of nothing more than a presentation of the mean profile with, perhaps, a comparison with some normal group. Few investigators have attempted the kinds of complex profile comparisons and scale interaction analyses employed by Goodstein et al. (1961). Third, many of the syndromes studied, such as alcoholism and delinquency, are themselves quite heterogeneous. The one thing all alcoholics have in common is that they drink more than someone thinks they should. Alcoholics can come from all races, religions, regions, and ranks of society. They may be bright or stupid, well educated or ignorant, aggressive or passive, elated or depressed. Averaging the CPI scores of such dissimilar individuals, one obtains the profile of a hypothetically average alcoholic that is not too dissimilar from the profile of the equally mythical average prison inmate, or average person with marital problems. For that matter, many individuals could be included in all of these samples, depending on what aspect of their multiple difficulties the investigator wishes to emphasize. The more heterogeneous the syndrome, the more such average profiles will lack distinctive features. Finally, the data on specific syndromes were often collected as a minor part of some larger project. For example, Canter (1963) reports data on the mean CPI scores of alcoholics in a study whose primary emphasis was on dissimulation. Since such investigations were not intended as normative studies, information was often not included concerning the groups' age, race, SES, education, and so forth.

Chemical dependencies. Addiction to various chemical substances is an increasingly serious problem in the United States. While the term "addict" was once reserved for the heroin user in the ghetto, there is increasing awareness that the problem is much broader. The use of hard drugs is spreading among suburbanites and military personnel, and the use of stimulants such as amphetamines and caffeine as well as depressants such as barbiturates and alcohol is growing. Moreover, addictions are not confined to those substances such as heroin that create physiological dependence; "psychological addiction" can also occur. With the increase in the extent and the breadth of the chemical dependency problems has come an increase in sociological and psychological research into their causes and cures.

Although there has been little CPI research on alcoholism as such, data on alcoholic patients at state hospitals have been reported in studies of dissimulation by Canter (1963), and studies of volunteering by Corotto (1963). The mean profiles of the samples of alcoholic patients reported in those investigations are quite similar. Patterns resemble those of other socially deviant groups, with a general lowering of the overall profile (see Figure 14). The major difference between the alcoholics' profiles and those of other psychiatric patients is in the *Cm* scale; the alcoholics had essentially normal *Cm* scores while the hospitalized psychiatric patients, who presumably were more disturbed and had had more bizarre experiences, had low *Cm* scores.

Hogan, Mankin, Conway, and Fox (1970) compared the CPI scores of four groups of undergraduates who differed in their use of marijuana. Their sample was composed of thirty-seven frequent users, twenty-three occasional users, forty-four nonusers, and forty-four principled nonusers. Significant differences were obtained on ten CPI scales. On most scales, the frequent users and the principled nonusers differed the most, with the other two groups falling in between. As a group, the marijuana users had *higher* scores than the nonusers on the factor 2 and factor 3 scales, but *lower* scores on the factor 1 measures. As might be expected, the marijuana users, all of whom were functioning adequately in college, had a much healthier profile than the hospitalized alcoholics. The only point of similarity was in their low scores on *Re, So,* and *Sc.*

Stewart and Livson (1966) hypothesized that cigarette smokers would have significantly lower *So* scores than nonsmokers, on the basis of their theory that smoking stems in part from rebelliousness. Their hypothesis was confirmed. Adult men and adult women who smoked each had mean *So* *T*-scores 8 points below those obtained by comparable groups of nonsmokers.

Those few studies represent just a beginning of the application of the CPI to the problem of dependence on chemical substances. However, it is interesting that, despite the vast diversity of samples and substances used, one consistent finding has emerged: in each sample the group that used the substance have below average scores on the Socialization scale.

Psychosomatic disorders. Two studies have contrasted patients believed to be suffering from psychophysiological disorders with symptom-free groups. In his follow-up of subjects in the Oakland Adolescent Growth Study, Stewart (1962) located ten men and ten women with such psychosomatic ailments as stomach ulcers, essential hypertension, migraine, neurodermatitis, spastic colitis, asthma, and arthritis. When the CPI scores of the psychosomatic men were compared with those obtained by the symptom-free group, the psychophysiological group was found to have significantly lower scores on *Wb, Sc,* and *Ie;* there was also a trend ($p < .10$) for them to be higher on *Cm*. The data for the women were similar; they had a strong trend ($p < .10$) for lower scores on *Wb* and *Sc* and significantly higher scores on *Cm.*

Unlike most investigators, who limit themselves to contrasting an abnormal with a normal group, Stewart also contrasted the CPI scores of his psychosomatic groups with his behavior disorder samples. He found the psychosomatic men to be significantly higher on *Cm,* and a trend ($p < .10$) for them to be higher on *So.* The psychosomatic women were significantly higher than their behaviorally maladjusted counterparts on both those scales, and there was a tendency ($p < .10$) for them to be higher on *Re,* as well. That pattern, showing patients with psychophysiological disorders to be higher on scales measuring socialization and superego strength, is consistent with theories of psychopathology that emphasize the role in psychosomatic disorders of repression and suppression of anger and other antisocial forms of behavior. Those data also underline the importance of the *Cm* scale in the differentiation of various types of psychopathology.

Stewart's success in obtaining meaningful differences using well-defined cases with a relatively homogeneous symptom syndrome would suggest that focusing on a single psychosomatic disorder would be even more fruitful. Weinberg, Mendelsohn, and Stunkard (1961) did not find this to be the case, however, although that may have been because of the disorder they chose to investigate: obesity. Comparing the CPI data of eighteen markedly obese men with a carefully matched male sample having normal weight, they failed to find any CPI scales significantly differentiating the two groups. The other tests in their battery also failed to discriminate the groups, and they concluded that there were no reliable personality differences between obese and nonobese men.

Similar conclusions were reached by Brown (1970), who investigated whether injured high school football players differed in personality from those not injured. In a sample of 186 players, he found no significant relation between CPI scores and the amount of time lost from practice due to injuries over the course of the season.

Defense mechanisms. Many psychosomatic disorders are thought to stem from repression of emotionally charged material; repressed anxiety or hostility are the most frequently cited culprits. Assuming this to be the case, Stewart's work would suggest that the CPI, and particularly the factor 1 scales, would be responsive to different styles of defense.

A program of research by Donn Byrne and his colleagues has focused on the dimension of *repression-sensitization.* According to Byrne, repressors are those who avoid anxiety-arousing stimuli, while sensitizers approach and attempt to control them. His revised Repression-Sensitization (*RS*) scale, composed of MMPI items, is a well-validated measure of that construct (Byrne, 1964). Byrne, Golightly, and Sheffield (1965) correlated the *RS* and CPI scores of ninety-one students; they report the scales most consistently relating to the repression-sensitization dimension are *Sy, Wb, Sc, To, Gi, Ac,* and *Ie.* Those correlations are all negative, ranging from $-.30$ to $-.49$, indicating that high scorers on those scales are more likely to use repressive defenses. With the exception of *Sy,* all those scales have high loadings on factor 1.

Proceeding from an entirely different conceptual base, Megargee and colleagues have also obtained data relevant to defenses. Megargee (1964, 1965, 1966d) set out to demonstrate that some violent criminals are characterized by excessive controls against the expression of hostility, while other more sociopathic, assaultive offenders are undercontrolled. In the course of that research, an Over-controlled Hostility (*OH*) scale was devised and validated by Megargee and his coworkers for the MMPI. The scale assesses inhibitions against strong hostile impulses (Megargee, 1969a; 1971; Megargee, Cook, and Mendelsohn, 1967; White, 1970). Significant positive correlations have been obtained between *OH* and the *Sc* ($r = +.40$) and *Gi* ($r = +.44$) scales of the CPI, while the measure bears a significant negative relation ($r = -.28$) with the *Sa* scale (Megargee, Cook, and Mendelsohn, 1967). Since repression is hypothesized to be a primary defense mechanism of the overcontrolled type, those data provide further evidence of an association between factor 1 scales and repressive defenses.

It is possible, however, that some of those associations may have been because both Byrne et al. and Megargee et al. used paper-and-pencil, MMPI-based measures of their constructs. Hirt and Cook (1962) had psychiatrists and psychologists sort military offenders into 1) a group manifesting no psychiatric disorder, 2) an acting-out group, and 3) a withdrawn group. The *Do, Sy, Sa, Wb, So, Sc, Gi, Cm,* and *Py* scales of the CPI were administered and the means of each possible pair of groups compared using *t* tests. Despite the fact that the acting-out and withdrawn groups could reasonably be assumed to differ in regard to their use of repressive defenses, none of those nine CPI scales differentiated the two groups significantly. Instead the test appeared to be more sensitive to general maladjustment, for the no-disease group was significantly higher than both deviant groups on scales *So* and *Sc,* and also higher than the withdrawn group on scales, *Do, Wb, Gi,* and *Py.* The no-disease group was significantly lower than the acting-out group on *Wb.* Thus the question of the relation between the use of repressive defenses and CPI scores remains open.

Marital adjustment. Surprisingly little work has been done on the relation of the CPI to marital adjustment. (Ziegler and Rodgers' research on family planning, reviewed in Chapter Fourteen, has yielded data relevant to personality patterns and marital roles.) Aller (1963) evaluated the marital adjustment of one hundred student couples at the University of Idaho. Correlating CPI scores with measures of adjustment, Aller found *Sc* and *Re* had significant correlations with adjustment in the husband. *Sc* correlated positively with adjustment in the wives. An interesting but statistically insignificant trend worth further study was for the wives' *To* and *Re* scores to correlate positively with their marital adjustment, while their *Sa* and *Do* scores had a negative correlation. It is also noteworthy that marital adjustment was more closely associated with scales measuring values than with the factor 2 scales assessing social poise, particularly in view of Hogan and Mankin's (1970) finding that it is the factor 2 scales that relate closest to interpersonal attraction outside marriage (see Chapter Fourteen).

Juvenile delinquency and criminality. Gough (1969b, p. 5) states that people with "delinquent, asocial tendencies" are one of the few problem groups with which the CPI has been found to have "special utility." As noted in Chapter Five, extensive research has established the validity of the *So* scale for detecting that behavior; this discussion deals with the patterns established by various types of delinquent on the test as a whole.

The primary source of data on male delinquents and criminals is the CPI *Manual,* in which mean scores are reported for three deviant samples: ninety-one

high school disciplinary problems, 142 young delinquents, and 194 prison inmates. The mean profiles for those three groups are quite similar (see Figure 15)
and resemble those of the alcoholics in Figure 14. The mean T-scores on most
scales fall below 50, as did those of the alcoholics. However, the profiles of the
asocial groups should be evaluated relative to the norms for high school students
rather than the national norms on which the profile sheets are based. Viewed in
that light, the depressed factor 2 scales are typical of those obtained by high
school boys. In the factor 1 scales, the three samples tend to be somewhat lower
than the high school average on Wb, To and Ac, and markedly lower on Re and
So. They also tend to be somewhat lower on the factor 3 and 4 scales. Thus the
data suggest that their social poise is no different from that of other young men
but that they are unconventional, lack mature values, and are unable to sublimate
or channel their nonconformity into creative or intellectual channels.

It is hazardous, however, to rely too heavily on normative data without
adequate control samples. Given the size of the samples, most of the differences
between the delinquent groups and the high school norms just discussed would
probably prove statistically significant if one computed the appropriate statistical
tests. However, knowing the statistical significance adds little to the meaningfulness of those differences when so many other factors such as the racial composition
of the samples, their socioeconomic level, the effects of institutionalization, and so
on, are left uncontrolled. For that reason, Richardson and Roebuck's (1965)'
comparison of delinquent boys with their nearest-aged nondelinquent male siblings is important, since IQ, social class, home environment, and a host of other
variables were carefully controlled. They found the CPI profiles of the delinquent
and nondelinquent Ss to be quite similar; significant differences were obtained
only on the Re and So scales.

Rusk (1969) found no CPI scales discriminated significantly between the
fifty delinquents and forty nondelinquent Mexican-American boys he tested. That
was probably because he matched the groups on age, SES, IQ, and geographical
origin, and made sure all the Ss came from deprived urban backgrounds and had
a history of family upheaval, hostility, and emotional disturbance.

In non-domestic studies, Mizushima and DeVos (1967), using a Japanese
translation of the CPI, compared thirty-six inmates of the Kurihama Reformatory for severe delinquents with sixty-four similarly aged students at a commer-
cial high school near Tokyo. The delinquents were significantly lower on the Do,
Wb, Re, So, Sc, To, Ac, Ai, Ie, Py, and Fe scales. Finding differences primarily
in the factor 1 and 3 scales lends cross-cultural support to the pattern noted in
Gough's data. The absolute elevations for the delinquents were five to ten T-score
points below the mean scores reported by Gough (1969b) for asocial American
samples. That probably indicates a cultural difference since the Japanese nondelinquents were also lower than their American counterparts on those scales.

In female delinquency, Gough (1969b) has provided normative data for
eighty-seven high school disciplinary cases, twenty-five young delinquents, and
338 prison inmates. Those data are reproduced in Figure 16. The profiles of the
disciplinary cases and the prison inmates are quite similar to one another and to
the male profiles reported by Gough (Figure 15). However, the young delinquents were considerably lower on the factor 1 and 3 scales. That may be because

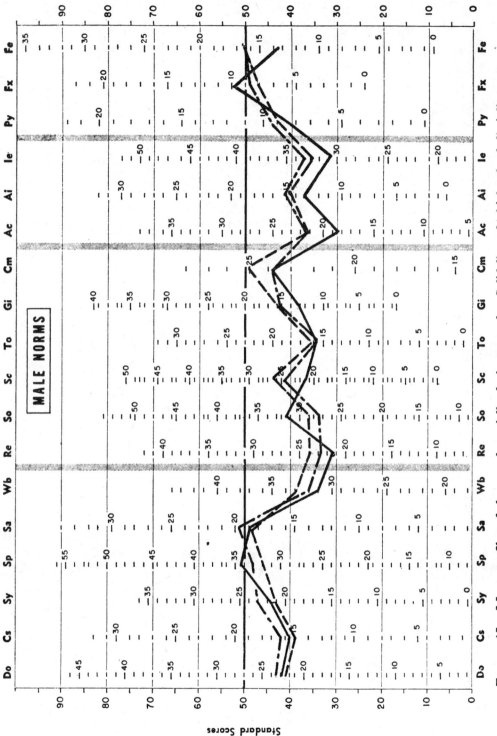

FIGURE 15. Mean profiles of three male socially deviant samples. Solid line: 91 high school disciplinary cases. Broken line: 142 young delinquents. Dot-dash line: 194 prison inmates. Data from Gough (1969b).

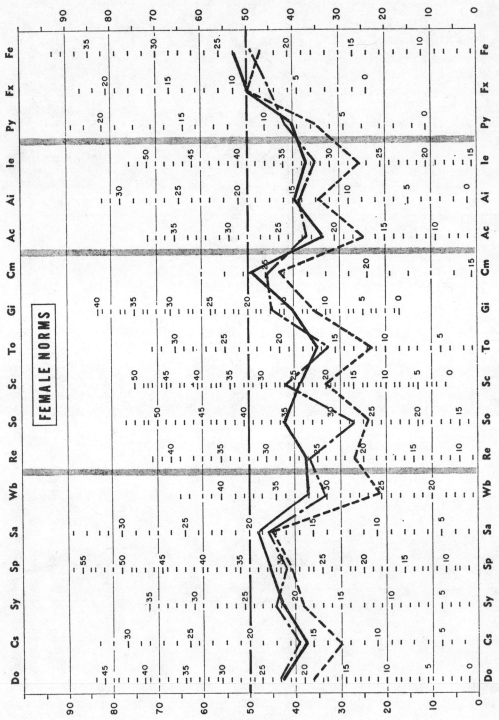

FIGURE 16. Mean profiles of three female socially deviant samples. Solid line: 87 high school disciplinary cases. Broken line: 25 young delinquents. Dot-dash line: 338 prison inmates. Data from Gough (1969b).

the sample was smaller and the data less reliable, but it is consistent with the present writer's observation that female delinquents tend to be more disturbed than their male counterparts. Much of female delinquency is composed of "status" offenses such as running away from home or engaging in sexual activity—behavior that is not illegal once the individual is over eighteen years of age. That overall pattern is often associated with emotional turmoil and family dissension, which may be why the delinquent girls' scores are lower than those of incarcerated adult women.

Tonra (1963) compared the CPI scores of thirty delinquent and thirty nondelinquent white Catholic girls matched for intelligence and socioeconomic level. The mean profile of the delinquent girls was almost identical to the profile of the 338 female prison inmates tested by Gough (1969b). When compared with the nondelinquent contrast group, the delinquents' scores were shown to be significantly lower on ten of the eighteen scales and significantly higher on two. Unlike the pattern observed for male delinquents, the delinquent girls were found to be significantly lower on all of factor 2 scales. In addition, they were lower on several factor 1 scales: *Re, So,* and *Ac,* as well as *Fx* and *Cm.* The delinquents were significantly higher on *Gi* and *Py.* The pattern was generally consistent with the observation that delinquent girls are more likely to have disturbed interpersonal relationships than are male delinquents.

Vincent (1961) has done extensive research on young unwed mothers using the CPI. In his studies he has compared the CPI scores of girls from broken homes with those of girls from intact homes, and he has investigated the differences between unwed mothers who give up their children for adoption and those who choose to raise them. Since in California, as well as many other jurisdictions, conceiving a child out of wedlock is cause for a minor to be declared delinquent by a juvenile court, the aspect of Vincent's data that will concern us here is his comparison of unwed mothers with single high school girls who were never pregnant (SNP). Two such comparisons were made, the first limited to girls from intact homes and the second to girls from broken homes. In the first, Vincent found unwed mothers scored significantly lower on *Do, Re, So,* and *Ac.* In the second, limited to girls from broken homes, the unwed mothers were lower on *So* and *Fe.* In his comparisons of girls from broken and unbroken homes (to be reviewed in detail below), Vincent found a number of scales discriminating, particularly those loading on factor 2. The relationship between broken homes and delinquency has been well-established (Rosenquist and Megargee, 1969), so Vincent's data raise the question about whether the pattern of differences on factor 2 scales noted by Tonra (1963) is specific to delinquency or in part an artifact of uncontrolled differences in the extent of broken homes. Unfortunately, those variables are so complexly and inextricably intertwined that a researcher who achieves experimental control sacrifices generality, and vice versa.

Hetherington and Feldman (1964) investigated the personality characteristics of college students who cheated on examinations administered under conditions that made cheating extremely easy. Of the seventy-eight men and women in the class, forty-six (59 per cent) cheated. On the CPI, the cheaters were found to be significantly lower on *Re, So, Ac, Ai,* and *Ie*—in short, on the scales dealing with ethical constraints and achievement motivation. An unexpected finding was that they were also significantly higher on *Sy*.

In general, the results of investigations of the CPI scores of individuals who have engaged in various sorts of antisocial or asocial behavior are fairly consistent. The scales loading on factor 1—particularly *Re* and *So,* and, to a somewhat lesser extent, *Ac*—consistently differentiate those engaging in deviant behavior. In some comparisons, especially those involving females, the factor 2 scales may also show significant differences.

In addition to making gross discriminations between delinquents and nondelinquents, the CPI has also been used to investigate the differences between different types of delinquents. One distinction that has been made in the literature on delinquency is between the solitary delinquent, who commits his offense alone, and the social delinquent, who commits his crimes in the company of others. Since the factor 2 scales relate to social effectiveness, several investigators have selected groups of solitary and social delinquents and administered the CPI to determine if those or other scales differentiate the two types. Using samples of social and solitary Japanese delinquents, Mizushima and DeVos found the social delinquents significantly higher on three factor 2 scales: *Sy, Sp,* and *Sa*. *Sp* and *Sa* are also two of the scales that differentiated Wilcock's (1964) sample of "individualized" criminals from his samples of "socialized" and "socialized aggressive" criminals who may have had accomplices. The individualized criminals were also significantly lower on *Ie* and higher on *Fe*. Richardson and Roebuck (1965) compared the CPI scores of social delinquents with those of "mixed" delinquents, who committed some offenses alone and some in the company of others. As might be expected in view of the greater similarity of the two samples, fewer scales differentiated them significantly. The one scale that did show a significant difference was, appropriately enough, Social Presence (*Sp*), which had also been significant in the other studies.

Researchers on delinquency also like to categorize offenders on the basis of whether the offense was a crime against property or against a person. Mizushima and DeVos (1967) subdivided their delinquent Japanese sample into eighteen convicted of thefts and fourteen convicted of crimes of violence and compared their CPI scores. They found the violent offenders to be significantly higher on *Sp* and *Sa,* and lower on *Fe*. There was some confounding with the social-solitary distinction, however, for the investigators noted that most of the violent offenders were social delinquents and most of the thieves solitary. Wilcock's (1964) study was even more confounded, so that there is no way of examining the differences between property and person offenders apart from the individual-social distinction.

Megargee (1966d) compared the *Sc* scores of a small sample of extremely assaultive delinquents (EA) with the scores of moderately assaultive delinquents to test his hypothesis that extremely violent individuals are often overcontrolled; the significantly higher *Sc* scores obtained by the EA group support his contention. He also compared the EA group with moderately assaultive and nonviolent delinquents on the other CPI scales and found the EAs to be significantly higher on *Wb* and *Ie*. There were insignificant trends for them to be higher on the other factor 3 scales, *To, Ai,* and *Fx*.

Other investigations which have examined differences between groups of asocial individuals include Hirt and Cook's (1962) comparison of acting-out, withdrawn, and normal military offenders described earlier, and Vincent's (1961) comparison of unwed mothers who kept their children with those who gave them up for adoption. In the latter study, Vincent found the unwed mothers who released their children for adoption were significantly higher on every CPI scale except *Fx* and *Fe* than those who retained them. That was consistent with Vincent's observations that the mothers who released their children were also more mature, better educated (39 per cent attending or completing college), and from higher SES families with a more favorable family background.

The CPI has been used in a variety of ways to predict parole success. In connection with the PICO project of the California Department of Corrections, Gough and two other psychologists made global evaluations of inmates' amenability to counseling based on their overall CPI profile. Later, the more amenable inmates were observed to have lower rates of parole violations than those deemed nonamenable (Rudoff, 1959; Rudoff and Bennett, 1958). Whether those differences are statistically significant is not immediately apparent from the technical reports, but the direction of the mean differences is certainly consistent from one sample to the next. Those data suggest that a clinician can make valid inferences from the CPI; however, they are of limited value to other potential users who do not know the basis for the clinicians' judgments.

A study by Gough, Wenk, and Rozynko (1965) provided a better test of the CPI's forecasting efficiency, both alone and in conjunction with other tests. Those investigators first compared the CPI scores of 183 California Youth Authority parole violators with 261 nonviolators. The parole violators were found to be significantly higher on *Sp* and *Sa* and significantly lower on *So* and *Sc*. That comparison was repeated on a second sample of 130 violators and 165 nonviolators; the parole violators were found to be significantly lower on *So, Sc,* and *Cm*. The investigators next sought to determine if a weighted combination of CPI scores, either alone or in conjunction with other measures, could improve on the predictions possible from *So* or *Sc* alone. Multiple regression equations were computed for the CPI alone; for the CPI in conjunction with the "base expectancy (BE) table" (an experience table based on case folder data used regularly by the Youth Authority); for the CPI with the MMPI; and for all three measures used individually and together. The best CPI-only formula was found to be: Parole success $= 45.078 - .353\,Sp - .182\,Sa + .532\,So + .224\,Sc$.

While that index significantly discriminated violators from nonviolators in both the original and cross-validating samples, it was less efficient than the BE table alone. The best predictor was found to be the BE used in conjunction with the CPI as follows: Parole success $= 21.328 - .411\,Sp + .308\,So + .236\,Sc + .435\,Cm + .444$ BE. On cross-validation this formula worked better than the BE, CPI, MMPI, the BE-MMPI combination, or all three combined. Used with the optimal cutting score, it correctly classified 63 per cent of the cross-validation sample; while not overly impressive, that figure is an improvement over the base rate prediction (56 per cent) and slightly exceeded the proportion of hits possible from the CPI alone (60 per cent), the CPI-MMPI combination (60 per cent), the BE alone (59 per cent), or the MMPI alone (56 per cent). (The combination of all three was of equal value—63 per cent—but obviously less efficient and more expensive.)

Social maturity. Gough (1966b) has also constructed an index for the appraisal of social maturity. Social maturity includes socialization, the construct assessed by *So,* but is broader. The chief difference is in the adherence to ordinary social rules under extraordinary circumstances. The person who is socially mature is receptive to change and may rebel against the established order if it becomes repressive; the person who is overly socialized—that is, not socially mature—will cling to the rules even when they are outmoded. Martin Luther King, for example, was well socialized, but not so oversocialized that he could not recognize the faults of the system and seek to change them; in this he manifested his social maturity.

The distinction between socialization and social maturity is then clearest at the upper end of the continuum, particularly during times of change. Unfortunately, that distinction is lost in much of the research literature because the emphasis is on the lower end of the continuum where the behavioral expectations do not differ. That emphasis was begun with the very derivation of the social maturity index. Given the description of the construct, one would expect well-socialized people who were accepting of change to be compared with well-socialized people who resisted change. Instead, Gough (1966b) derived two multiple regression equations by contrasting the CPI scores of 881 male juvenile delinquents with those of 2,146 nondelinquent males. The first equation, for use with hand calculators, involved only three variables: Social maturity No. $1 = 25.701 + .408\ Re + .478\ So - .296\ Gi$. The second, more exact equation, for use with computers, was: Social maturity No. $2 = 28.062 + .148\ Do + .334\ Re + .512\ So - .317\ Gi - .274\ Cm + .227\ Fx$. Both formulas were designed for use with raw scores on the scales.

In the validation of the social maturity index, delinquency continued to serve as a major criterion. The indices were first cross-validated by calculating index scores for 409 delinquents and 2,482 nondelinquents. The point-biserial correlations between equations 1 and 2 and delinquency were .60 and .63 respectively; those correlations exceeded the highest correlation for a single CPI scale $(So, r = .52)$. Since social maturity is one of Gough's culturally universal folk concepts, he next attempted a cross-cultural cross-validation comparing the scores of thirty-eight Italian male delinquents with those of 659 nondelinquent male Italians. The means on both equations differed significantly $(p < .01)$. In a subsequent study, Gough, DeVos, and Mizushima (1968) also found thirty-six delinquent Japanese boys scored significantly higher than 113 nondelinquents matched for SES and education $(p < .001)$.

However, Gough (1966b) also conducted validational studies on nondelinquent samples. He applied the equation to Hetherington and Feldman's (1964) data and found that college students who did not cheat scored significantly higher than those who cheated. Applied to high school students, the equations discriminated fifty students nominated by their principals as being high on responsibility from fifty-one others named as low. Analyses of the adjectives applied to high and low scorers by IPAR observers and peers yielded descriptions consistent with the construct. Further data were provided in a subsequent report (Gough, 1971). Gough had undergraduates scale the degree of social maturity exemplified by fourteen occupational groups; that yielded a reliable ranking of those fourteen occupations with respect to their social maturity. Machinists and sales supervisors were lowest; dentists and industrial research scientists highest. Not entirely by coincidence, Gough happened to have available CPI normative data on samples from each of those fourteen occupations, from which he computed social maturity equations. The rank order correlation between the perceived social maturity and the mean scores on the social maturity index was .83.

In a "serendipitous validity study," Lefcourt (1968) used the social maturity index to identify which of sixty-six students in an advanced psychology class had cut required reading material out of the library's copies. The CPI had been administered previously and scored for social maturity; only one of the sixty-six students fell below Gough's suggested cut-off score for identifying delinquents in his U.S. samples. Lefcourt was able to collect evidence that it was that one student who in fact had stolen the material from the library. Lefcourt was also able to glean a second criterion of social maturity from that class—namely, whether each student's term paper indicated he had not actually done the required research and was instead bluffing. Such papers were assigned a grade of D; the raters agreed on 98 per cent of the cases. Of the three people lowest on the index, two had grades of C− and one a grade of D. (The index scores of any other students with such grades were not reported.) Finally, the only two students who failed to come by and pick up their final exams and perhaps learn from their mistakes were also the two students with the lowest index scores.

The data thus show that the social maturity index can discriminate differences in socialization. Indeed, some of the studies indicate that it may do so better than does the Socialization scale. As yet, however, it remains to be seen whether it can detect the openness to constructive change that Gough maintains distinguishes the index from *So*.

Treatment Applications

PREDICTION OF RESPONSE TO COUNSELING

Despite the importance of predicting response to treatment, there has been surprisingly little systematic research on such a question using the full CPI. Of the few studies that have been performed, most have used only a few selected scales. Heilbrun (1961) investigated the characteristics of men and women who terminate counseling early. The CPI was not the primary instrument in that study, but Heilbrun did note in passing that women with high *Fe* scores and men with low *Fe* scores tended to terminate early, while low *Fe* women and high *Fe* men were more likely to stay in treatment. No other CPI scales were examined in that study. In a later study, Heilbrun (1962) examined the relationship between his Adjective Check List Counseling Readiness scale and the CPI *Sa, Re, Gi,* and *Py* scales. He predicted that *Sa* and *Gi* would be negatively related to counseling readiness and that *Re* and *Py* would be positively related. For 261 men, the correlations with all four scales were significant and negative, ranging from −.45 (*Py*) to −.80 (*Sa*). For 126 women, the correlations were also negative and those with *Gi, Re,* and *Py* were statistically significant, ranging from −.18 (*Py*) to −.51 (*Gi*). Heilbrun interpreted those data as indicating that self-acceptance in men and the desire to foster a good impression in women were most likely to lead to premature termination. The unanticipated negative correlations with *Re* were taken as indicating clients' general inability to assume responsibility; those for *Py* were interpreted as an indication that the person high on that scale wants to deal independently with his problems and hence is less ready for counseling. Further research is required to verify those speculations, not only because of the after the fact reasoning, but also because the accuracy of conclusions depends upon the validity of the ACL Counseling Readiness scale.

Leventhal (1968) investigated the relationship between his CPI Anxiety scale and counseling prognosis and report that high scorers have a poorer prognosis, improving more slowly and requiring more interviews to termination. The most thorough investigation of the relation of the entire CPI to counseling prognosis was conducted by the research staff of the California Department of Corrections in connection with the PICO (Pilot Intensive Counseling Organization) project. (Unfortunately, the reports of that project are not generally available. Those that the writer does have access to [Rudoff, 1959, and Rudoff and Bennett, 1958] do not contain enough data to permit an adequate evaluation of the ability of the CPI to forecast response to counseling.) In the PICO project, the CPI was used to assess the amenability to intensive counseling of Youth Authority wards. Amenability was initially evaluated by having three clinicians inspect each profile and make prognostic judgments; later (as reported in Chapter Eight), an Amenability scale was devised. The relation of those measures to the inmates' response to counseling is not included in the reports of the PICO project available to this writer. As noted, however, the inmates judged most amenable by the clinician did have the best post-release adjustment whether or not they had been intensively counseled.

Over all, the research on the prediction of response to treatment with the CPI has been promising in that most studies have found some significant relationships. However, the area has suffered greatly from a lack of sustained, systematic research. The one sustained effort, the PICO project, is of limited value because the results of the CPI evaluation program have not been adequately reported in the professional literature.

EVALUATION OF CHANGE IN TREATMENT

The CPI is used not only to predict the potential for improvement in treatment, but also to measure change after therapy or counseling has been completed. In such studies, the validity of the CPI is taken as established and the test is used as a yardstick by which the effectiveness of the treatment program is evaluated. Of course, in the case of failure to demonstrate change, therapists might be inclined to question the test. Since there is no way to determine whether the test or the treatment is at fault, the results that have been obtained will be described and the reader must draw his own conclusions.

Nichols and Beck (1960) used the CPI as one of several measures of client change after counseling at a university counseling service. Other measures included ratings made by therapists and by patients. For each measure the difference between the pre- and post-treatment scores was determined; those different scores were then factor analyzed. Of the six factors that emerged, two were clearly CPI factors. One was identifiable as the factor we have labeled factor 1, with high loadings from *Wb, Re, Sc, To, Gi,* and *Ac;* the second was factor 2, with high loadings from *Do, Sc, Sy, Sp,* and *Sa.* The amount of change on the factor 2 scales was significantly greater than that observed in an uncounseled nonclient group tested at the same intervals. It would appear from these data that the factor 2, and to a lesser extent the Factor 1, scales are the ones most responsive to the changes resulting from insight-oriented personal counseling. It is noteworthy that those CPI factors were independent of the clients' and therapists' ratings; however, this could well be due to the variance of the common method.

Shaver and Scheibe (1967) used the CPI to evaluate changes as a result of participating in a summer camp program, in chronic psychiatric adult patients, most of whom were schizophrenic. The CPI was administered before and after the program, and significant mean increases were found in *Cs, Sy, Sp, Sa, Cm,* and *Ac.* No control group was used.

The CPI was also used in the PICO project to evaluate change as a result of intensive counseling (Rudoff and Bennett, 1958). Matched cohorts of delinquents were assigned to either the regular California Youth Authority (CYA) program or to the regular program enriched by a program of intensive counseling. The CPI was administered on intake and again just before release. The staff first determined the amount of change in the mean CPI scores of the total group including both experimental and control *S*s. Significant improvement was noted on seventeen of the eighteen scales, the lone exception being *Cm.* (In this research an early prepublication form of the CPI was used. That version used the old scale designations and the old keying for many scales. To avoid confusion, the results are discussed using the modern scale names and scoring directions rather than those in the report.) To evaluate the effects of the experimental counseling program, the experimental and control groups were subdivided into amenable and nonamenable subgroups and their change scores compared. The improvement on any of the scales of the counseled subgroups was not found to be significantly greater than that of the groups in the regular program. Change was also evaluated by computing indices of profile similarity for each individual between the pretest and the posttest. Those analyses suggest greater change for the control group than the experimental. With that statistic, however, there is no indication whether the change is for the better or worse.

A global comparison was also obtained by following a suggestion of Gough's that the mean *T*-score on all scales except *Fe* be computed and used as an overall adjustment index. That index indicated improvement in all the various subgroups, but the experimentally counseled groups did not improve significantly more than the control groups (Rudoff and Bennett, 1958). It was perhaps because of those findings that a somewhat different technique was adopted by Warren and Palmer (1965) to evaluate the effects of another CYA program, the Community Treatment Project (CTP). While the PICO project had experimented with intensive counseling within an institutional setting, the CTP project emphasized differential treatment in a community setting by specially trained

CYA parole officers. In that project the CPI profiles of the forty-one experimental subjects and the 165 controls were submitted to Gough, who inspected each and then Q-sorted the profiles with respect to their social adjustment. Next he Q-sorted the profiles with respect to personal adjustment, casting them into a binomial distribution from best to poorest adjustment. That was done for both pretests and posttests. On both the posttest sorts, the experimental group was found to be significantly better-adjusted than the control. When the amount of improvement on each dimension was determined, it was also found that the experimental group significantly exceeded the control. According to Gough (personal communication, 1971), "This study was later repeated with a larger sample, permitting sort versus re-sort reliability checks on my judgments and more precise specification of trends. The outcomes were excellent on all fronts."

This procedure of Q-sorting profiles deserves special mention. As we have noted, one of the major problems in CPI research is preserving the holistic, configural use of the instrument by a clinician in a quantitative study. That procedure allows one to rigorously evaluate the test-clinician combination rather than the test alone. Hopefully, more such investigations will be forthcoming.

The CPI was also used by Rudoff and Piliavin (1969) to evaluate the effects of an experimental program of reduced caseloads and intensive casework services for mothers in the Aid to Needy Children program. The CPI was employed to help identify different types of clients as well as to evaluate personality change. The statistical comparison of before and after scale scores showed no statistical differences, but some minor differences were noted in the clinical interpretations of those profiles.

Given the diversity of samples studied, research designs employed, and treatment programs used, it is impossible to integrate the results of those few efforts to use the CPI as a measure of treatment effectiveness. Therapy outcome research is always a tricky business, fraught with difficulties in selecting adequate controls and separating meaningful change from the "hello-goodbye" effect. Investigators who have contrasted the outcome of a particular treatment with the results of some other treatment have naturally had a more difficult time demonstrating significant effects than have investigators who have compared treated with nontreated groups or who have simply demonstrated changes in test scores after counseling without using any contrast group whatsoever. For the CPI student, the most interesting aspect of such research is the diverse strategies employed by the different investigators, particularly the use of clinical interpretations of test patterns in addition to the unvarnished scale scores. The latter procedure is a much better approximation of the way the test is used in clinical practice and should be adopted in validity studies of the CPI in which there are good criterion measures available.

READINESS FOR RELEASE

Evaluation of response to treatment is of more than academic interest. It not only plays a central role in program evaluation, but is also important in determining whether a patient is ready to terminate treatment. The better one can predict his post-therapy behavior, the better one can make that determination.

Aside from the parole prediction studies already reviewed, the only study of such a problem was conducted by Lorei (1964), who administered the CPI to 104 consecutively admitted patients just prior to their release from a VA neuropsychiatric hospital. He correlated the scores on each of the eighteen scales with each patient's success in remaining nine months out of the hospital. None of the scales had significant point-biserial correlations with that criterion. No effort was made to determine whether combinations of scales or judgments based on overall profiles would have been more successful.

COUNSELOR CHARACTERISTICS

Although the CPI is generally applied to the recipients of treatment, it has also been used in the selection of counselors and in studies of counselor behavior. Covner (1969) compared the CPI profiles of successful and unsuccessful volunteer alcoholism counselors, many of whom were alcoholic themselves. Partly because of small sample sizes, few of the differences attained statistical significance. Covner did observe significantly lower Do scores and significantly higher Fe scores among the male counselors rated as most effective. One might infer from this that a rather passive and nondirective orientation was favored in his agency, although Bohn (1965) has reported that high and low Do counselors do not differ in directiveness.

Brams (1961) related a number of MMPI scales to the communication effectiveness of graduate student counselors. In addition to the standard scales, he scored the MMPI for four scales which, with some additions and modifications, are now included on the CPI: $Do, Cs, Re,$ and To. None correlated significantly with his measures of effectiveness of communication.

Freedman, Antenon, and Lister (1967) administered the CPI and Guilford Zimmerman Temperament Survey to thirty-seven counselors whose interview behavior was then rated on the Porter Interview Analysis scale. Multiple regression equations were computed between the tests and the scores for such interview behaviors as supporting, probing, evaluating, interpreting, and giving information. No first-order correlations between test scales and interview behavior were reported, but the multiple regression equations did show significant relationships between counselors' personality characteristics as assessed by those tests and their interview behavior.

Beech (1970) mailed CPIs and an unspecified questionnaire on employed styles of pastoral counseling to sixty-six Protestant ministers in Alberta. According to Beech, Gough had suggested two formulas defining the continuum from a) love to hostility, and b) permissiveness to restrictiveness: Love $= Sy + To + Cm + Fe$; Permissiveness $= Sa - Gi + Ai + Py + Fx$. Those formulas were applied to the ministers' CPIs; on the basis of median splits, four groups were formed: loving permissive, loving restrictive, hostile permissive, hostile restrictive. The counseling styles of the four groups, as determined by examination of their self-reports, were then examined. Beech's report of his findings seems to indicate a perfect congruence between counseling style and CPI results in the permissive-restrictive dimension. Of course, that simply means the ministers were consistent in their self-description, since no external observations of counseling style were used. No such congruence was found in the love-hostility dimension, apparently because all the ministers characterized themselves as loving.

It is generally difficult to come to any conclusions regarding the use of the CPI in selecting counselors. In general, the data show few relationships between the test and the various measures of counselor behavior, but serious shortcomings in the design, analysis, and reporting of several of such studies limits their meaningfulness.

Concluding Remarks

A comparison of this chapter with the preceding one demonstrates that there has been much less research done on the clinical use of the CPI than on its educational and vocational applications. The major reason for that is that the CPI was not designed for the assessment of psychopathology and that the clinician has available other instruments such as the MMPI which meet his needs better. The research on the clinical use of the CPI indicates that the test is not as effective when applied to disturbed groups. While maladjustment is manifested by low profiles, the inventory does not discriminate different patterns of maladjustment well and is of limited use in differential diagnosis. It is used most effectively with delinquents, criminals, and others whose problems stem from conflicts between individual and social values rather than intrapsychic conflicts.

Although the CPI is less useful than the MMPI in assessing neurotic tendencies and not as sensitive as the Rorschach in detecting signs of thought disorder, it may be used to supplement other, "more clinical" tests. Further research should be aimed at delineating the specific areas in which the CPI can contribute to the clinical battery. For example, it might be useful in assessing candidates for sensitivity training or encounter groups, since it was designed to discriminate patterns of interpersonal behavior among relatively well-functioning people. Its emphasis on positive functioning should make it possible to use the CPI to find strong points in an otherwise pathological personality. Its relation to educational and vocational achievement should make it of particular value in assessing the prognosis for profiting from vocational and educational therapy and rehabilitation programs.

CHAPTER 14

Application in Selected Research Problems

The CPI is a research tool favored by many investigators. The quantity and the quality of the research literature using the CPI vary greatly from area to area. Some problems, such as creativity, have received considerable attention, and several extensive programs of research using the CPI have been carried out. In other areas, the surface has been barely scratched and much research remains to be done. Although the conclusions in the newer areas are tentative at present, some are discussed here in the hope that the curiosity of others will be aroused sufficiently to perform additional studies.

Conformity

The discovery of the Nazi extermination camps after World War II stimulated research on conformity and obedience as psychologists attempted to discover how apparently ordinary humans could come to behave in such an inhuman fashion. One of the most stimulating investigations was Asch's (1951) account of how some subjects would deny the evidence of their senses to conform to the obviously erroneous opinion of the majority. While social psychologists quickly designed studies to explore the parameters of that phenomenon, personality researchers turned their attention to the characteristics of such conformists.

Crutchfield (1955) reported the results of the first such investigation using the fledgling CPI. Using an Asch-type situation, he measured the amount of yielding engaged in by fifty men, all of whom "were engaged in a profession (unspecified in Crutchfield's report, but probably military officers) in which leadership is one of the salient expected qualifications." Those conformity scores were correlated with the CPI; significant negative correlations ranging from −.30 to −.41 were obtained with scales *Sy, Re,* and *To* (see Table 24).

Table 24. RELATION OF CPI SCALES TO YIELDING IN ASCH-TYPE EXPERIMENTS

Significant Correlations[b]

	Crutchfield (1955)	Tuddenham (1959)				Harper (1964)	Hase and Goldberg (1967)
	50 Men	27 Adult Men	37 College Men	29 Adult Women	37 College Women	135 Student Nurses	174 College Women
Do		−.31		−.40			
Cs		−.78		−.51	−.33	−.17	−.22
Sy	−.30[a]			−.42			
Sp					−.41		
Sa							
Wb							
Re	−.30[a]	−.44					.18
So							.16
Sc							
To	−.30[a]					−.20	
Gi						.19	
Cm							.21
Ac		−.42					
Ai		−.58	−.41		−.45	−.19	
Ie							
Py		−.48					−.17
Fx					−.59		
Fe							.26

[a] Minimal estimate; Crutchfield reported significant negative correlations "ranging from −.30 to −.41" but did not identify which scale had which coefficient.
[b] $p < .05$.

Tuddenham (1959) studied the relationship between the CPI and yielding in four samples: twenty-seven adult men from the Oakland Adolescent Growth Study, twenty-nine adult women from the same study, thirty-seven college men, and thirty-seven college women. His results are presented in Table 24. Like Crutchfield, the statistically significant correlations that Tuddenham obtained were all in the negative direction. Moreover, the magnitude of many was substantial, ranging as high as −.78. However, the patterns differed considerably from one sample to the next, with one group having six significant correlations and the next only one. The scales bearing the strongest relationship to yielding in Tuddenham's study were *Cs* and *Ai,* both of which had noteworthy negative correlations in every sample except one. Harper (1964) performed a similar investigation using 135 student nurses. Only four scales correlated significantly, but two of the four were *Cs* and *Ai.* The magnitude of the correlations was much lower than in Tuddenham's study, however. Appley and Moeller (1963) divided forty-one women sophomores into three groups: high yielding, middle yielding, and low yielding, on the basis of their performance in an Asch situation. Analyses of variance indicate that none of the eighteen scales significantly differentiate the groups. However, the results of that study must be regarded with caution because some serious errors are present in the means reported for the three groups.[1] Hase and Goldberg (1967) used a paper-and-pencil measure of yielding; 174 college women responded to an opinion survey. Five weeks later, the questionnaire was readministered along with false information about the group means in the first session. The amount of shift toward the false mean was the measure of yielding. Hase and Goldberg reported the CPI scale correlating most closely with that index was the same scale that had correlated most consistently in the other studies: *Cs* ($r = -.24$).

Creativity

Achievement and creativity are obviously related, and one of the first problems confronting the researcher is distinguishing *creative* achievement—that is, original or innovative accomplishments from achievement in general. A man may do a great deal and do it very well, but, unless his approach is somehow unique, researchers would not consider him creative. In that sense an Auguste Renoir painting of a nude would be considered less creative than Marcel Duchamps' "Nude Descending a Staircase." That is not to say that the more creative work is necessarily better, but simply that it is more original, or less traditional.

Despite that, creativity does imply quality. There are many things that are different yet not considered creative. The speech patterns of a hebephrenic may be unique, but they are considered crazy rather than creative because they do not satisfy basic rules for communicability. But then wasn't James Joyce's stream-of-consciousness style regarded as unintelligible when introduced? The problem is whether unconventional works can be judged using conventional standards. Some may say no, and suspend judgment, but failure to apply any critical standards can lead to the absurd rhapsodies over the sensitivity, understanding and genius manifested in the random daubs of a chimpanzee. It is no accident that we have chosen artistic works as examples of creativity, for it is in the arts that judgments of creativity are probably the most subjective, and in which the influence of styles and fashions are most evident. If, for example, Andy Warhol is a creative genius because he painted a Campbell's Tomato Soup can, what then of that anonymous man who first designed the can Warhol painted? The criterion problem is thus evident.

It is partly because of such problems that many investigators have re-

---

[1] For example, a raw score of 14 on Communality is so low that its *T*-score equivalent is 0; nevertheless, *mean Cm* raw scores varying from 1.64 to 2.54, 12 points below the lowest tabled value, are reported. Similar impossible means are listed for two other scales (*Wb* and *So*), and the means on *Sc* and *Fe* also deviated suspiciously.

treated to studies of scientific creativity. Here they feel somewhat more confident of their judgment and here there are more external guidelines that can help the rater. It is debatable whether the Salk or Sabin polio vaccines represent a sufficiently innovative approach to call their achievements creative, but it can be determined whether the vaccines are effective in preventing the disease. Similarly, no one would have any great regard for Frank Lloyd Wright's Imperial Hotel in Tokyo or his E. J. Kaufman House at Bear Run, Pennsylvania, if the former had toppled at the first earthquake or the latter dropped into the waterfall over which it was built. While purists may argue, a solution must be pragmatically successful to be recognized as creative. No matter how unique the idea to go east by sailing west, if the *Nina, Pinta,* and *Santa Maria* had in fact fallen off the edge of the earth, Christopher Columbus would be remembered not as a creative navigator but as a foolish one.

Many resolve the problem by using the so-called "test of time," judging a man's work by how well it endures in later generations. Few now question the creativity of Darwin or Freud, but to their contemporaries the genius of their work is less evident; today some are understandably reluctant to bestow similar accolades on a man whose life's work is incomplete. Unfortunately, the psychological researcher cannot afford to wait until a man is dead, because by then his subject is singularly unresponsive. Moreover, men change with age. One wonders what the men whose lives are recorded in *A History of Psychology in Autobiography* (Boring and Lindzey, 1967), all of whom were over sixty at the time they wrote their memoirs, would have written had some prescient person invited them to participate in a similar volume when they were in their thirties. Most investigators of creativity have sacrificed the perspective of time and test their subjects while they are still young and productive. Indeed some have chosen their subjects on the basis of their creative *potential* rather than their creative *accomplishment*.

One thus has to continually question the universality of the studies done on creativity. Can the data on creative high school students be generalized to Nobel Prize winners? Has success changed the attitudes of the men whose professional reputations are now established? Do the findings on the creative painter apply to the poet or the physicist?

ARTISTS

As part of a program of research on creativity in various fields, thirty writers nominated by English professors as being unusually creative were studied at IPAR. They were contrasted with a group of California writers who were members of a writers association. In a preliminary report of the data obtained, Barron (1965) listed the mean CPI scores of the two groups. (See Figure 17.) No tests of significance were reported, but differences between group means of four or more T-score points were found on nine scales. Creative writers were four or more points *higher* on *Sa, To, Fx,* and *Fe* and *lower* on *Wb, So, Sc, Gi,* and *Ac.* Those and other data suggest that the more creative writers were more independent, unconventional, and less well-adjusted in the usual sense. The pattern suggests great ego-strength that permitted access to usually repressed material in conjunction with greater personal effectiveness. Similar patterns, but fewer eccentricities

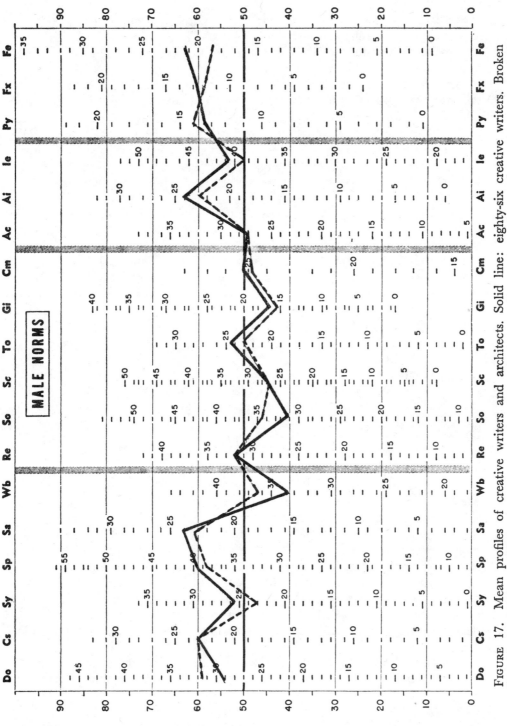

FIGURE 17. Mean profiles of creative writers and architects. Solid line: eighty-six creative writers. Broken line: forty creative architects.

are noted in samples of creative architects and mathematicians studied at IPAR.

The outstanding feature of the IPAR program is the fact that it has been able to intensively study individuals whose creative contribution in various fields is so outstanding that it has received national recognition. Not all research programs have been as fortunate in obtaining subjects, and most investigators have to content themselves with less stringent criteria of creative accomplishment, usually samples of students.

One such study was performed by Holland and Astin (1962) using Merit Scholarship finalists who had been tested during their senior year in high school. After those students had been in college three years, they were sent a form listing ten artistic accomplishments. They were asked to check off each accomplishment they had performed. Unfortunately, the form was heavily biased in favor of performing arts such as music, drama, and public speaking, and neglected creative writing and the graphic arts. Seven scales correlated significantly with that criterion among 681 boys and three did so among the 272 girls. The magnitude of those correlations was small, the highest being .22 (see Table 25). Most notable was the fact that in the male sample, all factor 2 scales correlated significantly with artistic achievement. That is quite contrary to the image of the lonely artist in his garret; one suspects that the correlations reflect the heavy emphasis on the performing arts in the questionnaire.

SCIENCE

General. The writer was not able to find any studies of the relationship between CPI scores and differences in general scientific creativity among mature scientists. There have been several studies using samples of students differing in general scientific achievements. Although the writer feels the results of those studies are relevant to a discussion of research on creativity using the CPI, it should be pointed out that some parents disagree, maintaining that those investigations, at best, are studying only *potential* or *possible* creativity.

Holland and Astin (1962) examined the scientific creativity of their 953 Merit finalists. Questionnaires were sent to the students on which they were asked if they had published or presented a scientific paper, received a research grant or fellowship, received any awards for scientific activities, invented a patentable device or constructed an original piece of apparatus. Only one of the thirty-six correlation coefficients was statistically significant, and it was quite small ($r = .13$). Such results contrast sharply with those obtained for artistic creativity. The difference may have been because of the greater rigor of the criterion of scientific achievement and because the sampling was made during the junior year while the bulk of undergraduate scientific research typically occurs during the senior year.

While Holland and Astin (1962) used scientific achievements during college as their criterion, two other investigations of science students focused on scientific potential. Garwood (1964) administered a battery of creativity tests to 105 young male science majors from three universities. She selected eighteen high and eighteen low creative *S*s on the basis of those scores and tested them with the CPI *Do, Cs, Sy, Sp, Sa, So, Sc, Gi, Ie,* and *Fx* scales. She predicted the highly creative group would be significantly higher on scales *Do, Cs, Sy, Sp, Sa, Ie,* and

Fx, and significantly lower on *So, Sc,* and *Gi.* One-tailed tests of the differences between the means supported seven of her ten hypotheses (see Table 25). Strong trends in the predicted direction were also noted for *Ie* ($p < .055$) and *Cs* ($p < .07$). It would appear from Garwood's data that social poise, extraversion, and verbal fluency are not limited to those students whose creativity is in the performing arts.

Parloff and Datta (1965) mailed CPIs to 572 male high school students who had competed in the 1963 Westinghouse Talent Search and scored above the eightieth percentile on a test of science aptitude. The 536 students who responded were divided into three groups on the basis of judges' ratings of individual research projects the students submitted. The first group consisted of 112 judged to have high potential creativity, the second of 137 judged to have moderate potential creativity, and the third of 287 with low potential creativity. The CPIs of each pair of groups were then compared; the results are included in Table 25.

In general, the profiles of all three groups were above average, as would be expected with such a select group of young people. The distinctive feature of the high creative groups' CPI pattern was the higher scores on several factor 1 scales, indicating, perhaps, stronger internalized values, and on the *Ie* scale, suggesting better application of intelligence. The lows differed from the other two primarily on the factor 3 scales, suggesting less independence and more rigidity in their thinking.

In a subsequent study, Parloff, Datta, Kleman, and Handlon (1968) factor analyzed the CPI scores of 938 adolescents who had successfully entered the twenty-second and twenty-fourth annual science searches and who had scored above the eightieth percentile on the science aptitude tests. They also factor analyzed the scores of 101 more creative and ninety-nine less creative adults. Four factors emerged; the first three identifiable as factors 1, 2, and 3, and the fourth a blend of factors 4 and 5. Parloff, calls factor 1 *disciplined effectiveness.* The factor scores showed an interesting difference between the adolescents and adults. The more creative adolescents were significantly higher on that factor than their less creative peers, while the reverse was found in the adult samples. Factor 2 was designated *assertive self-assurance;* the researchers report their creative groups' factor scores were significantly higher than those of their less creative groups on that factor in both their adolescent and adult samples. That finding is consistent with Holland and Astin's data on artistic achievement and Garwood's on scientific creativity, but not with Parloff and Datta's (1965) research. Factor 3 was called *adaptive autonomy.* In both samples the creative *S*s were significantly higher on that factor, which data are consistent with all other studies of scientific creativity reviewed here thus far. Factor 4, *humanitarian conscience,* failed to differentiate the creative from the noncreative *S*s in either age group.

Mathematics. The studies thus far have dealt with general scientific creativity among students. Helson (1967b) and Helson and Crutchfield (1970) have explored the personality factors associated with demonstrated creativity in mature mathematicians. They compared the CPI scores of thirty-four creative and twenty-nine less creative male mathematicians and the scores of eighteen creative and twenty-nine less creative female mathematicians. Ratings by fellow mathematicians and faculty members were used as the criteria of creativity. In both

sexes, the creative mathematicians were found to be significantly higher on the
Fx scale than their less innovative peers. In addition, the creative men were found
to be significantly lower on *Sc* and the creative women significantly lower on
Cm and *Ac*.

Helson (1967b) also reports some interesting sex differences. On both
So and *Sa* the creative men were higher than their comparison group but the
creative women were lower. One might speculate that those significant interactions stem from the masculine bias found in contemporary American culture. The
independent creative male scientist is pursuing a culturally valued life style, while
the career woman is in conflict with many implicit and explicit social mores. That
might explain her lower *So* scale scores. Similarly, social approval of the man's
and disapproval of the woman's independence could well foster the differences
noted on the Self-Assurance scale.

Engineering. McDermid (1965) correlated the CPI with supervisors'
ratings of the research efforts of fifty-eight engineers and technicians employed
by the Hammond Organ Company. The one scale that correlated significantly
with the criterion was *Ai* ($r = .27$).

Overall, there are considerable differences among those studies of scientific
creativity. Considering the variety of criteria and subject samples used in different investigations, that is not too surprising. Most investigators have chosen comparison groups that resemble their creative group in almost every respect except
originality of work. As a result, the differences found, even when statistically reliable, have generally been of small magnitude. Although those differences may
help one form hypotheses about the creative personality, they are too small to
suggest that the CPI could be used with any accuracy to predict creativity.

One of the few consistent trends so far is that factor 3 scales always attain
statistical significance. Even in studies in which only one scale was significant,
that scale was a factor 3 measure. Generally, we have suggested that that is because its scales, *To, Gi, Ai, Ie,* and *Py,* reflect independence of thought and rejection of pat, conventional solutions. *Ai* was, of course, derived to measure independent achievement, while *Py* was derived from the protocols of eminent psychological researchers. However, it would be amiss not to note that those scales
are also among those having the highest correlations with such measures of intelligence as the Concept Mastery Test. In view of the degree to which most of the
investigators have matched the intelligence levels of their creative and noncreative
samples, the writer would not be inclined to regard such a pattern as an artifact
of inellectual differences. Others who feel that the role of intelligence in creativity
has been underemphasized (McNemar, 1964) might be inclined to argue the
point, however.

MIXED ARTISTIC AND SCIENTIFIC CREATIVITY

The data reviewed thus far, while fragmentary, does not suggest any major differences between creative artists and creative scientists. Cellini, Da Vinci,
Freud, Schweitzer, and many others have made notable contributions in both art
and science, and even in this day of specialization there are many who are creative in both areas. Consequently, some investigations of creativity have not distinguished artistic from scientific achievement.

MacKinnon (1961a, 1961b, 1962, 1963, 1964; Hall and MacKinnon, 1969) and his associates at IPAR have conducted intensive and extensive research on the personality patterns of creative architects. Architecture was deliberately selected as a field that called for scientific and engineering skills as well as artistic talent. A well-designed house must be aesthetically satisfying, but on a cold morning it's more important for the heating system to work properly. In MacKinnon's ambitious study, professors of architecture nominated the most creative architects in the United States. Forty of such men were studied at IPAR. Two contrast groups were also studied. The first consisted of forty-three less-creative architects who had worked with the members of the creative group; the second of forty-one less creative men who had not worked with the members of the creative group. The rated creativity of the first group significantly exceeded that of the second, which in turn was significantly higher than that of the third. The samples were matched for age and locale.

The most creative group was significantly higher than the least creative group on five scales: *Sp, Sa, Py, Fx, Fe;* and significantly lower on *Wb, Re, So, Sc, To, Gi, Cm,* and *Ac*. The medium creative group generally fell between the other two. They were significantly higher than the highly creative group on *Cm*. When compared with the least creative group, the middle group was significantly higher on *Fe* and significantly lower on *Wb, Sc,* and *Gi* (Wallace Hall, personal communication, 1971).

The statistically significant correlations between the CPI scales and the ratings of creativity for the total sample of 124 are presented in Table 25. A positive correlation with the factor 3 scale Fx was found. (*Ai* and *Py* did not correlate significantly with creativity. All three groups of architects had elevated mean scores on those measures.) Most interesting are the negative correlations with the factor 1 scales. One could speculate that creative architects have less well-developed value systems. That is not the case; it is more accurate to state that they have strong, but highly *individual* value sysems and behave in accordance with those values, not worrying about whether others approve of their behavior. From that one would predict a high score for them on Gough's social maturity index.

In a subsequent study, Hall and MacKinnon (1969) used those data to derive and cross-validate a multiple regression equation for the prediction of creativity with the CPI. The total sample was divided into two subsamples of sixty-two architects matched for creative talent. A stepwise multiple regression equation was derived using the data from one of the samples, and cross-validated using information from the second. An arbitrary decision was made to limit the equation to three predictor variables. The best CPI equation was: Creativity $= .547$ $Sp - 1.015\ Ac + .990\ Fe$.

On cross-validation that equation correlated .47 with the criterion. The investigators also derived similar equations for other tests; while not as accurate as the equation derived for the SVIB, the CPI formula was superior to those derived for the MMPI, FIRO-B, the ACL, the Allport-Vernon-Lindzey Study of Values, and the Myers-Briggs Type Indicator.

The current concern over the failure to make adequate use of the creative resources of women gives added importance to a longitudinal investigation of Mills College seniors by Ravenna Helson (1967a). Helson had Mills faculty

Table 25. SUMMARY OF STATISTICALLY SIGNIFICANT FINDINGS[a] IN STUDIES INVESTIGATING THE RELATION OF THE CPI TO CREATIVITY

	Artistic Creativity		Scientific Creativity					
	Holland and Astin (1962)		GENERAL					
			Holland and Astin (1962)		Garwood (1964)	Parloff and Data (1965)		
	Significant[a] Correlations		Significant[a] Correlations		Significant[a] Differences Between Means	Significant[a] Differences Between Means		
	Boys 681	Girls 272	Boys 681	Girls 272	18 High Creative versus 18 Low Creative	112 High Creative versus 137 Moderate Creative	112 High Creative versus 287 Low Creative	137 Moderate Creative versus 287 Low Creative
Do	.22	.16			4.5			
Cs	.19							
Sy	.18				3.7			
Sp	.14				5.3			
Sa	.17				3.1			
Wb					NA[b]	+[c]		−[c]
Re					NA[b]			
So					−3.2			
Sc	−.09	−.11			−3.8	+		
To					NA[b]			
Gi					−4.4	+		
Cm	−.08				NA[b]		−[c]	
Ac					NA[b]			
Ai							+	+
Ic			.13			+	+	
Py				−.12	NA[b]		+	+
Fx								+
Fe					NA[b]			+

Table 25. Summary of Statistically Significant Findings[a] in Studies Investigating the Relation of the CPI to Creativity (Cont'd)

Scientific Creativity

	Mathematics — Helson (1967[b]); Helson and Crutchfield (1970) Significant[a] Correlations		Engineering — McDermid (1965) Significant[a] Correlations
	34 Creative versus 29 Noncreative Men	18 Creative versus 29 Noncreative Women	38 Male Engineers
Do			
Cs			
Sy			
Sp			
Sa			
Wb			
Re			
So			
Sc	−3.9		
To			
Cm		—[c]	
Ac		−3.5	
Ai			.27
Ie			
Py			
Fx	2.0	4.3	
Fe			

Table 25. Summary of Statistically Significant Findings[a] in Studies Investigating the Relation of the CPI to Creativity (Cont'd)

	Mixed Scientific and Artistic Creativity			Test of Creativity	
	MacKinnon (1964)	Helson (1967a)		Barron (1965)	Gough (1969b)
	Significant[a] Correlations	Significant[a] Correlations		Significant[a] Correlations	Significant[a] Correlations
	124 Male Architects	22 Creative Students versus 13 Noncreative Students— Women	Creative versus Noncreative Women After 5 Years	50 Military Officers	100 Males
Do				.29	.45
Cs					.29
Sy	.18				.27
Sp	.19				.26
Sa					.35
Wb	−.20				−.19
Re	−.20				
So	−.31			−.39	−.28
Sc	−.21				
To	−.23				
Gi	−.31				
Cm					
Ac	−.24				.19
Ai					.22
Ie		1.67			
Py			2.3		
Fx	.24				
Fe	.24				

[a] p < .05

[b] NA: Scale not administered.

[c] Magnitude of difference not reported.

members nominate the most creative members of the senior class. No distinctions were made about the type of creativity, be it artistic, scientific, or whatever. The twenty-two nominees were then assessed and their test scores on the CPI and many other instruments, compared with those of 113 less creative classmates. Aside from scales specifically designed to assess creative talent, few personality measures distinguished the two groups. The only CPI scale that did so was Py. Five years later, Helson (1967a) reevaluated the same Ss. Questionnaires demonstrated that those who had been nominated as most creative in college had continued to display a significantly higher level of creative activity after graduation. The creative Ss were again higher on the Py scale but the significance level of the difference dropped (from $p < .01$ to $p < .10$). However, another factor 3 scale, Fx, did attain statistical significance in the follow-up. Helson's data on creative women thus continued the trend for the factor 3 scales to be the most sensitive to differences in creativity.

Helson also classified the Ss who had been nominated as creative during college according to whether they had remained single and continued their creative activity, married and continued to function creatively, or married and become inactive. (Apparently none remained single and inactive.) She then compared the CPI scores of those subgroups and found the single creative women were higher than the others on To ($p < .01$), $Re, So, Ai,$ and Py ($p < .05$).

ORIGINALITY

Most of the studies reviewed thus far have used ratings of creative activity in school or in professional life as their criteria. Some researchers have preferred to use tests of originality or creativity. To some extent that is the end result of a "bootstraps" operation: creative people are studied and the data used to construct and validate tests of creativity which in turn are then used to select new Ss for further study. Most of such tests relate fairly directly to aesthetic preferences and cognitive associations; thus they select individuals who have tastes, preferences, and thought patterns similar to those of people who are distinguished for their creative accomplishments.

Barron (1955) used the CPI to help test certain hypotheses about creativity. A battery of eight tests of creativity and originality was administered to a sample of one hundred Air Force captains and the fifteen highest and fifteen lowest were selected. He then compared their scores on the CPI $Do, Sa,$ and Sc scales to test his hypotheses that creative individuals are more dominant and self-assertive, as well as less repressed. He found the creative Ss to be significantly higher on Do and lower on $Sc;$ the differences on Sa were not significant. Subsequently, Barron (1965) reported correlations between his originality scale and the CPI with the influence of intelligence, as assessed by the Concept Mastery Test, partialed out. For one hundred Air Force officers he found partial correlations of .29 for Do and $-.39$ for Sc.

In the CPI *Manual,* Gough (1969b) reports the correlations between the CPI and the Guilford Creativity Battery for a sample of one hundred males. Seven significant positive correlations and two negative ones emerged (see Table 25). The pattern of positive correlation with factor 3 scales and a negative correlation with Sc was again found. Most striking, however, was the fact that all the factor 2 scales had significant positive correlation with the criterion as in the Holland-Astin and the Garwood studies.

Littlejohn (1967)' set out to determine the generality of the association between creativity and a feminine interest pattern noted by MacKinnon (1961). She divided 324 ninth-grade boys and 332 ninth-grade girls into high and low creative groups on the basis of their scores on the Revised Art Scale of the Welsh Figure Preference Test. The CPI Femininity scale was administered and no difference was found between the two groups. It is possible to question the appropriateness of that young a sample as well as the relevance of the criterion measure.

It can be seen that the CPI has been related to various criteria of creativity in a number of quite different samples. More often than not, significant although modest relationships have been found, indicating that reliable personality differences exist between creative and noncreative people. The most consistent relationships are also the most plausible. The most pervasive pattern is for the more creative Ss to be higher on the factor 3 scales Fx, Ai, and Py, indicating a rejection of rigid, authoritarian, dogmatic approaches, in favor of an open, receptive attitude conducive to independent thought. They are also higher on Sp and Sa, a pattern typical of assertive, inner-directed individuals. By the same token, the more creative people are often found to be significantly lower on Cm and Sc, indicating once again their independence and unconventional attitudes. Yet the data also contain warnings against glib generalizations about the creative personality. While a number of significant associations have emerged—certainly more than have been found with many other tests such as the MMPI—the majority of correlations have not been statistically significant. Even the most reliable associations were obtained less than a third of the time. Perhaps factor scores, such as those used by Parloff, et al. would have reduced that scatter somewhat, for it does appear that, for the factor 3 scales a least, it is the common variance that is related most closely to creativity.

While the research reviewed was aimed at understanding the creative personality rather than the selection of personnel, the data suggest that improved prediction with the CPI might be accomplished using multiple regression formulas such as those developed by Hall and MacKinnon (1969), or through the construction of special creativity scales.

Achievement Orientation

Carney has constructed a score consisting of the mean of the T-scores on the five factor 2 scales. He refers to it as the AO or Achievement Orientation score. He has proposed that it represents a more stable and objective measure of achievement motivation than McClelland's TAT-based measure of need Achievement (n Ach)'. He has inferred from data he has collected that the AO score may represent an estimate of the more enduring trait of achievement motivation, while the projective measure is a "state" measure, sensitive to transitory changes. Whether or not that is the case, it is clear from the correlational data he presents that AO and n Ach cannot be regarded as parallel forms. In his construct validation of the AO score, Carney related the measure to many other variables. It is questionable whether the relationships he has obtained are adequate to support his claim that the score assesses achievement motivation in the sense that McClelland uses the term. Nevertheless the relationships between a factor 2 summary score and other variables have intrinsic interest for the CPI student.

SITUATIONAL INFLUENCES

Carney et al. (1966) obtained AO scores under relaxed conditions and conditions calculated to arouse achievement motivation. They found AO scores increased significantly when the instructions stressed the importance of the task or when administration of the CPI was preceded by failure on a math test. For the CPI user, the changes in those scores under different conditions are noteworthy.

TIME ESTIMATION

Carney (1963) found that men with high AO scores typically overestimate time intervals while those with low scores underestimate them; however, the reverse pattern was noted for women.

PERCEPTUAL BEHAVIOR

Carney (1963) reported a significant negative correlation between AO and the number of shifts in the Necker Cube illusion among eighteen men ($r = -.52$); among sixteen women this trend did not attain statistical significance ($r = .26$). More recently, Carney (1965) found a significant correlation ($r = .30$) between AO scores and field independence as measured by the Witkin rod-and-frame apparatus.

DEMOGRAPHIC VARIABLES

Carney and McKeachie (1963) found that, as they had predicted, Jews had higher AO scores than Protestants and Catholics. They also found students from higher socioeconomic strata had significantly higher scores than those with lower SES. That was contrary to their expectation but is not surprising in view of the fact that *Cs* is one of the five factor 2 scales.

SMOKING

In a number of groups, Carney (1967) consistently found a low but significant positive correlation ($r = .22$) between AO scores and smoking. He notes that smokers tend to describe themselves as extroverted. If that is indeed the case, it might account for such a pattern since many have suggested that factor 2 is essentially an extraversion factor.

AROUSAL

According to Carney (1965) AO correlates significantly with a number of physical measures of arousal including GSR readings during a mathematics test ($r = .30$), hand dynamometer readings during a test of intelligence and body strength ($r = .43$), and body temperature during exertion ($r = .52$).

Curvilinear relations have been found between AO and the proportion of sex chromatin (Barr bodies) found in buccal smears (Carney, 1967), and similar relationships have been reported between AO scores and ratings of the masculinity of the body structure in samples of male and female students.

It is difficult to integrate such diverse findings. Carney (1965, p. 865) suggests that the construct of achievement motivation may hold the fabric together but admits that "it is a slender thread at best." The present writer feels that a more promising approach would be to regard the AO score as a measure of social poise and assertiveness.

Medical and Physiological Research

Because of the close interrelation of personality variables and physiological functioning, the CPI in recent years has come into increasing use as a research tool in medical and physiological research. Carney's findings of significant relationships between his factor 2 summary score, AO, and such variables as smoking, somatotype, nuclear sex determination, GSR responsivity, and fluctuations in body temperature, have already been noted. In this discussion the use of the CPI in several psychophysiological investigations is described briefly. Most of the investigations reported here are pioneering efforts scrutinizing new areas. The results and their interpretation require much more research before their meaning and significance is clear. Since the *CPI* is of primary interest here, *we* shall not review each study in detail, but instead, focus on the role of the test in such new research efforts.

Serum cholesterol levels have been suggested as possible factors in cardiovascular disorders. Since personality variables have also been associated with various types of heart disease, Jenkins and his associates (1969) undertook an investigation of the relation of personality factors to serum cholesterol levels. In a sample of thirty-four San Francisco firemen he found significant positive correlations ranging from .35 to .46 between cholesterol level and scales *Re, So,* and *Sc.* In addition, a significant negative correlation (r = −.43) was found with *Sa.* From those data it appeared that the highly socialized, self-critical man is most likely to have the highest cholesterol level. Those high correlations were not replicated in a second study of 152 food-store workers. Through partial correlation, controlling for age, a low but significant association between *So* and cholesterol level was demonstrated. An interesting two-scale interaction pattern was demonstrated in this study when, after adjusting for age, it was found that the *S*s with high *So* and low *Sa* scores had the highest cholesterol levels, while those with low *So* and high *Sa* scores had the lowest.

Infantile colic is widely regarded as a psychosomatic response to stress on the part of the infant. Brown (1961) set out to determine whether the mothers of babies who developed colic during the first two or three months differed in their personality characteristics from mothers of noncolicky babies. Such a study would not only test the hypothesis that colic is the infant's response to a stressful environment created by an anxious or poorly adjusted mother, but also might indicate whether the CPI could be used to help identify such mothers in advance so that intervention by public health nurses or pediatricians could be planned. Brown administered the CPI and other instruments to new mothers at two hospitals on or about the fourth day after delivery. A follow-up conducted six to ten weeks later was used to determine the incidence of colic. On the basis of that follow-up, he formed two groups of nineteen mothers whose infants had developed colic and two contrast groups of fifty-eight mothers whose infants did not. In the first group he found the mothers of the children with colic were significantly lower on Wb, Sc, To, Gi, and Ai. All of those scales load on CPI factor 1 and suggest that those women had less well-developed values than did the other mothers. The results of the second comparison failed to replicate the first, however, for although the direction of the differences was the same, their magnitude was too small to be statistically reliable.

FAMILY PLANNING

The CPI has also been used in an ongoing program of research on family planning being conducted at the Cleveland Clinic by Ziegler and Rodgers and their associates (Ziegler, Rodgers, and Kriegsman, 1966; Ziegler, Rodgers, Kriegsman, and Martin, 1968; Ziegler, Rodgers, and Prentiss, 1969; Rodgers and Ziegler, 1968). One line of research there has focused on the before-and-after personality patterns of couples that elect for the man to have a vasectomy. Ziegler, Rodgers, and Kriegsman (1966) compared the CPI scores of forty-two men who chose vasectomies with those of forty-two men from couples using birth control pills. The only significant difference was that men scheduled for a vasectomy were significantly higher on the Socialization scale than the men in the comparison group. The wives' scores gave no support for the notion of greater female domination among the couples who had decided on a vasectomy. In a follow-up conducted a year later, significant increases were noted in the husbands' Sp scores and significant decreases in their So and Fe scores. However, another follow-up after three years showed no significant changes from the preoperative scores (Ziegler, Rodgers, and Prentiss, 1969).

The forty-two couples in the "pill" group served as Ss for another set of investigations aimed at illuminating the differences between couples who stop using oral contraceptives and those who continue their use (Rodgers and Ziegler, 1968; Ziegler, Rodgers, Kriegsman, and Martin, 1968). In that research, couples who abandoned the pill on medical advice or because they wanted a pregnancy were not included. The fifteen wives who continued using the pill were found to be significantly higher on the Sp, Sa, and Ai scales than the wives who discontinued. Their husband were found to be lower on the Gi, Ac, and So scales than the husbands of the women who discontinued. This suggested to the researchers that these men were less likely to take over the responsibility for contraception in order to please their wives. In the fifteen couples who continued using the pill there was an increase in the husbands' Cs, Ac, Ai, and Wb scores while the husbands

in the group that discontinued decreased on those scores over the four years of
the study.

In those longitudinal studies, the CPI, when periodically administered to
both spouses, was found to be a useful supplement to the data gathered from interviews and questionnaires. The results suggest that it would be useful in a variety of studies of marital interaction and adjustment.

Research has shown that dreaming typically occurs in cycles. Such dream
cycles are accompanied by rapid eye movements (REM) and a disturbance in
EEG pattern. Recently, Foulkes and Vogel (1965) demonstrated dreamlike
mentation at the onset of sleep with no REM and no EEG disturbances. In a
series of investigations, Foulkes and his co-workers have compared that dreamlike behavior (NREM mentation) with the more typical REM patterns. In those
investigations (Foulkes, Spear, and Symonds, 1966; Pivik and Foulkes, 1968a,
1968b) they have correlated the CPI with various aspects of that behavior, such
as the extent of dreamlike fantasy, the number of words used in reporting the
dream, the amount of NREM recall, and the time it takes the sleeper to orient
himself after being aroused. Foulkes, Spear, and Symonds (1966) reported significant correlations between such variables and several CPI scales. Generally,
those findings were not replicated by Pivik and Foulkes (1968a), who found only
six of seventy-two correlations between the CPI and various parameters of NREM
mentation statistically reliable. By comparing the personality variables associated
with REM and NREM mentation, the investigators hope to determine how similar the psychodynamics of the two forms of behavior are.

Lazarus, Speisman, Mordkoff, and Davison (1962) used the CPI to explore the personality patterns of college students with different autonomic reactions to the stress induced by seeing films of a primitive subincision rite. They
found that Ss with high So and Ai scores displayed stronger autonomic reactions
to stress than did those characterized by high scores on the factor 2 scales $Do, Cs,$
$Sp,$ and $Sa.$

Developmental Influences

Several studies have been performed examining the relationship between
the CPI and patterns of family life. The data from such studies can be used either
to formulate or to test hypotheses about the relationship between such patterns
and personality.

The CPI is used in a variety of ways in such studies. In Brown's study
(1961) of infantile colic, the CPI scores of the mothers were related to the development of colic on the part of their children. Vincent (1961) studied the effects of broken homes on the adjustment of adolescent girls. Contrasting the CPI
scores of fifty girls from broken homes with fifty girls from intact homes, he found
the girls from the broken homes significantly lower on $Do, Cs, Re,$ and $So.$ The
above Ss were all single girls who had never been pregnant. Vincent also compared the scores of fifty unwed mothers from broken homes with those of fifty

unwed mothers from unbroken homes. In that comparison, the girls from the broken homes were significantly lower on *So* but not on the other scales.

Further evidence for the association between socialization and broken homes is found in an investigation by Megargee, Parker, and Levine (1971). The CPI *So* scale was administered to 208 women and 280 men enrolled in introductory psychology classes at the University of Texas at Austin. On the basis of their *So* scores, the *S*s were divided into four groups: a) those with *T*-scores of 39 or less; b) those with *T*-scores from 40 to 49; c) those with *T*-scores from 50 to 59; and d) those with *T*-scores of 60 or above. The incidence of divorced parents was significantly higher in the groups with the lower *So* scores. Similarly, ratings of the overall adequacy of the parents' marriage and the happiness of their childhood increased dramatically from the low *So* to the high *So* groups. No differences in the incidence of firstborn or only-children were noted, however.

The effects of early parental absence were further investigated by Maruyama (1969), who compared the CPI scores of forty adolescent boys who had been separated from their parents from ages two to six with those of forty boys from intact families. He hypothesized that the former group would have a diminished sense of competence which would be manifested by lower scores on scales *Sa, Re,* and *Ai*. That hypothesis was confirmed. A second hypothesis—namely, that the separated boys would be less effective, and that that would be manifested through lower *Fe* scores—was not supported. Unfortunately, the design of the study confounded early parental absence with current deprivation, since all the boys in the early-parental-absence group were drawn from an institutional setting, while those in the early-intact group were still living at home.

Hill (1966a, 1967) also used University of Texas students in his study of the autobiographical correlates of the *Do, Re, So, Ac, Ai,* and *Ie* scales. Those CPI scales were administered to 350 male freshmen who were also asked to write structured autobiographies. The top and bottom 27 per cent on each scale were identified and their autobiographies compared on a number of dimensions dealing with the father, the mother, disciplinary practices, childhood, adolescence, and so forth. For five of the six scales, the autobiographical accounts were quite consistent with the expectations; the sixth was neutral in that regard. While Hill was primarily interested in construct validation of the scales, the data can also be studied to learn how certain childhood patterns relate to subsequent personality functioning.

Mitchell (1965) used the CPI to test the hypothesis that children's sex-role adjustment would be related to the adjustment of the same-sex parent. He administered the CPI *Do* and *Fe* scales to ninety-eight boys and one hundred and twenty-eight girls in the ninth grade and to their parents. For each married couple, he compared the husband's and wife's *Do* and *Fe* scores to determine whether or not they fell into the culturally approved pattern of compatibility (dominant, masculine father, and less dominant, feminine mother). In counselors' ratings of the children, he found that boys whose parents scored low on the index of conventional sex role consonance appeared more maladjusted than those whose parents were high on the measure. The patterns of parental dominance were also associated with general and individual parent disciplinary patterns. This study is noteworthy not only for its specific findings but also because of its methodological innovations, specifically the relating of differences in two-scale configurations in the parents to an independent measure of adjustment in children.

Leventhal (1970) used the CPI *Fe* scale to test certain notions about the origins of sex-role behavior. The assumption that children imitate their siblings' behavior suggested that in two-child families, men with sisters should be more feminine than men with brothers. Leventhal's study, however, showed that it was the men with older sisters who had the significantly lower *Fe* scores.

Political Participation

Milbrath and Klein (1962) administered shortened versions of the *Do, Sc, Sp, Sa,* and *So* scales to eighty-eight Washington lobbyists to determine the relationship between personality and different styles of participation in politics. Feeling they measured the same basic attributes, Milbrath and Klein shortened and combined *Sp, Sa, So,* and *Sc* into a single scale that they labeled *sociality.* They then correlated the scores on that combined scale and the scores on *Do* with various types of political activity. They found that *Do* correlated significantly with campaigning and participating in nonpolitical groups. The sociality scores, on the other hand, not only correlated significantly with those activities, but also with party activity, contributing funds to the party, and soliciting funds for the party. Neither scale related significantly to holding elective public office.

From this brief survey of the research applications of the CPI, it can be seen that it has been used in a variety of ways and found to relate to many variables ranging from physiological factors to political behavior. The developmental studies have shown that the CPI can be used to chart the effects of personality factors spanning two generations, while the longitudinal research reviewed in this and other chapters has demonstrated that it is sensitive to influences occurring over a number of years. Clearly, the data show the CPI to be a "wide-banned" instrument with many diverse applications.

Directions for Research

ᚨᚠᚨᚠᚨᚠᚨᚠᚨᚠᚨᚠᚨᚠᚨᚠᚨᚠᚨᚠᚨᚠᚨᚠᚨᚠᚨᚠᚨᚠᚨᚠᚨᚠᚨᚠᚨᚠ

One can be impressed by the wide variety of problems to which the CPI has been applied. The studies reviewed here have found significant associations between the CPI and various measures of achievement in elementary school, high school, and college, as well as in military and police training programs, medicine, dentistry, nursing, and teaching; moreover, the CPI can identify those who are likely to partake in extracurricular activities or cheat on exams. The inventory has been found to relate to leadership, managerial ability, employability, and adjustment. It can forecast juvenile delinquency, parole success, and can reliably discriminate alcoholics from marijuana and cigarette smokers. It has been found to relate to conformity, creativity, time estimation, physiological responsiveness to stress, blood serum patterns, political participation, marital adjustment, and to one's choice of family planning methods. The CPI can also be used to predict whether an infant is likely to suffer from colic, and it can chart the short and long term effects on such infants if the marriage should end in divorce.

Thus the CPI is clearly a "wide-band" instrument—one that is sensitive to a broad array of behavior patterns. In selecting a wide-band instrument one usually sacrifices validity. A psychologist interested only in intellectual functioning, for example, would be better advised to administer a narrower-band instrument such as the WAIS. The relation between band width and validity is not absolute. Despite its broad range of applicability, the CPI is quite valid in some areas such as the assessment of socialization and psychological femininity.

The CPI's range of application is not the most noteworthy aspect of the research literature, however, for other assessment devices such as the Rorschach and clinical interview have been applied to an even broader array of problems (although not with as much demonstrated empirical success). More noteworthy

247

is the fact that the CPI has been found capable of making long-range predictions, sometimes over a period of three or four years. Concurrent validation is all very well, but the true test of a personality assessment device is whether it can provide one with valid predictions of behavior early enough for appropriate action to be taken (Meehl, 1959; Myers, 1950). The CPI can, apparently, validly forecast high school graduation, college matriculation, and college graduation, particularly when used in conjunction with the sources of data. To be sure, some of the associations, although statistically significant, are small in magnitude. In that respect the CPI is reminiscent of a dog walking on his hind legs—he does not do it well, but it is remarkable that he does it at all.

Another noteworthy aspect of the literature is the success the CPI has enjoyed in other cultures. Psychologists have been skeptical about whether domestic assessment devices in general, and structured inventories in particular, can be exported successfully. The fact that it was so contrary to expectation makes the cross-cultural data even more impressive.[1] Whether it is due to the use of folk concepts, the item pool, the scale construction strategy, all of the above, or none of the above, it is clear that Gough has created a remarkably vigorous assessment advice.

If nothing else, the literature demonstrates the wide acceptance the CPI has found among applied psychologists in both their scientific and their professional roles. The most recent reviews in the *Mental Measurements Yearbooks* reflect that acceptance: In 1965, Kelly termed the CPI "one of the best, if not *the* best available instrument of its kind," and Goldberg's forthcoming review states, "At least for the next five years, the knowledgeable applied practitioner should be able to provide more valid nontest predictions from the CPI than from most other comparable instruments on the market today" (Goldberg, in press).

Such acceptance was hard won. When the CPI was first introduced, there was considerable skepticism regarding the usefulness of "paper-and-pencil" instruments. In 1953, Albert Ellis noted the field of personality assessment was virtually monopolized by projective techniques and that it was often assumed "that paper and pencil tests of personality are rarely employed by reputable clinicians." After surveying the literature on their use and validity Ellis concluded,

> "since personality inventories depend, in the last analysis, on printed questions, and since virtually no one claims for them the advantage of getting at unconscious and semiconscious material which effective clinical use of interview and projective methods are generally conceded to some extent to uncover, it is difficult to see why clinicians should spend considerable time first mastering and then using these inventories. The clinical psychologist who cannot, in the time it now takes a trained worker to administer, score and interpret a test like the MMPI according to the best recommendations of its authors, get much more pertinent, incisive, and depth-centered 'personality' material from a straight-

[1] Gough recalls one colleague who dismissed the early results on the validity of the Socialization scale in Europe as meaningless since "all Western cultures are alike." When the data from Costa Rica arrived, Gough rushed to show his colleague, who looked at them in consternation and cried, "Damn that United Fruit Company! They've Americanized the Costa Ricans!"

forward interview technique would hardly appear to be worth his salt" [Ellis, 1953, p. 48].

The fact that structured inventories are viewed more favorably in most quarters today is due in no small measure to the development of the CPI and the vigorous program of research undertaken with it.

What directions should be taken in future research with the CPI? The reader who is "worth his salt" has no doubt formulated several ideas. In the final pages are noted a few of the more pressing priorities.

Test Development

The primary need in the area of test development is for normative studies on representative samples of minority-group Americans. It is ironic that less is known about the CPI scores of black and brown Americans than about the score patterns of people from other nations. In recent years, research has been performed using Negro, Mexican-American, and American Indian subjects. The results of those studies are disquieting because they show that lower class minority-group members often obtain lower scores on most CPI scales. As the CPI wins increasing acceptance, the regression equations derived for the prediction of job performance, academic achievement, and the like, will no doubt be used more and more to screen applicants for various educational and vocational opportunities. If so, we might expect a high proportion of minority-group members to be rejected on the basis of those scores. There is therefore an urgent need for normative research on blacks and other minority-groups. (That is equally true of most other personality-assessment devices in current use.) As noted, some studies have been performed, but they have not used national samples stratified on the basis of age or socioeconomic status. The effects of race, SES, IQ, and other demographic variables on CPI scores should be sorted out.

If the present norms are not found suitable for use with minority-group members, there are several possible courses of action. Gynther (1971) has discovered that several MMPI scales discriminate against blacks, causing them to be rejected from police training programs in which the MMPI is a screening device. He recommends deriving new race-specific scales. For example, on the Sc (Schizophrenia) scale, normal blacks obtained a mean T-score of 80, falsely indicating serious disturbances. Gynther would create a new "black" Sc scale by contrasting the responses of normal and schizophrenic blacks. A similar procedure could be followed for the CPI. Or race-specific multiple regression formulas could be developed for various selection situations. Perhaps a correction factor built into the norms would be sufficient. Or it may be that the CPI in its present form is entirely suitable. Until large-scale normative research is undertaken and the extent of the problem, if any, determined, no corrective steps can be taken.

A similar but less pressing problem exists with respect to age. The applicability of the CPI to older groups should be determined. Some research has been done on changes in CPI scores as a function of age (Grupp, Ramseyer, and Richardson, 1968) and that needs to be pursued further.

Scale Validity

In our review of the validation of the eighteen CPI scales, wide discrepancies were apparent. Some scales such as *Do, So, Ac, Ai,* and *Fe* have had dozens of studies performed on them; others have languished in obscurity. The most obvious need is for better evidence regarding the validity of some of those neglected scales. In particular, the distinction between certain groups of similar scales such as *Sy* and *Sp, Ac* and *Ai,* and *Re, So,* and *Sc* needs to be sharpened through empirical research.

The individual interpretation of the CPI relies in part on configural patterns and curvilinear relationships. The empirical foundations for those interpretive principles are weak. More studies need to be performed to demonstrate how the meaning of one scale depends upon the elevation of another and determine whether the meaning of some scales such as *Sc* and *Fx* alters drastically at the extremes.

Another basic interpretive principle is that situational as well as personality factors should be considered in making predictions. Aside from the Dominance scale, for which the influence of the race, sex, and dominance level of the subject's task partner have been examined, there has been little if any exploration of the configural relations between CPI-assessed traits and situational factors. Such studies should have high priority.

Factorial Research

Numerous factor analyses of the CPI have all yielded essentially identical results. The author feels that further factor analyses of the CPI scales would be a waste of time. Scales have been developed for factors 1, 2, and 5 (*Fe*). Factor scales for factors 3 and 4 might be useful.

Relations With Other Variables

The adjectival analyses and the published correlations of the CPI with other inventories are both great assets to the CPI user. As new inventories are introduced, those tables in the *Manual* should be kept up to date.

The vast bulk of such research has used normal samples. It would be interesting to learn whether the same patterns of correlations, and more important, the same adjectives, could be applied to other groups, such as psychiatric patients who exhibit similar score characteristics.

Individual Interpretation

Although the CPI was designed to be used in individual interpretation, there are pitifully few studies testing the validity of clinicians' CPI interpretations. The problems of validating rich, complex, clinical interpretations are immense, as projective testers discovered some time ago (Megargee, 1966c), but somehow those problems must be tackled if one is to justify continuing the training of clinicians in such an art. In particular, we should determine those problems, populations, and settings which are most amenable to clinical interpretation, and those in which clinicians are most likely to err. If indeed certain talents are necessary to acquire interpretational skills, then it would be appropriate to devise selection devices to identify such clinicians. (Perhaps an actuarial CPI formula?)

Educational and Vocational Applications

The ability of the CPI to forecast academic and vocational achievement and the parameters that influence those predictions have been well-documented in the literature, and there is a surfeit of multiple regression formulas. It would be desirable if researchers would compare the validity and determine the generality of some of the prediction formulas already developed before rushing to compute new ones.

The bulk of the research in that area has been on the prediction of academic success in high school and college. In addition to their applied value, such studies also demonstrate the long-range forecasting ability of the CPI and illustrate how prediction is enhanced if the CPI is used in conjunction with other data. The author would suggest that researchers in those areas turn now from prediction studies to research, using the CPI to identifiy the personality dynamics associated with achievement at various IQ levels. Ideally, such investigations would examine not only the students, but also their parents. Studies designed to determine which students respond best to different instructional approaches would also be highly desirable.

Clinical Applications

The clinical use of the CPI would benefit greatly from the use of some of the multivariate approaches that have sparked the educational-vocational research. Additional use of multiple regression techniques and discriminant analyses is needed.

Because the CPI was developed for use with normal people, the author is skeptical about its usefulness in differential diagnosis of psychiatric patients, unless it is used as part of a clinical battery. Research on clinical assessment has shown the major problem with instruments designed to detect psychopathology, such as the Rorschach and MMPI, is that they may overestimate the extent of disturbances (Megargee, 1966c). Regression analyses using CPI scores in conjunction with more clinical instruments might show an improvement in the predictions that are possible from either instrument alone.

Thus far the CPI has been shown to be most useful in discriminating individuals who are primarily in conflict with society rather than with themselves. Low *So* scores characterize delinquents, criminals, unwed mothers, marijuana and cigarette smokers, bright underachievers, alcoholics, cheaters—and psychologists. A fruitful area for configural research would be studies such as Hogan's (1970) designed to determine what other variables influence the behavioral manifestation of low socialization. Such studies might also provide indications about whether the CPI could be used for the typological classification of antisocial individuals.

Other Research Applications

The range of other research applications of the CPI is limited only by the imagination of investigators. Thus far most of the studies have been exploratory in nature, designed simply to determine if there is a relation between CPI scale A and behavior pattern X. Further studies should pursue, replicate, and try to make sense out of those findings in order to answer the question, "Why should there be a correlation between A and X?"

As we have seen, much has been done with the CPI. Twenty-one years have passed since it was first copyrighted. Those years have been devoted to its development and to testing its potential abilities in various directions. At the age of twenty-one, the CPI has reached its maturity. There will be changes and refinements, hopefully for the better, but its basic character is fixed. Now, as with any young adult, it is time for the years of useful productivity to begin.

Item Composition of Selected CPI Scales

Standard Scales

DOMINANCE (*Do*)—forty-six items
> *True:* 53, 57, 162, 167, 179, 202, 207, 235, 267, 295, 303, 304, 310, 319, 320, 335, 346, 355, 359, 376, 403, 412, 448.
> *False:* 31, 54, 111, 113, 117, 177, 210, 233, 253, 258, 314, 315, 369, 370, 379, 383, 385, 390, 418, 424, 443, 452, 456.

CAPACITY FOR STATUS (*Cs*)—thirty-two items
> *True:* 17, 62, 72, 103, 154, 160, 167, 200, 201, 283, 287.
> *False:* 23, 25, 32, 40, 47, 49, 55, 68, 79, 94, 128, 137, 186, 190, 220, 227, 230, 233, 237, 258, 273.

SOCIABILITY (*Sy*)—thirty-six items
> *True:* 1, 4, 45, 50, 61, 84, 102, 107, 108, 126, 146, 163, 167, 197, 202, 216, 218, 228, 242, 269, 277, 283.
> *False:* 7, 64, 74, 83, 111, 121, 124, 134, 145, 188, 225, 258, 273, 284.

SOCIAL PRESENCE (*Sp*)—fifty-six items
> *True:* 4, 10, 30, 50, 77, 80, 93, 97, 102, 108, 148, 152, 170, 180, 197, 200, 208, 224, 231, 245, 251, 259, 275, 280, 296.
> *False:* 2, 5, 14, 23, 25, 47, 54, 58, 68, 69, 74, 76, 83, 92, 96, 98, 118, 123, 134, 137, 150, 156, 174, 177, 187, 192, 226, 227, 229, 282, 285.

SELF-ACCEPTANCE (*Sa*)—thirty-four items
> *True:* 21, 42, 86, 101, 104, 112, 138, 146, 179, 197, 198, 211, 216, 247, 275, 296, 300.
> *False:* 3, 7, 31, 38, 47, 69, 111, 121, 174, 177, 182, 185, 227, 233, 258, 284, 291.

SENSE OF WELL-BEING (*Wb*)—forty-four items

True: 224, 259, 276, 312, 313, 413.
False: 15, 54, 70, 89, 191, 236, 266, 297, 299, 301, 306, 308, 309, 318, 325, 330, 337, 341, 344, 351, 353, 358, 372, 375, 381, 388, 398, 406, 411, 415, 425, 430, 434, 437, 438, 449, 454, 455.

RESPONSIBILITY (*Re*)—forty-two items

True: 18, 22, 51, 61, 126, 138, 162, 179, 193, 212, 213, 221, 234, 235, 278, 283, 286.
False: 16, 20, 26, 36, 43, 49, 73, 75, 77, 90, 105, 113, 121, 129, 139, 164, 189, 205, 206, 210, 253, 261, 288, 294, 300.

SOCIALIZATION (*So*)—fifty-four items

True: 62, 123, 144, 168, 180, 192, 198, 212, 223, 245, 284, 317, 323, 334, 367, 373, 389, 394, 395, 409, 429, 439.
False: 12, 36, 93, 94, 156, 164, 170, 182, 184, 214, 257, 302, 327, 336, 338, 339, 345, 369, 385, 386, 393, 396, 398, 405, 416, 420, 428, 431, 435, 436, 444, 457.

SELF-CONTROL (*Sc*)—fifty items

True: 149, 168, 174, 223, 276, 286.
False: 4, 20, 29, 42, 44, 48, 53, 54, 57, 66, 78, 81, 91, 93, 102, 104, 114, 115, 120, 132, 146, 151, 170, 173, 178, 183, 185, 191, 196, 208, 211, 231, 243, 248, 251, 257, 267, 275, 292, 294, 296, 297, 298, 300.

TOLERANCE (*To*)—thirty-two items

True: 122, 172, 269.
False: 15, 20, 27, 33, 60, 67, 89, 94, 117, 134, 136, 139, 142, 151, 158, 176, 183, 184 ,206, 209, 219, 237, 241, 247, 257, 258, 266, 285, 294.

GOOD IMPRESSION (*Gi*)—forty items

True: 14, 103, 127, 133, 140, 165, 195, 222, 254.
False: 10, 30, 34, 38, 42, 44, 48, 56, 66, 70, 78, 81, 91, 101, 109, 120, 150, 153, 159, 170, 178, 203, 207, 231, 238, 248, 262, 268, 275, 289, 293.

COMMUNALITY (*Cm*)—twenty-eight items

True: 316, 322, 333, 342, 343, 348, 371, 410, 426, 427, 440, 445, 446, 447.
False: 307, 311, 321, 324, 332, 349, 350, 360, 366, 374, 378, 384, 401, 421.

ACHIEVEMENT VIA CONFORMANCE (*Ac*)—thirty-eight items

True: 6, 8, 46, 125, 135, 202, 228, 239, 246, 260, 264, 292.
False: 9, 20, 29, 36, 49, 119, 121, 145, 147, 157, 161, 164, 173, 175, 194, 214, 236, 243, 250, 251, 270, 271, 279, 281, 291, 299.

ACHIEVEMENT VIA INDEPENDENCE (*Ai*)—thirty-two items

True: 8, 50, 122.
False: 3, 5, 20, 37, 41, 52, 59, 63, 116, 117, 121, 130, 139, 141, 145, 169, 196, 204, 206, 225, 237, 241, 252, 255, 263, 265, 270, 273, 294.

INTELLECTUAL EFFICIENCY (*Ie*)—fifty-two items

True: 30, 50, 122, 152, 200, 228, 269, 283, 290, 356, 362, 368, 389, 391, 399, 407, 414, 432, 433.
False: 2, 20, 49, 64, 76, 92, 111, 121, 136, 141, 157, 164, 169, 184, 188, 205, 258, 265, 273, 298, 352, 365, 382, 392, 402, 417, 419, 422, 423, 434, 441, 450, 453.

PSYCHOLOGICAL-MINDEDNESS *(Py)*—twenty-two items
> *True:* 95, 166, 172, 207, 215, 234.
> *False:* 11, 12, 24, 54, 85, 88, 99, 118, 131, 145, 155, 185, 211, 226, 229, 282.

FLEXIBILITY *(Fx)*—twenty-two items
> *True:* 331.
> *False:* 305, 326, 328, 329, 340, 347, 354, 357, 361, 363, 364, 377, 380, 387, 397, 400, 404, 408, 442, 451, 458.

FEMININITY *(Fe)*—thirty-eight items
> *True:* 28, 35, 58, 64, 65, 71, 110, 115, 144, 181, 187, 217, 232, 240, 244, 272, 278.
> *False:* 13, 19, 38, 39, 78, 82, 87, 100, 106, 114, 123, 129, 143, 171, 199, 208, 210, 214, 249, 256, 274.

Abbreviated MMPI Scales

To estimate MMPI scale raw scores (without K corrections) from corresponding CPI abbreviated scales use this formula: $y = aX + b$, where y = estimated MMPI raw score and x = score on abbreviated CPI scales and a and b represent constants for each scale (Rodgers, 1966).

LIE *(CPI-L)*
> *True:* none
> *False:* 30, 66, 91, 120, 153, 197, 207, 373, 414.
> a = 1.068   b = 1.36

FREQUENCY *(CPI-F)*
> *True:* 2, 157, 183, 288, 306, 330, 372, 393, 423, 437, 454.
> *False:* 224, 312, 392.
> a = 1.927   b = 2.08

CORRECTION *(CPI-K)*
> *True:* 276.
> *False:* 10, 44, 60, 66, 111, 128, 133, 134, 142, 147, 150, 227.
> a = 1.609   b = 5.72

HYPOCHONDRIASIS *(CPI-Hs)*
> *True:* 298, 308, 411, 437, 459.
> *False:* 135, 138, 313, 407, 475.
> a = 2.456   b = 3.87

DEPRESSION *(CPI-D)*
> *True:* 54, 147, 150, 177, 299, 437, 453, 459.
> *False:* 21, 44, 50, 66, 114, 128, 130, 133, 197, 242, 245, 259, 280, 356, 358, 474, 475, 479.
> a = 1.675   b = 7.17

HYSTERIA *(CPI-Hy)*
> *True:* 54, 89, 107, 158, 337, 437, 455, 459.
> *False:* 21, 66, 111, 124, 128, 133, 135, 138, 142, 161, 176, 227, 245, 266, 342, 389, 457, 475.
> a = 1.773   b = 8.29

PSYCHOPATHIC DEVIATE *(CPI-Pd)*
> *True:* 20, 54, 94, 164, 173, 214, 257, 336, 353, 369, 386, 390, 393, 398, 423, 454.

False: 21, 37, 61, 111, 130, 134, 212, 227, 245, 267, 276, 290, 385, 389.
a = 1.275   b = 5.75

MASCULINITY-FEMINITY (*CPI-Mf*)
True: 8, 17, 72, 122, 217, 240, 244, 351.
False: 19, 49, 121, 128, 136, 143, 167, 172, 199, 205, 208, 209, 210, 249, 269, 373, 392, 474.
$a_m = 0.611$ $b_m = 18.07$
$a_f = 1.260$ $b_f = 15.69$

PARANOIA (*CPI-Pa*)
True: 91, 184, 220, 294, 353, 386, 398, 423.
False: 32, 142, 209, 212, 219, 241, 245, 266, 286.
a = 0.995   b = 4.70

PSYCHASTHENIA (*CPI-Pt*)
True: 54, 70, 91, 147, 151, 177, 187, 243, 257, 258, 309, 369, 383, 449, 455, 456.
False: 21, 50, 108, 135, 356.
a = 1.965   b = 1.48

SCHIZOPHRENIA (*CPI-Sc*)
True: 20, 54, 89, 91, 99, 137, 151, 175, 236, 285, 294, 297, 299, 309, 330, 336, 341, 353, 358, 398, 402, 423, 430, 449, 456.
False: 21, 290, 413.
a = 2.006   b = 3.19

HYPOMANIA (*CPI-Ma*)
True: 77, 117, 175, 294, 297, 336, 338, 341, 351, 386, 399, 402, 453, 479.
False: 111, 134, 148, 153, 227, 286, 373, 389.
a = 1.331   b = 5.10

SOCIAL INTROVERSION (*CPI-Si*)
True: 27, 54, 68, 124, 134, 142, 150, 188, 209, 227, 258, 286, 385, 422.
False: 1, 20, 108, 111, 143, 163, 167, 191, 200, 202, 206, 208, 218, 242, 243, 368.
a = 1.930   b = 1.84

Hase Experimental Scales

FACTOR SCALES

EXTROVERSION-INTROVERSION (*fEx*)
True: 108, 200, 216, 242, 259, 277, 346.
False: 33, 38, 58, 74, 83, 111, 124, 134, 159, 177, 186, 227, 272, 284, 385, 418.

HARMONIOUS CHILDHOOD (*fHa*)
True: 45, 168, 323, 367.
False: 299, 302, 420, 428, 453.

SURGENCY (*fSu*)
True: 1, 77, 102, 163, 167, 208, 218, 231, 251, 296, 395.
False: 69, 182, 318.

CONFORMITY-REBELLIOUSNESS (*fCo*)
True: 223.
False: 44, 80, 91, 114, 161, 173, 183, 214, 248, 250, 268, 275, 297, 336, 396, 435.

ASCENDENCE-SUBMISSION *(fAs)*
True: 39, 53, 179, 184, 202, 239, 267, 320, 359, 376, 412, 448.
False: 31, 379, 443.

SUPER EGO STRENGTH-NEUROTICISM *(fSe)*
True: 50.
False: 11, 54, 99, 121, 145, 176, 192, 194, 238, 243, 252, 257, 279, 298, 327, 331, 369, 405, 422, 456, 477.

ORTHODOXY-FLEXIBILITY *(fOr)*
True: 24, 35, 51, 68, 85, 88, 96, 98, 112, 123, 131, 230, 256, 273, 317, 328, 348, 361, 363, 370, 380, 383, 387, 409, 460, 478.
False: 228.

SELF-CONFIDENCE IN PUBLIC *(fSc)*
True: 52, 239, 319, 403.
False: 7, 40, 258, 314, 334, 429, 452.

AMIABILITY-IRRITABILITY *(fAm)*
True: 138.
False: 2, 64, 89, 178, 190, 236, 364, 425, 469.

SERENITY-DEPRESSION *(fSe)*
True: 245.
False: 12, 27, 76, 94, 185, 187, 232, 311, 341, 353, 365, 378, 416, 419, 441, 461, 465, 467.

EGO-STRENGTH-PSYCHOTICISM *(fPs)*
True: 13, 180.
False: 20, 92, 128, 151, 157, 158, 164, 206, 271, 294, 299, 302, 374, 390, 421, 423, 431, 444, 449, 454.

THEORETICAL SCALES

ACHIEVEMENT *(nAc)*
True: 6, 56, 112, 131, 181, 224, 256, 260, 264, 312, 316, 380, 382, 473.
False: 101, 145, 352.

AFFILIATION *(nAf)*
True: 1, 107, 167, 242, 287, 395.
False: 38, 74, 124, 332, 468.

DEFERENCE *(nDe)*
True: 3, 7, 11, 125, 127, 155, 165, 198, 223, 304, 314, 370, 462, 478.
False: none.

DOMINANCE *(nDo)*
True: 50, 53, 179, 200, 202, 319, 320, 346, 359, 376, 403, 412, 448.
False: 31, 379, 443.

EXHIBITION *(nEx)*
True: 4, 78, 93, 102, 108, 146, 231, 239, 267, 292, 296, 317, 435.
False: 186.

INFRAVOIDANCE *(nIn)*
True: 25, 40, 57, 58, 83, 85, 111, 134, 150, 159, 227, 258, 284, 285, 334, 348, 418, 422, 429, 452.
False: none.

NURTURANCE (nNu)

> *True:* 195, 240, 295, 433, 447.
> *False:* 16, 219, 315, 329, 374, 469.

ORDER (nOr)

> *True:* 24, 88, 166, 204, 229, 246, 328, 361, 364, 387, 408.
> *False:* 331.

PLAY (nPl)

> *True:* 9, 39, 77, 119, 143, 163, 185, 208, 218, 251, 280.
> *False:* 461.

UNDERSTANDING (nUn)

> *True:* 95, 140, 211, 215, 222, 228, 269, 283, 472.
> *False:* 2, 67, 281.

AUTONOMY (nAu)

> *True:* 36, 81, 148, 157, 180, 182, 194, 214, 250, 268, 275, 288, 302, 318, 336, 396, 421, 476.
> *False:* none.

RATIONAL SCALES

DOMINANCE ($R\ Dom$)

> *True:* 6, 37, 50, 53, 81, 102, 179, 180, 200, 202, 224, 239, 256, 267, 319, 320, 346, 355, 359, 376, 403, 412, 448, 476.
> *False:* 7, 11, 13, 25, 31, 111, 134, 177, 227, 258, 272, 335, 369, 379, 383, 385, 418, 429, 443, 452, 462.

SOCIABILITY ($r\ Soc$)

> *True:* 1, 21, 52, 77, 102, 108, 119, 143, 163, 167, 208, 218, 242, 251, 280, 287, 346, 395.
> *False:* 38, 40, 57, 74, 83, 109, 111, 124, 134, 156, 159, 182, 227, 236, 252, 284, 285, 286, 334, 416, 418, 461.

RESPONSIBILITY ($r\ Res$)

> *True:* 14, 51, 112, 149, 162, 181, 195, 221, 234, 235, 260, 278, 312, 323, 380, 389, 442, 473.
> *False:* 43, 49, 73, 101, 117, 120, 139, 145, 185, 203, 253, 262, 275, 297, 307, 331, 374, 388, 420.

PSYCHOLOGICAL-MINDEDNESS ($r\ Psy$)

> *True:* 127.
> *False:* 25, 47, 59, 69, 98, 106, 123, 136, 141, 176, 209, 219, 225, 226, 233, 252, 257, 282, 325, 329, 378, 416, 419, 425, 457, 458, 460, 469.

FEMININITY ($r\ Fem$)

> *True:* 28, 68, 88, 144, 160, 240, 244, 286, 287, 433, 480.
> *False:* 17, 33, 36, 82, 87, 95, 104, 129, 172, 196, 205, 210, 249, 269, 283, 291.

ACADEMIC ACHIEVEMENT ($r\ Ach$)

> *True:* 6, 50, 61, 84, 95, 103, 122, 140, 166, 181, 204, 222, 224, 228, 246, 256, 260, 269, 283, 292, 391, 408.
> *False:* 54, 94, 99, 116, 121, 145, 169, 185, 230, 326, 331, 352, 422, 436, 450, 456.

YIELDING-CONFORMITY *(r Con)*

>   *True:* 7, 58, 88, 127, 165, 198, 212, 223, 229, 255, 260, 263, 276, 290, 304, 305, 314, 348, 385, 387, 462, 478.
>   *False:* 29, 170, 250, 268, 275, 302, 339.

Other Scales

AMENABILITY *(Amen)*, (Rudoff, 1959).

>   *True:* 3, 7, 43, 44, 64, 74, 91, 111, 112, 121, 124, 147, 157, 170, 173, 174, 209, 213, 243, 266, 281, 284, 294, 317, 341, 345, 351, 361, 409, 416, 428, 436, 454.
>   *False:* 45, 168, 228, 276, 313, 411, 469.

ANXIETY *(Anx)*, (Leventhal, 1966).

>   *True:* 90, 94, 156, 158, 175, 183, 236, 285, 306, 321, 327, 353, 372, 378, 381, 390, 398.
>   *False:* 178, 190, 214, 246, 348.

EMPATHY *(Emp)*, (Hogan, 1969)

>   *True:* 4, 8, 52, 84, 86, 97, 100, 127, 191, 198, 239, 275, 287, 359, 403.
>   *False:* 25, 67, 79, 81, 98, 186, 194, 247, 255, 271, 361, 363, 364, 421, 442, 463.

FACTOR P: PERSON ORIENTATION *(Po)*, (Nichols and Schnell, 1963)

>   *True:* 45, 52, 53, 97, 108, 131, 146, 154, 163, 179, 200, 202, 216, 218, 239, 242, 256, 287, 292, 319, 320, 346, 359, 391, 403, 412, 448, 475.
>   *False:* 7, 13, 25, 38, 64, 68, 74, 79, 85, 182, 186, 188, 223, 227, 272, 314, 325, 383, 385, 418, 429, 452, 460.

FACTOR V: VALUE ORIENTATION *(Vo)*, (Nichols and Schnell, 1963)

>   *True:* 22, 46, 103, 127, 135, 138, 149, 165, 168, 174, 181, 195, 260, 276, 278, 313, 356, 362, 367, 371, 380, 392, 407, 413, 439, 451.
>   *False:* 20, 26, 29, 30, 32, 42, 44, 48, 49, 55, 60, 71, 77, 80, 81, 93, 101, 105, 106, 109, 114, 115, 117, 119, 120, 132, 141, 142, 153, 155, 157, 161, 164, 170, 175, 178, 183, 184, 185, 191, 194, 203, 206, 209, 214, 237, 247, 248, 250, 253, 262, 266, 268, 270, 275, 279, 282, 289, 291, 294, 297, 298, 299, 300, 302, 307, 336, 344, 351, 353, 375, 396, 398, 399, 406, 411, 419, 420, 428, 431, 436, 453, 454, 463, 468, 470, 474.

BARRON EGO-STRENGTH SCALE *(CPI-Es)*, (Goldberg, personal communication)

>   *True:* 62, 77, 107, 269, 356, 475.
>   *False:* 20, 54, 70, 74, 151, 173, 175, 232, 243, 298, 344, 358, 369, 385, 434, 441, 459.

Adjectives characterizing high-scoring and low-scoring men on the eighteen CPI scales

Do

High

ambitious
dominant
forceful
optimistic
planful
resourceful
responsible
self-confident
stable
stern

Low

apathetic
indifferent
interests narrow
irresponsible
pessimistic
restless
rigid
reckless
suggestible
submissive

Cs

High

discreet
forgiving
imaginative
independent
mature
opportunistic
pleasant
praising
progressive
reasonable

Low

bitter
gloomy
greedy
interests narrow
nagging
resentful
restless
tense
touchy
unkind

Sy

High

clever
confident
interests wide
logical
mature
outgoing
resourceful
reasonable
self-confident
sociable

Low

awkward
bitter
cold
complaining
confused
hard-hearted
interests narrow
quitting
shallow
unkind

Sp

High

adventurous
interests wide
pleasure-seeking
relaxed
self-confident
sharp-witted
unconventional
uninhibited
versatile
witty

Low

appreciative
cautious
cooperative
interests narrow
kind
mannerly
patient
prudish
serious
shy

Sa

High

confident
enterprising
egotistical
imaginative
opportunistic
outgoing
polished
self-confident
self-seeking
sophisticated

Low

bitter
commonplace
interests narrow
quitting
reckless
submissive
tense
unintelligent
withdrawn
self-denying

Wb

High

conservative
dependable
dependent
good-natured
inhibited
logical
pleasant

Re

capable
conscientious
dependable
reasonable
reliable
responsible
serious

So

adaptable
efficient
honest
inhibited
kind
organized
reasonable

Sc

considerate
dependable
hard-headed
logical
painstaking
precise
reasonable

To

forgiving
generous
good-natured
independent
informal
pleasant
reasonable

	poised	stable	sincere	reliable	soft-hearted
	praising	steady	thorough	self-controlled	thoughtful
	relaxed	thorough	wholesome	self-denying	unselfish
	sincere				
	anxious	careless	deceitful	conceited	affected
	blustery	disorderly	defensive	fault-finding	cold
	distractible	forgetful	headstrong	hasty	egotistical
	forgetful	irresponsible	irresponsible	headstrong	fussy
Low	hurried	lazy	mischievous	impulsive	hard-hearted
	impulsive	mischievous	outspoken	individualistic	self-centered
	mischievous	pleasure-seeking	quarrelsome	self-seeking	shallow
	quitting	reckless	rude	spunky	thankless
	shallow	show-off	sarcastic	temperamental	whiny
	restless	spendthrift	unconventional	unrealistic	fault-finding

	Gi	Cm	Ac	Ai
	adaptable	cautious	ambitious	foresighted
	changeable	conscientious	capable	independent
	considerate	deliberate	conscientious	informal
	kind	efficient	considerate	intelligent
High	self-denying	formal	intelligent	lazy
	soft-hearted	organized	logical	pleasant
	tactful	practical	mature	rational
	unselfish	responsible	reasonable	sarcastic
	warm	thorough	resourceful	touchy
	friendly	thrifty	responsible	versatile
	complaining	attractive	apathetic	affected
	dissatisfied	careless	distrustful	bossy
Low	fault-finding	courageous	hard-hearted	cautious

	Ie	Py	Fx	Fe
Low (Cont.)	hasty	daring	irresponsible	cool
	headstrong	distractible	pleasure-seeking	egotistical
	indifferent	forgetful	reckless	fearful
	nagging	leisurely	rude	frivolous
	pessimistic	pleasure-seeking	shallow	mannerly
	temperamental	reckless	shiftless	smug
	unkind	spendthrift	show-off	stern
High	capable	aloof	easy going	appreciative
	confident	evasive	fickle	complaining
	efficient	foresighted	independent	feminine
	foresighted	independent	lazy	formal
	independent	individualistic	optimistic	meek
	intelligent	persevering	pleasure-seeking	nervous
	reasonable	preoccupied	quick	self-denying
	self-controlled	reserved	sharp-witted	sensitive
	sophisticated	unfriendly	spendthrift	weak
	unaffected	wary	spontaneous	worrying
Low	awkward	active	determined	adventurous
	cold	cheerful	efficient	aggressive
	forgetful	energetic	hard-headed	clear-thinking
	hard-hearted	flirtatious	organized	daring
	interests narrow	humorous	planful	impulsive
	queer	kind	practical	masculine
	restless	opportunistic	stern	outgoing
	sensitive	outgoing	stubborn	pleasure-seeking
	shallow	sociable	stolid	showoff
	suggestible	talkative	thorough	strong

Adjectives characterizing high-scoring and low-scoring women on the eighteen CPI scales

	Do	Cs	Sy	Sp	Sa
High	aggressive	alert	aggressive	adventurous	adventurous
	bossy	clear-thinking	confident	daring	argumentative
	conceited	forceful	dominant	flirtatious	bossy
	confident	individualistic	energetic	mischievous	demanding
	demanding	ingenious	flirtatious	outgoing	determined
	dominant	insightful	intelligent	pleasure-seeking	dominant
	forceful	intelligent	interest wide	spontaneous	outgoing
	quick	interests wide	outgoing	versatile	sarcastic
	strong	logical	sociable	ingenious	talkative
	talkative	versatile	talkative	witty	witty
Low	cautious	absent-minded	cautious	cautious	cautious
	gentle	cautious	inhibited	conventional	conventional
	inhibited	meek	meek	fearful	gentle
	peaceable	mild	modest	gentle	mild
	quiet	retiring	quiet	reserved	modest
	reserved	shy	retiring	retiring	patient
	shy	simple	shy	sensitive	peaceable
	submissive	submissive	timid	submissive	shy
	trusting	timid	unassuming	timid	trusting
	unassuming	weak	withdrawn	withdrawn	unassuming

	Wb	Re	So	Sc	To
High	calm	conscientious	cautious	calm	calm
	capable	cooperative	clear-thinking	conservative	efficient
	clear-thinking	discreet	conservative	gentle	insightful
	fair-minded	foresighted	organized	moderate	leisurely
	informal	insightful	practical	modest	logical
	mature	planful	reasonable	patient	mature

	Gi	Cm	Ac	Ai
High	calm conservative mild moderate modest patient peaceable trusting understanding worrying changeable cynical frank	clear-thinking confident energetic humorous practical rational rigid stern strong realistic appreciative artistic awkward	conservative efficient idealistic enterprising obliging planful logical reliable reserved responsible adventurous careless easy-going	calm capable clear-thinking discreet intelligent logical mature original rational reflective awkward excitable foolish
Low	reasonable reliable tactful responsible arrogant awkward bitter careless hard-headed lazy obnoxious rebellious restless sarcastic obliging poised rational wise awkward defensive fault-finding hard-headed opinionated sarcastic self-pitying tactless unconventional unstable	reliable self-controlled unassuming wise defensive careless fickle foolish impulsive outspoken peculiar pleasure-seeking reckless uninhibited	peaceable quiet reserved self-controlled adventurous aggressive arrogant excitable impulsive rebellious restless sarcastic temperamental uninhibited	responsible self-controlled tactful understanding arrogant autocratic bitter defensive distrustful hard-headed infantile resentful restless sarcastic

Ie

Low (Cont.)
- moody
- pessimistic
- sarcastic
- shrewd
- stubborn
- temperamental
- witty

High
- capable
- clear-thinking
- confident
- efficient
- informal
- intelligent
- leisurely
- logical
- rational
- relaxed

Low
- absent-minded
- awkward
- interests narrow
- nervous
- pessimistic
- simple
- slow
- stubborn
- tense
- withdrawn

Py

Low (Cont.)
- feminine
- forgetful
- forgiving
- indifferent
- irresponsible
- unconventional
- undependable

High
- capable
- cool
- independent
- ingenious
- leisurely
- logical
- mischievous
- self-confident
- sharp-witted
- undependable

Low
- conventional
- generous
- honest
- kind
- praising
- tense
- trusting
- unassuming
- warm
- worrying

Fx

Low (Cont.)
- lazy
- irresponsible
- rebellious
- sarcastic
- unconventional
- uninhibited
- zany

High
- careless
- clever
- daring
- imaginative
- individualistic
- ingenious
- mischievous
- original
- pleasure-seeking
- sociable

Low
- cautious
- conscientious
- conservative
- defensive
- prudish
- rigid
- slow
- simple
- sincere
- self-punishing

Fe

Low (Cont.)
- immature
- infantile
- rattlebrained
- restless
- simple
- unrealistic
- unstable

High
- conscientious
- discreet
- generous
- gentle
- helpful
- mature
- self-controlled
- sympathetic
- tactful
- warm

Low
- coarse
- dissatisfied
- lazy
- masculine
- pleasure-seeking
- restless
- robust
- self-centered
- touchy
- tough

References

ABBOTT, K. A. "Harmony and Individualism: Changing Chinese Psycho-Social Functioning in Taipei and San Francisco." *Asian Folklore and Social Life Monographs*, 1970, *12*.

ADIS-CASTRO, G. "A Study of Selected Personality Dimensions by Means of the Questionnaire Method in a Latin American Culture." Unpublished doctoral dissertation, University of California, Berkeley, 1957.

ADORNO, T. W., FRENKEL-BRUNSWIK, E., LEVINSON, D. J., AND SANFORD, R. N. *The Authoritarian Personality*. New York: Harper and Row, 1950.

AIKEN, L. R., JR. "Personality Correlates of the Attitude toward Mathematics." *Journal of Educational Research*, 1963, *56*, 476–480.

ALLER, F. D. "Some Factors in Marital Adjustment and Academic Achievement of Married Students." *Personnel and Guidance Journal*, 1963, *41*, 609–616.

ALTROCCHI, J. "Dominance as a Factor in Interpersonal Choice and Perception." *Journal of Abnormal and Social Psychology*, 1959, *59*, 303–308.

ANASTASI, A. *Psychological Testing*. (3rd ed.) New York: Macmillan, 1968.

APPLEY, M. H., AND MOELLER, G. "Conforming Behavior and Personality Variables in College Women." *Journal of Abnormal and Social Psychology*, 1963, *66*, 284–290.

ARMILLA, J. "Predicting Self-Assessed Social Leadership in a New Culture with the MMPI." *Journal of Social Psychology*, 1967, *73*, 219–225.

ASCH, S. E. "Effects of Group Pressure upon the Modification and Distortion of Judgment." N. H. Guetzkow (Ed.), *Groups, Leadership, and Men*. Pittsburgh: Carnegie Press, 1951. Pp. 177–190.

ASTIN, A. W. "Personal and Environmental Factors Associated with College Dropouts Among High Aptitude Students." *Journal of Educational Psychology*, 1964, *55*, 219–227.

BARNETTE, W. L., JR. "A Structured and a Semi-structured Achievement Measure

Applied to a College Sample." *Educational and Psychological Measurement,* 1961, *21,* 647–656.

BARON, A. "The Use of Personality Factors as Criteria for Grouping Pupils for Instruction with the Programmed Material: English 2600." *Dissertation Abstracts,* 1968, *28*(10-A), 4038. (Abstract)

BARRON, F. "The Disposition toward Originality. *Journal of Abnormal and Social Psychology,* 1955, *51,* 478–485.

BARRON, F. "The Psychology of Creativity." In F. Barron, et al., *New Directions in Psychology: II.* New York: Holt, Rinehart, and Winston, 1965. Pp. 1–134.

BEECH, L. A. "The California Psychological Inventory as a Measurement of Permissiveness-Restrictiveness in Love-Hostility. *Psychological Reports,* 1970, *27,* 381–382.

BENDIG, A. W. "Comparison of the Validity of Two Temperament Scales in Predicting College Achievement." *Journal of Educational Research,* 1958, *51,* 605–609.

BENDIG, A. W., AND KLUGH, H. E. "A Validation of Gough's *Hr* Scale in Predicting Academic Achievement." *Educational and Psychological Measurement,* 1956, *16,* 516–523.

BENJAMIN, J. A. "A Study of the Social Psychological Factors Related to the Academic Success of Negro High School Students." *Dissertation Abstracts International,* 1970, *30*(8-A), 3543. (Abstract)

BENNETT, C. S. "Relationship between Selected Personality Variables and Improvement in Academic Achievement for Underachieving Eighth-Grade Boys in a Residential School." *Dissertation Abstracts International,* 1970, *30*(8-A), 3272–3273.

BIELIAUSKAS, V. J., MIRANDA, S. B., AND LANSKY, L. M. "Obviousness of Two Masculinity-Femininity Tests." *Journal of Consulting and Clinical Psychology,* 1968, *32,* 314–318.

BIENEN, S. M., AND MAGOON, T. M. "ACL Adjectives Associated with Differential Status on CPI Scales." *Personnel and Guidance Journal,* 1965, *44,* 286–291.

BLOCK, J. *The Challenge of Response Sets.* New York: Appleton-Century-Crofts, 1965.

BOFFEY, T. M. "Nixon Administration Accused of Downgrading Science." *Science,* 1970, *169,* 265.

BOGARD, H. M. "Union and Management Trainees—A Comparative Study of Personality and Occupational Choice." *Journal of Applied Psychology,* 1960, *44,* 56–63.

BOHN, M. J. "Counselor Behavior as a Function of Counselor Dominance, Counselor Experience, and Client Type." *Journal of Counseling Psychology,* 1965, *12,* 346–352.

BORING, E. G., AND LINDZEY, G. *A History of Psychology in Autobiography.* Vol. 5. New York: Appleton-Century-Crofts, 1967.

BOUCHARD, T. J., JR. "Personality, Problem-Solving Procedure, and Performance in Small Groups." *Journal of Applied Psychology Monograph,* 1969, *53,* No. 1, Part 2, 1–29.

BRAMS, J. M. "Counselor Characteristics and Effectiveness of Communication in Counseling." *Journal of Counseling Psychology,* 1961, *8,* 25–30.

BROWN, M. "Attitudes and Personality Characteristics of Mothers and Their Relation to Infantile Colic." Unpublished doctoral dissertation, Vanderbilt University, Nashville, Tennessee, 1961.

BROWN, R. B. "Personality Characteristics Related to Injuries in Football." *Dissertation Abstracts International,* 1970, *30*(9-A), 3758–3759. (Abstract)

BUTT, D. S., AND FISKE, D. W. "Comparison of Strategies in Developing Scales for

Dominance." *Psychological Bulletin,* 1968, *70,* 505–519.

BYRNE, D. "Repression-Sensitization as a Dimension of Personality." In B. A. Maher (Ed.), *Progress in Experimental Personality Research.* Vol. 1. New York: Academic Press, 1964. Pp. 169–220.

BYRNE, D., GOLIGHTLY, C., AND SHEFFIELD, J. "The Repression-sensitization Scale as a Measure of Adjustment: Relationship with the CPI." *Journal of Consulting Psychology,* 1965, *29,* 586–589.

CAMPBELL, D. T. "Recommendations for APA Test Standards Regarding Construct, Trait, or Discriminant Validity." *American Psychologist,* 1960, *15,* 546–553.

CAMPBELL, D. T., AND FISKE, D. W. "Convergent and Discriminant Validation by the Multitrait-Multimethod Matrix." *Psychological Bulletin,* 1959, *56,* 81–105. Reprinted in E. I. Megargee (Ed.), *Research in Clinical Assessment.* New York: Harper and Row, 1966. Pp. 89–110.

CANTER, F. M. "Simulation on the California Psychological Inventory and the Adjustment of the Simulator." *Journal of Consulting Psychology,* 1963, *27,* 253–256. Reprinted in E. I. Megargee (Ed.), *Research in Clinical Assessment.* New York: Harper and Row, 1966. Pp. 213–217.

CAPRETTA, P. J., JONES, R. L., SIEGEL, L., AND SIEGEL, L. C. "Some Noncognitive Characteristics of Honors Program Candidates." *Journal of Educational Psychology,* 1963, *54,* 268–276.

CARNEY, R. E. "Achievement Motivation, Anxiety, and Perceptual Control." *Perceptual and Motor Skills,* 1963, *17,* 287–292.

CARNEY, R. E. "Research with a Recently Developed Measure of Achievement Motivation." *Perceptual and Motor Skills,* 1965, *21,* 438.

CARNEY, R. E. "The Effect of Situational Variables on the Measurement of Achievement Motivation." *Educational and Psychological Measurement,* 1966, *26,* 675–690.

CARNEY, R. E. "Sex Chromatin, Body Masculinity, Achievement Motivation, and Smoking Behavior." *Psychological Reports,* 1967, *20,* 859–866.

CARNEY, R. E., MANN, P. A., AND MC CORMICK, R. P. "Validation of an Objective Measure of Achievement Motivation." *Psychological Reports,* 1966, *19,* 243–248.

CARNEY, R. E., AND MC KEACHIE, W. J. "Religion, Sex, Social Class, Probability of Success, and Student Personality." *Journal for the Scientific Study of Religion,* 1963, *3,* 32–42.

CARNEY, R. E., AND MC KEACHIE, W. J. "Personality, Sex, Subject Matter and Student Ratings." *The Psychological Record,* 1966, *16,* 137–144.

CARSON, G. L., AND PARKER, C. A. "Leadership and Profiles on the MMPI and CPI." *Journal of College Student Personnel,* 1966, *7* (January), 14–18.

CATTELL, R. B. "The Description of Personality: 2. Basic Traits Resolved into Clusters." *Journal of Abnormal and Social Psychology,* 1943, *38,* 476–507.

CATTELL, R. B. *Description and Measurement of Personality.* Yonkers-on-Hudson, New York: World Book Company, 1946.

CATTELL, R. B. *Personality and Motivation Structure and Measurement.* New York: World Book Company, 1957.

CATTELL, R. B. *Handbook Supplement for Form C of the Sixteen Personality Factor Test.* Champaign, Illinois: Institute for Personality and Ability Testing, 1962.

CATTELL, R. B., EBER, H. W., AND TATSUOKA, M. M. *Handbook for the Sixteen Personality Factor Questionnaire.* Champaign, Illinois: Institute for Personality and Ability Testing, 1970.

CATTELL, R. B., AND EBER, H. W. *Handbook for the Sixteen Personality Factor Ques-*

tionnaire (the Sixteen PF). Champaign, Illinois: Institute for Personality and Ability Testing, 1957.

CHAPMAN, L. J., AND CHAPMAN, J. P. "Genesis of Popular but Erroneous Psychodiagnostic Observations." *Journal of Abnormal Psychology,* 1967, *72,* 193–204.

CHAPMAN, L. J., AND CHAPMAN, J. P. "Illusory Correlation as an Obstacle to the Use of Valid Psychodiagnostic Signs." *Journal of Abnormal Psychology,* 1969, *74,* 271–280.

CHEN, M. K., PODSHADLEY, D. W., AND SCHROCK, J. G. "A Factorial Study of Some Psychological, Vocational Interest, and Mental Ability Variables as Predictors of Success in Dental School." *Journal of Applied Psychology,* 1967, *51,* 236–241.

COLLINS, D. J. "Psychological Selection of Drill Sergeants: An Exploratory Attempt in a New Program." *Military Medicine,* 1967, *132*(9), 713–715.

COROTTO, L. B. "An Exploratory Study of the Personality Characteristics of Alcoholic Patients Who Volunteer for Continued Treatment." *Quarterly Journal of Studies on Alcohol,* 1963, *24,* 432–442.

COVNER, B. J. "Screening Alcoholic and Nonalcoholic Applicants for Volunteer Counselor Positions." *Quarterly Journal of Studies on Alcohol,* 1969, *30,* 420–425.

CRITES, J. O. "The California Psychological Inventory: I. As a Measure of the Normal Personality." *Journal of Counseling Psychology,* 1964a, *11,* 199–202.

CRITES, J. O. "The California Psychological Inventory: II. As a Measure of Client Personalities." *Journal of Counseling Psychology,* 1964b, *11,* 229–306.

CRITES, J. O., BECHTOLDT, H. P., GOODSTEIN, L. D, AND HEILBRUN, A. B., JR. "A Factor Analysis of the California Psychological Inventory" *Journal of Applied Psychology,* 1961, *45,* 408–414.

CRONBACH, L. J. "Review of the California Psychological Inventory." In O. K. Buros (Ed.), *The Fifth Mental Measurements Yearbook.* Highland Park, N.J.: Gryphon Press, 1959. Pp. 97–99.

CRONBACH, L. J. *Essentials of Psychological Testing.* (Second ed.) New York: Harper and Row, 1960.

CRONBACH, L. J. *Essentials of Psychological Testing.* (Third ed.) New York: Harper and Row, 1970.

CRONBACH, L. J., AND GLESER, G. C. *Psychological Tests and Personnel Decisions.* (Second ed.) Urbana, Illinois: University of Illinois Press, 1965.

CRONBACH, L. J., AND MEEHL, P. E. "Construct Validity in Psychological Tests." *Psychological Bulletin,* 1955, *22,* 281–302. Reprinted in E. I. Megargee (Ed.), *Research in Clinical Assessment.* New York: Harper and Row, 1966. Pp. 68–88.

CRUTCHFIELD, R. S. "Conformity and Character." *American Psychologist,* 1955, *10,* 191–198.

DAHLSTROM, W. G., AND WELSH, G. S. *An MMPI Handbook.* Minneapolis: University of Minnesota Press, 1960.

DATEL, W. E. "Socialization Scale Norms on Military Samples." *Military Medicine,* 1962, *27,* 740–744.

DATEL, W. E., HALL, F. D., AND RUFE, C. P. "Measurement of Achievement Motivation in Army Security Agency Foreign Language Candidates. *Educational and Psychological Measurement,* 1965, *25,* 539–545.

DAVIDS, A. "Psychological Characteristics of High School Male and Female Potential Scientists in Comparison with Academic Underarchievers." *Psychology in the Schools,* 1966, *3,* 79–87.

DEMOS, G. D., AND WEIJOLA, M. J. "Achievement-personality Criteria as Selectors of Participants and Predictors of Success in Special Programs in Higher Education." *California Journal of Educational Research*, 1966, *17*, 186–192.

DICKEN, C. F. "Simulated Patterns on the California Psychological Inventory." *Journal of Counseling Psychology*, 1960, *7*, 24–31.

DICKEN, C. F. "Convergent and Discriminant Validity of the California Psychological Inventory." *Educational and Psychological Measurement*, 1963a, *23*, 449–459.

DICKEN, C. F. "Good Impression, Social Desirability, and Acquiescence as Suppressor Variables." *Educational and Psychological Measurement*, 1963b, *23*, 699–720. Reprinted in E. I. Megargee (Ed.), *Research in Clinical Assessment*. New York: Harper and Row, 1966.

DINITZ, S., KAY, B., AND RECKLESS, W. C. "Delinquency Proneness and School Achievement." *Educational Research Bulletin*, 1957, *36*, 131–136.

DINITZ, S., RECKLESS, W. C., AND KAY, B. "A Self-gradient Among Potential Delinquents." *Journal of Criminal Law, Criminology, and Police Science*, 1958, *49*, 230–233.

DINITZ, S., SCARPITTI, F. R., AND RECKLESS, W. C. "Delinquency Vulnerability: A Cross Group and Longitudinal Analysis." *American Sociological Review*, 1962, *27*, 515–517.

DOMINO, G. "Differential Prediction of Academic Achievement in Conforming and Independent Settings." *Journal of Educational Psychology*, 1968, *59*, 256–260.

DONALD, E. P. "Personality Scale Analysis of New Admissions to a Reformatory." Unpublished master's thesis, Ohio State University, 1955. Cited by Gough, H. G., in "Theory and Measurement of Socialization." *Journal of Consulting Psychology*, 1960, *24*, 23–30.

DRAPER, N. R., AND SMITH, H. *Applied Regression Analysis*. New York: John Wiley, 1966.

DURFLINGER, G. W. "Academic and Personality Differences between Students Who Do Complete the Elementary Teaching Credential Program and Those Who Do Not." *Educational and Psychological Measurement*, 1963a, *23*, 775–783.

DURFLINGER, G. W. "Personality Correlates of Success in Student Teaching." *Educational and Psychological Measurement*, 1963b, *23*, 383–390.

EDWARDS, A. L. *The Social Desirability Variable in Personality Assessment and Research*. New York: Dryden, 1957.

ELLIOTT, L. L. "WAF Performance on the California Psychological Inventory." Wright Air Development Division Technical Note 60-218, Lackland AFB, Air Research and Development Command, 1960.

ELLIS, A. "Recent Research with Personality Inventories." *Journal of Consulting Psychology*, 1953, *17*, 45–49.

ELLSWORTH, L. "Some Remarks on the Characteristics of Minority Youngsters." In experiment in higher education staff, *Higher Education for the Disadvantaged: A Commentary*. East St. Louis: Southern Illinois University, 1968. Pp. 44–51.

FENELON, J. R., AND MEGARGEE, E. I. "Influence of Race on the Manifestation of Leadership." *Journal of Applied Psychology*, 1971, *55*, 353–358.

FINK, M. B. "Self-Concept as It Relates to Academic Under-Achievement." *California Journal of Educational Research*, 1952, *13*, 57–62.

FINK, M. B. "Objectification of Data Used in Under-Achievement Self-Concept Studies." *California Journal of Educational Research*, 1962, *13*, 105–112.

FISHER, J. "The 'Twisted Pear' and the Prediction of Behavior." *Journal of Consulting Psychology*, 1959, *23*, 400–405. Reprinted in E. I. Megargee (Ed.), *Research in Clinical Assessment*. New York: Harper and Row, 1966. Pp. 151–160.

FLAHERTY, M. R., AND REUTZEL, E. "Personality Traits of High and Low Achievers in College." *Journal of Educational Research,* 1965, *58,* 409–411.

FOULKES, D., AND VOGEL, G. "Mental Activity at Sleep Onset." *Journal of Abnormal Psychology,* 1965, *70,* 231–243.

FOULKES, D., SPEAR, P. S., AND SYMONDS, J. D. "Individual Differences in Mental Activity at Sleep Onset." *Journal of Abnormal Psychology,* 1966, *71,* 280–286.

FRANKEL, P. S. "The Relationship of Self-concept, Sex Role Attitudes, and the Development of Achievement Need in Women." *Dissertation Abstracts International,* 1970, *30*(7-B), 3371–3372. (Abstract)

FREEDMAN, S. A., ANTENEN, W. W., AND LISTER, J. L. "Counselor Behavior and Personality Characteristics." *Counselor Education and Supervision,* 1967, *7*(1), 26–30.

GARWOOD, D. S. "Personality Factors Related to Creativity in Young Scientists." *Journal of Abnormal and Social Psychology,* 1964, *68,* 413–419.

GENDRE, F. "Évaluation de la Personalité et Situation de Sélection." *Bulletin D'Études et Recherches Psychologiques,* 1966, *15,* 259–361.

GILL, L. J., AND SPILKA, B. "Some Non-intellectual Correlates of Academic Achievement among Mexican-American Secondary School Students." *Journal of Educational Psychology,* 1962, *53,* 144–149.

GLUECK, S., AND GLUECK, E. *Unraveling Juvenile Delinquency.* New York: Commonwealth Fund, 1950.

GOLDBERG, L. R. "Simple Models or Simple Processes? Some Research on Clinical Judgments." *American Psychologist,* 1968, *23,* 483–496.

GOLDBERG, L. R. "The Search for Configural Relationships in Personality Assessment: The Diagnosis of Psychosis Versus Neurosis from the MMPI." *Multivariate Behavioral Research,* 1969, *4,* 523–536.

GOLDBERG, L. R. *Why Measure that Trait? An Historical Analysis of Personality Scales and Inventories.* Address presented at the meetings of the Western Psychological Association, Los Angeles, California, April, 1970.

GOLDBERG, L. R. "Parameters of Personality Inventory Construction and Utilization: A Comparison of Prediction Strategies and Tactics." Unpublished mimeographed Paper. Oregon Research Institute, 1971.

GOLDBERG, L. R. "Review of the California Psychological Inventory." In O. K. Buros (Ed.), *The Seventh Mental Measurements Yearbook.* Highland Park, New Jersey: Gryphon Press (in press).

GOLDBERG, L. R., AND HASE, H. D. "Strategies and Tactics of Personality Inventory Construction: An Empirical Investigation." *Oregon Research Institute Research Monograph,* 1967, *7,* No. 1.

GOLDBERG, L. R., AND RORER, L. G. "Test-retest Item Statistics for the California Psychological Inventory." *Oregon Research Institute Research Monograph,* 1964, *4,* No. 1.

GOLDBERG, L. R., RORER, L. G., AND GREENE, M. M. "The Usefulness of 'Stylistic' Scales as Potential Suppressor or Moderator Variables in Predictions of the CPI." *Oregon Research Institute Research Bulletin,* 1970, *10,* No. 3.

GOLDBERG, L. R., AND RUST, P. "Intra-individual Variability in the MMPI-CPI Common Item Pool." *Oregon Research Institute Research Bulletin,* 1963, *3*(3).

GOODSTEIN, L. D., CRITES, J. O., HEILBRUN, A. B., JR., AND REMPEL, P. P. "The Use of the California Psychological Inventory in a University Counseling Service" *Journal of Counseling Psychology,* 1961, *8,* 147–153.

GOODSTEIN, L. D., AND SCHRADER, W. J. "An Empirically-derived Managerial Key for the California Psychological Inventory." *Journal of Applied Psychology*, 1963, *47*, 42–45.

GOUGH, H. G. "A New Dimension of Status: I. Development of a Personality Scale." *American Sociological Review*, 1948a, *13*, 401–409.

GOUGH, H. G. "A New Dimension of Status: II. Relationship of the *St* Scale to Other Variables." *American Sociological Review*, 1948b, *13*, 534–537.

GOUGH, H. G. "A Sociological Theory of Psychopathy." *American Journal of Sociology*, 1948c, *53*, 359–366.

GOUGH, H. G. "A New Dimension of Status: III. Discrepancies between the *St* Scale and 'Objective' Status." *American Sociological Review*, 1949a, *14*, 275–281.

GOUGH, H. G. "A Short Social Status Inventory." *Journal of Educational Psychology*, 1949b, *40*, 52–56.

GOUGH, H. G. "The Development of a Rigidity Scale." Unpublished mimeographed manuscript, Institute of Personality Assessment and Research, Berkeley, California, 1951a.

GOUGH, H. G. "Studies of Social Intolerance: I. Some Psychological and Sociological Correlates of Anti-Semitism." *Journal of Social Psychology*, 1951b, *33*, 237–246.

GOUGH, H. G. "Studies of Social Intolerance: II. A Personality Scale for Anti-Semitism." *Journal of Social Psychology*, 1951c, *33*, 247–255.

GOUGH, H. G. "Studies of Social Intolerance: III. Relationship of the *Pr* Scale to Other Variables." *Journal of Social Psychology*, 1951d, *33*, 257–262.

GOUGH, H. G. "Studies of Social Intolerance: IV. Related Social Attitudes." *Journal of Social Psychology*, 1951e, *33*, 263–269.

GOUGH, H. G. "Identifying Psychological Femininity." *Educational and Psychological Measurement*, 1952a, *12*(3), 427–439.

GOUGH, H. G. "On Making a Good Impression." *Journal of Educational Research*, 1952b, *46*, 33–42.

GOUGH, H. G. "Predicting Social Participation." *The Journal of Social Psychology*, 1952c, *35*, 227–233.

GOUGH, H. G. "The Construction of a Personality Scale to Predict Scholastic Achievement." *Journal of Applied Psychology*, 1953a, *37*(5), 361–366.

GOUGH, H. G. "A Nonintellectual Intelligence Test." *Journal of Consulting Psychology*, 1953b, *42*(4), 242–246.

GOUGH, H. G. "What Determines the Academic Achievement of High School Students?" *Journal of Educational Research*, 1953c, *46*(5), 321–331.

GOUGH, H. G. "Some Common Misconceptions about Neuroticism." *Journal of Consulting Psychology*, 1954, *18*(4), 287–292.

GOUGH, H. G. *Manual for the California Psychological Inventory.* (First Ed.) Palo Alto, California: Consulting Psychologists Press, 1957.

GOUGH, H. G. *Manual for the California Psychological Inventory.* (Rev. ed.) Palo Alto, California: Consulting Psychologists Press, 1960.

GOUGH, H. G. "Factors Related to Differential Achievement among Gifted Persons." Unpublished paper, Institute of Personality Assessment and Research, University of California, Berkeley, 1963.

GOUGH, H. G. "Academic Achievement in High School as Predicted from the California Psychological Inventory." *Journal of Educational Psychology*, 1964a, *65*, 174–180.

GOUGH, H. G. "Achievement in the First Course in Psychology as Predicted by the California Psychological Inventory." *Journal of Psychology*, 1964b, *57*, 419–430.

GOUGH, H. G. "A Cross-cultural Study of Achievement Motivation." *Journal of Applied Psychology,* 1964c, *48*(3), 191–196.

GOUGH, H. G. "Conceptual Analysis of Psychological Test Scores and Other Diagnostic Variables." *Journal of Abnormal Psychology,* 1965a, *70,* 294–302.

GOUGH, H. G. "Cross-cultural Validation of a Measure of Asocial Behavior." *Psychological Reports,* 1965b, *17,* 379–387.

GOUGH, H. G. "Some Thoughts on Test Usage and Test Development." Paper read at symposium on "Personality Measurement: What We've Learned: What We Need to Learn." American Personnel and Guidance Association, Minneapolis, Minnesota. April, 1965c.

GOUGH, H. G. "A Cross-cultural Analysis of the CPI-Femininity Scale." *Journal of Consulting Psychology,* 1966a, *30*(2), 136–141.

GOUGH, H. G. "Appraisal of Social Maturity by Means of the CPI." *Journal of Abnormal Psychology,* 1966b, *71,* 189–195.

GOUGH, H. G. "Graduation from High School as Predicted from the California Psychological Inventory." *Psychology in the Schools,* 1966c, *3*(3), 208–216.

GOUGH, H. G. "An Interpreter's Syllabus for the California Psychological Inventory." In P. McReynolds (Ed.), *Advances in Psychological Assessment.* Vol. 1. Palo Alto, California: Science and Behavior Books, 1968a. Pp. 55–79.

GOUGH, H. G. "College Attendance among High-aptitude Students as Predicted by the California Psychological Inventory." *Journal of Counseling Psychology,* 1968b, *15,* 269–278.

GOUGH, H. G. "Cross-cultural Studies of Socialization." In S. D. Peizer (Chm.), Cross-cultural Approaches to the Study of Delinquency." Symposium presented at the American Psychological Association, San Francisco, September, 1968c.

GOUGH, H. G. "A Leadership Index on the California Psychological Inventory." *Journal of Counseling Psychology,* 1969a, *16,* 283–289.

GOUGH, H. G. *Manual for the California Psychological Inventory.* (Rev. ed.) Palo Alto, California: Consulting Psychologists Press, 1969b.

GOUGH, H. G. "Scoring High on an Index of Social Maturity." *Journal of Abnormal Psychology,* 1971, *77,* 236–241.

GOUGH, H. G., CHUN, K., AND CHUNG, Y. E. "Validation of the CPI Femininity Scale in Korea." *Psychological Reports,* 1968, *22,* 155–160.

GOUGH, H. G., DE VOS, G., AND MIZUSHIMA, K. "Japanese Validation of the CPI Social Maturity Index." *Psychological Reports,* 1968, *22,* 143–146.

GOUGH, H. G., DURFLINGER, G. W., AND HILL, R. E., JR. "Predicting Performance in Student Teaching from the California Psychological Inventory." *Journal of Educational Psychology,* 1968, *59*(2), 119–127.

GOUGH, H. G., AND FINK, M. B. "Scholastic Achievement among Students of Average Ability, as Predicted from the California Psychological Inventory." *Psychology in the Schools,* 1964, *1*(4), 375–380.

GOUGH, H. G., AND HALL, W. B. "Prediction of Performance in Medical School from the California Psychological Inventory." *Journal of Applied Psychology,* 1964, *48,* 218–226.

GOUGH, H. G., AND HEILBRUN, A. L. *The Adjective Check List Manual.* Palo Alto, California: Consulting Psychologists Press, 1965.

GOUGH, H. G., AND KIRK, B. A. "Achievement in Dental School as Related to Personality and Aptitude Variables." *Measurement and Evaluation in Guidance,* 1970, *2,* 225–233.

GOUGH, H. G., MC CLOSKY, H., AND MEEHL, P. E. "A Personality Scale for Dominance." *Journal of Abnormal and Social Psychology,* 1951, *46,* 360–366.

GOUGH, H. G., MC CLOSKY, H., AND MEEHL, P. E. "A Personality Scale for Social Responsibility." *Journal of Abnormal and Social Psychology,* 1952, *47,* 73–80.

GOUGH, H. G., MC KEE, M. G., AND YANDEL, R. J. *Adjective Check List Analyses of a Number of Selected Psychometric and Assessment Variables.* Unpublished mimeographed paper, Maxwell Air Force Base, Alabama: Officer Education and Research Laboratory, Air Force Personnel and Training Research Center, Air Force Personnel and Development Command, 1955.

GOUGH, H. G., AND PETERSON, D. R. "The Identification and Measurement of Predispositional Factors in Crime and Delinquency." *Journal of Consulting Psychology,* 1952, *16,* 207–212.

GOUGH, H. G., AND SANDHU, H. S. "Validation of the CPI Socialization Scale in India." *Journal of Abnormal and Social Psychology,* 1964, *68,* 544–547.

GOUGH, H. G., WENK, E. A., AND ROZYNKO, V. V. "Parole Outcome as Predicted from the CPI, the MMPI, and a Base Expectancy Table." *Journal of Abnormal Psychology,* 1965, *70,* 432–441.

GRIFFIN, M. L., AND FLAHERTY, M. R. "Correlation of CPI Traits with Academic Achievement." *Educational and Psychological Measurement,* 1964, *24,* 369–372.

GRUPP, S., RAMSEYER, G., AND RICHARDSON, J. "The Effect of Age on Four Scales of the California Psychological Inventory." *Journal of General Psychology,* 1968, *78,* 183–187.

GYNTHER, M. "Different Cultures . . . Different Norms?" Paper delivered at the Sixth Annual MMPI Symposium, Minneapolis, Minnesota, April 7, 1971.

HALL, W. B., AND MACKINNON, D. W. "Personality Inventories as Predictors of Creativity among Architects." *Journal of Applied Psychology,* 1969, *53,* 322–326.

HARPER, F. B. W. "The California Psychological Inventory as a Predictor of Yielding Behavior in Women." *Journal of Psychology,* 1964, *58,* 187–190.

HASE, H. D. "The Predictive Validity of Different Methods of Deriving Personality Inventory Scales." Unpublished doctoral dissertation, University of Oregon, 1965.

HASE, H. D., AND GOLDBERG, L. R. "Comparative Validity of Different Strategies of Constructing Personality Inventory Scales." *Psychological Bulletin,* 1967, *67,* 231–248.

HATHAWAY, S. R. "MMPI: Professional Use by Professional People." *American Psychologist,* 1964, *19,* 204–210. Reprinted in E. I. Megargee (Ed.), *Research in Clinical Assessment.* New York: Harper and Row, 1966. Pp. 164–174.

HEILBRUN, A. B., JR. "Male and Female Personality Correlates of Early Termination in Counseling." *Journal of Counseling Psychology,* 1961, *8,* 31–36.

HEILBRUN, A. B., JR. "Psychological Factors Related to Counseling Readiness and Implications for Counselor Behavior." *Journal of Counseling Psychology,* 1962, *9,* 353–358.

HEILBRUN, A. B., JR., DANIEL, J. L., GOODSTEIN, L. D., STEPHENSON, R. R., AND CRITES, J. O. "The Validity of Two-Scale Pattern Interpretation on the California Psychological Inventory." *Journal of Applied Psychology,* 1962, *46,* 409–416.

HELSON, R. "Personality Characteristics and Developmental History of Creative College Women." *Genetic Psychology Monographs,* 1967a, *76,* 205–256.

HELSON, R. "Sex Differences in Creative Style." *Journal of Personality*, 1967b, *35*, 214–233.

HELSON, R., AND CRUTCHFIELD, R. S. "Mathematicians: The Creative Researcher and the Average Ph.D." *Journal of Consulting and Clinical Psychology*, 1970, *34*, 250–257.

HETHERINGTON, E., AND FELDMAN, S. "College Cheating as a Function of Subject and Situational Variables." *Journal of Educational Psychology*, 1964, *55*, 212–218.

HICKS, C. R. *Fundamental Concepts in the Design of Experiments.* New York: Holt, Rinehart, and Winston, 1964.

HILGARD, E. R., AND LAVES, L. W. "Lack of Correlation between the CPI and Hypnotic Susceptibility." *Journal of Consulting Psychology*, 1962, *26*(4), 331–335.

HILL, A. H. "Autobiographical Correlates of Achievement Motivation in Men and Women." *Psychological Reports*, 1966a, *18*(3), 811–817.

HILL, A. H. "A Longitudinal Study of Attrition among High Aptitude College Students." *Journal of Educational Research*, 1966b, *60*, 166–173.

HILL, A. H. "Use of a Structured Autobiography in the Construct Validation of Personality Scales." *Journal of Consulting Psychology*, 1967, *31*, 551–556.

HILL, R. E., JR. "Dichotomous Prediction of Student Teaching Excellence Employing Selected CPI Scales." *Journal of Educational Research*, 1960, *53*, 349–351.

HILL, R. E., JR. "An Investigation of the CPI Empirically Keyed for Dichotomous Prediction of Student Teacher Excellence." In E. M. Huddleston (Ed.), *The 18th Yearbook of the National Council on Measurements used in Education.* Ames, Iowa: NCME, 1961, Pp. 107–109.

HILLS, D. A. "The California Psychological Inventory Flexibility Scale, Motivation Instructions, and Some Measures of Behavioral Rigidity." Unpublished doctoral dissertation, State University of Iowa, Iowa City, 1960.

HIRT, M. L., AND COOK, R. A. "The Effectiveness of the California Psychological Inventory to Predict Psychiatric Determinations of Socialization." *Journal of Clinical Psychology*, 1962, *18*, 176–177.

HOGAN, R. "Development of an Empathy Scale." *Journal of Consulting and Clinical Psychology*, 1969, *33*(3), 307–316.

HOGAN, R. "A Dimensoin of Moral Judgment." *Journal of Consulting and Clinical Psychology*, 1970, *35*, 205–212.

HOGAN, R. "A Study of Police Effectiveness." *Personnel Psychology* (in press).

HOGAN, R., AND DICKSTEIN, E. "A Dimension of Maturity: Moral Judgment." Report No. 96, Center for Social Organization of Schools, The Johns Hopkins University, March, 1971.

HOGAN, R., AND MANKIN, D. "Determinants of Interpersonal Attraction: A Clarification." *Psychological Reports*, 1970, *26*, 235–238.

HOGAN, R., MANKIN, D., CONWAY, J., AND FOX, S. "Personality Correlates of Undergraduate Marijuana Use." *Journal of Consulting and Clinical Psychology*, 1970, *35*, 58–63.

HOLLAND, J. L. "The Prediction of College Grades from the California Psychological Inventory and the Scholastic Aptitude Test." *Journal of Educational Psychology*, 1959, *50*, 135–142.

HOLLAND, J. L., AND ASTIN, A. W. "The Prediction of the Academic, Artistic, Scientific and Social Achievements of Undergraduates of Superior Scholastic Aptitude." *Journal of Educational Psychology*, 1962, *53*, 132–143.

HOWELL, M. A. "Personal Effectiveness of Physicians in a Federal Health Organization." *Journal of Applied Psychology*, 1966, *50*, 451–459.

JACKSON, D. N., AND MESSICK, S. "Content and Style in Personality Assessment." *Psychological Bulletin*, 1958, *55*, 243–251.

JENKINS, C. D., ET AL. "Psychological Traits and Serum Lipids." *Psychosomatic Medicine*, 1969, *31*(2), 115–128.

JENSEN, A. R. "Authoritarian Attitudes and Personality Maladjustment." *Journal of Abnormal and Social Psychology*, 1957, *54*, 303–311.

JOHNSON, R. T., AND FRANDSEN, A. N. "California Psychological Inventory Profile of Student Leaders." *Personnel and Guidance Journal*, 1962, *41*, 343–345.

JONES, C. A., JR. "The Effects of Intellectualization and Identification upon Psychological Stress Reaction." Unpublished doctoral dissertation, University of California, Berkeley, 1963.

JONES, R. R., AND GOLDBERG, L. R. "An Alphabetical List of CPI Items with Corresponding MMPI Numbers." *ORI Technical Reports*, 1964, *4*(1).

KALIS, B. L., TOCCHINI, J. J., AND THOMASSEN, P. R. A Correlation Study between Personality Tests and Dental Student Performance." *Journal of the American Dental Association*, 1962, *64*, 656–670.

KEIMOWITZ, R. I., AND ANSBACHER, H. L. "Personality and Achievement in Mathematics." *Journal of Individual Psychology*, 1960, *16*, 84–87.

KELLY, E. L. "Review of the California Psychological Inventory." In O. K. Buros (Ed.), *The Sixth Mental Measurements Yearbook.* Highland Park, N.J.: Gryphon Press, 1965. Pp. 168–170.

KIPNIS, D. "Social Immaturity, Intellectual Ability, and Adjustive Behavior in College." *Journal of Applied Psychology*, 1968, *52*, 71–80.

KIRK, B. A., CUMMINGS, R. W., AND HACKETT, H. H. "Personal and Vocational Characteristics of Dental Students." *Personnel and Guidance Journal*, 1963, *41*, 522–527.

KLEINMUNTZ, B. *Personality Measurement: An Introduction.* Homewood, Illinois: Dorsey Press, 1967.

KNAPP, R. R. "A Reevaluation of the Validity of MMPI Scales of Dominance and Social Responsibility." *Educational and Psychological Measurement*, 1960, *20*, 381–386.

KNAPP, R. R. "Personality Correlates and Delinquency Rates of a Navy Sample." *Journal of Applied Psychology*, 1963, *47*, 68–71.

KNAPP, R. R. "Value and Personality Differences between Offenders and Nonoffenders." *Journal of Applied Psychology*, 1964, *48*, 59–62.

KOENIG, K., AND MC KEACHIE, W. J. "Personality and Independent Study." *Journal of Educational Psychology*, 1959, *50*, 132–134.

KOHFELD, D. L., AND WEITZEL, W. "Some Relations Between Personality Factors and Social Facilitation." *Journal of Experimental Research In Personality*, 1969, *3*, 287–292.

KORMAN, M., STUBBLEFIELD, R. L., AND MARTIN, L. W. "Patterns of Success in Medical School and Their Correlates." *Journal of Medical Education*, 1968, *43*, 405–411.

KURTINES, W., AND HOGAN, R. "Sources of Conformity in Unsocialized College Students." Unpublished mimeographed manuscript, Department of Psychology, The Johns Hopkins University, 1971.

LA GRONE, C. W. "Sex and Personality Differences in Relation to Feeling for Direction." *Journal of General Psychology*, 1969, *81*, 23–33.

LAZARUS, R. S., SPEISMAN, J. C., MORDKOFF, A. M., AND DAVISON, L. A. "A Laboratory Study of Psychological Stress Produced by a Motion Picture Film." *Psychological Monographs*, 1962, *76*(34, Whole No. 553).

LEFCOURT, H. M. "Serendipitous Validity Study of Gough's Social Maturity Index." *Journal of Consulting and Clinical Psychology*, 1968, *32*, 85–86.

LESSINGER, L. M., AND MARTINSON, R. A. "The Use of California Psychological Inventory with Gifted Pupils." *Personnel and Guidance Journal*, 1961, *39*, 572–575.

LETON, D. A., AND WALTER, S. "A Factor Analysis of the California Psychological Inventory and Minnesota Counseling Inventory." *California Journal of Educational Research*, 1962, *13*, 126–133.

LEVENTHAL, A. M. "An Anxiety Scale for the CPI." *Journal of Clinical Psychology*, 1966, *22*, 459–461.

LEVENTHAL, A. M. "Additional Technical Data on the CPI Anxiety Scale." *Journal of Counseling Psychology*, 1968, *15*(5, Pt. 1), 479–480.

LEVENTHAL, G. S. "Influence of Brothers and Sisters on Sex-role Behavior." *Journal of Personality and Social Psychology*, 1970, *16*, 452–465.

LEVIN, J., AND KARNI, E. S. "Demonstration of Cross-cultural Invariance of the California Psychological Inventory in America and Israel by the Guttman-Lingoes Smallest Space Analysis." *Journal of Cross-Cultural Psychology*, 1970, *1*, 253–260.

LICHTENSTEIN, E., AND BRYAN, J. G. "CPI Correlates of the Need for Approval." *Journal of Clinical Psychology*, 1966, *22*, 453–455.

LIDDLE, G. "The California Psychological Inventory and Certain Social and Personal Factors." *Journal of Educational Psychology*, 1958, *49*, 144–149.

LINTON, T. E. "The CPI as a Predictor of Academic Success." *Alberta Journal of Educational Research*, 1967, *13*, 59–64.

LIPP, L., ERICKSON, R., AND SKEEN, D. "Intellectual Efficiency: A Construct Validation Study." *Educational and Psychological Measurement*, 1968, *28*, 595–597.

LITTLEJOHN, M. T. "Creativity and Masculinity-Femininity in Ninth-graders." *Perceptual and Motor Skills*, 1967, *25*, 737–743.

LOREI, T. W. "Prediction of Length of Stay out of the Hospital for Released Psychiatric Patients." *Journal of Consulting Psychology*, 1964, *28*, 358–363.

LUTTRELL, J. M. "The Relationship of Selected Nonintellectual Factors to Achievement Levels of Home Economics Majors." Unpublished master's thesis, Florida State University, School of Home Economics, 1969.

MAC KINNON, D. W. "Fostering Creativity in Students of Engineering." *Journal of Engineering Education*, 1961a, *52*, 129–142.

MAC KINNON, D. W. "The Personality Correlates of Creativity: A Study of American Architects." Paper presented at the Fourteenth International Congress of Applied Psychology, Copenhagen, Denmark, August 13, 1961b.

MAC KINNON, D. W. "The Nature and Nurture of Creative Talent." *American Psychologist*, 1962, *17*, 484–495.

MAC KINNON, D. W. "Creativity and Images of the Self." In R. W. White (Ed.), *The Study of Lives*. Englewood Cliffs, N.J.: Prentice-Hall, 1963. Pp. 250–279.

MAC KINNON, D. W. "The Creativity of Architects." In D. W. Taylor and F. Barron (Eds.), *Widening Horizons in Creativity*. New York: Wiley, 1964. Pp. 359–378.

MAHONEY, T. A., JERDEE, T. H., AND NASH, A. N. *The Identification of Management Potential: A Research Approach to Management Development*. Dubuque, Iowa: W. C. Brown, 1961.

MARUYAMA, Y. "The Sense of Competence in Middle Adolescent Boys." *Dissertation Abstracts International*, 1969, *30*(5-B), 2405–2406. (Abstract)

MASON, E. P. "Comparison of Personality Characteristics of Junior High Students from American Indian, Mexican, and Caucasian Ethnic Backgrounds."

Journal of Social Psychology, 1967, *73,* 145–155.

MASON, E. P., ADAMS, H. L., AND BLOOD, D. F. "Personality Characteristics of Gifted College Freshmen." In *Proceedings of the Seventy-third Annual Convention of the American Psychological Association.* Washington: APA, 1965. Pp. 301–302.

MASON, E. P., ADAMS, H. L., AND BLOOD, D. F. "Personality Characteristics of Gifted College Freshmen." *Psychology in the Schools,* 1966, *3,* 360–365.

MASON, E. P., AND BLOOD, D. F. "Cross-validation Studies of Personality Characteristics of Gifted College Freshmen." In *Proceedings of the Seventy-fourth Annual Convention of the American Psychological Association.* Washington: APA, 1966. Pp. 283–284.

MC CARTHY, D., ANTHONY, R. J., AND DOMINO, G. "A Comparison of the CPI, Franck, MMPI, and WAIS Masculinity-Feminity Indexes." *Journal of Consulting and Clinical Psychology,* 1970, *35,* 414–416.

MC CLOUD, W. T. "Student Characteristics Associated with Use and Nonuse of the Washington State University Student Counseling Services." *Dissertation Abstracts,* 1969, *29*(9-A), 2964. (Abstract)

MC DERMID, C. D. "Some Correlates of Creativity in Engineering Personnel." *Journal of Applied Psychology,* 1965, *49,* 14–19.

MC NEMAR, Q. *Psychological Statistics.* (Third ed.) New York: John Wiley and Sons, 1962.

MC NEMAR, Q. "Lost, Our Intelligence? Why?" *American Psychologist,* 1964, *19,* 871–882.

MEEHL, P. E. "The Dynamics of 'Structured' Personality Tests." *Journal of Clinical Psychology,* 1945, *1,* 297–303.

MEEHL, P. E. "When Shall We Use Our Heads Instead of the Formula?" *Journal of Counseling Psychology,* 1957, *4,* 268–273. Reprinted in E. I. Megargee (Ed.), *Research in Clinical Assessment.* New York: Harper and Row, 1966. Pp. 651–656.

MEEHL, P. E. "Some Ruminations on the Validation of Clinical Procedures." *Canadian Journal of Psychology,* 1959, *13,* 102–128. Reprinted in E. I. Megargee (Ed.), *Research in Clinical Assessment.* New York: Harper and Row, 1966. Pp. 8–27.

MEEHL, P., AND ROSEN, A. "Antecedent Probability and the Efficiency of Psychometric Signs, Patterns or Cutting Scores." *Psychological Bulletin,* 1955, *52,* 194–216. Reprinted in E. I. Megargee (Ed.), *Research in Clinical Assessment.* New York: Harper and Row, 1966. Pp. 129–150.

MEGARGEE, E. I. *Undercontrol and Overcontrol in Assaultive and Homicidal Adolescents.* Doctoral dissertation, University of California, Berkeley. Ann Arbor, Mich.: University Microfilms, 1964. No. 64-9923.

MEGARGEE, E. I. "Assault with Intent to Kill." *Trans-Action,* 1965, *2*(6), 27–31.

MEGARGEE, E. I. "The Edwards *SD* Scale: A Measure of Dissimulation or Adjustment?" *Journal of Consulting Psychology,* 1966a, *30,* 566.

MEGARGEE, E. I. "Estimation of CPI Scores from MMPI Protocols." *Journal of Clinical Psychology,* 1966b, *22,* 456–458.

MEGARGEE, E. I. (Ed.), *Research in Clinical Assessment.* New York: Harper and Row, 1966c.

MEGARGEE, E. I. "Undercontrolled and Overcontrolled Personality Types in Extreme Anti-Social Aggression." *Psychological Monographs,* 1966d, *80*(3, Whole No. 611).

MEGARGEE, E. I. "Conscientious Objectors' Scores on the MMPI *O-H* (Overcontrolled Hostility) Scale." *Proceedings of the Seventy-seventh Annual Convention of the American Psychological Association.* Washington: APA, 1969a. Pp. 507–508.

MEGARGEE, E. I. "Influence of Sex Roles on the Manifestation of Leadership." *Journal of Applied Psychology,* 1969b, *53,* 377–382.

MEGARGEE, E. I. "The Prediction of Violence from Psychological Tests." In C. D. Spielberger (Ed.), *Current Topics in Clinical and Community Psychology,* Vol. II. New York: Academic Press, 1970. Pp. 97–156.

MEGARGEE, E. I. "The Role of Inhibition in the Assessment and Understanding of Violence." In J. E. Singer (Ed.), *The Control of Aggression and Violence: Cognitive and Physiological Factors.* New York: Academic Press, 1971. Pp. 125–147.

MEGARGEE, E. I., BOGART, P., AND ANDERSON, D. J. "The Prediction of Leadership in a Simulated Industrial Task." *Journal of Applied Psychology,* 1966, *50,* 292–295.

MEGARGEE, E. I., COOK, P. E., AND MENDELSOHN, G. A. "Development and Evaluation of an MMPI Scale of Assaultiveness in Overcontrolled Individuals." *Journal of Abnormal Psychology,* 1967, *72,* 519–528.

MEGARGEE, E. I., AND MENDELSOHN, G. A. "A Cross-validation of Twelve MMPI Indices of Hostility and Control." *Journal of Abnormal and Social Psychology,* 1962, *65,* 431–438. Reprinted in E. I. Megargee (Ed.), *Research in Clinical Assessment.* New York: Harper and Row, 1966. Pp. 282–291.

MEGARGEE, E. I., AND MENZIES, E. "The Assessment and Dynamics of Aggression." In P. McReynolds (Ed.), *Advances in Psychological Assessment,* Vol. 2. Palo Alto: Science and Behavior Books, 1971.

MEGARGEE, E. I., PARKER, G. V. C., AND LEVINE, R. V. "The Relationship of Familial and Social Factors to Socialization in Middle Class College Students." *Journal of Abnormal Psychology,* 1971, *77*(1), 76–89.

MILBRATH, L. W., AND KLEIN, W. "Personality Correlates of Political Participation." *Acta Sociologica,* 1962, *6,* 53–66.

MITCHELL, L. H. "Dominance and Femininity as Factors of the Sex Role Adjustment of Parents and Children." Unpublished doctoral dissertation, University of California, Berkeley, 1965.

MITCHELL, J. V. "A Comparison of the First and Second Order Dimensions of the 16 PF and CPI Inventories." *Journal of Social Psychology,* 1963, *61,* 151–166.

MITCHELL, J. V., JR, AND PIERCE-JONES, J. "A Factor Analysis of Gough's California Psychological Inventory." *Journal of Consulting Psychology,* 1960, *24,* 453–456.

MIZUSHIMA, K., AND DEVOS, G. "An Application of the California Psychological Inventory in a Study of Japanese Delinquency." *Journal of Social Psychology,* 1967, *71,* 45–51.

MORGAN, H. H. "A Psychometric Comparison of Achieving and Nonachieving College Students of High Ability." *Journal of Consulting Psychology,* 1952, *16,* 292–298.

MYERS, C. R. "Prediction in Clinical Psychology." *Canadian Journal of Psychology,* 1950, *4,* 97–108. Reprinted in E. I. Megargee (Ed.), *Research in Clinical Assessment.* New York: Harper and Row, 1966. Pp. 39–47.

NICHOLS, R. C. "Subtle, Obvious and Stereotype Measures of Masculinity-Femininity." *Educational and Psychological Measurement,* 1962, *22,* 449–461.

NICHOLS, R. C. "Nonintellective Predictors of Achievement in College." *Educational and Psychological Measurement,* 1966, *26,* 899–915.

NICHOLS, R. C., AND BECK, K. W. "Factors in Psychotherapy Change." *Journal of Consulting Psychology,* 1960, *24,* 388–399.

NICHOLS, R. C., AND SCHNELL, R. R. "Factor Scales for the California Psychological Inventory." *Journal of Consulting Psychology,* 1963, *27,* 228–235.

NORFLEET, M. A. "Personality Characteristics of Achieving and Underachieving High Ability Senior Women." *Personnel and Guidance Journal,* 1968, *46*(10), 976–980.

NUNNALLY, J. C. *Psychometric Theory.* New York: McGraw-Hill, 1967.

OLMSTEAD, D. W., AND MONACHESI, E. D. "A Validity Check on MMPI Scales of Responsibility and Dominance." *Journal of Abnormal and Social Psychology,* 1956, *53,* 140–141.

PARKER, G. V. C., AND MEGARGEE, E. I. "Factor Analytic Studies of the Adjective Check List." *Proceedings of the Seventy-fifth Annual Convention of the American Psychological Association.* Washington, D.C.: APA, 1967. Pp. 211–212.

PARLOFF, M., AND DATTA, L. E. "Personality Characteristics of the Potentially Creative Scientist." In *Science and Psychoanalysis,* Vol. III. New York: Grune & Stratton, 1965. Pp. 91–106.

PARLOFF, M. B., DATTA, L. E., KLEMAN, M., AND HANDLON, H. H. "Personality Characteristics which Differentiate Creative Male Adolescents and Adults." *Journal of Personality,* 1968, *36,* 528–552.

PETERSON, D. R., QUAY, H. C., AND ANDERSON, A. C. "Extending the Construct Validity of a Socialization Scale." *Journal of Consulting Psychology,* 1959, *23,* 182.

PIERCE, J. V. "Personality and Achievement Among Able High School Boys." *Journal of Individual Psychology,* 1961, *17,* 102–107.

PIERCE-JONES, J., MITCHELL, J. V., JR., AND KING, F. J. "Configurational Invariance in the California Psychological Inventory." *Journal of Experimental Education,* 1962, *31*(1), 65–71.

PIVIK, T., AND FOULKES, D. "NREM Mentation: Relation to Personality, Orientation Time, and Time of Night." *Journal of Consulting and Clinical Psychology,* 1968a, *32,* 144–151.

PIVIK, T., AND FOULKES, D. "NREM Mentation: Relation to Personality, Orientation Time, and Time of Night." *Psychophysiology,* 1968b, *4,* 372.

PLANT, W. T., AND MINIUM, E. W. "Differential Personality Development in Young Adults of Markedly Different Aptitude Levels." *Journal of Educational Psychology,* 1967, *58,* 141–152.

PURKEY, W. W. "Measured and Professed Personality Characteristics of Gifted High School Students and Analysis of Their Congruence." *Journal of Educational Research,* 1966, *60,* 99–103.

QUERY, W. T. "CPI Factors and Success of Seminary Students." *Psychological Reports,* 1966, *18,* 665–666.

RAWLS, D. J., AND RAWLS, J. R. "Personality Characteristics and Personal History Data of Successful and Less Successful Executives." *Psychological Reports,* 1968, *23*(3, Part 2), 1032–1034.

RECKLESS, W. C., DINITZ, S., AND KAY, B. "The Self Component in Potential Delinquency and Potential Nondelinquency. *American Sociological Review,* 1957, *22,* 566–570.

REED, C. F., AND CUADRA, C. A. "The Role-taking Hypothesis in Delinquency." *Journal of Consulting Psychology,* 1957, *21,* 386–390.

RICHARDSON, H., AND ROEBUCK, J. "Minnesota Multiphasic Personality Inventory and California Psychological Inventory Differences between Delinquents and Their Nondelinquent Siblings." In *Proceedings of the Seventy-third Annual*

Convention of the American Psychological Association. Washington, D.C.: American Psychological Association, 1965. Pp. 255–256.

RODGERS, D. A. "Estimation of MMPI Profiles from CPI Data." *Journal of Consulting Psychology,* 1966, *30,* 89.

RODGERS, D. A., AND ZIEGLER, F. J. "Social Role Theory, the Marital Relationship, and the use of Ovulation Suppressors." *Journal of Marriage and the Family,* 1968, *30,* 584–591.

ROGERS, M. S., AND SHURE, G. H. "An Empirical Evaluation of the Effect of Item Overlap on Factorial Stability." *Journal of Psychology,* 1965, *60,* 221–223.

RORER, L. G. "The Great Response Style Myth." *Psychological Review,* 1965, *63,* 129–156.

RORER, L. G., AND GOLDBERG, L. R. "Acquiescence in the MMPI?" *Educational and Psychological Measurement,* 1965, *25,* 801–817. Reprinted in E. I. Megargee (Ed.), *Research in Clinical Assessment.* New York: Harper and Row, 1966. Pp. 236–248.

ROSENBERG, L. A. "Idealization of Self and Social Adjustment." *Journal of Consulting Psychology,* 1962, *26,* 487.

ROSENBERG, L. A., MC HENRY, T. B., ROSENBERG, A. M., AND NICHOLS, R. C. "The Prediction of Academic Achievement with the California Psychological Inventory." *Journal of Applied Psychology,* 1962, *46,* 385–388.

ROSENQUIST, C. M., AND MEGARGEE, E. I. *Delinquency in Three Cultures.* Austin: University of Texas Press, 1969.

RUBINROIT, C. D. "Leadership in Dyadic Groups as a Function of Dominance and Ethnic Composition." Unpublished doctoral dissertation, University of Texas at Austin, 1970.

RUDOFF, A. "The PICO Project: A Measurement of Casework in Corrections. Second Technical Report of Preliminary Findings." Tracy, California: Deuel Vocational Institution, 1959. (Mimeo.)

RUDOFF, A., AND BENNETT, L. "PICO: A Measure of Casework in Corrections. First Technical Report of Preliminary Findings." Deuel Vocational Institution, California State Department of Corrections, 1958. (Mimeo.)

RUDOFF, A., AND PILIAVIN, I. "An Aid to Needy Children Program: A Study of Types and Responses to Casework Services." *Community Mental Health Journal,* 1969, *5*(1), 20–28.

RUSK, M. T. "A Study of Delinquency among Urban Mexican-American Youth." *Dissertation Abstracts International,* 1969, *30*(5-A), 1877–1878. (Abstract)

SARBIN, T. R., WENK, E. A., AND SHERWOOD, D. W. "An Effort to Identify Assault-prone Offenders." *Journal of Research in Crime and Delinquency,* 1968, *5,* 66–71.

SCARPITTI, F. R., MURRAY, E., DINITZ, S., AND RECKLESS, W. C. "The 'Good Boy' in a High Delinquency Area: Four Years Later." *American Sociological Review,* 1960, *25,* 555–558.

SCHWARTZ, M. L., DENNERLL, R. D., AND LIN, Y. G. "Neuropsychological and Psychosocial Predictors of Employability in Epilepsy." *Journal of Clinical Psychology,* 1968, *24,* 174–177.

SHAVER, P. R., AND SCHEIBE, K. E. "Transformation of Social Identity: A Study of Chronic Mental Patients and College Volunteers in a Summer Camp Setting." *Journal of Psychology,* 1967, *66,* 19–37.

SHNEIDMAN, E. S. "Suggestions for the Delineation of Validation Studies." *Journal of Projective Techniques,* 1959, *23,* 259–262. Reprinted in E. I. Megargee (Ed.), *Research in Clinical Assessment.* New York: Harper and Row, 1966. Pp. 5–7.

SHURE, G. H., AND ROGERS, M. S. "Personality Factor Stability for Three Ability Levels." *Journal of Psychology*, 1963, *55*, 445–456.

SIEGMAN, A. W. "Personality Variables Associated with Admitted Criminal Behavior." *Journal of Consulting Psychology*, 1962, *26*, 199.

SMELSER, W. T. "Dominance as a Factor in Achievement and Perception in Cooperative Problem-Solving Interactions." *Journal of Abnormal and Social Psychology*, 1961, *62*, 535–542.

SNIDER, J. G. "Academic Achievement and Underachievement in a Canadian High School as Predicted from the California Psychological Inventory." *Psychology in the Schools*, 1966a, *3*, 370–372.

SNIDER, J. G. "The Canadian High School Achievement Syndrome as Indicated by the California Psychological Inventory." *Ontario Journal of Educational Research*, 1966b, *9*, 43–47.

SNIDER, J. G., AND LINTON, T. E. "The Predictive Value of the California Psychological Inventory in Discriminating Between the Personality Patterns of High School Achievers and Underachievers." *Ontario Journal of Educational Research*, 1964, *6*, 107–115.

SOUTHERN, M. L., AND PLANT, W. T. "Personality Characteristics of Very Bright Adults." *Journal of Social Psychology*, 1968, *75*, 119–126.

SPIELBERGER, C. D., GORSUCH, R. L., AND LUSHENE, R. E. *The State-trait Anxiety Inventory (Test Manual)*. Palo Alto, California: Consulting Psychologists Press, 1970.

SPRINGOB, H. K., AND STRUENING, E. L. "A Factor Analysis of the California Psychological Inventory on a High School Population." *Journal of Counseling Psychology*, 1964, *11*, 173–179.

STANDRIDGE, C. G. "The Predictive Value of Nonintellectual Factors and Their Influence on Academic Achievement." *Dissertation Abstracts*, 1968, *29*(5-A), 1458. (Abstract)

STEIN, K. B., GOUGH, H. G., AND SARBIN, T. R. "The Dimensionality of the CPI Socialization Scale and an Empirically Derived Typology among Delinquent and Nondelinquent Boys." *Multivariate Behavioral Research*, 1966, *1*, 197–208.

STEIN, K. B., VADUM, A. C., AND SARBIN, T. R. "Socialization and Delinquency: A Study of False Negatives and False Positives in Prediction." *Psychological Record*, 1970, *20*, 353–364.

STEWART, L. H. "Social and Emotional Adjustment during Adolescence as Related to the Development of Psychosomatic Illness in Adulthood." *Genetic Psychology Monographs*, 1962, *65*, 175–215.

STEWART, L., AND LIVSON, N. "Smoking and Rebelliousness: A Longitudinal Study from Childhood to Maturity." *Journal of Consulting Psychology*, 1966, *30*, 225–229.

STRONG, E. K., JR. *Vocational Interests of Men and Women*. Stanford, California: Stanford University Press, 1943.

SWISDAK, B., AND FLAHERTY, M. R. "A Study of Personality Differences between College Graduates and Dropouts." *Journal of Psychology*, 1964, *57*, 25–28.

THOMSON, W. D. "Predicting Practical Nursing Course Grades from the California Psychological Inventory and the Differential Aptitude Tests." Unpublished master's thesis, Graduate Department of Education, Brigham Young University, 1969.

THORNDIKE, R. L. "Review of the California Psychological Inventory." In O. K. Buros (Ed.), *Fifth Mental Measurements Yearbook*. Highland Park, N.J.: Gryphon Press, 1959. P. 99.

THORNE, G. "Discriminations Within the Delinquency Continuum Using Gough's Socialization Scale." *Journal of Consulting Psychology*, 1963, *27*, 183.

TOLOR, A. "A Comparison of Several Measures of Psychosexual Disturbance." *Journal of Projective Techniques*, 1957, *21*, 313–317.

TONRA, M. S. "Differentiation between a Female Delinquent and a Nondelinquent Group on the Socialization Scale of the California Psychological Inventory." Unpublished master's thesis, Fordham University, 1963.

TRIMBLE, J. E. "Psychosocial Characteristics of Employed and Unemployed Western Oklahoma Male American Indians." Doctoral dissertation, University of Oklahoma, 1969. Ann Arbor, Michigan: University Microfilms, 1969. No. 69–17, 832 .

TRITES, D., KUREK, A., AND COBB, B. "Personality and Achievement of Air Traffic Controllers." *Aerospace Medicine*, 1967, *38*, 1145–1150.

TUDDENHAM, R. "Correlates of Yielding to a Distorted Group Norm." *Journal of Personality*, 1959, *27*, 272–284.

VELDMAN, D. J., AND KELLY, S. J. "Personality Correlates of a Composite Criterion of Teaching Effectiveness." *Alberta Journal of Educational Research*, 1965, *11*, 102–107.

VELDMAN, D. J., AND PIERCE-JONES, J. "Sex Differences in Factor Structure in the CPI." *Journal of Consulting Psychology*, 1964, *28*, 93.

VINCENT, C. *Unmarried Mothers*. New York: Free Press of Glencoe, 1961.

VINGOE, F. J. "Note on the Validity of the California Psychological Inventory." *Journal of Consulting and Clinical Psychology*, 1968, *32*, 725–727.

VITZ, P. C., AND JOHNSTON, D. "Masculinity of Smokers and the Masculinity of Cigarette Images." *Journal of Applied Psychology*, 1965, *49*, 155–159.

WARREN, M. Q., AND PALMER, T. B. "Community of Treatment Project: An Evaluation of Community Treatment for Delinquents." Fourth progress report. CTP Research Report No. 6. Community Treatment Project: Sacramento, California, 1965. (Mimeo.)

WEBB, A. P. "Sex-role Preferences and Adjustment in Early Adolescents." *Child Development*, 1963, *34*, 609–618.

WEBSTER, H. "Derivation and Use of the Masculinity-Femininity Variable." *Journal of Clinical Psychology*, 1953, *9*, 33–36.

WEINBERG, N., MENDELSOHN, M., AND STUNKARD, A. "A Failure to Find Distinctive Personality Features in a Group of Obese Men." *American Journal of Psychiatry*, 1961, *117*, 1035–1037.

WERNICK, R. "The Modern-style Mind Reader." *Life*, September 12, 1955, 97–108.

WHITE, W. C. "Selective Modeling in Youthful Offenders with High and Low O-H (Overcontrolled-Hostility) Personality Types." Unpublished doctoral dissertation, Florida State University, 1970.

WILCOCK, K. D. "Neurotic Differences between Individualized and Socialized Criminals." *Journal of Consulting Psychology*, 1964, *28*, 141–145.

WINKELMAN, S. L. "California Psychological Inventory Profile Patterns of Underachievers, Average Achievers, and Overachievers." Unpublished doctoral dissertation, University of Maryland, 1963.

YOUNG, R. K., BENSON, W. N., AND HOLTZMAN, W. H. "Change in Attitudes Toward the Negro in a Southern University." *Journal of Abnormal and Social Psychology*, 1960, *60*, 131–135.

ZDEP, S. M. "Intragroup Reinforcement and Its Effect on Leadership Behavior." *Organizational Behavior and Human Performance*, 1969, *4*, 284–298.

ZIEGLER, F. J., RODGERS, D. A., AND KRIEGSMAN, S. A. "Effect of Vasectomy on Psychological Functioning." *Psychosomatic Medicine,* 1966, *28,* 50–63.

ZIEGLER, F. J., RODGERS, D. A., KRIEGSMAN, S. A., AND MARTIN, P. L. "Ovulation Suppressors, Psychological Functioning, and Marital Adjustment." *Journal of the American Medical Association,* 1968, *204,* 849–853.

ZIEGLER, F. J., RODGERS, D. A., AND PRENTISS, R. J. "Psychosocial Response to Vasectomy." *Archives of General Psychiatry,* 1969, *21,* 46–54.

ZUCKERMAN, M., LEVITT, E. E., AND LUBIN, B. "Concurrent and Construct Validity of Direct and Indirect Measures of Dependency." *Journal of Consulting Psychology,* 1961, *25,* 316–323.

Author Index

Subject Index

A

Accident-proneness, 212

Achievement, academic, 16–17, 72, 74, 81, 85, 88, 153; in college, 75, 78–79, 179–189; in elementary school, 161–162; in high school, 74–75, 79, 117, 162–179; in specific courses, 74–75, 78, 79, 83, 88, 162, 180, 182, 186–187, 198–199, 233–234. See also Overachieving and Underachieving

Achievement orientation, 187, 240–242

Adjectival analyses, 17, 123–126, 145, 250, 260–268

Adjustment, 111–112, 121, 125, 142, 148; personal and social, 52, 54, 108, 110, 205–225; marital, 213, 244–245; sex role, 244–245; specific syndromes, 210–221; vocational education, 52, 54, 108, 110, 205, 210

Administration, 5

Aggressiveness, 64, 66–67, 130, 208, 212–213, 218

Anti-Semitism, 67–68

Anxiety, 6, 68, 97–98, 120, 123, 146, 148, 222, 259

Applications of CPI: in developmental research, 65, 227–246; in educational and vocational assessment, 160–204, 251; in family counseling, 149–153; in insight analysis, 153–154; in medical and physiological research, 242, 245; in parole prediction, 7, 219–220; in Peace Corps selection, 23; in prediction of posthospital adjustment, 54–55; in evaluation of treatment effectiveness, 222–225

Asch paradigm, 43, 71, 80, 227–229

Authoritarianism, 67, 77, 89, 197, 240

Autonomic response to stress, 51–52, 241, 244

B

Base rates, influence of, 156–157

Blind analysis, 128, 130

C

Cheating, 65, 217–218, 221

Class I scales, 6, 28, 39–55, 105, 111–112, 140, 203, 208

Class II scales, 6, 28, 56–71, 105, 111, 140, 203

Class III scales, 6, 28, 72–100, 105, 111, 140, 208

Class IV scales, 6, 28–29, 86–93, 105, 140

Clinical acumen, 128–130

Clinical assessment, 205–226, 251

Clinical folklore, 127, 146, 154–155

College matriculation, 75, 79, 172–175, 248

Community Treatment Project, 223–224

Conceptual analysis, 2, 17, 19–20, 27–28, 77, 102–155, 158

Configural interpretation, 70, 76, 124, 129–131, 142, 145–149, 154–155, 250–252

Conformity, 43, 71–72, 76, 80, 112, 123, 142, 197, 227–249

Construction of CPI, 21–100; item arrangement in, 16, 25, 36–37; item pool, 25; item selection in, 16, 25–28, 36–37; minority groups in, 29, 33; profile sheet in, 17, 28, 105; role of theory in, 10–11, 13, 22; selection of variables in, 7, 10–15; standardization, 4, 28–29, 33–35; strategy of, 15–20, 25–28; time estimation in, 241

Counseling, 150, 154, 221–226; response to, 97–98, 219, 221–223

Counselor effectiveness, 225–226

CPI *Manual,* 4, 7, 29, 38, 50, 57, 81, 84–85, 88, 92, 105, 118–119, 123–124, 130, 135, 204, 208, 213, 239, 250

Creativity, 17, 75–76, 80–81, 84–85, 88, 90, 229–240; in architecture, 230–231, 235, 238; in art, 229–232, 234–236, 238–239; in engineering, 234, 237; in mathematics, 233–234; in science, 230, 232–239; in writing, 230–231

Crime, 30, 48, 50, 52, 54, 59–60, 62–64, 66–67, 91–92, 212–216, 218, 251. See also Delinquency and Samples

Cross-cultural applicability of CPI, 19, 28

Cross-cultural research, 12, 14, 19, 28, 33, 59, 61–62, 75, 104–105, 163, 177–179, 248; in Austria, 62; in Canada, 75, 79, 82, 167, 177–179; in Costa Rica, 62, 248; in France, 62, 92; in Germany, 62; in India, 62; in Israel, 62, 64, 104; in Italy, 62, 75, 82, 92, 163–164, 177, 220; in Japan, 62; in Korea, 92; in Norway, 92; in Puerto Rico, 62; in South Africa, 62; in Switzerland, 62, 109; in Taiwan, 62; in Turkey, 92; in Venezuela, 92

D

Defense mechanisms, 212–213

Delinquency, 48, 50, 58–65, 91–92, 97, 117, 125, 128, 150, 205, 213–223, 251

Dependency, 43

Dissimulation, 22; and faking bad, 71, 132–140; and faking good, 34, 54, 68–70, 132–140; and malingering, 32, 52–55, 71, 132–140; and nonresponsive answering, 32, 70–71, 132–140. See also Scales, Communality, Good impression, Well being

Dogmatism, 67, 77, 89, 121, 240

Dominance, 5, 13, 16, 43, 68, 70, 73

Dropping out, 17, 172–173, 175, 177, 179

Drug usage, 210–212; alcohol, 52, 54, 59, 211; cigarettes, 93, 211, 241; marijuana, 59, 64, 99, 211, 251

E

Empathy, 6, 86, 154

Employability, 203–204

Extracurricular activities, participation in, 47–48, 182

F

Factor analytic methods, 24, 105, 108–110

Factor structure, 104–126, 250; factor 1 in, 6, 99, 110–112, 116–117, 119–120, 125–126, 150, 172, 174, 182, 188, 208, 210–211, 213–214, 217–218, 223, 233, 235, 243, 250; factor 2 in, 6, 99, 112, 116, 120–121, 125–126, 142, 150, 172, 182, 187–188, 199, 203, 208, 211, 213–214, 217–218, 223, 232–233, 240–242, 244, 250; factor 3 in, 6, 112–113, 121–122, 126, 142, 144, 148, 150, 180, 182, 196, 197, 208, 211, 214, 218, 233–235, 239–240, 250; factor 4 in, 6, 112–114, 122, 126, 142, 144, 150, 214, 233, 250; factor 5 in, 6, 112, 114–116, 122–123, 126, 142, 144, 150, 233, 250

Family-planning methods, 213, 243–244

"Folk-concept" theory, 5, 12–14, 16, 18–20, 25, 33, 45, 77, 86

G

Graduation, high school, 17, 74, 79, 172, 174–175, 177, 179, 248; college, 17, 75, 78–79, 185–186, 248

H

Honors participation, 88, 186–188

I

IPAR, 43, 50–51, 54, 57, 66, 90, 98, 124, 230–232, 235

Independent thinking, 50, 76, 78–79, 112, 121–122, 126, 142, 144, 180

Individual interpretation, 17, 28, 117, 124, 127–155, 250–251; determination of validity of, 132–140; elevation of scores in, 140, 145; preliminary steps in, 131–132; profile analyses in, 140–144; scale analyses in, 144–145; training in, 127–130

Intelligence, influence on prediction of achievement with CPI, 74–80, 82–84, 88, 162–163, 180–181

Interpersonal adequacy, 6, 13, 17, 52, 112, 120–121, 148, 150, 153

Introversion-Extroversion, 112